SCOTTISH HISTORY SOCIETY

FIFTH SERIES

VOLUME 18

James Wilson,
Journal of My Life and
Everyday Doings

The photograph shows James Wilson, author of the Journal, standing next to his wife, Katie. Their two children, Alexander and Margaret, are standing beside their grandfather, James Wilson (senior).

JOURNAL OF MY LIFE AND EVERYDAY DOINGS
1879-81, 1885-92

James Wilson, farmer in Banffshire

edited by
Peter Hillis

EDINBURGH

Printed for the Scottish History Society

The date of 2005 on the spine refers to the nominal year
in the Society's annual series of publications.

British Library Cataloguing-in-Publication Data:
A catalogue record for this book is available
from the British Library.

ISBN 978-0-906245-27-0
Printed in Great Britain

CONTENTS

PREFACE

I first met James Wilson's granddaughter, Edith Lowrie, in May 2003 during a visit to Fordyce while working on a research project which examined the relationship between church and people in every major denomination within Fordyce and the neighbouring parish of Portsoy. Family letters, diaries and journals often contain detailed comments on religion with the Sunday sermon attracting particular criticism, discussion and debate. Therefore, I reacted with the pleasure known to historians, on coming across a previously undiscovered but valuable source, when George Christie, an Elder in Fordyce Parish Church, recommended Wilson's Journal for its insightful observations on religion, churches and their ministers. We arranged to meet in George's house but, having been told that Edith lived in sheltered accommodation in Huntly, I was not expecting to meet a sprightly eighty year old whose presents for her eightieth birthday included a ride on a motorcycle, one mile for every year of her life, between Portnockie and Aberlour. Much of Wilson's energy has passed on to his granddaughter with the connections between the past and present evident in many other areas. The Wilson family had been friendly with George Christie's grandparents and James Wilson travelled to Aberlour, albeit much more slowly, to work on two local farms and later for his 'honeymoon'.

In May 2003, we visited the farms and landmarks central to Wilson's life: Knowes where he farmed; Backies, home of his great friend, Willie McWillie; Cornhill, site of the local station and market; the neighbouring farms of Ardiecow and Oathillock; Kirkton, where his wife Katie Duncan spent her early years; Deskford and Fordyce Churches where he worshipped; Deskford Cemetery where he was buried and Newpark, farmed by his friends, the Hendry family. These locations and the area's natural beauty provide a continuing link with Wilson's Journal. The farms continue as working farms, but with larger fields, different farm houses and fewer workers than in Wilson's time.

It would not have been possible to produce this volume without the help and support of many people. The Journal, poems, essays, papers and short story are reproduced with kind permission of Edith Lowrie. James Wilson's Foreword is reproduced with the kind permission of his great granddaughter, Anne Robson. Information on the local area was generously provided by George Christie and David McWilliam. Drew Calderhead, Leonie Docherty and Brian Lochrin of the Jordanhill Campus at Strathclyde University helped with the illustrations and graphics. The map of the north east of Scotland and the area around Knowes is reproduced with permission of the National Library of Scotland. Linda Harris at the University of Strathclyde provided helpful comments on Wilson's poems and Graham Holton compiled the index. Elspeth Donaldson typed the Introduction and Bob Munro gave valuable advice on the first drafts. However, special thanks are due to Linda Nicolson who did a magnificent job in typing the Journal, poems and lectures.

This book is dedicated to the Wilson Family, past and present.

Peter Hillis
Glasgow
November 2007

GLOSSARY

Ayvels	Same meaning as yavals, ground on which a crop of grain is grown for the second year.
Bannocks	Round flat cakes of oat, barley or pease meal baked on a girdle.
Ben	The inner or better room in a house.
Blinding	Gravel to put smooth surface on a road.
Boll	One boll or bole equalled six bushels with one
bushel	being the dry measure of eight gallons of grain.
Braird	First shoots of growing grain.
Brose	Dish of oatmeal mixed with hot water pease meal on a girdle.
Clyack	The last sheaf of corn to be cut at the harvest. The clyack sheaf was also the last sheaf of harvest to be
put	on top of the last rick.
Cinder	A strong stimulant.
Colls	Hay cocks.
Cushies	Wood pigeons.
Driving	To transport in a cart or wagon.
Dulse	Edible seaweed.
Fast day	Thursday or Friday before Communion Sunday. A special church service was held on fast day.
Fastern-Even	Shrove Tuesday.
Finger and toe	Disease of turnips in which the tap root branches. The tap root is the strong main root stretching down vertically from the plant.
Forms	Benches.
Frosted	To sharpen the points of a horse's shoe that it may not slip on ice.
Furs	Furrows.
Gully looking (weather)	Threatening (weather).
Gimmers	Young ewes.
Girnal	Meal chest.
Graip	Four pronged fork.
H.M.I.S.	Her Majesty's Inspector of Schools.
Happin-in	Digging in or covering (the dung).

I.R.O.	Inland Revenue Officer.
Keepers	Animals kept for fattening.
Marnin Fair	Fair named after St Marnan or Marnoch, after whom the parish is also named. The Fair was held on the second Tuesday of March and it became an annual market for horses and cattle.
Marrows	Best parts.
Mavis	Song thrush.
Orra	Odd.
Orra Man	Odd job man.
Paling	Fencing.
Peter Fair	Local fair and market held in Rathven in July.
Put in the cries	Proclaiming the marriage banns.
Queys	Heifers.
Rank	Uncomposted dung.
Scuffle	Horse drawn hoe.
Shalt	Working horse, smaller than a Clydesdale, often used to pull a gig.
Sprotts	Coarse reedy plants growing in clumps on wet ground.
Stirk	A yearling or young cow.
Suppering (the horses)	Giving horses their last meal of the day.
Sward	The grassy surface of land.
Swingletree	Cross piece of the plough to which the traces of the horse are attached.
Tailers	Tail chains by which a horse hauls a wagon.
Tares	Mixture of oats, vetches and peas cut with a scythe as extra feed for milk cows and feeding cattle.
Thete	The traces for attaching a horse to a farm implement via a swingletree.
Tory	The leatherjacket grub that attacks the roots of crops.
Tramp Colls	A number of hay colls put into one and tramped hard in order that the hay may be further dried.
Turred	Thatch and/or turfs being blown off roofs.
Venison	Animals hunted, beasts of the chase.
Working grieve	Overseer of a farm who also worked the farm.
Wreathes (of snow)	Snowdrifts.
Yarr	Corn spurrey.
Yavals	Ground on which a crop of grain is grown for the second year running.

MEASUREMENTS

FOR DISTANCE		
SCOTS	**IMPERIAL EQUIVALENT**	**METRIC EQUIVALENT**
1 inch	1 inch	2.54 cms
1 ell = 37 inches	3 feet 1inch	93.98 cms
1 fall = 6 ells	18 feet 6 inches	5m 63.88 cms
1 chain = 4 falls	74 feet	22m 55.52 cms
1 mile = 80 chains	1 mile 213 yards 1 foot	1 km 804m 41.6 cms

FOR AREA		
SCOTS	**IMPERIAL EQUIVALENT**	**METRIC EQUIVALENT**
1 acre	1.26 acres	0.51hectares

MONEY

STERLING (OLD)	**STERLING (NEW)**
1 farthing	0.104 pence
1 halfpenny = 2 farthings	0.209 pence
1 penny = 2 halfpennies	0.417 pence
1 shilling = 12 pennies	5 pence
1 pound = 20 shillings = 240 pennies	1 pound = 100 pence
1 guinea = 21 shillings	1 pound 5 pence

SCOTS QUARTER DAYS

Candlemas	2nd February
Whitsun	15th May
Lammas	1st August
Martinmas	11th November

LIST OF ILLUSTRATIONS

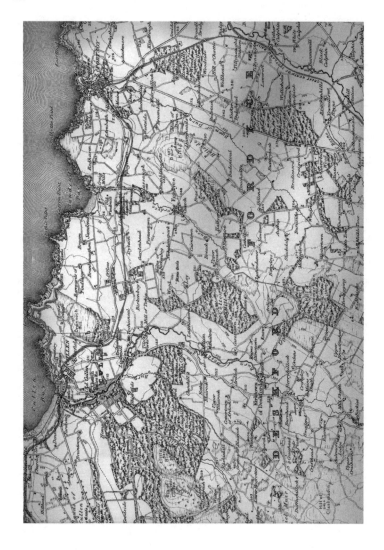

1871, Ordnance Survey Map, Banffshire, 1:10860. Knowes was not marked on the original map, but has been added for this volume using the spelling of Knows (as in Knows of Deskford). Knows is located just to the east of Kirktown of Deskford.

Reproduced by permission of the Trustees of the National Library of Scotland.

INTRODUCTION

James Wilson was born at Upper Knowes, now Knowes, on the nineteenth of June, 1859 and baptised eleven days later. He was the only son of James and Mary Wilson, nee Bidie, in a family of twelve children, although two sisters died in infancy of diphtheria. The surviving sisters were Janet, Isabella, Jane, Margaret, Ann, Elisabeth, Catherine, Mary and Joanna (Joan). The 1881 Census recorded that James's and Mary's grandson, William, also lived at Upper Knowes.[1] Upper Knowes was rented from the Seafield Estates to James Wilson, senior, with his son somewhat contentiously taking over the tack in 1888. Wilson spent the early years of his working life helping his father farm Upper Knowes and in 1889 he married Catherine (Katie) Duncan from the neighbouring farm of Kirkton. They had two children, Alexander, known as Duncan after his mother's maiden name, and Margaret. Wilson left Upper Knowes to farm at Burns in 1900, but Catherine died twelve years later. He then moved to live with his daughter and son-in-law who farmed at Parklea, becoming a prominent member of the local community serving as Clerk to the School Board and a Justice of the Peace. In 1929, Wilson married his second wife, Betty Wallace, but he died in 1937 and was buried alongside Catherine in Deskford Churchyard.

Wilson began writing his Journal in January 1879 when he was nineteen years old and the entries continued until 1892. The volume covering the period between January 1882 and June 1885 is missing, but the extant three volumes provide a detailed record of rural life in late nineteenth-century Scotland. Wilson also kept a separate book that recorded many of his poems, essays, short stories, selected correspondence and lectures given to local organisations such as the Deskford Mutual Improvement Society. Towards the end of his life Wilson wrote what he called a 'Foreword',[2] which recounts various influences on his life such as his early schooling, neighbours, farming

---

[1] 1881 Census for Scotland, vol. 151.
[2] See p. 29 below.

and his reasons for keeping the Journal. It was not common for working people in Scotland during the nineteenth century to keep diaries or journals and the critical biography of the working class contains few by Scottish farmers.[3] However, there was something of a tradition in keeping a diary or journal in the Deskford area since Wilson's friend, Willie McWillie, kept a diary between 1881 and 1887. This unpublished and relatively short account with many gaps stands in contrast to one regularly kept by his uncle, Robert McWillie, from 1826-1876. These diaries are currently unpublished.

Knowes lies close to the centre of Deskford parish in Banffshire. Located in the North East of Scotland, Banffshire is bounded to the south by Moray and Aberdeenshire, and to the north by the Moray Firth, which can be seen from Knowes. It is said that, on his tour of Scotland, Dr. Johnson pulled down the blinds of his carriage while passing through Deskford.[4] Had Dr. Johnston deigned to keep the blinds open, he would have seen an area of great natural beauty within its fifteen square miles bounded by Grange, Rathven, Cullen and Fordyce. Fordyce became an ecclesiastical centre with its church, originally associated with St. Talarician (or Tarquin), dating back to the sixth century. In the seventeenth century Deskford became a separate parish with the remains of the original church forming one corner of the present churchyard. The church in which James Wilson often worshipped was built in 1872.[5]

Standing on Greenhill, one viewpoint in the parish at 240 metres, the view looks out over Knowes, the burn of Deskford and on towards the village itself which today consists of houses, a farm, church and churchyard. Streams flowing through small glens and ravines edged by woodlands of fir, ash, oak, beech and larch augment the burn of Deskford as it flows through the parish on its way to the sea. In the land beyond the burn, agriculture has created a patchwork pattern of fields and hedges that slope towards the burn with farm buildings punctuating the landscape. These farms stand as a testimony to generations of farmers who turned moss and heath into cultivated land. Over the centuries, farmers have worked the soil described as 'a black loam upon a hard clay bottom' which, according to the *New Statistical Account*, 'renders draining, in almost all parts of the Parish, of the greatest necessity and importance, and it has of late been much resorted

[3] J. Burnett, D. Vincent & D. Mayall, (eds.), *The Autobiography of the Working Class, 1790-1900*, 2 vols. (Brighton, 1984).
[4] J. Sinclair, *The Statistical Account of Scotland*, 20 vols. (Edinburgh, 1791-1799), iv, 361.
[5] D. Finlay, *Banffshire Churches* (Banff, 1994), 19.

to, and with much advantage'.[6] The name Deskford originated in 'chess fure', meaning a cold place to the south, in this case of Cullen and the coast, so explaining the numerous references in Wilson's Journal to 'driving tiles' and 'draining'. Nonetheless, the cold and wet climate was not detrimental to 'the general health and longevity of the inhabitants'.[7]

Draining was only one of several changes which transformed Scottish agriculture at the end of the eighteenth century. The traditional view of an agricultural revolution has been challenged by Whittington who has argued that from the early seventeenth century farming methods, techniques and attitudes were changing with the process one of continuous evolution as opposed to a revolution.[8] Tom Devine, however, viewed the 1760s and 1770s as crucial decades with 68 per cent of parishes in Ayrshire, Angus, Fife and Lanarkshire reporting in *The Statistical Account* that change first became established in these decades.[9] Whether the timescale was long or short, change affected all areas of agriculture. The advance of large scale pastoral farming replaced many smaller farms and the traditional infields and outfields which characterised the ferm touns. Farmers enclosed fields with ditches and hedges while the land was drained and treated with fertilisers such as lime and bonemeal. Crop rotation further increased yields with selective breeding improving the quality of livestock. New machines, such as the horse drawn hoe and seed-drill, aided ploughing, sowing, reaping and harvesting with the later introduction of steam driven threshers and winnowers taking some of the hard physical labour out of traditional harvesting methods.

The changes came at a human cost with large numbers of small tenant farmers and cottars displaced 'in a manner very reminiscent of the Highland Clearances', but without a significant drop in population and subsequent social unrest.[10] This is partly explained by important local variations in agricultural reform. Tenant displacement reached its height in upland areas where arable farming struggled to produce significant returns, most notably in southern parishes of Lanarkshire and Ayrshire, the hill country of Angus and areas bordering the Highlands. Moreover, the process of tenant removal was often 'absorbed within the broader

---

[6] *New Statistical Account of Scotland* [*NSA*], 15 vols. (Edinburgh, 1845), xiii, 65.
[7] *NSA*, xiii, 64.
[8] G. Whittington, 'Was There a Scottish Agricultural Revolution?' in A. Cooke, I. Donnachie, A. MacSween & C.A. Whatley (eds.), *Modern Scottish History, 1707 to the Present*, 3 vols. (East Linton, 1998), iii, 82.
[9] T.M. Devine, *The Transformation of Rural Scotland, Social Change and the Agrarian Economy* (Edinburgh, 1994), 43.
[10] Devine, *Transformation of Rural Scotland*, 50.

and more familiar mechanism of the regular re-letting of farms'. Devine characterised this process as 'clearance by stealth'.[11] The situation facing cottars was more problematic. Cottars formed a numerically important group within rural society supplying labour to tenant farmers in return for which they were provided with a small holding. By the early nineteenth century, many cottar families had been displaced by the consolidation of small holdings into larger farms in a process more akin to Highland clearance. In Boindie, Banffshire, 'the introduction of large farms, joined to the exclusion of the families of servants and customers, has operated in reducing the population …', while a decline in population in Gartly from 1800 people in 1793 to 979 in 1831 'can only be imputed to the principal tenants extending their farms and removing their cottagers'. The neighbouring counties of Elgin and Nairn witnessed a similar decline. In Rafford, 'the principal cause' of the decrease 'has been the uniting of a number of small farms into one' and in Auldearn 'the enlargement of farms' led to people leaving the village.[12] The potential for subsequent unrest was defused by an expansion of the labour market elsewhere in the rural economy and as a result of the emerging industrial revolution. An expanding network of small to medium-sized market towns and increasing demand for skilled workers created new job opportunities. Moreover, many cottars continued to work the land in a variety of skilled and unskilled occupations such as agricultural labourers, farm servants and ploughmen.

By the 1830s, the method of employing farm labour had fixed into a pattern which, as Malcolm Gray has demonstrated, was to continue into the twentieth century.[13] Unmarried men and women were hired for periods of six months with married couples for one year. Hiring was normally arranged at the Whitsun and Martinmas feeing markets with individual arrangements struck between farmer and labourer. Wage rates varied in line with supply and demand, the strength of the rural economy alongside the reputation of both the employer and employee. Unmarried farm servants lived either on the farm or in bothies, with married servants and their families often accommodated in farm cottages. In parts of Banffshire, however, the nature of the local agricultural economy supported a continuing number of crofters and small holders who supplemented the ready supply of farm servants.

[11] Devine, *Transformation of Rural Scotland*, 122.
[12] *NSA*, xiii, 13, 98, 230, 252.
[13] M. Gray, 'Farm Workers in North East Scotland', in T.M. Devine (ed.), *Farm Servants and Labour in Lowland Scotland, 1770-1914* (Edinburgh, 1984), 16.

Irrespective of status, it was long and tiring toil with ploughmen, regarded as a group apart, starting work at 4.00 a.m. or earlier to feed, yoke and take the horses to the field for up to ten hours ploughing. The day ended with grooming and suppering back at the stables.

The process of agricultural change in Banffshire and Deskford followed national trends, but warns against over generalisations. In Banffshire, the Earl of Findlater initiated agricultural improvements. Overseers from England were placed on farms in Lower Banffshire with many smaller holdings consolidated into single farms leased for long periods. Fields were enclosed with stone walls or fences and Findlater was the first to introduce turnip husbandry and sown grass into the county. Arguably the most significant innovation followed the famine of 1782, with the widespread adoption of Aberdeen Angus cattle. This placed 'Aberdeenshire and Banffshire at the head of beef producing counties'.[14] Crops included oats, barley and turnips with sheep grazing alternately on the high and low ground depending on the season, but 'it is by cattle that agriculture of the two counties flourishes'.[15] The average size of farm remained small (although many small holdings had disappeared) with few yielding a rent in excess of £200 per annum. The majority of farms were let at under £100 per annum.

The description given in the *New Statistical Account* by the Reverend George Innes of Deskford demonstrates that, on the whole, agricultural changes in the parish fitted into the more general pattern. 'Great improvements', Innes wrote, 'have been of late made in the way of draining and cultivation'. Aided by a quarry in the parish, 'lime and bone manure are both used with excellent effect ... Considerable quantities of fish manure are likewise used ...'. The 'breeds of cattle and sheep are of a mixed kind' while arable farming consisted 'of grain of all kinds, potatoes, turnips, hay and pasture and flax'.[16] A distillery at Glenglassaugh consumed much of the local barley crop and the rope works in Portsoy required a steady supply of flax.

The population fell between 1790 and 1811 due, 'most probably, to the diminution of the number of crofters and sub-tenants'.[17] However, Deskford illustrated the continuing diversity in farm sizes throughout Banffshire. The 1881 Census recorded farm and croft sizes with Wilson's tenancy at Upper Knowes covering 72 acres which included part of the neighbouring farm of Ardiecow, added to Knowes in the 1870s. This made Knowes a medium-sized farm, as shown in

[14] W. Watt, *A History of Aberdeen and Banff* (Edinburgh, 1890), 331.
[15] Watt, *Aberdeen and Banff*, 334.
[16] *NSA*, xiii, 71.
[17] *NSA*, xiii, 69.

the table below which lists each croft and farm in the parish as documented in the1881 Census.[18]

Croft/Farm Acreage, Deskford, 1881			
Croft/Farm	No. of Acres	Croft/Farm	No. of Acres
Ardoch Croft	8	Knowes	75
Ardiecow	200	Lambscroft	7
Ardoch Farm	170	Langland	96
Backies	97	Langland Burn	150
Balmore	101	Leichestown	112
Black Hillock	33	Little Cultain	50
Blairock Croft	–	Little Moss Side	14
Bloomfedd	32	Little Skeith	27
Bogetra	76	Inaltrie	155
Bracehead	20	Mid Skeith	101
Braeside	29	Moss Side	100
Broadrashes	43	Nether Blairock	146
Burn Heads	105	Oathillock	54
Burns	70	Ordens	110
Careston	136	Podhead	30
Clochmacreich	150	Poolside	8
Clump Croft	15	Skeith	200
Clune	100	Squardoch	21
Craibstone	112	Squardoch	75
Craiglug	15	Stripeside	18
Croftgloy	102	Swailend	59
Duffieshilloch	50	The Field	8
Faceyhill	11	Todholes	39
Faceyhill	21	Todside	8
Faceyhill	20	Upper Blairock	140
Faceyhill	21	Upper Braeside	29
Gateside	15	Upper Craibston	6
George Taylor	197	Upper Knowes	72
Grans of Blairock	20	Upper Skeith	60
Greenhill	75	Wardleys	7
Greystone	12	Wellcroft	2
Hoggie	20	Woodside	27
Kirkton	135		

[18] 1881 Census for Scotland, vol. 151. The spelling of farm names is as recorded in the Census, but this sometimes does not match either the contemporary or present day spelling e.g. Knowes is sometimes spelled as Knows.

Wilson appreciated the advantages of large farms despite, or perhaps because of, Knowes' medium size. He outlined the main benefits of large farms in a paper, reprinted in Appendix 2, given to the Ballindalloch Mutual Improvement Association in January 1886. He commented on the improved breed of cattle in place of the 'thin scraggy animals that might have seen pasturing the fields some forty or fifty years ago'. The shorthorn or Aberdeen Angus of the 1880s produced more quality beef as a result of improvements brought about 'entirely' by the large farmers. The same group had taken the initiative in forming agricultural societies, introduced 'new and labour-saving implements', improved soil quality and generally benefited the local community by, for example, giving 'more work to local tradesmen'. Wilson, was perhaps over critical of the extent to which his and other similarly sized farms contributed to agricultural improvements, but he made strenuous efforts to control costs by keeping as much work as possible 'in house'.

Agricultural improvements opened up previously uncultivated parts of Deskford which encouraged more people to settle the land. Consequently, between 1831 and 1861 the population increased from 828 to 1031, but in the following two decades the number fell to 849.[19] This resulted from a complex combination of 'push' and 'pull' factors involving a decline in prices for many agricultural products, emigration to Australia and North America and migration to the local market towns such as Cullen and Portsoy. Portsoy's development in the nineteenth century provides strong support for Tom Devine's argument that small market towns played a crucial role in the rural economy.[20] Situated approximately seven miles from Knowes, Portsoy became the local nexus for trade, commerce and industry. Continual improvements to the harbour led to it becoming the principal port in Banffshire with locally grown grain the major export. The multi-storeyed grain stores built on the quayside have now been converted into shops, flats and premises for small businesses. Portsoy also featured a diverse range of industries including rope, engineering and flax works. Commercial enterprises included banks and insurance companies with the allied professions of lawyers, merchants and agents. The town's coastal location supported a thriving fishing industry also found in the neighbouring village of Sandend. In 1859, the Banff railway linked with Portsoy to improve access to Aberdeen and other

[19] F. Groome, *Ordnance Gazetteer of Scotland*, 4 vols. (Edinburgh, 1883), ii, 352.
[20] T.M.Devine, *The Transformation of Rural Scotland* (Edinburgh, 1994), 151.

areas in the north east.[21] Portsoy's growing prosperity was matched by an expanding population from 1720 in 1841 to 2090 in 1881 as people moved from the surrounding areas in search of work.[22]

Portsoy's development did not take place at significant expense to Deskford which continued to provide varied goods and services. It had a library, in which Wilson played a prominent role, public school and museum. The 1881 census recorded many skilled trades such as masons, blacksmiths, carpenters, tailors, shoemakers, a draper, farrier and cartwright. Wilson was a member of Deskford Parish Church in the 1870s and 1880s, but there was also a Free Church congregation in the Parish. James MacIntosh, who ministered in the Parish Church between 1843 and 1890, had been born in the neighbouring parish, Ordiquhill, but his successor, George Park, hailed from Inverurie.[23] Wilson provides a detailed account in his Journal of Park's ordination to Deskford.

The railway passed through Cornhill on its way to Portsoy. Cornhill Station is now a family home standing next to the old agricultural market where Wilson and other local farmers dealt in crops and livestock. In January 1880, Wilson described one of the worst accidents in nineteenth-century Scotland:

> In the newspapers this week is an account of the fearful accident which happened last Sunday night 28th December viz. the blowing down of a part of the Tay Bridge at the moment the train was crossing it. There were about 75 persons in the train at the time; but whether the bridge was blown down before the train came or the train blown over taking the bridge with it will never be rightly known, as none have been left to tell the tale.

Wilson probably did not realise it at the time, but the Tay Bridge disaster was an omen for less certain times in agriculture. As Gavin Sprott has noted, the period before 1880 was one of 'high farming' with investment in new methods, crops, livestock and machinery allied to rising farm incomes.[24] However, the early 1880s witnessed an agricultural depression with falling prices: barley prices fell from 30/- per quarter in 1883 to 25/- in 1893; oats sold for less than 5/- per quarter in 1895 than they had in 1883 and between 1883 and 1895 fatstock prices fell by twenty per cent.[25] North East Scotland survived the downturn better than many

---

[21] J. Slater, *Portsoy in Points and Pictures* (Falkirk, 1980), 24.

[22] Groome, *Ordnance Gazetteer*, vi, 224.

[23] H. Scott, *Fasti Ecclesiae Scoticanae*, 8 vols. (Edinburgh, 1926), vi, 286.

[24] G. Sprott, 'Lowland Country Life', in T.M. Devine & R.J. Finlay (eds.), *Scotland in the Twentieth Century* (Edinburgh, 1996), 170.

[25] T.M. Devine, 'Scottish Farm Labour in the Era of Agricultural Depression, 1875-1900', in Devine (ed.), *Farm Servants and Labour in Rural Scotland*, 243.

other areas partly due to the quality of its cattle, high standards of husbandry, a diverse product range and robust local markets, such as the Glenglassaugh Distillery, for barley. Nonetheless, the low returns on investment made Wilson question farming as a career. In his 'Foreword', written towards the end of his life, he admitted that 'although I was put to the plough at the early age of 14, I must confess that my heart was never truly in my work' and he regretted not fulfilling his ambition to enter the civil service. His interest in farming grew on taking over more responsibility for Knowes, so that looking back on his life he could say 'that I have never in the slightest degree regretted my choice...'. Entries in later volumes of the Journal bear out this transformation as Wilson records more fully the many aspects of farming, especially yields and prices. His own success as a farmer is evident in the yields quoted in the Journal with, for example, those for barley coming close to the official weight of 56 lbs per bushel.

Knowes and Deskford put their own stamp on wider changes to agriculture. Local specialisms in cattle rearing ran parallel to more general changes in arable production with diversity an important, if not foolproof, protection against falling prices and foreign competition. Small farms and crofts, such as Poolside, co-existed with those over 150 acres, exemplified by Maltrie and Ardoch, with Knowes located close to the centre of this spectrum. Although agricultural products were exported by rail and sea, the local area remained vitally important by providing a ready market and diverse range of goods and services. This in turn supported a network of skilled craftsmen and employment opportunities for farm servants. Farming practices in 1880 were very different from those described in *The Statistical Account of Scotland* at the end of the eighteenth century, but the parish remained one, which in today's terms would be called 'an area of outstanding natural beauty', and this was a seminal influence on Wilson's life.

Wilson compiled his Journal on Monday evenings giving only one relatively small clue at the time as to the motivation. 'This account of my daily life', he wrote in 1888, 'is intended to be something which I may peruse in after years with pleasure and profit ...'. His 'Foreword' provided a fuller explanation which linked keeping a diary to his belief in self improvement. It was not only 'a means of improving one's writing and comprehension, but it also makes one take more particular note of men and passing events ... I could not advise any young person who wishes to improve themselves during their leisure hours in any better way than by keeping a diary'. On his own admission early entries 'were extremely meagre, two or three lines sometimes sufficing for a week, and the whole month of January occupying one small page. As time slipped past however and my vocabulary increased I went into far more detail—a holiday—a Picnic—or an entertainment of any sort providing adequate copy'. This 'copy' gives the reader a glimpse of a life based on attitudes and values very different from those portrayed as important and dominant by so much of today's media. Wilson's motivations for keeping the Journal separate it from many earlier working class 'autobiographies' which sprung from spiritual assumptions about the 'significance of the inner lives of ordinary men and women, and about the necessity of understanding human identity in the dimension of time'. This self analysis was written down to support fellow believers with a particular concern for the 'moral development of both the author and his readers'.[26] A second more general motivation lay in the desire to record both the threats and opportunities created by social, economic and political change. A formal written record might help keep alive passing traditions, but it would also balance the views of elite groups in society whose interests were often at variance to those of the working class. Wilson records a spiritual and moral life; but these do not appear to have been the primary reasons for keeping the Journal. Politics receives only passing reference. Wilson kept his Journal to improve his education and to provide a personal retrospective on a life which revolved around the naturally recurring events of the farming year. The Journal ends suddenly in January 1892 although in the preceding week he wrote, 'what with nursing and other little odds and ends I have got no time to write any since the New Year'. By this time Wilson had two young children and the demands of a young family allied to running the farm meant there was little time left to write. Moreover, he had kept a meticulous record for over a decade.

Wilson had a profound regard for the land. His care and concern for the natural environment went well beyond its worth as a source of employment and income, witnessed in the evocative language used to describe the area around Knowes. In April 1881, he wrote:

> I had finished my Journal writing for the week, and had my book put past, but after suppering my horses I beheld a scene which has compelled me again to resume my pen. The sun had been set for half an hour behind the hill of Maud and the curtain of night was drawing its folds of darkness over the earth. Scarcely a breath of wind stirred the air and as I stood on the old dyke beside the peat stack and gazed around me, I beheld what to my eyes seemed a most beautiful picture, and listened to what to my ears reckoned

---

[26] J. Burnett, D. Vincent & D. Mayall (eds.), *The Autobiography of the Working Class, 1790-1900*, 2 vols. (Brighton, 1984), i, p. xiii.

the sweetest music. All along the hill side and wherever you turned your eyes, numbers of bonfires were shedding their ruddy glow and lighting up the gathering gloom, while above them the smoke was eddying and circling and rising in columns in the still evening air. Over the Clunehill could be seen the sea lying so calm and still like a glassy mirror, and instead of the deep blue, appearing under the darkness overhead, a bluish white; while far away in the distance the Sutherland hills could be dimly discerned their towering heads still capped with snow. Such was the scene on which my eyes did feast, while the treat provided for my ears was not a whit less worthy of notice ... Far and near could be heard the sharp 'pe-wit' of the lapwing, or 'pese weep' as we more commonly call it, great numbers of which are now preparing their nests in the fields around. The plaintive cry of the curlew could also be heard far away on the hill side ... In the field close at hand I could hear the pleasant chirp of the partridge as it called its mate ... The blackbird and the mavis seemed to vie with each other which would produce the sweetest song, and all the other members of the sylvan choir, each in its own peculiar key yet all blending together in sweetest harmony, were pouring forth in joyful strains their evening lay.[27]

There was no contradiction in Wilson's eyes between nature as a source of wonder and income. The land was there to be worked in a timeless pattern dictated by the seasons with no respite, even during the winter months. One week in December 1888 included ploughing 'in the forenoon', protecting 'the turnips we pulled the day before from snow', threshing and winnowing corn, collecting tiles for draining and cleaning harnesses. Harvest time was a particularly busy time of year for Wilson and his neighbours over whom he cast a professional, if critical, eye. 'The past week', he wrote in October 1886, 'has been a good harvest week, and the greater bulk of the stooks have now disappeared, excepting our neighbour Ardiecow, who has only got the half of it cut. His corn is very very green this year. We got other two stacks in on Tuesday afternoon. Wednesday was a grand day. We turned over the clean land stooks in the morning and by dinner time they were in very good order ... We have 18 stacks in all. Thursday was Cornhill market day ... There was a very small turn out, being harvest-time ...'.

The prices for agricultural products were a constant concern and the Journal provides a detailed record of the local market. A retrospect on 1885 noted, 'fodder is everywhere scarce, and has been selling at

---

[27] The full description of the area around Knowes was written on 4 April 1881, see p. 100 below.

high prices. But if straw be dear, the grain has been as cheap. I never saw the barley so low in price. We got only 23/6 for ours'. By 1889, prices had improved with 'grain of every kind ... certainly fetching good prices, and since harvest it has always been rising. At the present time good dry oats of the standard weight is selling at 17/- while barley 54lbs per bushel is 25/-. The weight is also most satisfactory, our barley being 56 and some of the oats 43'. Prices were, however, affected by foreign competition. In 1888, there was 'some indications of grain falling in price, a great amount of foreign stuff being brought in', and one year later Wilson speculated on the reasons for cheap beef. The cause was 'to be found I think in the tremendous amount of imported meat. And not only has the dead meat import been very heavy, but a large number of lean cattle have also been brought into this country. Cattle food being abundant, the supply of home loan cattle was found inadequate to the demand. Large numbers were therefore imported, more especially from Canada'. These imports reached Deskford when, in January 1892, Wilson 'was up one evening seeing Ardiecow's Canadians. He has not got them very fat yet, but he is thinking of selling them as his turnips are going done'.

Tight control of costs, efficient husbandry and diverse products, including honey, helped Knowes remain profitable although there were times, notably during 1886, when future prospects looked bleak. 'I have been thinking for some time back', he wrote, 'that I might do worse than start for Australia myself by another year. Willie will soon be able to do the work, and there will be no use for us both at home. And then farming here is such a poor job. It is hard work and little pay, with the prospect that very soon there will be no pay at all'. Thoughts of immigration were brought into sharper focus since his sister, Mary, and her husband left Deskford for Australia in June 1886.

Downward pressure on prices forced Wilson and other farmers to seek a reduction in rents. In October 1886, Wilson travelled the short distance to Cullen House in an attempt to 'make a new bargain with "The Laird". There is a break in the lease next Whitsunday, and the times have so greatly altered since five years ago, that we think it absolutely necessary that there should be some reduction in the rent. I did not get great encouragement however, Mr. Bryden was very civil, but he could not see his way at all to let down the rent. The land was too dear perhaps, but it was not dearer than our neighbours he said'. Labour costs were kept to a minimum on most farms through utilising the family as the chief source of labour supplemented, with varying degrees of success, by hired hands. Wilson and his Uncle Limes, so called because he farmed at Limestones beside the local lime quarry, 'went over to Peter Fair on Friday (July 1888) ... The supply of harvest hands was fully equal to the demand. Men to cut and build were getting £4.10/-, bandsters from £3.10/- to £4 and women from £2.10/- to £3'. Labour relations could prove fraught when on one occasion he came home and was rather astonished when 'they told me that the bandster had run off. I was not much disappointed however as he was very useless ... Next day was Cornhill market so I went over and engaged another man. There were plenty of hands to be got'.

The weather could prove to be just as problematic as hired help, but with more serious consequences. The Journal provides a detailed record of local weather conditions which appear to support claims that today's climate is warmer and wetter. The winter of 1880 was particularly harsh and looking out to a frozen landscape Wilson feared

that the weather will now frighten us. On Thursday sleet and rain fell the most of the day, and although toward night the snow sank a little I never thought it was to be a right-thaw, there being always a white mist about the hills. On Friday the wind changed from east to north and we had occasional showers of sleet and snow. The turnips however being bare and being quite fresh we took advantage of them and secured six loads. About four o'clock snow began to fall very thickly and there being at the same time a good breeze of wind it also commenced to blow. As night set in the wind increased and the snow thickened and at seven o'clock when I went out to supper the horses, it was a fearful night indeed. Thus had it continued to fall and drift throughout the night and next day until twelve o'clock, when it cleared, but the wind still keeping strong, drifting continued until Sunday morning.

Blizzards in December could be expected, but they were less expected in the summer when on June 1888

we have experienced weather the like of which was never remembered by the oldest person living. We had thirty-six hours of rainfall, commencing on Saturday night, and on Sunday morning it turned to snow, continuing the most of the day. By afternoon there was two inches all over, there being also a strong gale of wind, and having all the appearance of a day in March. I have read of someone saying, 'the summer had set in with its usual severity' and I am sure that the leafy month of June has commenced severe enough this year whatever. I see by the newspapers that in the upland districts a considerable depth of snow fell; while wreathes in some cases two feet deep were found. From four to nine inches was reported from different places. Cattle parks must have suffered severely, and I heard of a case of one dying from exposure. I do not think that turnips will be injured as there was not much frost with it. One morning in the first of the week was extremely frosty however, there being ice on the water. With such weather, most vegetation could not be expected.

Challenges thrown up by family relationships closely matched those posed by the weather and the Wilson household was not immune from timeless disputes over property and the suitability of potential wives or husbands. In March 1887, Wilson successfully applied to be a 'working grieve' on Balliemulloch Farm near Aberlour. His friend, Willie McWillie, reflected on how Wilson was missed in the Deskford area:

> My friend James Wilson has just left. He stayed for a few hours on his way home from being engaged as working grieve at Balliemaulloch. He has £15 of wages. I regret his leaving very much. I hope he will like his new place for he deserves a good one.[28]

On the twenty third of April the Deskford Mutual Improvement Association 'had a meeting ... about the present that was to be given to J. Wilson. It was agreed to get Chambers' Encyclopedia if sufficient money could be raised, and failing that a chain and locket would be given'.[29]

In his Journal Wilson often fails to explain this move and similar decisions at the time, and it only transpired later that the move to Speyside stemmed from umbrage at not being given control of Knowes. Nonetheless, Wilson's huff is the historian's gain as he painted a vivid picture of life in and around Aberlour on land dominated by Ballindalloch Estate. At 170 acres, Balliemulloch was over twice the size of Knowes and was rented to the Richardson family who employed Wilson for one year with a 'get out' clause after six months. His wages were £30, but the move was not successful. Wilson admitted to being homesick, a feeling accentuated by the ways in which Balliemulloch was (mis)managed:

> I cannot say that I am liking Balliemulloch very well yet. There are too many mistresses and they take by far too much interference. The tools and implements about the place are also completely done, and to speak of new ones would be out of the question. We are also very poorly fed, it being nothing uncommon to get porridge three times a day and always twice.

The final straw broke in November over a dispute concerning the wages owed to one hired hand. 'On Thursday evening', noted Wilson, 'I asked for Currie's wages as he was going to Keith market on Friday and was not coming back. They kept 2/- off for every day he wanted. They had no right I think to keep off as much as his wages only ran to

---

[28] 'The Diary of Willie McWillie, 1881-1887', (unpublished), 22 March 1887 and 26 April 1887.

[29] 'Diary of William McWillie', 26 October 1887.

1/6 a day but they are the meanest, greediest folk I ever saw'. Consequently, Wilson moved to work at Georgetown, Inveravon, also near Aberlour. He lived in a bothy and described both accommodation and work as 'a change for the better in every respect ... I am also liking the bothy far better than expected. The woman keeps everything clean and tidy and seems to be a good cook. We have brose in the morning, potatoes for dinner, and porridge for supper, but of course she would cook anything we like to give her'. Pride of place on the farm went to 'a herd of over 40 Aberdeen Angus cattle ... Of course they are kept in grand order and it seems to be the cattleman's hobby to tell of the noble blood of his "black skins".' Despite the unpleasant experience of life and work at Balliemulloch, Wilson entered fully into the community life in Speyside. He became an active member of Ballindalloch Mutual Improvement Society. His paper to the Society, quoted above, on the advantages of large farms may have been influenced by his work at Georgetown. As a regular worshipper at Aberlour Parish Church, he held the sermons given by John Smith Sloss, the recently ordained minister, in high regard. [30]

In exploring the area his inquisitive mind noted local landmarks especially farms, crofts and the land. In July 1887, he and the foreman from Balliemulloch set out to see Glenlivet, travelling along the turnpike road as the ground over the hillside was too wet. Their route can be retraced today and the landmarks described in the Journal are still visible. The route took them past Glen Fairclas Distillery, down towards Ballindalloch Castle and Dalnashaugh Inn. The road then turned down Avon Side with farms such as Craggan and Drumin spaced out along each side of the river. Turning up Glenlivet they 'came in sight of the Distillery of Minmore belonging Major Smith' where Wilson was impressed with the bonded stores which he paced at 'forty-two yards inside'. Other visitors might have been more impressed with the final product, but as a tee-totaller Wilson made no such admission. The modern day visitor to Minmore, or now Glenlivet Distillery which is owned by Pernod, is given a taste of whiskies produced using water from Josie's Well to feed the mash tun as it did over a century ago. Carrying on along the road they viewed the Morange at the foot of Ben Rinnes noting how its farms were 'of the smaller size'. On another occasion he climbed Ben Rinnes from where he could see Knowes far in the distance. Their journey ended at Tomnavoulin with its 'School and Schoolhouse, where William Lorimer was sometime Schoolmaster, while across the water is the

---

[30] Scott, *Fasti*, vi, 336.

Roman Catholic Chapel'. The road continued onto Tomintoul and is now best known for featuring in road reports when it is blocked by snow. The fact that this walk exceeded 14 miles was not worthy of comment since walking this distance was nothing out of the ordinary.

Disagreement over who should manage Knowes led to Wilson moving to the Aberlour area and his determination to return under his own conditions emphasises his resolute if not stubborn personality. In October 1887, Wilson received a letter from his uncle which contained a request from his parents that he should return home. Willie McWillie visited Knowes and noted that Wilson was being greatly missed:

> Spent the evening of the 25th very pleasantly at Knowes. Mr. and Mrs. Wilson want James to come home again, they feel the want of him very much. I have written and told him so.[31]

Wilson had, however, 'quite made up my mind … that I will not go home to be on the same footing as I left. I think I could manage things fully better than Father now and if he cannot see his way to make ends meet, and is willing to give me the management for his and Mother's sake I might go home, but when once I am away, I would be better to take another half year whatever. One is always learning something'. This battle of wills continued until the following spring when, on a visit home, his conditions were met:

> Father is complaining greatly on his loss of sight, and about not being able to go to the markets, and he is sorely put about as to how the seed is to be got in. I was sorry to see him troubling himself so much, and he got me to promise that I would come home at Whitsunday again. He is to go down to Cullen House and get my name put in to the tack, and Willie is going to be put to learn a trade. I will be much benefited, however, by the year I have been away from home. I have seen and learned much which I would not have done otherwise.

A further pull factor was, nevertheless, at work. Over the months and years visits to Kirkton became more frequent and the references to Katie Duncan increased until in October 1888 he asked for her hand in marriage. 'Of course I was impetuous and wanted an answer there and then, but no—I must wait. —She must have time, but on Friday evening she would let me know her decision'. After perhaps an anxious wait, Friday arrived and 'it was with a beating heart, that I knocked at the door of Kirkton … Katie herself answered my call, came out and shut the door. This with her warm hand clasp somewhat reassured me. The night being chilly I threw my overcoat around her shoulders, and led her into the garden, and there at the upper end,

[31] 'Diary of William McWillie', 6 November 1887.

with her head reclining on my shoulder; —with the October wind sighing among the trees, and the crescent moon with her pale silvery light looking down upon us, as if to witness our plighted troth, she whispered in my ear that her heart was a' my ain'. They were married in July 1889, travelling to Aberlour for a 'honeymoon' which turned into something of a 'busman's holiday' with time spent inspecting Ballindalloch Estate and the local farms, including Balliemulloch, where the crops were looking 'remarkably well, but their turnips very backward'. It would be interesting to speculate how many of today's honeymooners spend a Sunday in the same way as the newly wedded Mr. and Mrs. Wilson who 'breakfasted at eight o'clock, and was much pleased with the size of the Aberlour eggs, and the sweetness of its honey. Remembering the maxim that 'a Sabbath well spent, brings a week of content, and health for the toils the morrow', we spent the forenoon in reading the Scriptures, meditation and prayer. At twelve o'clock we repaired to the Established Church to hear Mr. Sloss'. After lunch they visited a farm where 'Katie was delighted with the clean and tidy appearance of the whole premises, more especially the dairy …'. This was followed by a walk to Aberlour Mains Farm with a view across to Knockando. They ended the day by attending the Episcopal Church in Aberlour.

Wilson's thoughts on his honeymoon reveal the deep affection and love which he felt for Katie, 'and so our holiday was ended. I will not say our honeymoon. God grant that it will never end'. This did not conflict with his more traditional expectations of the relationship between husband and wife established from day one of the marriage when '… I took good care to rise first in case Katie should "don the breeks"'. Farming remained an ever present concern, despite the occasion, since after breakfast '… I went out to have a look at Mr. Ross' stock and crops'. Further insights into his thoughts on marriage came in a birthday present of Mrs Craik's *A Woman's Thoughts About Women*, given to Katie several months before their wedding.[32] Wilson had 'a favour for Mrs. Craik's writings and this one has in no degree lessened my estimation of their sterling work'. At one level the book confirms a stereotype of Victorian women by eschewing equality in its acceptance that women were ' "the weaker vessel" with dependence upon one we love being perhaps the sweetest thing in the world'.[33] However, Mrs. Craik aimed her book at single women who, she urged, should embrace self dependence, quoting the example of two young women who

---

[32] Mrs Craik, *A Woman's Thoughts About Women. By the Author of John Halifax, Gentleman etc.* (London, 1858).
[33] Mrs Craik, *A Woman's Thoughts*, 23.

successfully ran the family business after the death of their father. Craik reserved particular criticism for idleness and concluded a chapter entitled, 'Something to Do', with the following homily:

> But—and when her place is vacant on earth, this will be said of her assuredly, both here and Otherwhere— 'She has done what she could'.[34]

This also encapsulated Wilson's expectation of a wife's role within a loving relationship.

At the same time, when Wilson was recording the events surrounding his engagement, he referred to 'the disgraceful conduct of Joan ... Of all the shame and disgrace caused by the conduct of her, whom I shall never countenance as a Sister, I shall make no more mention here'. It transpired later that the 'disgraceful conduct' was pregnancy before marriage. From this point on Wilson turned his back on Joan until her death from a throat infection in October 1890, but illegitimate births were by no means uncommon, as illustrated by the many cases of 'antenuptial fornication' recorded in the kirk session minutes of Fordyce Parish Church. In December 1872, Jane Wighton of Redlythe Farm compeared before the session 'and gave Joseph Tait as the father of her illegitimate child. Satisfactory evidence was produced as to the paternity. Jane Wighton was admonished and continued, and the Clerk was instructed to cause the said Joseph Tait to be summonded to appear here at the next meeting of session'. There was no record of his appearance, but in January 1873 'compeared Jane Wighton ... She was suitably admonished and restored to privileges'.[35] This case highlighted the close knit nature of rural society since Jane Wighton was the daughter of James Wighton from whom Wilson bought crop seed, and one elder hearing the case was Wilson's uncle who farmed at Limestones. The inhabitants of Burns, where Wilson farmed after leaving Knowes, could not escape censure when in April 1881, 'compeared Elspet Cumming, Servant at Burns, Fordyce, confessing that she is with child, and giving as the partner of her guilt James Flaws, formerly of Burns and now in Strath of Brydoch, Alvah. The Clerk was instructed to cite him to appear at next meeting of session'. Both James Flaws and Elspet Cumming later 'professed penitence' and were 'absolved from Church censure'.[36]

[34] Mrs Craik, *A Woman's Thoughts*, 21.
[35] National Archives of Scotland, Fordyce Parish Church, Kirk Session Minutes, 9/12/1872 and 13/1/1873, CH2 (1) 14/5.
[36] Fordyce Kirk Session Minutes, 8/4/1881, 29/4/1881, 1/8/1881 and 8/12/1881. There are no extant records for Deskford Parish Church after 1858 so it was not possible to find any reference to Joan Wilson appearing before the kirk session.

Wilson characterised the social conservatism which pervaded rural society in contrast to support for political liberalism. During the 1885 general election campaign a political meeting was held in Deskford School addressed by 'Mr. Darling the Conservative candidate for Banffshire … Mr. Darling was received with cheers and hisses, and during his speech he was repeatedly interrupted. His speech was wholly taken up criticising the foreign policy of the Liberals and defending the Church. He is a fluent speaker and a nice looking man, but I do not think his speech would have gained him any supporters'. Consequently, the Journal expresses little surprise when the Liberal candidate won by a majority of 173 votes.

Debates on perceived low levels of literacy currently dominate Scottish education with present standards unflatteringly compared to a past golden age dominated by the lad o' pairts. Wilson's copperplate handwriting and the fluency of his Journal, lectures, poems and short stories suggest an advanced education, but he received a relatively short education in Deskford School. In the 'Foreword' Wilson described the subjects which he studied, his teachers and fellow pupils. Mr William Smith from Banff, 'although of extremely meagre stature … was every inch a man, as well as a gentleman. He was a most beautiful writer, and for many years he proved himself to be a good all round teacher, sending not a few of his pupils direct to University…'. However, 'after the vigour and enthusiasm of youth had somewhat subsided I have heard it alleged that he did turn just somewhat lazy, and also somewhat fond of a wee drappie'. Wilson did not regard himself as 'a brilliant scholar. The learning of my lessons I am certain required far more time and study than was bestowed by many of my school-mates in the same subjects, but once I had fully mastered them, I seemed to have not only the ability of retaining, but also improving on them'. These subjects included the traditional 3Rs of reading, writing and arithmetic alongside religious education which concentrated on learning the Shorter Catechism. Wilson also studied Latin which, 'although perhaps of little or no practical value to me in later life, still I never regretted spending part of my school days in the study of this dead language, for in English literature there are so many Latin phrases used, that I certainly have enjoyed it'. Of more practical use was the Mensuration and Book-Keeping which 'after leaving school I often followed … up on my own account, and to this day nothing gives me greater pleasure than to measure a few fields or even a whole farm when asked to do so by any of my friends or neighbours'.

In and beyond Deskford the prevailing culture placed great value on the parish school and the importance of continuing education through self improvement. Wilson demonstrated this through his involvement in the Deskford Library and the Deskford Mutual Improvement Association. The Deskford Association formed part of a national network providing a forum for people to meet and debate current affairs and more general issues. Wilson was a regular contributor and kept a record of his essays and lectures. These cover a wide range of topics and are reprinted in Appendix 2. He also addressed the Vale of Deskford Temperance Society giving a general paper on temperance in 1889 and later speaking against the motion, 'is a teetotal farmer justified in selling barley to a distillery?' Wilson did in fact supply barley to the local distillery at Glenglassaugh, but these lectures encapsulate many of his attitudes and beliefs, for example, in the efficient use of time, enjoyment derived from the spring and support for temperance.

The spirit of mutual improvement spread to running the local library in the evenings. In July 1885, Wilson and a friend 'went over to Kirkton on Friday evening and opened the Library. There was but a small attendance, as this is scarcely the season for reading. It is intended to call in all the Books belonging to the Library next month to have them all re-arranged, and get a new catalogue printed'. His own reading included Dickens, Scott, Burns, MacDonald and Samuel Smiles' *Self Help*. Smiles was given a strong endorsement in line with Wilson's commitment to self improvement. 'A better book', wrote Wilson, 'I never read in my life … It contains so many practical lessons, and so many illustrious examples of what others have done, by their perseverance; courage; industry; economy; honesty; energy; application; decision of character; truthfulness; accuracy and punctuality; that beyond any other book I have ever read, it ought to be the means of stimulating us to diligence in business, to self improvement; and to earnest striving to follow those who have left such well defined footprints, on the sands of time'. *Self Help* became one of the most popular books in the nineteenth century with the fourth edition reprinted fifty times between 1859 and 1907.[37] The book's central theme was summed up by the opening sentence which quoted the maxim, 'heaven helps those who help themselves' to which Smiles added his own advice supported by profiles of notable 'self helpers' such as James Watt and Isambard Kingdom Brunel.

Self help did not imply selfishness since a sense of community and mutual support runs through Wilson's Journal. He helped his neighbours at key times of the farming year, 'we were at Ardiecow on the 6th October, 1889 and gave them a day's cutting with the reaper. We were also back yesterday the 15th and gave them a spell at leading,

[37] S. Smiles, *Self Help*, (London, 1859).

the crop is not heavy. On Thursday we were at Limestones leading. They have a splendid crop and as the weather for the last few days has been remarkably fine it was in splendid condition'. Wilson kept a paternal watch over Backies, which had been farmed by his friend Willie McWillie until his death in 1888 when the tack transferred to his sister. In November 1888, 'I went passed Backies and got a drive with Miss McWillie. She was wanting me to buy Irish calves for her but there were none in the market'. The New Year brought 'an invitation from Mrs Riddoch to go up for dinner along with Alick Duncan and Miss A. McWillie. After enjoying Mrs Riddoch's hospitality we went up to see Annie's "stock", her cattle being indeed well worth inspection. She has got the other 12 Irish calves, but they are fair dearer this year each costing close on £7 while last year they were bought at 5 guineas'.

In an age before television, the cinema and other modern leisure activities, mutuality and self help were the watchwords for entertainment. The Journal records a diverse and rich variety of leisure activities which often revolved around the community, friends and the Church. The list is impressively long: agricultural flower and vegetable shows; picnics; soirees; concerts; Burns Nights; dances; visiting friends and neighbours; trips to Aberdeen; walking; parties alongside the above mentioned lectures to the Mutual Improvement Association. Willie McWillie's diary emphasises the value placed on visiting friends in their home:

> Did not feel very well on Sunday and did not go to Church. Our old servant Maggie Duncan and her husband George Geddes was here in the afternoon. James Wilson of Knowes came across to tea and stayed the evening. We discussed several not very Sunday topics, Chill plows and the best method of applying farmyard manure were two of the subjects discussed. He advised me to try this method of heading my diary, he has adopted this style and likes it very well. If it was not for his Mother and Father he is minded to go to Australia. I would feel a great loss if he did.[38]

The Deskford Annual Picnic featured as a notable local event with Wilson's lively description reflecting his enjoyment of the occasion:

> In the evening (August 1881) I went over to Kirkton to get the orchard in trim for our Annual Pic-nic. We cut the grass, set the seats, and put up a swing ... By three o'clock ... a goodly company of lads and lasses gay all in holiday attire and bent on merry making, had assembled beneath the spreading boughs of the giant ash, that rears its towering head on the

---

[38] 'Diary of William McWillie', 30 December 1886.

level haugh by the burnside. The afternoon was all that could be desired and the turnout was fully an average. By 3.30 our musicians, viz. Messrs. Johnstone, Geddes, Duncan and Black had their fiddles tuned and we enjoyed a few reels and schottisches. About half past four Mr. Smith, School Master, was called to the Chair and after a few remarks by him, a sumptuous tea was served out by the stewards and stewardesses, who afterwards enjoyed their own cup by the dykeside. Dancing was now entered into with great zest, all the Contra Dances—Rory O' More, Loch Leven, Strip the Willow and others ... Those who were not inclined for dancing amused themselves with various games, while old Aunt Sally, and the Swing, was a source of great amusement to the youngsters.

Times of happiness were balanced by illness and death. The death of his great friend, Willie McWillie, in June 1888 and his mother three months later made a deep impression on Wilson. Both deaths resulted from long and painful illnesses in an age without antibiotics and treatments developed by later advances in medicine. The reaction to these deaths also highlights the seminal role which faith played in his life. 'Oh that God', he lamented after Willie McWillie's death, 'would deeply impress on my mind, the most solemn lesson taught by the death of my friend; so that by leading a holy and devoted life, I may be able from my heart to say, "Let me die the death of the righteous, and let my last end be like his".' Faith also determined the reaction to life threatening events such as that in August 1879 when he was struck by lightning while furring up turnips. He completely recovered and could not 'feel too grateful to God, whom his great mercy spared me, as I earnestly hope (as the apostle says) to live, not unto ourselves, but unto him who saved us, and washed us in his blood'. Consequently, the epitaph, 'No Cross, No Crown', was carved on the bottom plinth of his and Katie's gravestone.

Faith was nurtured by regular attendance at Sunday worship in Deskford Parish Church, but following the common practice he also attended other churches, notably Deskford Free Church and Fordyce Parish Church where the Hendry family from Newpark Farm joined him. His Presbyterian beliefs did not preclude attendance, albeit rarely, at Episcopalian and Roman Catholic services. Wilson epitomised the critical attention paid to the sermon, which was central to Sunday worship. Some sermons drew praise:

I was at Church on Sunday ... We had Mr. McLachlan, Inveravon, preaching. He really is a grand preacher, and we got an excellent sermon from him. His text was Proverbs XI, 30. 'The fruits of the righteous is a tree of life'. We ought to learn from this he said that everyone bore fruit of some sort,

either good or bad. Without Christianity however it was
impossible to bear such fruit as that described in the text ...

Other ministers and sermons were less impressive:

> James McKenzie came down to see me in the afternoon. I
> went up and had tea with him, and then went to the Service at
> the Brig O' Avon. It was Mr. Robertson's assistant who
> preached. He seems to be a very earnest man, but has a bad
> delivery and is terribly confined to the paper.

Notwithstanding his strong faith he kept a perhaps surprisingly
open mind in the debate between evolutionists and the account of
creation given in Genesis. During one week in September 1885 he
read Chambers's *Vestigis of the Natural History of Creation* noting that it
aimed 'to show that the world was not created in six days, as the Bible
would lead us to believe'. Wilson then went on to describe Chambers's
theory of evolution which stated that 'the world must have been in
existence countless ages before man appeared on the scene' while
animals 'have been gradually progressing from the more simple forms
of life', evidence for which could be found in 'the testimony of the
rocks'. Wilson's perceptive observations of the natural world may have
influenced his attitude towards evolution which seemed 'to be very
natural, but how it can be reconciled to the testimony of revelation
which tells us that the world with all the beasts and birds and creeping
things were created in the space of six days, I cannot as yet perceive'.

Religion, the land, self improvement, family, friends and
community were the lynchpins of Wilson's life. Readers of the Journal
will form their own impressions about his character and personality,
but his granddaughter remembers a stern man who insisted that she
attended the afternoon sunday school held in his house at Parklea
instead of joining her friends on the beach at Sandend. Old age
brought fading eyesight and the need for his son-in-law to read aloud
the newspaper with any noise made by the children greeted with a
sharp 'whist'. Some of his writing reflects this sternness, especially his
attitude towards his sister and strong moral tone. And yet the Journal
and poems reveal a more private side to his personality expressed
through a profound attachment to the land, high regard for friendships,
alongside love for his wife and family. However, the historical
importance of the Journal largely lies in the wide ranging observations
on life in rural Scotland which go some way to countering Gavin
Sprott's well founded claim that lowland agriculture and society is a
'considerable, yet in many ways an under-developed, subject area'.[39]

---

[39] G. Sprott, 'Lowland Society and Agriculture', in Cooke *et al* (eds.), *Modern Scottish
History, 1707 to the Present*, ii, 188.

Nevertheless, such a personal account by one person begs the question of the extent to which it reflects prevailing attitudes and practices.

Autobiographies, diaries and journals describing middle class life in urban Scotland were relatively common throughout the nineteenth century, sharing with Wilson an emphasis on religious worship. Born and brought up in Glasgow's prosperous West End, J.J. Bell remembered the streets of Hillhead on Sunday mornings as families joined the procession winding its way to the local Churches with 'scenes almost spectacular in their respectability. Every Mama wore a Sunday bonnet and carried an umbrella—or parasol, if the summer sun were shining; almost every daddy, bearded and black-coated, wore a silk hat ...'.[40] Sir Michael Connal, industrialist and philanthropist, was described by his biographer as having a 'very deep' religious life. 'He lived in the spirit of the 139th Psalm—in the light of God'. Connal's own diary expanded on this influence:

> ... the Christian in all the duties and opportunities of the situation in which he may be placed is bound to have God's glory constantly in view by the consideration that the part allotted him is God's, and that in it, however dark it be as to its ultimate end for God, he is bound to exercise all knowledge and refinement, adorning with the graces of the Christian every duty he is engaged in ...[41]

This did not imply an uncritical faith as demonstrated in the critical analysis of sermons, with one preached by Dr. Candlish labelled as 'reprehensible' and 'speculative'.[42]

Many middle class families helped maintain a profitable postal service by their voluminous correspondence. The chemist and industrialist, Walter Crum, wrote regularly to his wife and daughters, often quoting at length the Sunday sermon with one extract running to four and a half pages. On 21 August 1864, he wrote to his daughter, 'the sermon was excellent throughout, with a few fine passages and so expressed as to secure continued attention. It was on the fall of Eve ...'.[43] Women, who comprised the majority of church-goers, were also sharp observers of Sunday worship. Helen McFie, wife of a sugar refiner, built her life around family, home and religion. The practice of Sunday worship was not broken by winter weather or travelling abroad. If snow blocked the roads around the family's country estate in

---

[40] J.J. Bell, *I Remember* (Edinburgh, 1932), 42.
[41] J.G. Gibson (ed.), *Diary of Sir Michael Connal* (Glasgow, 1895), xvii.
[42] Gibson (ed.), *Diary of Sir Michael Connal, 50.*
[43] GUA, Letter from Walter Crum to his daughter Mary, 21/8/1864, 1073/3/17.

Dumfries, then a service was held in the drawing room. And back in Edinburgh:

> 21 April (1864) Thursday. Fast Day. Forenoon Dr. Bruce's.
> Afternoon Mr. Davidson's, Mr. Andrew Bonnar preached.
> 24 April Sunday. Went to Dr. Bruce's morning, afternoon and evening. Dr. B. preached on the agony of Christ in Gethsemane being actually suffering instead of his people. Mr Gibson assisted him.[44]

Working class autobiographies were less common than middle class diaries and journals, but the diaries kept by an anonymous farm servant in Meikleforce in 1830 and by a millwright in Dundee share many similarities with Wilson's Journal, especially in their emphasis on religion and mutual improvement. The diary of the farm servant is in fact a second hand account given by his parish priest of the original manuscript.[45] The diary concentrates its account on each Sunday, consequently, a more accurate title would have been 'Sunday Diary' or 'Spiritual Diary' since it makes little reference to events outwith going to Church, as characterised by the entry for 3 January 1830:

> Attended Divine Service. Sermon, Psalm XXXIX, 4. This sermon was calculated to impress on the mind with the remembrance of the uncertainty of life, and to think what would have been our case had we been summoned before our Judge, and that some who were this day last year in their pews in Church fresh and blooming are now laid in their graves. This brings to my mind the death of ... Spent the rest of the day in meditation and reading.

The farm servant did not provide a description of rural life to match that given by Wilson in his Journal. The diary of John Sturrock, a millwright in Dundee, gives a full account of his life between 1864–1865 with religion at its core.[46] Sundays, notwithstanding interruptions, were spent attending two or three services. On 11 December 1865 he 'got up at half past eight. Went to Mr. Ewing's Church in the forenoon, Mr. Adamson's, Wallacetown, in the afternoon, who I must say is in my opinion a dry preacher. I was intending to go and hear Miss Armstrong in the evening but was prevented by J. Wright coming in, as we must always have an hour or two's conversation when we get the opportunity, we had almost two hours tonight on two or three different subjects. I then went and heard Mr. McGregor of Free St. Peter's ... He gave a most eloquent and impressive sermon on Romans 14, 7 and 8:

[44] GUA, Private Journal of Helen McFie (nee Wahab), 1864–1865, DC 120/1/10.
[45] C. Low, 'Diary of a Farm Servant Sixty Five Years Ago', *The Scottish Standard Bearer*, February 1895.
[46] C.A. Whatley (ed.), *The Diary of John Sturrock* (East Linton, 1996).

"For no man liveth to himself and no man dieth to himself. For whether we live, we live unto the Lord, and whether we die, we die unto the Lord". It would be well for us if we would keep these words more in mind than we do but alas! Our guilty hearts will think nothing but this world and its vanities'.[47] Wilson shared these sentiments and would have found further common ground in Sturrock's concern for self improvement through reading and attendance at drawing class. They both epitomised nineteenth-century respectability and its dislike of idleness, concerned to ensure that leisure time was turned to 'particular advantage' instead of being trifled away.[48] They were less unanimous over the Roman Catholic Church whose services Sturrock described as 'a piece of merest trumpery'[49] in contrast to Wilson's comments on attending a Roman Catholic chapel in Aberdeen:

> The walls also round about with all the pillars supporting the arches, are all decorated and adorned with paintings and sculptor of such a style and in such a manner as the Church of Rome knows only too well. We got however a fairly good address from The Revd. Mr. Stropani, while the music was first class but for the rest of the service I could neither make head nor tail of it.

The Roman Catholic Church had a more established presence in the North East and minimal Irish immigration prevented the religious tensions which arose in Dundee and Glasgow.

In a short story entitled, 'Rustic Courtship or Farm Life in Banffshire', Wilson expanded on the importance of respectability in his description of the Brown family who were central to the narrative:

> By retailing some groceries to her neighbours, by boarding one of the female teachers in her room end, and by dint of the strictest economy, she (Mrs. Brown) had managed to bring up her family in a most respectable manner, making it a strong point, that every one of them should go regularly to Church and Sunday School.

The story also drew strongly on Wilson's own courtship and his knowledge of the area around Deskford with fictitious places such as Fordyce barely disguised from actual locations. A full version of the story is given in Appendix 3. A selection of his poems, chosen to illustrate their range, variety, influence of faith, family, friends, farming and nature, appears in Appendix 1. His poetry displays some skill with language and some thoughts on the human condition. Overall it is variable in standard, but shows a developing skill in the poet as a writer

[47] Whatley (ed.), *Diary of John Sturrock*, 43-4.
[48] Whatley (ed.), *Diary of John Sturrock*, 29.
[49] Whatley (ed.), *Diary of John Sturrock*, 45.

alongside a maturing human being. Robert Burns, religion, the prevailing culture of the time and nature heavily influence the poems. Wilson's life was not radically different to that of his contemporaries. He stands out, however, for leaving such a detailed account of rural Scotland at a time when agriculture was entering a new era. The quality of his writing, his poems and lectures, further enhance his importance. The Journal may lack gossipy detail and it begins somewhat repetitiously, but perseverance by the reader is rewarded by insights into so many aspects of rural society. There is much to capture the imagination of the general reader alongside those with more specialist interests: the weather for environmental historians; observations on religion for church historians; agricultural practices for students of farming; estate management within land economy; treatment of human and animal illnesses for students of medicine and veterinary science; the quality of his writing for educationalists and his use of leisure time for those studying social history. Taken as a whole, however, the Journal provides a rare insight into an important part of Scottish society.

Editor's note
Wilson wrote his Journal in four large notebooks each exceeding two hundred pages. A separate volume contains his essays, lectures and poems alongside some later correspondence. The only extant copy of the Journals is a facsimile copy taken in the early 1960s from the originals. These facsimiles cover Volumes 1, 3 and 4 but exclude the second volume covering the period 1882-1885 which, despite extensive searches, cannot be traced. The facsimile copy is held by James Wilson's granddaughter, Edith Lowrie. The original Journals were taken to Canada by a relative where they were lost. Edith Lowrie also holds Wilson's original volume with his lectures, poems and correspondence.

Wilson's text required only very minor editing. There have been some changes to the punctuation, layout of the text and spelling: for example, he spelt colour as color. Placenames presented a greater difficulty since there is considerable variation in the spelling between different sources and within the Journal. For example, Knowes is sometimes referred to as Upper Knowes, but at other times as Knowes. In some maps it is spelled as Knows. As a general rule, Wilson's spelling of placenames has been followed except when the writing was unclear and in this case the modern spelling has been used. Towards the end of his Journal, Wilson began to put sub-headings at the top of each page. They do not always relate to the entire content of each page and for the purpose of consistency have been omitted from the edition. Otherwise the text remains very much as Wilson wrote it.

Wilson's poetry presented a difficulty in that he both composed poems and copied the works of other poets into his Journal. Wilson was careful to acknowledge works which were not his own and those featured in the appendix were composed by him notwithstanding the occasional external influence. For example, Wilson's, 'The Water Mill', is based on the poem, 'The Lesson of the Water Mill', by Sarah Doudney. The poems featured in this publication were selected to illustrate important themes and interests including family, friends, nature, religion and different types of poetry.

A Journal of my Life
April 4

filled up three quarters of potato oats, and started
for Pokey to get an exchange of seed. He
selected a bushful of Sandwich oats, grown on
Tweedie of Tincherly, and weighing 45 lbs. finished
our own furrows without A4. On Wednesday
afternoon I again tried the plough. It was still
very hard, and I was only able to plough down
hill. Thursday was also very frosty, so in the forenoon I went over to the smiddy and got the
filly shod. In the afternoon I was ploughing
clover land. On both Friday and Saturday I
ploughed all day, although still rather hard in
the mornings. On Sunday afternoon Father
went over to Newbigging to see Mark Wilson
who has lately returned from Dumreca and
is thought to be dying of consumption.
Mrs Riddell Bachus and Miss Anna A Mills
came over on a visit. Today it has been
fresh and warm and quite spring like. And
I expect it may have long continued. I hope

And every-day Doings
April 4

the filly in the plough a few turns in the
forenoon, when she went very well.
I had finished my funeral writing for the
week, and had my tools put past, but after my
my horses I tried a name which has compelled
me again to resume my pen. The sun had then
set for half an hour behind the hill of Maud, and
the curtain of night was drawing its folds of
darkness over the earth. Scarcely a breath of wind
stirred the air, and as I stood on the old dyke
beside the peat stacks, and gazed around on
I beheld what to my eyes seemed a beautiful
picture; and listened to what may was reckoned
the sweetest music. All along the hill side and
where-ever you turned your eyes numbers of bonfires
were shedding their ruddy glow, and lighting up
the gathering gloom, while above them the smoke
was eddying and curling, and rising in columns
in the still evening air. Over the Clumhill
could be seen the sea lying so calm and still.

Pages from Wilson's Journal, April 4 1881.

Artist's impression of Knowes Farm, circa 1880 (artist unknown.)

JAMES WILSON'S FOREWORD

Before perusing the following pages, might I be allowed to state a few of the reasons that have led me to indite what is contained therein?[1] Personally I have always had a keen desire to know something of my forbears, and so by committing to writing all that I know of my parents, grandparents etc., I may be able to satisfy a like desire in some of those who follow after. Another reason is that I may be able to record some of the more outstanding events that have occurred, during my long and not altogether uneventful life.

The many accidents in which I have been involved, during my daily occupation, or when driving alone, or in company with my better half, any one of which might easily have proved fatal, ought most assuredly to fill my heart with gratitude to the wise and loving Father who has so often, and seemingly so miraculously protected and spared me. The very act of recording these events ought surely to strengthen our faith and to deepen our belief in the precious words of the great dramatist 'There is a Divinity that shapes our ends, rough hew them how we will'.

In my younger days I was a member of two Mutual Improvement Societies one in Deskford and the other in Inveravon. During the years I attended these most useful meetings I wrote and delivered several essays and other papers. In later years I have given speeches at 'Burnsnichts' or when presenting School Prizes etc., etc.

I have also tried my hand at the composition of verse. During most of my life it has been my practice to make extracts from the books I have read. From 1879-1892 I also kept a diary writing regularly once a week and filling four volumes. Extracts from these will be inserted in the following pages, whilst the other items will be given in full. To gather all these together and place them in order within the covers of this volume will thus be my aim and ambition and if the perusal   of

---

[1] 'Foreword' was the term used by James Wilson to describe this retrospective on his life. Here it is used as a Foreword to his Journal for the overview provided on his life, neighbours and the Deskford area.

these pages at any future time should be the means of inducing anyone
to follow the steps I have taken and so obtain a measure of the pleasure
and satisfaction that has fallen to my lot, my labour of love will
certainly not have been in vain.

... [half page missing] no doubt thinking that he was being treated
unjustly and being at the same time of a rather stubborn nature, the
teacher failed entirely to make David comply with his demands.
Consequently a hand to hand tussle ensued, and both combatants were
seen rolling on the floor. It was always a doubtful question which of
them had the best or the worst of it, but Mr. Brander during the
scrummage had unfortunately torn off one of David's trouser buttons.
On regaining his feet and perceiving this David sternly demanded that
'you'll shew on that button again afore I move oot o' this'. The
teacher took no heed for a time, but David kept so persistently to his
demand that ultimately Mr. Brander had to climb down so far as to
say, 'go through to the housekeeper and she will attend to you'.

On another occasion a nephew of my own, William Bidie from
The Backies, a young stout fellow of 19 or so went boldly up and took
a younger boy out of Mr. Brander's hands saying, 'Ye'll nae lay anither
han on Sandy, ye've gein him ower muckle already'. The teacher at
once desisted making no remonstrations. Another episode which
occurred when I was under Mr. Brander's tuition has fixed itself upon
my memory. On every Monday so many questions of the Shorter
Catechism had always to be repeated. On one particular, Monday
Mackenzie MacIntosh and myself had failed to repeat satisfactorily. We
were told in the most peremptory manner, 'go to your seats and learn
your catechism correctly'. Before being dismissed for dinner we were
again called up. Now this hour before dinner was usually employed in
copying the headlines of our copy-books. While Mackenzie and I
were repeating our 'questions' or answers rather Mr. Brander was
leaning over one of the big girl's shoulders showing her how to hold
her pen properly. I managed to repeat my task without any very
flagrant mistake, but my school-fellow was laboriously striving to wade
through Effectual Calling but making sorry progress. Seeing that 'The
Maister's' back was completely turned to us I held up the Catechism
before Mackenzie's eyes when he reeled it off without a hitch.

Like Mr. Malinson of George McDonald fame and like many
another dominie of those days, Mr. Brander had seemingly the
ambition of being able to wag his paw in a pulpit some day, and
accordingly he had for some years been attending the Divinity Hall.
When absent on these occasions he had of course to provide a
substitute.

Having finished his studies he was appointed to a charge in a mining village in Lanarkshire. During his residence there, a Miss Lorimer, a Deskford lady, was employed as his housekeeper. After several years however he gave up his charge, married his housekeeper and retired to the South of England where he died leaving a widow and one son.

Mr. Brander's successor was a Mr. William Smith who belonged to Banff. Although of extremely meagre stature, Mr. Smith was every inch a man, as well as a gentleman. He was a most beautiful writer, and for many years he proved himself to be a good all round teacher, sending not a few of his pupils direct to the University. The most distinguished of these has undoubtably been Professor Ashley Mackintosh of Aberdeen, the youngest son of the Rev. Dr. Mackintosh who for over 40 years was the respected Minister of Deskford. As Chairman at social meetings Mr. Smith had few equals.

I have said that Mr. Smith proved himself to be an excellent teacher for many years, but after the vigour and enthusiasm of youth had somewhat subsided I have heard it alleged that he did turn just somewhat lazy, and also somewhat fond of 'a wee drappie'. When first coming to Deskford and for many years his mother kept house for him, but after her decease he married a Miss Wilson, a niece of Dr. MacIntosh's. After his retiral about the year 1903 the family went to reside at Nairn. Both Mr. Smith and his spouse are now deceased but the son and daughter still survive.

Nothing of any particular note falls to be recorded of these latter years I spent at school. My own personal opinion, is that in no degree could I ever have been called a brilliant scholar. The learning of my lessons I am certain required far more time and study than what was bestowed by many of my school-mates on the same subjects, but once I had fully mastered them I seemed to have not only the ability of retaining, but also of improving on them.

When I was about 12 years of age Mr. Smith suggested that I should commence to learn Latin and this I did, mastering The Rudiments and part of Caesar. Although perhaps of little or no practical value to me in after life, still I never regretted spending part of my school days in the study of this dead language, for in English Literature there are so many Latin phrases used, that I have certainly enjoyed its perusal better through my having a slight knowledge of their meaning. During the last six months I was at School Mensuration and Book Keeping were my principle studies, land measuring having a special attraction for me. After leaving School, I often followed this up on my own account and to this day nothing gives me greater pleasure than to measure a few fields or even a whole farm when asked to do so by any of my friends or neighbours.

I might here mention a few of my school-mates with whom I continued to have intercourse in after years. First among these must be Alex and George Duncan of Kirkton Farm who were afterwards to become my brothers-in-law. Their mother had been extremely delicate and two years after George was born she was taken from them leaving 4 girls as well as the two boys. My mother and Mrs. Duncan had been extremely intimate however, and so after Mrs. Duncan's decease she continued to take a very motherly interest in the whole family.

Many a summer evening were Alex and George visitors to Knowes, and for many years Fastern-even or bannocky day was never allowed to pass without their coming up the brae to enjoy the fun and frolic.[2] My mother seemed to be an expert at telling our several fortunes. When the eggs were being broken to make the bannocks, we each selected one. The white of the egg was carefully poured into a tumbler and a little water added. My mother then held up the glass between her and the light, and having previously learned who was supposed to be our best girls, she was thus able to make some rather telling hits.

When about 16 years of age George was sent to the North of Scotland Bank at Cullen being afterwards transferred to the Head Office in Aberdeen. Relieving an agent in Fraserburgh he had the misfortune of being put in a damp bed, and this was the beginning of a decline from which he succumbed in 1888 being then only 33 years of age.

On leaving School, Alex was put to work on the farm and continued to do so until his father's death in 1891 when he succeeded to the tenancy. He improved the farm greatly by draining and deep ploughing, and he paid most particular attention to his cattle and horses, the latter being his special hobby. His second eldest sister, Mary, having married Mr. Alex Ross of Hillfolds, Ordiquhill, in 1880, Catherine having come to Knowes in 1889 and Jessie the eldest having married Mr. Joseph McConnachie, Esq. of India, Elspet a twin sister with Catherine was consequently left alone for housekeeper. In 1890 however, she died of cancer in the breast, and Cathy Ross, a niece, came to Kirkton. About two years later as she got married to William Smith of Badenhammer and now of Broadbeg, her elder sister, Alice, took her place. My brother-in-law had never been a very robust man and in the Spring of 1907 he turned very poorly and died in the month of July.

At Oathillock, a neighbouring farm to Knowes, there were in those days two families Mackay by name. When a father died leaving two

---

[2] Fastern-even, Shrove Tuesday; bannocks, round flat cakes of oat, barley or pease meal baked on a girdle.

sons it was very customary at that time to divide the holding between them, and such was the case here. John, the elder brother, had a very large family, but several of them were sadly deficient both mentally and physically and ultimately became quite helpless. The family of the younger brother, Sandy, was of quite a different caste. The oldest son was a graduate of Aberdeen University and ultimately became Rector of Rothesay Academy. The one nearest my age was James, and both of us being somewhat musically inclined, many a meeting was convened for the purpose of practicing on the Concertina, said meetings being not infrequently held at the foot of a stack in the cornyard. When about 15 years of age James was apprenticed to a draper in Dufftown, afterwards serving with Provost Smith in Cullen, and while there he was appointed Precentor in the Established Church, a post which he filled with much acceptance. After several years he went to Buckie and established a business of his own, and gradually increasing it from time to time until now it is not only one of the largest warehouses in Buckie, but one of the largest in the County of Banff.

Another school-mate of mine was Alex Murray. His parents were a worthy couple who lived in the village of Berryhillock, his mother being a rather noted personality in the district, and known locally as lucky Murray. At hatches, matches and despatches, Lucky's attendance was reckoned to be almost indispensable. She was of a most genial and jovial disposition, and never put forward the slightest objections to a wee bit cinder amongst her last cup of tea.[3] Alex was their youngest boy and they managed to send him to Aberdeen University. After several appointments he was selected as Head Master for Birnie, Morayshire, and here he remained until he retired a few years ago.

Adam Longmore of Cottartown was a little bit older than myself. He was pupil teacher to Mr. Smith, and also became a graduate of Aberdeen University. During the greater part of his teaching days he was first at Badenscoth and then at the Parish School of Auchterless. John his brother died several years ago.

At the farm of Berryleys, Fordyce, a large family of boys of the name of Christie was reared. They all came to Deskford School and as they had to pass Knowes on their way thither, they were my daily companions. Sandy, the eldest, was a draper in London. William for many years was School Master at Skene, and lived at Dyce after his retirement. James was a Minister somewhere in Kincardineshire. John and Stewart, the youngest, kept public houses in Glasgow. George learned to be a cabinet maker but died young, whilst the only survivor

---

[3] cinder, a strong stimulant

of them all now is Thomas, who for many years was a railway guard in the South of Scotland.

William Murray the only son of James Murray of Ardiecow was only a short time at Deskford School as he obtained a Murray and Minty bursary tenable at the Parish School of Fordyce. After leaving School he was employed as a clerk at the Banff Brewery, and remained there for a considerable number of years. When the Brewery was discontinued, he took a shop with a grocer's licence at the south end of High Street. He was three times married, and had four at least of a family. Sad to relate however, his mind became unhinged, and he died several years ago in Ladybridge Asylum. He had four sisters, Maggie, Jeanie, Nellie and Mary—nice decent quiet girls. They all came to Deskford School and were my sisters' companions. Maggie and Jeanie were never married and died at a comparatively early age, at the beautiful Speyside village of Aberlour, to which their Father had removed at Whitsunday 1879. Mary, the youngest, married a baker in Aberdeen, a Mr. Catto, but she is now deceased. Nellie, the only survivor, is the wife of Mr. Morrison, a boot and shoe manufacturer in Aberdeen.

Sandy, William and John Wright from Greenhill were also my school-mates. Sandy in his younger days went to farm service, married a farmer's daughter from Marnoch and then became tenant of the farm of Burnfield in Rothiemay. He died only a few months ago. After their father's death, William and John became tenants of Croftgloy, Deskford, where John still remains, his brother having died less than a year ago. Several of the boys Milne from Burns of Deskford were also School companions. Sandy, the eldest, succeeded his father in the tenancy of Burns. He married Elsie McKenzie of Broadloy by whom he had two sons and a daughter. The eldest son is now farmer at Carnoch, whilst the younger succeeded to Burns at his father's death some three years ago. The only daughter, Barbara, graduated at Aberdeen University, but being rather delicate she came home to recuperate for a time. Coming over to Fordyce as one of a party from Deskford, who were Amateur Theatricals, Mr. Dickson our Minister had kindly offered to motor several of the ladies home. Miss Milne happened to be his last passenger, but if this was his first visit to Burns it certainly was not his last, and Miss Barbara now presides at the Manse of Fordyce with a girl and boy both of School age. Sandy's brother, Willie, was about ages with me. He became tenant at Carnoch at the same time as I went to Burns and his sister, Jane, went along with him as housekeeper. Another sister, Barbara, who was a teacher, also resided there.

There was seemingly consumption in the family however, for Willie and Barbara both succumbed to that malady within a few days of each other. Frank, a younger brother, was also at School with me, but before going to the university he was several years at Fordyce Academy. After graduating M.A. at Aberdeen he attended the Divinity Hall and ultimately emigrated to Australia. As a token of how small the world really is, the first door that Mr. Milne knocked at in Melbourne was opened by my eldest sister, Jessie, like himself a native of this beautiful Parish of Deskford. The house belonged to some mutual friends from Cullen and my sister was just visiting there at the time. A good many years ago Mr. Milne paid a visit to his native county, when we had the pleasure of a call from him at Burns.

Three of Dr. MacIntosh's sons were also pupils at Deskford School during my time, viz Mackenzie, Frank and Ashly. MacKenzie was a rather wild sort of boy, but very fond of all sorts of animals. Amongst his pets were dogs of all sorts and sizes from a mastiff to a grey-hound. A young roe deer was a great attraction for a week or ten days, but confinement and the lack of its mother's attention proved too much for it. After School days MacKenzie could never settle down to any occupation being of a rather restless sort of disposition, and he at length went out to Canada to his brother, William, who was a farmer there. Whether he be now alive I am unable to say.

Frank was entirely different from his elder brother being quiet and gentle. He went to Aberdeen University and ultimately went in for medicine. After practicing in several districts in Scotland, he has been settled for several years in the Mainland of Orkney. He has never married. Ashly, the youngest of the family, was a remarkably brilliant scholar and carried everything before him at Aberdeen and Cambridge. His ambition had seemingly been the Indian Civil Service but being failed in one of his exams he turned his attention to medicine and surgery. He has been a Professor for many years at Aberdeen Royal Infirmary but retired a few months ago. Like his brother Frank, Ashly has remained in single blessedness, but his youngest sister, Edith, has I am certain made a most efficient housekeeper.

Nellie the other sister married a cousin of her own, a Mr. Emslie, a stockbroker in London. He has been dead now for several years but Mrs. Emslie still resides with her two daughters somewhere in Surrey.

The Lorimer family in Kirkton were also pupils with me under Mr. Brander and Mr. Smith. James, the eldest, would only have been a few years with me as he was several years older. When his School days were over he started to learn to be a shoemaker along with his father and at his father's decease he carried on the business and that very successfully too. A new dwelling house and workshop were built during his father's lifetime, also in the village.

James has proved himself to be a noted horticulturalist, his garden being always a model of neatness while a goodly proportion of the prizes at the Annual Flower Show usually fell to his share. His apiary was also one of the largest in the district and his services were not infrequently in request as a judge of honey at neighbouring Exhibitions.

James Lorimer, the elder, was a rather noted character in his day. He was for many years grave-digger and beadle and bellman at the Parish Church but sad to relate his fondness for the Auld Kirk not infrequently led to his downfall. Sometimes after a burst of more than ordinary indulgence, he would determine to mend his ways, and have nothing more to do with the accursed drink. He would join the ranks of the Total Abstainers, sign the pledge and was extremely eloquent over the most degrading influence of all intoxicating liquor. He would declare with the greatest gusto that every glass a man took was just a nail in his coffin. This would continue for a short time, but I rather fear there had been a good many nails in the poor man's coffin.

The Morrison twins, John and Alec, from the Clunehill were a few years younger than I. After his School days, John continued to work on the farm, and ultimately married Helen Jane Stephen of Briggs by whom he had four sons and one daughter. He has been deceased now for several years, while his widow and eldest son carry on the farm. Alec the twin brother, being a cripple through an accident when a child, was sent to the North of Scotland Bank in Cullen for a few years. The general merchant's shop in Berryhillock being vacant, he became tenant of the same and carried on a successful business there for a good many years. When Mr. Garden left Raemore for Brankenenthum, Mr. Morrison was appointed Clerk to the School Board, and it was when he died in 1899 that I received the appointment.

John Longmore, Cottartown, a brother of Adam previously mentioned would have been two years my junior. Most of the boys at School usually had nick-names, and John had the noted distinction of being known in these early days as 'Satan'. He remained at home with his parents working the small farm of Cottartown. At their decease he married a Miss Clark also of Deskford by whom he had three sons and two daughters all of which have done remarkably well. The eldest, Adam, is still at home, one is a teacher and the other is a county organiser under The College of Agriculture. Both the daughters became teachers, one is married abroad, while the other is the wife of Mr. Beveridge, presently Head master of Deskford School.

Last among those who were nearly of an age with myself, I must mention Willie McWillie of Langlinburn.[4] He was never a school-mate

---

[4] The McWillie family also farmed at Langlinburn

of mine however, having received all his education under Mr. Mitchell at the Free Church School. In after years however, he became one of- if not the closest and most intimate of my friends. When my uncle George Bidie left Backies old Mr. McWillie took it for his son George. George however, was of a rather flichteresome disposition and after a few years he went abroad. William, the youngest son, then took his place with Annie, his youngest sister, as housekeeper. When I was about 19 years of age a Course of Entertainments was organised in Deskford for the purpose of starting a public library for the Parish. Willie McWillie and I were appointed joint librarians and so a friendship was commenced that lasted until my friend died in 1888.

I will make no further comments on our friendship here, as several extracts from my Diary will be given later on.

From the time I left School and commenced to work on the little farm until I reached the age of 20 or thereby, there is not very much of importance to relate. Although I was put to the plough at the early age of 14, I must confess that my heart at first was never truly in my work. The education I had received at the village School had seemingly been the means of creating a desire for more. My great ambition was that I might in time be able to improve myself so that at some future period, the Civil Service or some such vocation might possibly open up for me. When I came to realise the miserable returns that were being obtained by the hard and incessant work on the little farm, I do not think that I can be greatly blamed for turning my thoughts towards something that might not only be somewhat more in accordance with my tastes and desires.

At this time my Father would have been about 60 years of age, and so when I considered that he could not for long be able to carry on the work of the farm unaided, and as I was the only boy in the family, I had perforce to put my inclinations into the background and resolutely put my hand to the plough instead of that diminutive implement or weapon that is said to be 'mightier than the sword'. I can truly say however, that I have never in the slightest degree regretted my choice. As no one I expect even has who has kept to the straight line of duty. Although as I have said the farm of Upper Knowes was a miserable poor holding as regards soil condition and houses, and as farming during the '80s and '90s was very far from being lucrative even on good farms, still I am truly thankful to be able to relate that from a pecuniary point of view I have been blessed far beyond my sanguine expectations.

As the years went by, and when hard work and perseverance was beginning to allow our heads to get a little above the water, I began to be thoroughly interested in everything pertaining to agriculture, the draining, liming and managing of the land and improving the breed of cattle and horses and the feeding of the livestock etc., etc., and now after 50 year's experience I often say that had I my life to begin over again I would be nothing else than a farmer. That farming is one of the healthiest occupations cannot be denied, but it has also much to recommend it besides. You may at times, when a push is on, have to work from dawn to dark, and it may be a thoroughly tired man that lays his head down upon the pillow at night, but it is then too that you truly recognise the truth of the saying, 'the sleep of the labouring man is sweet' and it then too that you appreciate its sweetness to the full. At other times however, when the more pressing work has been accomplished you can often take a few days or even a week off without much loss or inconvenience. But once again, and here I think is or ought to be the supreme attraction of farming. Who has the opportunity of being brought so often and so close to the very heart of Nature in all her moods and phases?

If the lesson of the sower and the seed, or 'first the blade then the ear, and then the full corn in the ear', appeals to any one, it surely must do so in a far more realistic manner to him who is daily and hourly in the very midst of Nature. Then think of the charm and delight of a morning in April, when as Burns so rapturously puts it, 'now in her green mantle' etc., etc.

In the early summer our two indigenous wild shrubs in the northern climes viz the gorse and the broom are truly gorgeous to behold and a sense of never failing pleasure to the farmer whose mind is in unison with Nature. Then in the Autumn again when the golden grain has been safely garnered, when the long rows of stacks have been securely protected by thatch and rape, when the plough is once more turning over the brown furrows, a leisurely stroll over the fields at this season compels one to admit that it is truly good to be alive, and truly grand to be a farmer.

This may be looked upon however, as a digression.

Prior to the early seventies, the farm of Ardiecow consisted of two holdings, the larger or western part being tenanted by a John Murray an old bachelor, whilst the eastern part was farmed by James Murray, a nephew of John's and whose family I have already mentioned. In the family of which John formed a part there were twins and triplets, all daughters, and a rather amusing incident is related concerning the same. About 2 years after the twins were born the farmer was working in the barn one day when a message came out to him that he had got another daughter. 'Weel, weel' says he without stopping his work, 'I've had that afore'. In a short time the messenger returns to the barn with the intelligence that twin daughters had appeared. 'Weel, weel', says the farmer again, 'I've had that afore' and still continued his work.

Again the messenger returned with the news that a third daughter had been sent him, 'Noo I never had that afore', says he, 'I will need to gang in noo'.

At that time the farm of Ardiecow came down the hill almost close to the houses of Upper Knowes. Old John Murray having died about 1871, a rearrangement of marches was made. 30 acres of the lower fields were added to Knowes while James, the nephew, got the whole of the remainder. This additional land to Knowes was extremely wet and dirty however, and it was several years before it was got into satisfactory condition.

At that time the houses at Knowes were in a rather dilapidated condition being extremely low, and except a small part at the end of the Dwelling House which was tiled, mostly all covered with thatch. All the fields on Knowes were also sadly in need of draining. That being so I often tried to induce my Father to look for a better farm but to little purpose. We did go and inspect several, Slackdale, Rothmackenzie, the High Farm of Glenbarry etc., but in my Father's opinion there were always serious drawbacks. Clunehill of Rathven was the only one he could find no fault with and an offer for it was sent to the Factor, but we were not successful.

Seeing that it was unlikely that I would ever be able to persuade my Father to leave his native place, and the lease expiring at Whit 1882, a new bargain was arranged with Lord Seafield the landlord Proprietor. The rent was fixed at £45 free of interest, a new dwelling house was built, and the old dwelling house and all others got new roofs and tiles put on. The landlord only provided the material for repairing the office houses however, the workmanship having to be all done at our own expense and many a long day did I spend causeying. Drain pipes were also laid and they were to be given free of charge if we would cut the drains and lay the pipes to the Ground Officer's satisfaction. We made an effort to put in as many as we could every winter, but as no money was available to pay for the cutting, my Father and I wrought at them ourselves draining in the forenoon and going to the plough in the afternoon. The soil on Knowes being of no great depth and the subsoil being hard, close, stony clay, the work of drainage was not only hard but the progress we made was extremely slow. After persevering for four years I began to see that the 19 year lease would be finished before we were able to drain one third of the land. There being a break in the lease at the expiry of 5 years I tried to persuade my Father to apply to the Factor for some assistance, but all my pleading was in vain his contention being that it would be of no use. As I persisted however, he at length suggested that I should go down to Cullen House myself and lay the matter before the Factor. Never having been in the Estate Office in my life before, it was with not a little trepidation that I presented myself before Mr. Bryson who was Factor for Lady Seafield at that time. Having stated my errand, the lease was at once produced, and the terms read over, much emphasis being laid on the large sum of money that Lady Seafield had expended on houses and her generosity in providing drain pipes for free etc.,etc. 'No, no young man you must go home and persevere, Lady Seafield could never see her way to make any further advances', says the Factor. 'Well, well', say I, as I turned about to leave, 'I will just need to go and try and make a living somewhere else, for I see no prospect yonder'. As I said this with a rather determined sort of expression, it seemed to appeal somewhat to Mr. Bryson. 'Stay a minute', says he. Mr. Michie, the Ground Officer, was now called into the Factor's private room. 'Is the land on the farm of Upper Knowes in a very wet condition'? Mr Bryson asked of Mr. Michie who at once replied, 'yes, sir it is extremely wet'. 'You will go up Mr. Michie and report'. I thanked the Factor kindly and took my leave. On coming out at the door, Mr. Michie accompanied me. 'Will you be at home on Wednesday afternoon'? He asked. 'I will make a point of that', say I.

Mr. Michie came up as he promised and I accompanied him over the fields pointing out what my Father and I had already done. 'You will commence at once and drive pipes', says he. There being a few inches of snow on the ground no ploughing could be done so I drove pipes every day for two weeks on end.

The drains were let to a Mr. Cameron, a contractor from Cullen. They commenced at one side of the farm and went right across to the other. There was a lot of frost during that winter and when the thaw came in March, strong breezes soon dried everything up. There was scarcely a drop of water seen in the bottom of any of these drains but the improvement they made to the soil was truly marvellous.

After getting the land dry I commenced and limed every shift as it came to be sown out in grass giving it from 12 to 15 bolls per acre.[5] This along with the draining and extra manuring, made the soil more tender and much easier wrought, and by the end of the lease in 1901, the whole farm was growing good, profitable crops.

I must now retrace my steps somewhat. In January 1879, I commenced to keep a Diary of my daily doings. Monday evening of each week was set aside for this express purpose, and with only a few exceptions I continued the practice for almost 10 years.[6] At first my entries were extremely meagre, two or three lines sometimes sufficing

---

[5] Boll, one bole equalled six bushels with one bushel being the dry measure of eight gallons of grain.
[6] The diary was in fact kept for thirteen years.

for a week, and the whole month of January in the first year only occupying one small page. As time slipped past however and my vocabulary increased, I went in for far more detail, a holiday, a Pic-nic, an entertainment of any sort providing adequate 'copy'.

My personal experience of keeping a Diary has led me to form a very high opinion of its usefulness. It is not only a practical means of improving ones writing and composition, but it also makes one take more particular note of men and passing events so as to be able to record our impressions of the same. I have also on several occasions found it extremely useful in ascertaining the exact date of any important event that might have occurred in those bygone years. I could not advise any young person who wishes to improve themselves during their leisure hours, in any better way, than by keeping a diary.

Under February 3 1879 I find the following extract:

No sign of fresh weather yet. Doing nothing but threshing and getting turnips. We have a course of entertainments in Deskford just now, the second of which came off on the evening of Friday last in the form of a lecture, given by the Rev. Mr. Anderson of Bondye. His subject was 'Travels in Italy'. In the course of his lecture he gave a description of St. Peters Cathedral, Rome, the length of which he stated as being over 600 feet and the breadth 456 feet.

The perusal of my Diary is also a source of never failing pleasure to me, bringing to mind a flood of memories that Old Father Time had done his best to cover up with his ever widening wings. The feeling thus formed, must I think be somewhat similar to that felt by parents, when members of the family long absent once more assemble around the parental hearth. The escapades and foibles of each, forgotten it may be by the youngsters, are recounted by the parents, the doings of their youthful years, their School days and their adolescence are all rehearsed in detail, making the parents even, feel younger and ever so much happier.

VOLUME ONE
1 JANUARY 1879-29 DECEMBER 1881

James Wilson
Upper Knowes
Deskford
January 1ˢᵗ 1879
A Journal of My Life and Everyday Doings

1879 January
1ˢᵗ

We have a very severe snow storm, which commenced on 8 December. Snow to the depth of 2 feet. I was at the funeral today of Ann Lawerence, Broadrashes. There was a ball last night at Ardoch.

6ᵗʰ

Very frosty. We are holding this as Xmas as yesterday was Sunday. I was over at Cornhill Station today, seeing about a train which is coming from Edinburgh. It did not come and I went past Limestones.

13ᵗʰ

Weather always stormy. On Saturday and yesterday about 4 inches more snow fell and last night there was a good deal of blowing.

20ᵗʰ

A few days of last week were fresh but it is not like to be a right thaw.

27ᵗʰ

The frost has been more severe last week than any we have yet had. We were driving away some corn in the first of the week. [1] The roads are very slippery.

---

[1] driving, to transport in a cart or wagon.

1879 February
3*rd*

No sign of fresh weather yet. Doing nothing but threshing and getting turnips. We have a course of entertainments in Deskford just now, the second of which came off on the evening of Friday last in the form of a lecture, given by the Rev. Mr. Anderson of Bondye. His subject was 'Travels in Italy'. In the course of his lecture he gave a description of St. Peters Cathedral, Rome, the length of which he stated as being over 600 feet and the breadth 456 feet.

The trial of the City of Glasgow Bank of Directors was finished on Saturday having lasted two weeks. Two of them have got eighteen, and the other five, eight months imprisonment.

10*th*

Two days in the end of the week were fresh but yesterday was frosty again. Today (Monday) is soft and foggy. Mary Wilson was over from Limestones on Friday.

17*th*

The past week has been soft throughout but never like a right fresh. A few have been ploughing the most of the week, and the most of people have been trying it. We tried it on Wednesday but it would not work, the frost in several places being too hard. The bad weather however does not seem to be all past yet. Yesterday it snowed a little all day and today it has never cleared while it has also been blowing very hard.

It is indeed now getting rather threatning, this being the eleventh week since the snow came on.

The third of our 'Course of Entertainment' came off on the evening of Friday last in the form of a concert. There was a good supply both of vocal and instrumental music, comprising four comic singers from Cullen the Misses Ker's who performed on the violin and piano and a choir, led by Mr. Reid.

24*th*

Another week of very hard frost, there was to be a meeting of the committee on Tuesday night but it was a bad night and I did not go. We held our fourth Entertainment on Friday night, there being a full house. Mrs. Michie, Cullen House, gave a fine display of views with a magic lantern. Mr. McCulloch, Grange, Miss Ker and Mr. Garden, then gave readings. Mr. McCulloch gave some songs and violin music and Mr. Reid and choir gave a few Scottish songs. Mr. Kitchen, Clune, performed the duties of the chair in excellent style, and altogether the meeting was a perfect success.

Our troops have got a severe defeat in the South of Africa at Cape Colony, on the 18th of January there being about 500 soldiers and 30 officers slain.

Father and Uncle were at Cullen today paying their rent. Tomorrow is Fastern-even and Joan and I are going to Oathillock to our tea and bannocks.[2]

1879 March
3rd

The first two days of last week were frosty but on Wednesday it turned fresh, a good deal of rain falling that night. It has been fresh since except a little frost in the mornings. Mary went away to Edinburgh on Thursday, Father accompanying her to Aberdeen. He returned on Saturday. I went with them to Portsoy Station, and when I came home I went to the funeral of Mason Milton who died on Tuesday last.

On Friday I got the plough started having been twelve weeks out of it except a few hours on 12th February. Joan and I were at Cullen yesterday (Sunday) at William Reid's. We went to the Free Church in the forenoon where Mr. Morgan preached on Judas Iscariot. At night we went to the hall where Mr. Scott preached.

They had splendid singing led by James Mackay and accompanied by the harmonium. Father was at the Smiddy today getting the young mare shoed. The Steam Mill is to thrash at Kirktown tomorrow.

10th

The past week has been dry and windy and the snow is gradually disappearing. Have been ploughing lea all the week, will have another week's work.

I was at Kirktown on Thursday at the Steam Mill.

The last of our course of Entertainments was held on Friday night Mr. Ker presiding. It was a lecture delivered by Mr. Stuart, H.M.S. His subject was 'The Orkney Islands' and it was a perfect treat.

I see by the newspapers that the 'Ameer' of Afghanistan whose country we are a war with just now is dead. His son, Yahoob Khan is to reign in his stead and as he is on friendly terms with our Government, the war will in all probability come to an end.

17th

After 12 days of fine Spring weather with the ground coming into fine condition for sowing, we are again in the middle of a very heavy snow

---

[2] bannocks, round flat cakes of oat, barley or pease meal baked on a girdle.

storm. On the afternoon of the 11th it became cold and stormy, and one morning there was at least 3 inches of snow. All that day and the next, it kept falling nearly without intermission, while at the same time there was a strong East wind causing it to drift into all sheltered places, and blocking roads and railways to a serious extent. There was a meeting in the School on the evening of Friday last to consider the renewal of the Library which has been lying for the last 12 years or more unused. It was resolved however to have it opened again and the proceeds of the recent 'Course of Entertainments' to be used to purchase new Books. There was also a committee of five appointed to take charge of the Library, and William McWillie and I were appointed joint Librarians. We were over on Saturday afternoon taking a list of the present Books, and there are about 152 volumes. The Library is at present in the Board Room, Kirktown, it having been transferred from Tailor Reid's Berryhillock in the course of last summer. The Entertainments just past have proved quite a success, there being realised in all £10:0:10 and after deducting all expenses leaving a surplus of more than £4.00.[3]

I was the only one at Church yesterday. There was a very thin attendance the roads being so bad.

24th

Four days of last week were very foggy, while at the same time there fell a drissling rain. The snow however slowly disappeared, and by Friday a few ploughs were at work. We ploughed a ridge on the Hill on Saturday afternoon, none of the rest being clear of snow. Sunday and today, however have again been very frosty, and it was afternoon before the plough would work. The Spring must now be a late one and dry fresh days are anxiously looked for by every one. Benjie Farquhar was over this afternoon for some turnips, he has bought a few from us, as his is entirely done. They were at Banff on Saturday with Jessie Hay and they are going to the Infirmary with her tomorrow.

She has got a very sore leg, and is quite unable to walk. I was to have gone to Finnygaud on Sunday last but the roads being so bad I did not go. I intend going next one.

I was over at Limestones on Tuesday. It was Marnin Fair and Uncle was at the market. Mary has been very bad with her eyes for some time past. She had been at Banff with them and they are still very sore.[4]

---

[3] Wilson used various abbreviations when recording money and these have been followed in this edition.

[4] Marnin Fair, fair named after St Marnan or Marnoch, after whom the Parish is also named. The fair was held on the second Tuesday of March and it became an annual market for horses and cattle.

31ˢᵗ

Saturday last was the day fixed for letting the farms of Leitcheston, Ardiecow and Wintertown. It is not known yet who has got any of them. Joan and I went over to Finnygaud on Saturday afternoon and returned on Sunday evening. Joan went to Church but I did not. The day was rather showery. Jemmie is always very busy. He has not been a Sunday at home for four or five weeks. Their Uncle, the Smith at the Knowes, has been very unwell for a long time and the Doctors fear he has got heart disease. Last week the frost was very severe, and the plough would not work. On Saturday however, it again relaxed its hold, and we have had three fine days. Surely we have now seen the last of the snow and frost, and I hope we may soon have days, which will enable us to say that the Spring is come indeed. We have three days ploughing of lea yet and it must be a fortnight at all events before any can be sown.

1879 April
7ᵗʰ

The past week has been a busy one. It was fine days and every one was pushing the work forward with the greatest energy. We have still a little lea to plough but we were three days at the clean ground. We will however get plenty of time to plough the lea for it has rained a great deal this afternoon and the clean ground will be very wet for a few days. The Farm of Ardiecow has been let to Mr. McIntosh. He is to make a sheep farm of it, and only keep one pair of horses.

James Murray has got a small farm on Spey side beside the village of Aberlour. His sale at Ardiecow is to be on 19ᵗʰ of May. Leitcheston has been let to Mr. McCombie a man from Bauds of Cullen, and James Mitchel, Netherton, has got his place. Uncle George was in past tonight on his way home from Swailend. John Reid is away to Aberdeen to the Circuit Court as a witness in the case of forgery by Stuart of Keith against Lewis Milne.

14ᵗʰ

The past week has been a bad one. The weather, which broke on Monday continued wet for the next two days, and since it has been cold and showery.

I was at Cullen on Tuesday afternoon, and saw Miss Kitchen as I was coming home. Leitcheston has got it nearly all sowed. No one else has commenced in this district yet.

Friday last was the first night the Library was open, but there was not a large turn out, there being about ten members joined, two ladies being among the numbers. James Robb died last week, and Father and

Mother were to go up the day of the funeral but it was a wet day and they did not go.

They were up today however, and are only newly arrived home. They had 'Rosie' and got Kirktown gig. I had the young mare in the plough all day. She goes very well, but is a little keen.

Thursday last was Cornhill market, there was a good turn out of cattle but a very stiff sale. Cultain has got a horsefoal last week.

21st

We commenced sowing today, and the ground is now in fine condition for the seed. The most of people however commenced in the end of the week but until Friday it was not in good season the first of the week being cold and showery.

Jessie Wilson was over on Wednesday afternoon. There was a meeting that night, of the Ratepayers for the purpose of electing members for the School Board, and although there had been a great word before of getting new members, the old ones were all elected. Mr. Stevenson, Ordens, being the only other one proposed, and he stated that if no other one were nominated, he would give in, and so save a poll. Jessie Cowie came over on Thursday along with Maggie Longmire who was on her way home from Finnygaud. She went home on Saturday and Joan went with her to Limestones. I went over to Clashendamer on Sunday afternoon to ask for Jessie Hay, who is in the Infirmary, Banff with a sore leg. Her mother however was just away seeing her and was not come home.

28th

There were only two dry days last week, Monday and Thursday. We were busy sowing on these while the ground was fine and dry. On Wednesday however, it was wet, there being cold sleety showers as all day, but not to such an extent as to stop the harrows until nearly evening, when we had to stop.

Thursday morning was also wet, but it cleared up and I went to the plough, the rest of the day being dry. Father was down at the roup at Leitcheston but bought nothing. It was very stiff sale and did not last long. They have got a few acres of land beside Buckie. Miss Katie Duncan was up that afternoon, she was saying they sowed all their barley the day before.

Friday was our fast day. We had Mr. Grant, Fordyce, both in the fore and afternoon.

Saturday was wet and misty. We were winnowing grass seed in the forenoon and in the afternoon. I filled in the furs of the turnips land.[5]

Father, Mother and I were at Church on Sunday. It was very wet, raining heavily the whole day. Our Minister had Mr. McVicar, Ordiquhill, assisting him and we got a beautiful discourse from him in the afternoon. The ground today was very wet. We took up the remainder of the turnips and went to the plough in the afternoon.

We will have abundance of turnips, but there is every appearance that we will require them for sometime yet, as the grass has hardly yet got a green shade. While many have their cattle already out, their winter keep being done. But although we may be thinking the winter that is past has been a severe one, yet when compared with what they have had in the Highlands, it has been comparatively slight for I was noticing today that on the tops of the hills there is not a black speck yet to be seen.

1879 May
5th

We resumed sowing on Tuesday and have been busy at it everyday since, but until Friday the land was not in very good condition. Friday and Saturday however, were very dry days, and we finished grass seeds and all on Saturday night.

I was over on Tuesday afternoon at Limestones for some boxwood. They were busy sowing. Mary's eyes are keeping a little better but I did not see her as she was away at Portsoy, and was not come home when I left although nearly eleven o'clock.

I was busy last week getting the garden in order, and Father went to the harrows an afternoon for one so that I got it finished.

Aleck Duncan and George were up at their tea on Sunday afternoon. The first Monday of May is a Bank holiday but he had got other two days. He is always liking fine to stop in Aberdeen.

12th

Last week we experienced another snow storm. The wind was North, North West accompanied with tremendous showers of snow and rain while it was also piercing cold. Vegetation made no progress at all in fact it was rather the reverse for the grass was not looking so green as it did the week before while everyone has their cattle out their winter keep being done. We have a week's turnips yet.

Last week I was grubbing and harrowing the turnip land and we have got a piece for Swedes ready.

---

[5] furs, furrows.

On Saturday I made drills for the potatoes. Father was down that day at the sale at Bogton. The cattle and horses were of first-class quality and sold pretty well but he bought nothing.

The Library was open on Friday last when a few more members joined. William Wilson came over tonight. He is going to stop until the term. He was tending cattle at Milton Duff Distillery but as they are sold off he is out of work. He has got a place however beside Inverness as cattleman at a diary.

Wednesday last was the day of the poll for the School Board. There were six candidates and Mr. Ker proved the unsuccessful one while Mr. Cowie, Inaltrie, was at the top of the poll. He had 84 votes.

19th

We planted the potatoes on Tuesday last. The day was warm and there was a little thunder with a very heavy thunder shower in the middle of the day. Father was at Portsoy, for manure.

On Wednesday it rained the whole forenoon exceedingly heavy. We could get nothing done at all outside. So we were cleaning some of the harness.

On Thursday Willie Wilson and I went up to William McBain's to cast the turfs.   I went over to Kirkton in the evening.

Friday was Cullen market but none of us was down at it. The fees however, were about £2 down and a great many not engaged. I went down to Dytach in the afternoon with two queys for William Hay and I went past Newton as I came home and got some nice flowers from the Miss Geddes's.[6]

On Saturday I was ploughing and grubbing but the ground was not too dry. A good few were drilling today.

Sunday was a very fine day.

On Monday we started to gather weeds and Father and I were both at the roup at Ardiecow in the afternoon. The cattle sold very well but the horses and other things realised but very little. Father bought a young calf and a few other things.

26th

The past week has been warmer with more growth but it was also very soft, there being hardly a whole dry day. It has been very unfavourable for the sowing of turnips, nevertheless everyone is pushing forward, the season being so far advanced, and I think with a few dry days the most of the Swedes in this locality would be got down.

[6] queys, heifers.

Tuesday I was drilling the whole day, while Father was putting out dung. The afternoon was a little wet.

On Wednesday morning we had a cow taken ill in calving, so I went off for the farrier. By the time I got back they had got one calf, and in a short time after she had another, but both were dead. The cow however, is keeping better. Father was at the shops of Tochineal today, he went to buy a cow but did not get one. The cattle sold very well, but the horses were very cheap.

Thursday forenoon was very wet but it cleared at twelve o'clock and I went to assist James Murray to drive some of his things to Cornhill Station. He was taking everything by the railway. The new tenant arrived with all his baggage late on Saturday night.

Friday was a very fine day and we got the half of the Swedes sowed in pretty good condition.

1879 June
2nd

The past week has been exceedingly wet and we have not been but a few hours in the 'yoke' all the week. Monday forenoon was dry, and I was harrowing and grubbing. We sowed the remainder of the Swedes that morning before breakfast. We were up very early, getting the carriage cart in order for Uncle George as he was going to flit George from Auchinharlick to Muttonbrae. The rain however, came on at dinner time and we had to give them a trace from Kirkton to Ardiecow as the roads had turned very soft.

Tuesday morning was a little soft but it cleared up and we went to Portsoy for two loads of manure.

On Wednesday morning we winnowed the last of the crop and Father went with it to the Mill, while I went a few hours to plough. The rain however, came on again in the afternoon, and during the night it rained a great deal.

On Thursday Father and I went to Keith market, and bought a cow, and a calf. There were a good few cattle and a pretty brisk sale. It is a black polled cow we have bought.

Friday and Saturday were both very soft.

Willie Cowie and Sandy came over on Sunday morning when they said that they had got no turnips down and had the most of it to roll. Mr. & Mrs. Farquhar were over in the afternoon. Jessie Hay is still in the Infirmary. They were saying that Joan Cowie and Jessie Ann Strachan were both proclaimed on Sunday. Father has been over at Limestones tonight and is only now come home.

9ᵗʰ

Last week until Friday was very soft and cold and the land was so wet that nothing could be done amongst it at all. We were at Cullen on Thursday along with other 13 carts, for sand to mix cement, with which a bridge is to be built over the Hoggie Burn at Broadrashes.

Friday and Saturday were both dry days and I was in the plough.

Today it has been very warm, but there has been a close mist all day, so that the land has not dried much. I have been grubbing all day but the land is very wet. I see that the Swedes are coming through the ground but the plants are not very healthy looking.

16ᵗʰ

We have had a whole week of foggy weather and no appearance of it clearing up yet. It has however, been very warm and vegetation of every kind has made rapid progress.

On Thursday forenoon I was harrowing while the rest were gathering weeds, but as the ground was rather wet I did not harrow much on it, and in the afternoon I commenced to drill.

Wednesday I drilled all day while Father was putting out dung. In the afternoon I covered in about 30 drills which we got sowed at night.

On Thursday we were both putting out dung in the forenoon while in the afternoon I was 'happin in'.[7]

There was a great deal of thunder that day and there came a shower in the afternoon which prevented us from getting our turnips sowed that night.

On Friday I drilled the remainder of the field and then covered them all in. It turned out a fine dry day and we got them all sowed in pretty good condition. The Library was open on that night and Willie McWillie brought down the new books from the F C Manse. They are very nice like books comprising the whole of the Waverley Novels in 25 volumes with other 8 larger books by George McDonald. There were 9 new members joined.

On Saturday I was grubbing and harrowing on the piece at the back of the house, but some of it was still very wet. In the afternoon there was a great deal of thunder and lightning and a little rain. George Stephen and Kate came down from Keith and they awaited at Clochmacruich until the rain went over.

On Sunday William Reid came up from Cullen, and him, George, Kate, Father Joan and I were all at Church.

Today I was in the drill plough all day, while Father was putting out dung. There has been a close mist all day consequently the ground

---

[7] Happin in, digging in or covering (the dung).

has dried very little. The threshing mill and cart shed at Towie were burned to the ground on the night of Wednesday last, the cause of the fire is unknown.

23rd

Tuesday last was wet and we did nothing amongst the land.

Wednesday however, was dry and Father and I were both putting out dung in the forenoon, while in the afternoon I was covering in, but we did not get them sown that night.

On Thursday I covered in the remainder of them and ploughed the 'end-rigs', while Father got them sowed. We finished on Friday forenoon and in the afternoon Joan and I was up at William McBain's setting the turfs.

On Saturday we were shearing the sheep and carting the young mare. She was very quiet and gave us no trouble. Katie Cowie of Finnygaud came over in the evening. Their Uncle, at the Knowes, died on Friday morning.

We had late sermon on Sunday, as our Minister had to go to Rathven. Their Minister has left just now and they have not got another.

Today I was over at Hoggie grubbing their turnip land and Joseph McKay was in the afternoon harrowing. During the past week the weather has been warm, but turnips are not doing well, there being complaints everywhere of them eating off with the fly. Uncle of Limestones and Mary were at Cullen today. They were in past as they went home and they are away home just now.

30th

I was over at a meeting on Tuesday evening arranging about our Deskford Annual Pic-nic when it was fixed to come off on Wednesday 9th July. Aleck Milne and I were appointed to ask the use of the Orchard from Mr. McIntosh which he very kindly granted. We then went down and asked Mr. Smith to be Chairman when we were again successful.

On Wednesday I was up at Ardiecow giving them a days drilling, and they have not got the turnips all finished yet. They made me go up when I unyolked to get my tea when I got a sight of Miss Mackintosh for the first time. She appears to be a very nice girl.

On Friday I was over at a meeting to get the tickets for the Pic-nic, but there was no tickets come. They came down with the 'Post' on Saturday night. I started that afternoon for Keith, and arrived there about five o'clock. After I had got tea and rested a little I went out to make some purchases, and also to get any 'cards' taken.

On Sunday George and I went to church. In the afternoon we went out to see the falls of Tarnash which are out the turnpike road the way of Huntly. We called in to see Miss Fraser as we went up past, when she accompanied us, Kate and the bairns also coming along. It was a very pretty place and I thought it well worth going to see. At six o'clock I started for home, and arrived rather tired about nine.

On Monday we went to the moss, and set the half of the peats and spread the rest. I got my Pic-nic tickets as I came past Kirktown, and went up with Miss Mackintosh's ticket (as she is to be a stewardess) in the evening, which she accepted.

1879 July
7th

The past week has been soft, some rain falling almost everyday. Tuesday was very wet. In the forenoon we painted one of the carts, the wright having painted the other and given it new shafts. In the afternoon I was cleaning some of the harness.

On Wednesday forenoon I was at the Smiddy, while in the afternoon I went down a short while to the Fordyce Pic-nic. It was showery and the ground got very wet making dancing almost an impossibility, and altogether it was not nearly so lively as in former years.

On Thursday I ploughed a corner of fallow land and in the afternoon we removed two cairns of stones in the den. In the evening we went over of Cornhill Station to meet Jane. (We had got a letter on Tuesday saying she had got her holidays and was going to spend them with us). We were rather late however, for we met her at Newmill, so she returned with us to the Station for her luggage and we arrived home about ten o'clock when all were very glad to see her.

On Friday we were running and hoeing the potatoes.

On Saturday we went to Portsoy, for two loads of coals from the 'Smith'. We got home about twelve o'clock and unyolked when I had them over in the afternoon.

On Sunday we were all at church except Joan. In the afternoon Jane, Joan & I went over to Limestones and Father went over with us to Muttonbrae to see Gran. She is always getting weaker.

On Monday we started to hoe the turnips and the last few days there is a great improvement on them and I hope in a few days they will be nearly all ready for the hoe. Uncle of Limestones and Father were at Cullen today and Uncle is thinking of getting up some new houses.

14ᵗʰ

On Monday last Mother and Jane went up to Keith with George in the Brewery Cart.

On Tuesday Father went up for them when Kate and the bairns came along with them. I was hoeing the most of the day, but in the afternoon there came a few peals of thunder and an extraordinary shower which put a stop to the hoe that night.

On Wednesday morning I awoke with little expectation of seeing a dry day but wishing for one all the same, as our Pic-nic was to come off that afternoon. This morning however, was very misty while at the same time there fell a drissiling rain. About ten o'clock the mist cleared off and Father and I went down to the 'Den' to cast out a small bit drain. We came home at twelve o'clock and by that time the rain was on again when I began to fear that our Pic-nic, for one year was to be a failure. I dressed myself however, and went over about two o'clock, when 'Lo' to the delight of everyone it began to clear, and by three o'clock the Orchard (in which it has been held for the past six years) presented a lively scene. For about an hour dancing was engaged in, to the excellent violin music of Messrs. Stephen, Johnstone, Geddes and Fordyce. Mr. Smith was then proposed to take the chair and he having made a few remarks an excellent tea was served out by a number of stewards and stewardesses. Everyone having got their appetite appeased the musicians again tuned their 'fickle friens', and in a short time, all were again 'tripping the light fantastic toe'. Dancing and games were now engaged in with great spirit, until about seven o'clock when we had a good heavy shower. It cleared however, for about an hour, when there came another shower but it did not last long. The ground however, wet before, became now so soft that dancing became almost an impossibility and having danced a few Highland reels and votes of thanks having been proposed for Mr. Mackintosh for the use of the Orchard, and others, the company dismissed everyone sorry that the weather should have spoiled a Pic-nic which had before always proved a success.

On Thursday morning everyone was rather tried and sleepy. Father and I went over to Cornhill market with a fat cow, which we sold. There were not many fat cattle, and the few that were in pretty good demand.

On Friday we were busy at the hoe, and in the evening I went over to open the Library. There was also a meeting that night to settle up about the Pic-nic, when we squared up better than was expected.

On Saturday we were all at the hoe.

On Sunday George came down with a machine for Kate, and bought Willie Mann the shoemaker with him. We were all at the church on Sunday expect Kate. In the afternoon George and Jimmie

Cowie came over, and when they were starting for home their horse got refractory and backed so until I thought they would not get away.

21*st*

The past week, has for the most part been dry, and although we have had scarcely any sunshine, it has been a good deal warmer and consequently there has been some growth.

On Monday Joan and I were at the moss setting the remainder of the peats. Father went with us and the cart, and took home a few of the first set ones but they were not very dry.

On Thursday we were busy at the hoe, as they were now requiring singling. Jane, Joan and I were up that night at our tea at Ardiecow (what none of us I suppose ever were before).

On Wednesday we managed to get the Swedes all hoed by six o'clock. The Bogmuchal Pic-nic came off that afternoon and a splendid night they got. Miss McIntosh, Ardiecow, was over at it, and I also saw a few more from this place going over in the afternoon.

On Thursday we were all very sorry as Jane had again to leave us for Duchally House. She went to Portsoy to catch the first train, and that she might get a through ticket for Perth. Father and Joan went with her, Joan accompanying her to Cornhill.

On Friday afternoon we went up for two loads of turfs and on Saturday we got home other four, Helen and I stopping and setting up the bottoms. Friday and Saturday were both very misty, but little rain falling.

On Sunday however, there was a good deal of rain fell and it has also been very wet today, with still no appearance of clearing.

28*th*

The weather for the past eight days has been exceedingly wet, there having been rain more or less everyday. We got nothing done on Monday and Tuesday but on Wednesday afternoon it cleared up while it was also very warm. Maggie and Jeannie Duguid were up that afternoon on a visit. Maggie got her holidays just now as her sister is going to be married to Mr. Templeton, Grantown. The marriage is to be on Friday.

On Thursday we were at the hoe but it was showery and they did not work well.

Friday was 'Peter Fair', and Father went over to it with Uncle of Limestones.[8] I was hoeing in the afternoon and in the afternoon I started to 'run' but the rain coming on I was obliged to loose.

We were hoeing on Saturday forenoon but the afternoon was wet.

Sunday however, was a fine dry day. Mr. & Mrs. Farquhar came over to their tea in the afternoon. Jessie Hay is out of the Infirmary now and is staying over at her grandmothers, but poor girl she is no better, nor is she expected to get better, as the bone of her leg is said to be souring.

The wet and dull weather, with the want of sunshine, is keeping everything terribly back and the harvest must now be very late. The barley here about is coming into ear, but there is no appearance of shooting among the oats yet. Barley and corn after lea will be a good crop but clean land will in general be very light, the 'yarr' having in many places completely choked it.[9] Turnips I fear are to be a bad crop. The early ones are by far the best (and by good luck we got all the Swedes sowed pretty early) but those sown first after the rain, were in mostly every case all eaten off by the fly, and had to be re-sown while those that were not sown again are in general blankly. We did not sow any twice but they have been all very stiff to come, and some pieces of them will be thin.

1879 August
4th

The weather is now getting rather serious as it still continues to be very wet. Everything is being spoiled with excess of moisture. The turnips in wet land are all getting yellow and there are still a good breadth of them to single. There is none of the hay in this district cut yet, and no doubt the heavy crops are being spoiled by the wet. Oats are just beginning to come into ear, but are making no progress. Corn after lea however is lengthening out considerably and in general will be a heavy crop, the only thing being wanting sunshine to bring it to maturity.

We were busy at the hoe last week whenever it was dry.

On Tuesday night I went over to the shoemakers and saw Miss McIntosh as I was passing.

On Friday forenoon it was a perfect spate. The afternoon however, was hard and dry. In the evening I went up to Ardiecow with some journals I had got a read of from Miss McIntosh and spent a very pleasant evening.

---

[8] Peter Fair, local fair and market held in July in Rathven.
[9] yarr, corn spurrey.

Saturday was dry and windy. We hoed a few drills of the Swedes the second time.

On Sunday afternoon Joan and I were over at Clashendamer at our tea.

Today it has been wet, while at the same time there has been a close mist, we were at the hoe but it was working very badly.

11th

The past week has been exceptionally wet, there being not one whole dry day, but plenty whole wet ones.

Tuesday was foggy with a good deal of rain. We hoed a few hours in the forenoon, but had to give it up for a bad job. In the afternoon I went over to the Smiddy with the young mare.

Wednesday was just a spate out and out. Thursday was a little dryer.

Friday was the Cattle Show at Keith. Joan and I were going up, and we were going to get a drive with Miss McIntosh Ardiecow, but it was a bad like morning so we did not go. It turned out a fine day however and I was rather disappointed. Father and I went to Portsoy for two loads of coals for Tailor Reid. There was a menagerie in the town but we did not stop to see it. I was over in the evening at the Library, but there were very few, attended.

There was not much rain on Saturday. We were driving home brushwood from the Cotton Hill, for firewood as they have nearly everything burned up, and there is little prospects of us getting many peats this year.

Sunday morning was soft but it cleared up in the afternoon and was fine and warm. We started the hoe again on Monday but they were still some wet.

The people from The Lodge were over deer shooting and I went along with them. We had a grand day's sport shooting one deer in the Cotton Hill, and another in the Green Hill.

18th

We have had a week of very fine weather, and it has done a great deal of good.

On Tuesday we were busy all day at the hoe.

On Wednesday we had a strong gail of wind, and we were afraid it would end in rain, but it kept off and Thursday was about the finest day we have had this season. This was the day of the 'Berry Market', and the Cornhill Flower Show was also held that day. Father was over at the market and Joan and Miss McIntosh went over to the Show in the afternoon. There was an extraordinary number of people and a very good show.

We were to cut the hay on Friday, but as the morning was foggy we went to the moss to turn the peats when we managed to get eight loads of pretty dry ones, and turned the most of the others. I went up to a hoeing match in the evening at Maxwell Lyon's, when I got the 5th prize.

On Saturday we got the man Brander who works on the roads, and started to cut the hay. We got a fine day, and got the most of it cut, but about six o'clock the rain was on and I think it had rained the most of the night for next morning everything was very wet like, while it was still raining with a close fog. George Bidie came over in the morning to tell us that Granny had died at 4 o'clock in the morning. She had been very ill since Tuesday. She is to be buried at Deskford on Wednesday. She is 83 years of age.

Monday morning was soft, but the rest of the day was fine. We started to hoe the Swedes a second time and in the afternoon we cut out the hay.

27th

I have always since I commenced, written my Journal on Monday evening, but on Monday last an event occurred which nearly brought all my Journal writing and everything else to a sudden termination. About three o'clock Father and I went away to the turnips. He went down to scuffle the yellow ones beside the bogs while I was furring up the Swedes on the hillock. About a quarter past four, and just as I had turned in at the top of a drill, there came a very vivid flash of lightning followed almost instantaneously by the loudest peal of thunder I ever heard. Both the mare and I were a little startled coming so unexpectedly for I had heard no thunder that day before. I did not stop however, and the mare went down the drill pretty fast. When turning at the end I saw we were to have a shower, and before I was half up it was on, accompanied by very large hail. I had not gone very far, when the mare stood up and turned around to get her back to the rain as the wind was right on her face. I went to take her by the head for fear she would come round on the plough but she stood still, so I went right in before her until the shower would go over. When I did this she came forward and put her nose close to my neck behind my left ear. We had stood thus for little more than a minute, when we were both struck with the lightning, both falling just as we had stood, but I neither heard, saw nor knew anything. I did not even know of falling. I had lain, as far as I could afterwards learn, about five minutes, and when consciousness began to return I at once knew, that I had been struck with the lightning. Although, I could not tell one part as being more painful than another, I could neither move hand nor foot, and in these few minutes I did verily believe that I would never rise again.

On regaining consciousness my first words were a prayer to God asking forgiveness for past sins, and of thankfulness for sparing me even although it were but for a few minutes. My thoughts however, soon turned, and a longing desire to live, and to look around once more on this fair world seized hold of one, and in these few minutes, oh how sweet did life seem to one.

With these thoughts came the desire to rise, and with an effort I managed to raise myself to my elbow, when I turned to see if the mare had shared the same fate as myself, and there she was lying still and motionless with her head resting almost on my feet, and as I thought quite dead. Surely that stroke was sent as a solemn warning, to remind one how short and uncertain our life here on earth is. Oh may we lay to heart the things that belong to our everlasting peace, and strive more earnestly than we have done to lead a better life, that we may be ready to depart whenever He sees fit to call us. My next thoughts were to look for Father, and on turning round I saw him coming slowly up with Willie, nearly at the top of the yellow turnips. It seems that the second peal of thunder had startled his mare, and springing forward she had dragged him over and pulled the reins out of his hands. She had however turned on to the lea, and the harrow sticking fast, the swingletree broke, and she came home unhurt.[10] When he got to his feet he saw that the mare was home and so he went over to Willie as he was a good deal frightened, and had come up with him as far as I have before mentioned before he saw me. He came to me then however, as fast as he could, and by the time he came up I had got to my feet. We then tried to get off some of the mare's harness as she was beginning by this time to show some signs of returning animation and was blowing terribly at the nose. I soon felt however, my legs giving way and said that I would be obliged to go home, as I felt, that if I stayed much longer I would soon be unable to do so.

I went home accordingly and prepared to go to bed when on taking off my stockings, it appeared that the circulation of the blood in my feet had completely stopped, from the top of my boots downwards being as white as milk. I told them to rub them with their hands which they did for a good while. They then took warm water and a cloth and rubbed them, and in about an hour they had returned to their natural warmth. I did not as you may suppose sleep very much that night and next day I still felt a little deranged. After that however, I was completely recovered and I am sure I cannot feel too grateful to God, who in his great mercy spared me as I earnestly hope (as the apostle

---

[10] swingletree, cross piece of the plough to which the traces of the horse are attached.

says) to live, not unto ourselves, but unto him who saved us, and washed us in his blood.

The mare however, was to share a sadder fate. They got the farrier to her on Monday night when he bled her, and on Tuesday we thought her a little better, but on Wednesday she was a great deal worse and we thought all day that she was just dying, so in the evening, as we thought it would be an act of charity to put the poor beast out of pain. I went over for Cultain who came over and shot her.

On Thursday we dug a hole and buried her just where she lay and there we saw the last of poor old 'Jane'. She was just a month older than me being 20 past but she could eat as well and work as well as ever she did.

1879 September
8th

I have let a week slip without writing my 'Journal' and the only excuse I can make is that we have been rather busy and also that the evenings are such, so that very little can be done in them, being as we would say half light—half dark. The weather has now changed a good deal for the better, the past week having been pretty dry.

On Monday we 'took in' the hay which was in colls and put it into tramp colls in the cornyard , it being in very good order.[11]

Father and Mother were up at Keith on Tuesday to the funeral of Maggie Imlach.

She had died on Saturday. Mother went up to see Kate as she has been unwell for sometime. The Doctor says she had just got cold and it had seated on her lungs, and she is also very weak. We heard however, from George today and she is a little better.

On Wednesday we were scuffling and hoeing among the turnips, and on Thursday afternoon we got the seed hay thrashed in splendid condition. We have not much seed however, and it is a little dark in the colour. I had it down to Carestown's loft on Friday morning.

On Friday afternoon we went over to the Smiddy to get the young mare shod, but the Smith was away at the moss, so we had to go back on Saturday morning. The wood roup in the Cotton Hill was on that day and Father bought two lots. It was hardly so dear as in former years.

John Cowie, Finnygaud, came over on Saturday night.

On Sunday John, Mrs. and Miss Hendry, Newpark, came up and went to church with us. It was a beautiful day, and we had Mr. McVicar, Ordiquhill, preaching to us.

---

[11] colls, hay cocks; tramp colls, a number of hay colls put into one and tramped hard in order that the hay may be further dried.

Today we were driving home the wood from the Cotton Hill and in the afternoon we had the young mare in the drill plough furring up some turnips but she was very quiet. George Gray, Little Cultain, died on Saturday evening. He has been very bad for sometime past, as he could keep nothing on his stomach. He is to be buried at Grange on Wednesday.

15th

We have had another week of fine dry weather but still very little sunshine. The crops however, have made good progress and barley is now assuming a yellowish colour. Oats are to be a good deal later for except those on clean land they are scarcely begun to mix. Turnips have improved a little but they have still a great deal to do. We have been busy all the week driving peats, and the good weather has also made a great improvement on them, indeed they are far drier than ever we expected to see them this year.

We have had the young mare to the moss, mostly every day. She is very quiet and goes splendid in the cart.

One Thursday Joan, Nellie and I were in the moss all day. We wheeled out the dry peats to the end of the lair and then set up the wet ones.

I was deer hunting in the Cotton Hill on Saturday but we were very unfortunate, getting but one solitary woodcock for our day's spoil.

On Sunday Joan and I went down to Fordyce Church. We went in past Newpark and went down to church with them. Mary Wilson and Jessie were both in church so we went up past with them. After tea we went over to Knowiemoor to see their garden, as it had got a prize for being second best within three miles of Cornhill. It is in very good order and laid off with much taste. We got no one about the place but the servant, all the rest being down at Brodiesord at the sermon. As we were taking a look through the garden John Main came in about, and so we had to go down with him, to get a sight of his garden and houses. He has got a very nice dwelling house, and his garden was well worth going to see. His office houses are also very compact, and he has everything about them very tidy.

22nd

After the long continuance of wet weather (which kept people's spirits and everything else in such depression) everyone is highly pleased with the delightful weather we are now enjoying. Still it cannot be called bright weather, getting as we do only occasional glimpses of the sun, yet for the past three weeks it has been very mild and warm, and I believe it has been the best weather we possibly could have had for had it turned very dry after so much wet the ground would have got so hard that nothing would have grown. The farmers on the coast side have all commenced harvest, and I hear that Clune and Inaltrie are to commence tomorrow.

On Thursday we got home all the peats except a few loads of wet ones. We went up for two loads for Mr. Smith.

On Wednesday morning and in the afternoon we look home some turfs. On Thursday we got home all the dry ones, and set up those that were wet.

On Friday and Saturday we were turning and hoeing the turnips at the back of the house. This morning we went up for two loads of the peats we left. Before we got to the moss it came on a heavy rain and kept raining until we were nearly home, when we were wet through. The afternoon however was dry and I was furring up the turnips.

29th

The weather all last week has been very good for harvest work, but only a few have as yet commenced. Kirkton and Raimore began on Friday and a few more have begun today.

On Tuesday we had a very strong gail of wind from the south west, and there are reports of barley, when it was ripe, being rather severely shaken.

On Wednesday we were building the hays. The wind had it all turned over and we were anxious to get it up. Joseph McKay came over and gave us a hand and we got a fine day.

On Thursday we took home the remainder of the peats, and in the afternoon we were driving turfs.

We were over on Friday helping Sandy McKay to thrash and build his hay. In the evening I went down to Newpark to get slips of some roses, and was entertained by Miss Hendry with some excellent music on the piano.

On Saturday night and Sunday morning a good deal of rain fell. Father and I were at church but the roads were very soft. We were cutting our sprotts today and a splendid crop they are.[12] I went down to Cullen in the afternoon and bought a lamp for the Library.

1879 October
6th

We commenced the harvest on Wednesday last, by cutting a piece of the barley. There came a very heavy shower in the afternoon, which stopped us for that night.

---

[12] sprotts, coarse reedy plants growing in clumps on wet ground.

Thursday and Friday were both fine forcy days and we kept busy at the sythe. We cut a small piece of corn on Friday afternoon and on Saturday we cut out the barley. There was some of it very ripe but as it is getting so late in the year we thought it better to be taking it. The corn has made very little progress in ripening to appearance during the past week and there is scarcely any corn cut in this district yet, but it has been fine weather for filling and it may be better that it looks.

Sunday was hasy and warm, and it was eleven o'clock today before we got commenced to cut.

Old Mrs. Hendry, Cairnton, died on Friday last, and she is to be buried at Fordyce on Tuesday. A letter came to Father today.

13th

The past week has been very good harvest weather, but the harvest work is progressing but very slowly everyone keeping back thinking it too green.

Until Friday it was very quiet and warm, and there was always a very strong dew in the mornings.

On Tuesday and Wednesday we were cutting at the clean land on the farthest knowe, and on Thursday we cut the piece clean land on the hill.

On Friday we led the barley, but it was not in too fine condition. I am sure it is not going to turn out well as it went into too little bulk in the stack. Today we were cutting the corn in the den, it being a splendid crop. They commenced harvest on Ardiecow this morning.

20th

The weather during the past week has been cold and stormy, while a few days were rather wet, but as there as always a good breese of wind it was not long in drying up. We did not cut a great deal during the week as we were always thinking the lea too green, but this stormy weather has made us easier pleased.

I was over at Oathillock on Monday afternoon, binding. They have got a cutting machine this year, but it does not make a very good job and it is very heavy on the horses. It is one of Hornsby's make and this is the third year it has wrought.

We went over with our horses on Wednesday afternoon, as it was too hard on their own going all day. They were a little keen at the first but it soon made them enough.

On Saturday we cut the most of the lea corn on the hill.

Father was at the church of Cullen on Sunday officiating at their sacrament as they have too few elders of their own.

On Monday we started the two sythes to cut clean before us. We have Andrew Stephen and Mrs. Bremner, the foreman of Carestown's wife. We had not cut two hours however, before the rain came on and we were obliged to come home. James Gray was just taking clyack and so I went over and asked if he would give us a day of his machine, as we were making no job of the cutting with the sythes.[13] This he was very willing to do, and as it was clearing up for this time we went off and cut some wads, and by three o'clock we were started, and by six we had got a good bit of it down. His machine is very light on the horses, and makes first class work.

27th

On Tuesday James Gray came up about nine o'clock and gave us another day of his machine. We hardly made a halt all day, and by night we had got the field we were at nearly all cut. We had Joseph McKay over giving us a hand.

On Wednesday we cut until ten o'clock, we then started the loading, and got in all the clean land except some in the den. We did not cut any more all the week, it being so very green, and as the weather was fine we thought we would leave it a few days to ripen.

On Thursday Alex Mackay took it all in and Cultain took clyack. The most of them have got it all cut in the end of the parish except Nether Blairock and Moss-side. On Saturday we went up and gave William McBain a day's cutting. He has not got much done yet, but I think his corn is every bit as ripe as ours.

On Sunday afternoon we had Mr. and Mrs. Farquhar and Uncle George over at tea. Our Sacrament is to be next Sunday but owing to the harvest, there is to be no fast day.

The frost, the last three mornings has been very severe. I saw ice on the water today, and in sheltered places it kept white all day.

1879 November
3rd

The weather, although now a little cold and stormy, is still very good for this day of the year. A few stooks are still to be seen in the parish, although they are now getting rather thin, while a few have commenced the plough. We had Andrew Stephen on Tuesday, and

---

[13] clyack, the last sheaf of corn to be cut at the harvest. The clyack sheaf was also the last sheaf of harvest to be put on top of the last rick.

we led all day. We took in the lea on the hill, and the half of the field of lea on Ardiecow.

Wednesday forenoon was wet, and we got nothing done, it cleared up however, by twelve o'clock so, we started to cut the piece green corn we had left. It was a little thin on the ground, but was very rank and strong, and had it only been ripe would have been a beautiful crop.

We started the leading again on Thursday morning, and got in all we had ready by four o'clock. We then took the sythes, and succeeded in taking clyack, although it was a little dark before we got finished.

On Friday we went up to William McBain's for two loads of divots to cover the potatoes. We were going to lift them on Saturday but the morning was very cold and stormy, and we did not try them.

Sunday was our sacrament when Father, Mother and I were at church. Our minister had no one assisting him. George Duncan has his holidays just now, and him and Aleck were up at their tea in the afternoon. Today we manged to get in the remainder of the crop. The clean land went into very little bulk in the stack, but the lea was a good crop, and stood out fine. We have 13 oat stacks and 2 barley ones.

10*th*

We lifted our potatoes on Tuesday and Wednesday, but they are a very deficient crop, being extremely small. They are however, of pretty good quality.

On Thursday the steam mill was at Carestown thrashing barley, and we were down assisting them. There was a very poor out-turn of barley, being only about a third of what he had last year. I commenced the plough on Friday. The stubbles are in grand order for ploughing being fine and dry.

On Saturday we got the most of the stacks thatched, as the day was fine and quiet during the rest of the week however, there was a good breese of wind, doing extremely well both with stooks and stacks.

I think the harvest now completely finished in Deskford, but I see by the newspapers, that in the upper districts there is still a good deal to do.

On Sunday the weather changed it being cold and showery. I was going over to Limestones in the afternoon, but as it was wet I did not go.

I was over at the Shoemakers one night, and was in past Ardiecow coming home, when we had a dance. They finished the harvest on Saturday last.

17*th*

On Monday afternoon and Tuesday forenoon, I was at the steam mill at Ordens. Him and Carestown have been driving their barley to Glenglassaugh Distillery during the week. Carestown had only 22 quarters being little more than a quarter off the acre, and it was 50 lbs per bushel.[14] Ordens to appearance turned out a little better but it is only 49 lbs per bushel.

On Tuesday afternoon we were tidying up the corn yard.

Wednesday was Hallow Fair Fordyce, and a cold stormy day it was. Father was down a few hours, but I was in the plough all day. The fees were a good deal down, and a great many were not engaged.

On Thursday I was driving out dung. Father was over at Cornhill Station for some oil-cake, and went past Limestones to ask for Aunt, who has been very poorly for sometime, she was however, keeping a little better. Cornhill market was that day. Cattle were in more demand, and prices were also a little better than last month.

On Friday I was in the plough. I went down to Kirktown in the evening and opened the Library when there was a proposal to get up some readings during the winter. The weather during the week with the exception of Wednesday has been all that could be desired.

On Friday and Saturday there was a pretty sharp frost, but yesterday and today it has all disappeared and we have had two fine fresh busy days.

24th

The good weather which we have been enjoying during the past 3 months, came to an end on Friday, and since then we have had a good deal of rain.

On Tuesday and Wednesday, I was at the plough. On Tuesday night I went down to Inaltrie to get my hair cut. Father was at Portknockie on Thursday with a load of turfs for Janet Reach, I took a few loads of turnips in the forenoon and in the afternoon went over to the Smiddy with Fanny to get her shoes removed. Alex Ross came up that night and we gave her a clip as she is very bad for sweating.

On Friday I was in the plough but the afternoon was rather wet.

Saturday was wet all day and I did not yolk the plough. We were winnowing some corn in the afternoon, and in the afternoon I had it over to the mill.

Sunday forenoon was wet and the afternoon showery. I was not at church as James Murdoch is in bed. Father and Mother were up at

---

[14] One bushel equalled 11.648 gallons or 52.916 litres. The official weight for barley was 56 lbs per bushel.

Ardiecow at their tea. I see that Donald has now got his sheep down. Today I was in the plough.

1879 December
1st

I was over on Tuesday assisting at the steam mill at Kirktown, but we did not do a large day's work. The barley had been a little heated, making it clap in the stack, and causing it to be very bad to thrash. The outturn of grain was also like other peoples—very poor. The rest of the week I was mostly at the plough, the weather being good.

Saturday was very cold and frosty. I was over in the afternoon, at the Smiddy and the meal mill.

Sunday was stormy, some good showers of hail falling during the day. In the afternoon, I went over to Limestones. He has not got his mill finished yet as the wright has never come to put in the doors and windows. Aunt is a little better, but she is getting very frail now. Today it has been very stormy snow falling nearly all day. In the morning the frost was too hard for the plough so we went to Tochineal for some tiles, and also went back again in the afternoon.

9th

The snow storm which commenced on Saturday the 29th November has continued during the week with increased severity, the frost in the first of the week being far more severe than what is generally expected at this season of the year. The snow has come on a week earlier than last year, and owing to the lateness of the harvest the work is not nearly so far forward as at this date last year. We had all the stubble and four acres of lea ploughed last year e're the storm commenced, but we have four acres of stubbles yet to plough. On Tuesday a little snow fell, and except thrashing an hour in the morning I was cleaning harness all day.

Wednesday was our thanksgiving day for the harvest. Mary Wilson, Limestones came over and went to church with us. We had Mr. Brochie, Cullen officiating, who gave us a splendid discourse from the text, 'for as long as the earth endureth seed time and harvest shall not cease'. In the afternoon James Gray, and his better half 'Janet', came up to tea.

On Thursday taking in a stack and thrashing was the most of our days work.

On Friday and Saturday a good deal of snow fell making a depth of about six inches over all.

Sunday was quiet and frosty. Joan and I were at church. Yesterday was a little soft throughout the day, but not like a right-thaw. I was driving out dung all day, and in the evening went over to the shoemakers to get my boots mended and thus leaving the writing of any 'diary' (if I my so call it) for tonight. Today it has been soft, with sleety showers, and a good deal of the snow has disappeared, but I am still in doubts if it is to last long.

15th

As I conjectured the thaw on Tuesday did not last long, the frost on Wednesday morning being intense. It relaxed however, a little during the day and also the two following days, but with little effect.

On Saturday however, a stormy breeze of wind sprung up from the south west which continued yesterday all day and today every particle of the snow has mostly disappeared.

On Wednesday we were thrashing and taking home some turnips. Later in the byre putting a young calf to suck.

Miss Duncan and George Duncan are practicing on the piano and violin. We were taken 'ben' to hear some of their new pieces which they rendered in first class style.[15] There is nothing delights me more than to sit and listen to music, especially when performed in such an excellent manner as Miss Duncan is capable of.

19th

The first week of winter weather. Still it can not be called bad weather. Quiet frosty days have been the general rule with sometimes a slight thaw. There has been no ploughing however, and thrashing corn and pulling turnips has been the most of our work.

Tuesday was very frosty. We were pulling and taking home turnips. In the afternoon I went down to Cullen and bought a calf from Anderson the Carter. The price was £21.17/6. A soiree was to be held that night in the Free Church being the anniversary of the ordination of the Revd. Mr. Forgan. I therefore waited a short time and went in to see what sort of an affair it would be. There was a large choir accompanyed by a harmonium and the singing was good. An address delivered by the Revd. Mr. Stockdale, Grange, on harmony was very good, and also one by a minister from Aberdeen but the others were not worth much. By the time we got out the wind had risen greatly, while it was also pitch dark and raining heavily. I looked out for a lassie and managed to pick one up, but unfortunately she had not got an umbrella. With the rosy cheeks, the golden ringlets, laughing blue eyes, and merry chat of Helen McHattie however, I was quite content. The road was most excessively slippery, and walking was both slow and dangerous.

---

[15] ben, the inner or better room in a house.

It rained nearly all day on Wednesday. I went over in the afternoon to the Smiddy with the old plough to be repaired.

Thursday was again frosty. We were pulling turnips.

On Friday morning I went to the Smiddy got one of the mares frosted, and went to Cullen in the afternoon for the calf.[16] The day was terrible cold and frosty.

On Saturday forenoon I went over to Limestones for a load of old barley straw for bedding. In the afternoon we were thrashing.

I was not at church on Sunday. Father, Joan and Willie were. Today I was pulling turnips and cleaning some of the harness.

26ᵗʰ

Grim John Frost has relaxed his hold, and again the plough is merrily going. Yesterday and today were fine days, fresh and happy. The rest of the week however, was very frosty.

On Tuesday we were thrashing.

Wednesday we took home the turnips I pulled on Monday. It was that day very like snow. I went up to Ardiecow in the evening. I had sent away an order to Messrs. Campbell and Co., Glasgow, for a Melodeon and I was expecting it that night. Don was to bring it from Cornhill Station. It came alright and I was highly delighted with its appearance. During the past few weeks I have been receiving invitations, many and pressing me to go and spend my New Year in the Scottish capital. I did not think however, that it was at all possible for me to go this year, and made many objections why I could not come.

On Thursday night however, I received a letter from Annie, with money to pay my way up and back. After that I had nothing to say, all my objections had been swept away, and Father having given his consent, I at once sat down and penned a letter to Annie saying I would come.

I intend going to Keith on Friday night, and starting with the first train on Saturday morning. I have been sporting a little with my gun these frosty days but a pheasant and a rabbit has been all the venison.[17]

On Saturday afternoon we were winnowing.

Yesterday morning I was delighted to find it fresh. Father, Willie and I were at church. The minister preached from the text, 'today if ye will hear his voice, harden not your hearts' and made touching reference to the close of the year. This forenoon I was in the plough. In the afternoon we had two loads of corn down to Millton and took home some turnips.

---

[16] frosted, to sharpen the points of a horse's shoe that it may not slip on ice.

[17] venison, in this context venison means the animals hunted or beasts of the chase.

29th

Thursday night—nine o'clock— as I start tomorrow for Keith en route for Edinburgh I take this opportunity of writing, as I will not have time again until …

[Presumably Wilson meant his return. The Journal does not describe the events between 'again until' and 'The frost which', although there are no missing pages.]

The frost which was so severe in the first of the week relaxed its hold on Tuesday and I got to the plough again.

On Wednesday there was a meeting of the Committee to distribute the tickets for the entertainments, when it was seen that it would be impossible to have the first night sooner than the 3^{rd of} January.

On Thursday we had the steam mill, when we were lucky to get a good day. We thrashed two stacks of barley and three of oats. The out turn of barley was poor, being scarcely two quarters off the acre, but the oats were very good.

We were at Oathillock on Friday giving them a hand but I think his barley turned out rather better. I was over that night at a soiree in Bogmuchals and gave them a reading and two recitations. Mary and Joseph Mackay went over with Joan and I went in past Ardiecow for Miss McIntosh. The School was rather crowded but I was greatly pleased with the whole proceedings. We went to Portsoy on Saturday with the barley when it only weighed 48 lbs the bushel.

31st

The last two days of the year have been fresh and warm, and on both of them I was at the plough.

On Tuesday I was ploughing stubbles, but on Wednesday I was at the lea. It is over in the 'den' and I am ploughing it with one fur. Joan and I are going to a ball at Ardoch tonight an account of which I will give next week.

It was my intention when I commenced to write this 'Account of my every day life', to do so every week, and if possible every Monday. Circumstances however often prevented me from writing on Monday but except twice (as far as I can recall) I have succeeded in writing a little every week.

I will now close by saying farewell to 1879 hoping that the year 1880 may prove brighter than its predecessor in more respects than one.

A Journal of My Life and Every Day Doings

1880 January
5ᵗʰ

1879 is now past and gone, and we have entered on a new year, I may say a new decade.

As the days and weeks of the year just commenced, go swiftly past, may it be our earnest endeavour to strive, towards some improvement so that when the year shall have run its course, we may be able to look back and say 'we have not altogether lived in vain'.

Joan and I were at a ball at Ardoch on the last night of the year. As I had not a partner I waited to get company with the shoemaker Mr. Thomson, and it was nearly eleven o'clock before we got there. By that time they were merry at the dancing, and indeed the dance was kept up with great spirit throughout the night. There was also an abundant supply of refreshments served out by the Committee, and a few ladies and gentlemen entertained us with some excellent songs.

On Thursday I was at the plough all day.

On Friday I was also at the plough. Uncle George and Mr. and Mrs. Mackintosh were down that night at tea. In the newspaper this week is an account of the fearful accident which happened last Sunday night 28ᵗʰ December viz. the blowing down of a part of the Tay Bridge at the moment the train was crossing it. There were about 75 persons in the train at the time, but whether the bridge was blown down before the train came, or the train blown over taking the bridge with it will never be rightly known, as none have been left to tell the tale. During the week every means have been employed to recover the bodies, but as yet very few have been got. There was a strong gale of wind here at the time and a good deal of damage in the form of stacks being blown over and houses turred was done.[18]

Today being 'Auld Yule' I was not in the yoke. In the evening Miss Mackintosh, Don and Willie came down to tea, and we spent a forenight at the cards.

12ᵗʰ

The first of the week was fresh and I was in the plough.

On Friday however, a strong frost set in and today it is still very hard. On Friday night the first of 'The Course of Entertainments' came off in the form of readings, recitations and songs, and proved a perfect

---

[18] turred, in this context, thatch and/or turfs being blown off roofs.

success. Among the readers we had Mr. Sutherland, Portknockie, who kept the audience in a perfect roar. Mr. Wilson, Glenglassaugh, was also much appreciated for his singing.

Mr. & Mrs. Farquhar were over on Sunday afternoon when they were saying they were thinking of giving up their farm and taking a house in Keith.

19th

The past week has been very stormy. In the first of the week there was a hard bare frost, but on Friday morning there came a fall of snow of nearly 5 inches.

On Tuesday and Wednesday we were driving out dung.

On Thursday Father and I were at the steam mill at Ardiecow. He was obliged to take it as he could get no water to thrash. In the evening Joan and I went up to tea, when two of the Miss Geddes, Johnny, and Mr. Keir, Fordyce, were there. Miss Geddes and Miss Mackintosh gave us some excellent music on the piano and we had a nice dance with Don playing fiddle.

On Friday I went over and opened the Library. There was a meeting of Committee afterwards when it was agreed to have readings etc. on 30th January instead of a concert as was formerly proposed.

On Sunday afternoon I went over to Limestones to ask for Aunt. She is very frail now and scarcely able to rise from her chair.

26th

Although the past week has been mostly fresh it was Saturday before the plough would work and even then the frost was not altogether out.

On Tuesday we winnowed some corn we had in the mill, and I then had it over to Berryhillock. The roads were extraordinary slippery.

On Wednesday Alex Ross came in past in the evening. We had been over looking at the farm of Hillfolds which is for let just now. I went over on Thursday evening to Newton to see Johnny Geddes when Miss E. Geddes (who was to leave for Aberdeen today) entertained us with some music on the piano. She has made great improvement since last I saw her.

The second of our 'Course of Entertainments' came off on Friday evening and was in the form of a lecture delivered by Rev. Mr. McIntyre , Portknockie. His subject was 'Origin of Proverbs' which he treated in a very humorous and attractive manner. Mr Mackintosh, presided and at the close proposed a hearty vote of thanks to the lecturer which was warmly responded to.

On Saturday I was in the plough all day. Father was over at a wood roup in the Bogs of Skeith, but it was a very stiff sale.

On Sunday the frost was again very hard. William Reid, Cullen, was up in the afternoon.

Today the frost has relaxed a little but not so much as to let the plough work.

1880 February
2nd

As the weather during the past week has been fine, I was busy at the plough and got a good bit turned over. I went over to the Free Manse on Tuesday to see about the new books we are getting for the Library, and it was arranged that Miss Mita Ker, who is in London should buy them as she came through Edinburgh from the same bookseller, as we got the others.

On Friday I attended a meeting of 'Committee of Entertainments', when it was agreed to have readings on the 6th, a lecture on the 13th and then finish up with a concert.

9th

Fine weather still continues, and the work is being pushed forward with all dispatch. A great ploughing match came off at Slackdale on Wednesday last when 68 ploughs appeared on the ground. The day was fine, and consequently there was a large turn out of spectators. The ground however, was not very equal, and of course I had the bad luck to fall among the stones. There was some first class work G. Geddes, Cottonhill, being the champion, and so becomes the owner of the Highland Society's medal. Only two prizes came to Deskford. A Duncan, Kirktown, being 10th and J. Clarke, Mid Skeith, 15th.

On Thursday Joan and I were over at Kirktown at our tea. Joseph and Mary Ann McKay and James Smith, Blairock, were the company.

The third Entertainment came off on Friday. Mr. Kitchen, Clune, was in the Chair and did his duties well, but altogether it was no great success.

On Saturday I was ploughing at clear land as the lea was getting very dry.

Mrs. Biddie, Backies, died on 29th January and Father was at her funeral on Monday last.

16th

I was in the plough everyday during the week the weather being fine.
On Monday Alex Ross and I went up to Raemore to ask Mr. Garden for Chairman to our concert. He would have been very willing to oblige us but as he has been unwell for sometime he was unable to comply.

Tuesday was Fastern-even new style, but we did not hold it. In the evening I went up to Ardiecow and got some bannocks.

Mr. Thomson the shoemaker and Mr. Geddes, Newton, being also there. The Rev. Mr. Boyd, F.C. Minister, Portosy, gave a lecture on Friday night as our fourth Entertainment. His subject was 'Popular Tales', but it was of no great interest. Mr. Ker was in Chair.

Thursday was Cornhill market. Father went over with two cattle and sold them. There was a large attendance but prices back from what they were last market. Helen Stephen was proclaimed in church yesterday, her intended's name being George Gray.

23rd

The opening of the Library being postponed, owing to the lecture, I went over and opened it on Monday night. It was a terrible night of wind and rain, and very few attended. The wind was indeed excessive and I see by the newspapers that a great deal of damage attended with loss of life, has been done to shipping especially on the East Coast.

I was in the plough all the rest of the week the weather being fine.

On Tuesday night Alex Ross and I went up to the Free Manse to make out the programme for the Concert, and it was past nine o'clock before we got through.

On Friday afternoon I though it was going to be a bad night, and was not a little anxious you may be sure, but there was a good breeze of wind and cleared up. Mary Wilson, Limestones, came over in the afternoon and went over with us. I had to go away however, a good deal earlier as I had to take the piano down from the Free Manse. I got the merchant of Berryhillock's spring cart, but we had rather a difficult job getting it in over. As the night kept up fine, there was a large turnout, three times as many as on any former night. Although some of our singers did not appear, we got on nicely the Misses Ker contributing largely with music on the violin and piano. Mr. Kitchen, Clune, performed the duties of the Chair in a very creditable manner and I think I may say that on the whole it proved a success.

Saturday afternoon was wet and I did not get to the plough.

Sunday was also wet all day, a good deal of rain falling.

Today however, it was again dry, and in the forenoon I was in the plough, while in the afternoon I was taking home some turnips.

1880 March
1st

The weather during the past week has been rough and stormy, the winds on some days being very strong.

On Monday night the miller came up from Milton and invited Joan and I to Helen's marriage on Saturday. I was hardly expecting to get but was none the less proud of being bidden.

On Tuesday the young mare grew unwell and we had to send for the farrier. He stayed all the afternoon with her but next day she was all right, and I went to the plough in the forenoon. In the afternoon Father went over to Limestones to meet Mother who was at Finnygaud. In the evening I went down to Fordyce to a service which was held in the Established Church. I went in past for Cultain and they had just commenced when we got down. They have been getting their Church all re-seated and otherwise improved and this service was held in honour of its being completed, but I was so highly delighted with the whole affair, that I think an account of it deserves a clean page.

1880 March
1ˢᵗ

Fordyce Soiree

Tea having been served out by an active band of stewards (there were no stewardesses and I think they were better without them) the Chairman, Mr. Grant gave an opening address, the chief feature of which was, his thanking the congregation for their liberal support towards the improvement of the church.

The choir then, under the leadership of Mr. Largue sung a hymn, which they also did between each of the speeches throughout the evening, and in a style which I have never heard equalled. Mr. Anderson minister of the Parish Church of Gartly was the first to address us. His subject was 'The solemn, and important trust, committed to us, as rational beings, in the case of an immortal soul' and he reminded us that we having but one life to live, and that a very short one, and that the well being of our eternal soul depended on how we spent that life, it behoved us so to live that we might ensure its safety.

In the course of his speech he also stated that, obedience, diligence, and truth, were three of the principal attributes of a good life.

The next speaker was Mr. Simmons U.P. minister, Portsoy. He has a very weak voice, but he gave us a capital discourse on 'How to make home happy' giving as his opinion that Piety, Industry, and Economy, were three things which would greatly tend to the increase of happiness at home.

The next to address us was Mr. Stuart, H.M.S. Inspector of Schools, who gave us a very eloquent speech on 'language', and in the course of which he stated, that it had been proved beyond doubt that Hebrew was the language spoken by our first parents in the Garden of Eden, and also that a child if left to itself would speak pure Hebrew.

There was then an interval and a service of fruit, there after Mr. Watt, Fetteresso, addressed us. He is rather an old man, and his subject was 'Christian Missions' which he handled in a very interesting manner, speaking mostly on those in India and Africa. The last speaker although not the least was Mr. Mackay, Cullen, his subject being 'The duty of Christian usefulness'.

We then got a speech from Mr. Anderson, Reporter Office, Portsoy, who proposed a vote of thanks to Mr. Grant, for presiding, Mr. Stuart then proposed a hearty vote of thanks to Mr. Largue and his choir, which was heartily responded to.

The choir then gave a parting hymn. Mr. Grant pronounced the blessing, and we dismissed.

On Friday evening I went over to a meeting, held in the School, for the purpose of settling up the entertainments, when it was seen that the whole drawings amounted to nearly £8, leaving a surplus of nearly £4 after paying all expenses.

Saturday morning was very rough and stormy heavy showers of rain, and hail falling at intervals. By mid-day however, it hardened up, and at one o'clock Joan and I set out for Milton.

They were married at the Church, the bridegroom and his people meeting us there.[19] We got back to Milton by three o'clock when a splendid dinner awaited us, and to which thirty-five sat down. Dinner being past, the fiddlers were got into tune, and we started the dancing but as none of his people were dancers, we got it all to ourselves. During the evening we were favoured with some splendid songs by Andrew Stephen and Miss Badenoch. Tea was served about seven o'clock, thereafter we had a few more reels, but it being Saturday night we finished up about half past ten. George Stephen who was down from Keith at it, came up with us and stayed all night.

Next morning it was very wet, but soon cleared up, when Father, Geordie, and I went to church.

8th

During the past week we have been enjoying delightful spring weather—indeed I fear it is a little too fine, to last long. Of all the seasons of the year I like Spring the best, for then, the songs of the birds being new, have greater charm and the grass springing so fresh and green is more pleasing to the eye than when more advanced. What a contrast there is between the mornings now and those during winter, and how pleasant it is to listen, as the day is dawning to the sweet

---

[19] Possibly the wedding of Helen Stephen and George Gray proclaimed on 16th February.

music of the feathered minstrels, as each in its own peculiar strain, pours forth its morning song of praise.

Everyone has been busy during the week ploughing clean land, and it is now in first class order. We will have two days ploughing yet before we be close to the turnips. I went down to Newpark on Tuesday evening to see Miss Hendry, when she gave us some fine music on the piano.

On Wednesday Father went over to take a look at the farm of Slackdale, which is for let just now. There is very good land on it, although some of it is rather wet, but the houses are in a most wretched condition and would require a great deal of repair. Mr. Donaldson who is leaving at Whitsunday, is going to Paris to be a missionary and he has been in Aberdeen studying the most of the winter. There was a Negro Entertainment given in the School on Friday evening, by some young men from Cullen, but as the night was not very good I did not go over.

On Sunday morning Jessie Cowie with Willie and Sandy, came over with the machine. They all went to church with Joan and I, and we took a look through the churchyard as we came down. Johnny Geddes, Newton, came over in the afternoon.

15th

We had fine weather in the first of the week, but on Thursday it turned cold and stormy.

On Friday night, a good deal of rain fell, and we have had a little every day since. On Tuesday I went up and spent a forenight at Ardiecow.

Thursday was Cornhill market. Father went over to buy a calving cow, but did not get one to suit him. I was in the plough all day, and got the piece clean land at the back of the house finished, and was not any sorry for the same, for it was very hard.

I went over on Friday night and opened the Library but it was a wet night, and few attended.

On Saturday we went to Portsoy for a load of manure and some coals, as we are getting the steam mill to thrash out the crop.

On Sunday Joan and I went down to Newpark, and went to church with them. There is a great improvement on the church now, the seats being far wider and more comfortable than formerly.

Today I was filling in the furs of the lea. By the newspapers I see they are sowing in early places.

22nd

The past week has been dry, with a little frost in the mornings, while some of the days were very warm. On Tuesday I went over to

Limestones, and went with Uncle to Marnin Fair. He had over the brown mare for sale, but like many more, had to bring her home again. There was a great turn out of horses, but no sale. I went down past Finnygaud, and staid a few hours. We got back to Limestones about half past six o'clock, and it being Fastern-even they were baking some bannocks.

I was in the plough on Wednesday. The steam mill was at Kirktown on Thursday and I was over giving them a hand.

On Friday we were driving the remaining stacks into the cornyard, and by seven o'clock Mr. Imlach had his thrashing machine set up along side ready to thrash them. We got a fine day on Saturday for the job, and they were finished and off by twelve o'clock. In the afternoon I was ploughing a piece on the Hill for potatoes.

Swailend and Burnheads commenced that day to sow.

29th

Today we were going to sow the lea in the Den but as the morning was rather gully looking, we went to the plough.[20] It cleared up however, and we sowed it in the afternoon. Carestown and Kirktown were also sowing, the ground being now in first class condition for the seed.

The weather during the past week has been very dry and every one has been very busy sowing. There has however, been severe frosts at night and it was always nine o'clock in the morning before the harrows would work.

On Tuesday and Wednesday I was harrowing in the 'den'.

On Thursday we sowed the half of the lea below the houses, and for the next two days I had work harrowing at it.

Today I sowed the rest of the lea, there being no frost in the morning. Owing to the frost there has been no growth during the week indeed the grass is not so green as it was a fortnight ago.

Kate and the bairns have been down staying all the week and they are all looking pretty well.

1880 April
5th

We have had a week of rather showery weather, consequently very little has been sown. The moisture however, has done good, and the grass is again assuming a green shade.

On Tuesday afternoon Father went to the harrows, while I commenced to get the flowers in the garden put into trim. About five

---

[20] gully looking, threatening (weather).

o'clock I took my supper, and set off for Limestones for a few potatoes of a special variety which they have got from Devonshire.

On Wednesday I got the lea harrowed out. Miss McIntosh came down in the evening for some flowers which I had promised her, and of course I had to carry the basket up the brae. We planted a few of them but it got dark and we had to lay them aside. Mr. Kier, Fordyce, was there. He had been staying a day or two. It is reported that he is going to take up shop in Fordyce on his own account.

Thursday forenoon was rainy. In the morning we winnowed the grass seed. Father then went to Swailend for seed barley, while I went to Muttonbrae for the grass seed riddle. In the afternoon I went to the plough.

I was ploughing on Friday and Saturday and both were showery. I was not at church on Sunday.

John Cowie was over from Finnygaud. In the afternoon Joan and I went over to our tea at Newton.

Today we sowed the barley, and it being a fine, dry day it was in grand trim for the harrows.

The farms which were for let have all got tenants now. Auchip has been let to a Morayshire man, Mr. McDonald, formerly blacksmith at Blackjug has got Slackdale, and a man named Duncan is coming to Clashendamer.

12th

On Tuesday last we sowed the clean land at the back of the house, and on Wednesday we sowed the grass seed. Thursday was Cornhill market. Father was not over, but it was a rather stiff sale. I went over in the evening to Clashendamer for a red currant bush and some rhubarb.

On Friday I was ploughing and harrowing a piece on the Hill for potatoes. In the afternoon Miss Duncan and Miss Katie Duncan came up to tea, and in the evening I went over with them to open the Library. After I got through I went in past Kirktown with a book, when we had a dance.

On Saturday morning Father went away to the Smithy with one of the horses while I started to roll with the other, but it grew wet and I had to unyoke. In the afternoon although still rather wet and misty I went over to the hill and made the potatoe drills.

Mr. and Mrs. Farquhar were over at tea on Sunday afternoon. His sale is fixed for the 8th of May.

Today I was harrowing some of the turnip land in the forenoon, while in the afternoon I was in the roller.

19ᵗʰ

Rather showery weather has prevailed during the past week, and the grass is looking fresh and green, bringing to one's mind the commencement of the old Scotch song 'Now in her green mantle blythe Nature arrays'.

Tuesday was a nice dry day, and we would have got all the potatoes planted had we not fallen short of seed.

Wednesday forenoon was wet, and we were winnowing some corn. It being dry in the afternoon we had it down to Milton, and when we returned took home the remainder of the turnips. Johnny Geddes, Newton, was over in the evening, selling tickets for a Social meeting, which was to be held at Fordyce on Friday night, but I did not buy any.

I was ploughing clean land on Thursday. In the afternoon I went down to Cullen to get my watch repaired as she had been stopped for a few days. As I came home I went in past the Clune to see Miss Kitchen, and it was, it was—well just rather late before I got home.

On Friday forenoon I ploughed the last of the clean land. It was a nice fresh day and as I stood at the end of the ridge, looking around me, and admiring the beauties of Nature, it came into my head, that I might try and compose a few verses on Spring. I commenced, as I went my rounds at the plough, I succeeded in putting together, after many revisals and alterations, the few lines which follow.

Spring
Some praise the beauty of the flowers
As beneath a summer sun,
They scatter fragrance all around,
In the merry month of June.

Some love the Autumn of the year;
When ripe fruit the earth doth crown,
And the green leaves change their lovely shade,
To red and russet brown.

Cold surly Winter, others say
Is the best of all the year,
For then comes merry Xmas round,
With joy and right good cheer.

And they love to see the ice-bound stream,
And the snowflakes as they go
To wrap up old Mother Earth in her shroud
Of white and fleecy snow.

But of all the seasons of the year,
I love sweet Spring the dearest,
For then the fields are fresh and green,
And all Nature looks her fairest.

How pleasant it is in a fresh spring morn,
To hearken the wee birds sing;
As each tiny minstrel adding its note,
Makes wood and valley ring.

But Spring is the time for busy work,
As no idlers then should be;
For the soil must be ploughed and harrowed and sowed
If a full crop we would see.

How I love to see in an April morn,
All the white sacks dotting the field;
With the sower sowing the seed, as in faith
He expects it a crop to yield.

Our Youth is the spring-time of our lives,
And we all our seed do sow;
Be they good or bad they shall all take root,
And in after years shall grow.

And as, if in Spring we mispend our time,
And sow not the proper seeds;
In harvest the fields will no ripe fruit show
But a mess of noxious weeds.

Even so in our youth if we do not
Our words and actions guard;
Our after-life will no pleasure yield
But sorrow be all our reward.

But oh! May it always be our aim,
As the years of youth fly past;
To sow in our hands, no seed but the good
And time, for truth shall last.

So that when the harvest of life shall come
And our seed to fruition hath grown;
The tares may be easily rooted up
When not tares have at all been sown.[21]

---

[21] tares, mixture of oats, vetches and peas cut with a scythe as extra feed for milk cows and feeding cattle.

Today we sowed the remainder of the crop, and I was in the harrows all day. In the evening I went over to the F.C. Manse, to arrange about purchasing a few more books for the Library.

26th

The weather during the past week has been cold and stormy with frequent showers of sleet and rain. Vegetation has not made much progress, owing to the cold, and braird is looking far best on land which is not rolled.[22]

On Tuesday I was in the harrows. In the afternoon I was sowing grass seed but there was a very strong wind making it a rather difficult job. I went over in the evening to Oathillock and got some nice flowers from Miss Mackay.

Wednesday forenoon was very wet. It cleared up however, about eleven o'clock, a strong gale of wind sprang up and by three o'clock it was as dry as I got to the roller.

On Thursday I was harrowing among the turnip land. Don Mackintosh came down and paid me the price of the pasture and spent the evening.

Friday was our fast day, and we had Mr Leidingham, Boyndie, both in the fore and afternoon.[23]

I was cross ploughing on Saturday all day.

Father, Mother and I were at church on Sunday. Our minister had Mr. McVicar, Oridiquhill assisting him and he gave us a splendid discourse in the afternoon from the parable of the marriage feast.

This morning as the land was too wet to plough, I went down to Cullen for my watch. In the afternoon I went to the plough.

On Sunday morning as Mr. & Mrs. Mackintosh were going to chapel and when they were a little below Cultain, the mare came down breaking both the shafts and throwing them all out on the road. Maggie and Willie were also in the machine at the time. I went up in the evening to ask about them, but none of them was any hurt in the least.

I see by the newspapers that the gale on Wednesday has done a great deal of damage on the east coast, and that a great many lives have also been lost.

1880 May
3rd

---

[22] braird, first shoots of growing grain.
[23] fast day, Thursday or Friday before Communion Sunday. Special church services were held on fast days.

The stormy weather which I reported last week, took a change for the better on Thursday last, the weather since then being fresh and warm, Saturday the first day of May being exceptionally fine. Grass is now looking well and with a few more warm days there would be a good bite for the cattle.

There are some reports of the 'tory' being at work, but a continuance of this weather would soon put the braird beyond its reach.[24]

On Tuesday I was cross ploughing. In the evening I went up to Ardiecow to assist them to cast the 'shelti' as the farrier was going to burn and blister one of its legs.[25]

Wednesday was a misty rainy day. I was at the plough in the forenoon, but as it continued wet I did not yoke again. Father went over to the School House, Ordiquhill to buy a calf, which we saw advertised but it was just sold a few hours before he got there.

He went to Portsoy on Thursday for two loads of manure, when we also got a calf. As we were coming out of the town William Seivwright the shoemaker came up with us, and told us that his brother George had been killed the day before. He had gone away to the Mill with a few sacks of corn and it is supposed that the horse having started he had jumped from the cart and had slipped his foot when the wheel of the cart went over his breast. He survived for about an hour, and was perfectly sensible that he would never recover. Truly in the midst of life we are in death.

On Friday and Saturday I was busy at the plough. Today Father was in the roller while I was driving out dung.

10th

The weather during the last eight days has been cold and dry, and during the whole of the week I have been busy making at the turnip land. I went over on Thursday morning to Limestones for their brown mare to give us a pull with the grubber and I had her home again on Saturday. The roup at Clashendamer was on that day. Father was over at it and bought a few small things but it was a rather stiff sale.

17th

The weather still continues dry and work is getting on apace. We commenced to drill on Tuesday afternoon and on Wednesday I was in the drill plough all day. I went over that evening to the Newton to see Johnny Geddes.

---

[24] tory, the leatherjacket grub that attacks the roots of crops.
[25] shelti, Shetland pony.

On Thursday Kirktown and a few others commenced to dung and in the evening I saw them sowing. Today I harrowed down the drills which got dung in the end of the year, sowed the manure, and in the afternoon covered them in. Sowing them in the evening.

24th

During the past week I have been very busy as Father has been unable to work with a sore back.

On Tuesday I was putting out dung all day. In the evening I went up to Ardiecow and had a shot with Don McIntosh's rifle.

On Wednesday I got them 'happin in' and after getting my supper started to sow them, it being nine o'clock before I got through.

On Thursday morning I harrowed down the potatoe drills, and the rest of the day I was in the drill plough. I unyoked however, at five o'clock, as I had to go to Cornhill Station to meet Maggie who was coming from Edinburgh. She arrived all right but very tried. I would easily have known Jemmie but Mary I never would have known.

Friday was Cullen market but there were very few went past this for it. Father went down a few hours with Uncle of Limestones, but feeing was very stiff.

On Saturday morning I made drills until half past ten. I then unyoked and went over to the roup at Auchip. Father, Mother and Maggie being also over. There was a great turn out of people and the sale was brisk. Father bought a lot of pailing posts and I bought a grindstone and a bag of staples.

I was at Church yesterday and was a little surprised to hear Alex Ross and Mary Duncan proclaimed for the third and last time. The marriage is to be on Thursday I hear.

Today I have been among the dung while Father went over for the things bought at the sale.

31st

The weather during the month of May has been very cold and dry. Consequently vegetation has not made great progress and pasture in many places is getting exceedingly bare. It has however been very suitable for cleaning the turnip land and work is a great deal further advanced than at this date last year. I see that our earliest sown turnips are all through the ground and as yet are looking pretty healthy. The weather however, is not very favourable for their growth, it being always too cold and windy. During the first three days of last week we had extraordinary gales of wind with severe drought. We were at Portsoy on Tuesday for manure, and the clouds of dust on the roads were something fearful.

On Wednesday we sowed some yellow turnips, but it was not a good job getting the manure sowed, the wind being so high.

On Friday we got a few more sowed for which we had not dung. The day was quiet and cloudy, and I think there had been thunder on the air. About half past five o'clock there came a tremendous shower of rain and hail. Although it was rather cold we were very thankful for it, and as we have had a few more showers since they will do an immense good.

I was in the drill plough on Saturday

On Sunday morning Geordy Cowie and Annie came over in the machine. Mary Watson, Limestones, also came over and we all went to church together. About seven o'clock they started for home Maggie and the bairns accompanying them. Father went over to Finnygaud with the cart today to bring them home and as I write I see them coming down the brae of Ardiecow. I was putting out dung all day.

1880 June
7th

The month of June opened rather favourably. The first three days being dry and warm. It did not continue long however, for since Thursday it has been rough and stormy, with cold showers from the N.W. The moisture however has done good as the land was getting exceedingly dry.

On Tuesday last I was covering in dung all day until four o'clock, after which I was sowing the turnips.

Father and I were both putting out dung on Wednesday forenoon. I covered it in, in the afternoon Father then sowing the turnips while I went to the Smithy.

On Thursday we got all the turnips sowed except the end-rigs.

On Friday I was driving some stones off the lea.

I ploughed the end-rigs on Saturday forenoon. In the afternoon I went up to Ardiecow to see them sheep shearing. They are very active with the scissors, Miss MacIntosh (who was taking an active part) sometimes succeeding in sending out one in less than ten minutes. As looking on however, would hardly do, I got hold of a scissors and commenced work, and by half past eight o'clock I had managed to clip about a score, 120 having been shorn altogether.

Today I drilled covered in and sowed the whole of the end-rigs.

14th

The first of last week was cold, but on Thursday the wind shifted round to the South and since then the weather has been warmer. Turnips which during the cold weather were almost at a stand still, have again started to grow, whilst sowing is all but completed. Potatoes, which have made great progress during the last few days, are looking healthy and seem to be coming up very equal. Although we have as yet plenty of pasture, it is in general very bare, whilst the hay crop is to be very light.

On Tuesday last Uncle of Limestones with Mrs. Barrie (who is paying them a visit just now) Mary, and Mr. William Barrie came over to visit us. They intended to drive down the length of Cullen to give Mr. Barrie a sight of the place, but it being the brown mare they had in the machine and as she is rather slow in action, we exchanged her for 'Rosie', whilst Uncle stayed with Father and I got on for driver. We drove past Kilnhillock where Mary bought two pigs, and then on to Mr. Michie's where we unyoked. We then took a stroll through the policies of Cullen House visiting the nursery, the pond and the flower garden. We afterwards went down to Cullen, taking a look at the harbour and gathering some dulse visited the Coffee Room (which is indeed a rather tidy little place) and got back to Mr. Michie's where a nice tea was awaiting us.[26] It was now time to start for home which we reached about half past nine, having spent a very delightful afternoon.

On Wednesday I was ploughing and harrowing a piece, which we are going to fallow on 'the hill'.

Thursday was Cornhill market and Father went over and bought a calf. In the evening I went over to Limestones, it being late or rather early before I got home.

On Saturday afternoon James Gray and William who arrived from America on Thursday, came up to tea along with Mrs. and Miss Hendry, Cairnton. William Gray is a good deal altered since he left, and is altogether a perfect Yankee.

Joan and I were in the moss today spreading the peats.

21st

The weather during the past week has been warm and dry and everyone is anxiously looking for a shower. Indeed if rain does not come and that very soon crops of every kind will be spoiled. Cereals as yet are looking well but will soon suffer from lack of moisture. In early districts barley is coming into ear. Turnips are coming on but slowly, and hoeing has not commenced in this district yet. The only cases of second sowing I have heard of has been Ardiecow and Clune.

Tuesday—We were driving stones off the hill in the forenoon. In the afternoon I was washing the carts. Mary Cowie and Uncle and Aunt of Finnygaud were over that day.

[26] dulse, edible seaweed.

On Wednesday morning Father went over to the Smiddy to get the shaft of one of the carts mended which I had broke the night before while washing them, letting one of the wheels fall on it, and squeezing my own toes at the same time. In the evening I went down an errand to the wrights. He was not in, so I went down to the Clune to see Miss Kitchen. He is going to get up new offices this summer. Joan, Annie and I went to the moss on Thursday to set the peats. The day was exceedingly warm, we had a long day's work and consequently before we got finished everyone using rather freely, the expression 'Oh my back'.

On Friday we were drawing straw all day. In the afternoon Uncle and Aunt of Limestones, Mrs. Barry and Mary came over to see us.

I was cleaning the harness on Saturday.

Today we commenced to thatch the back of the mill. The day was quick and hazy, with a slight dew falling at times.

28th

Nice warm weather still continues; and after a season of rather protracted drought, we have at last been favoured with a few genial showers, the most of it having fallen this afternoon. Hoeing has been general during the week, although we only commenced today.

On Tuesday last we finished our thatching, not in the least sorry to get through with such a dirty job.

I was at the Smiddy on Wednesday getting one of the mares shoed.

On Thursday afternoon we went up to the moss for two loads of peats, and found them wonderfully dry. In the evening I went up to Ardiecow to get my hair cropped. We got home other two loads of peats on Friday; in the afternoon I was cleaning at the harness.

We were rather early astir on Saturday morning as Maggie was that day going to return to Edinburgh. It was a nice morning and we were in plenty of time for the train. We had both the carts, as we were going to take out two loads of coal for the blacksmith.

When we came out of church on Sunday Joan and I went up to the Backies with Maggie Reid. Willie McWillie and Annie came also past with us, but it being a showery afternoon we could hardly get out to look about us.

This forenoon I was in the scuffle harrow, while Joan and Father commenced to hoe.

1880 July
5th

No more cry for rain, no lack of moisture now. Rain has fallen every day during the week, more or less, and on some days we had tremendous downpours, so I think we should now have sufficient moisture to last at least a month.

Tuesday was showery but we were hoeing all day.

On Wednesday there was a close mist and a drizzling rain, and we hoed the most of the day. I was going down to see the Fordyce Pic-nic, which was held that afternoon, but it being rather wet I did not go.

We only had a few hours on Thursday the most of the day being wet. In the evening I went over to a meeting, held in the Public School, to arrange for the Deskford Pic-nic. There was a large turn out, the Pic-nic being fixed to be held on 21st current.

On Friday we hoed until three o'clock, when there came a few peals of thunder, and thereafter some tremendous showers of rain.

We just hoed an hour on Saturday morning, the rest of the day being very wet with a close fog.

The weather during the past week has been characterised by tremendous falls of rain. Although we have been thinking, we were getting our own share of it, still it has done little damage here besides in many places. In Aberdeenshire and the South of Banffshire, on Wednesday it had been extraordinary, a great many bridges having been taken away by the flood, and turnip fields completely destroyed.

12th

We have got very little hoed during the week, the land being always too wet.

On Wednesday afternoon I went down to Fordyce to see the Pic-nic and Poultry Show. The Show was good and the evening being fine we had a nice dance, with a good supply of young ladies.

On Thursday evening I went over to Cornhill Station to meet Lizzie and her family who are paying us a visit just now. She has four, the youngest being only six months.

On Saturday I started for Finnygaud going past Hillfolds to see Sandy Ross and Mary Duncan, or as I should say Mr. & Mrs. Ross. There is a nice dwelling house, and most of the land looks to be good. I arrived at Finnygaud at half past ten, when they were nearly all to bed.

Sunday was rather wet all day, so that I could hardly get out to see the crops. The roads were now very wet, and it was ten o'clock before I got home.

This forenoon has also been wet, but we were at the hoe in the afternoon. In the evening I went up to Ardiecow with a stewardess ticket for Miss MacKintosh for the Deskford Pic-nic.

19th

The past eight days has been warm and showery and crops of every kind have advanced rapidly. Turnips are looking well, but the land has been always rather wet to get them rightly cleaned. We have been very busy hoeing all the week, as they were getting very rank, we finished singling on Friday.

On Tuesday night James Stevenson came in past just newly arrived from America. James is no more settled than ever he was, and I would not wonder though he be off again before long.

On Wednesday evening I went over to Oakhillock with Miss McKay's presentation ticket for the Pic-nic. She has been very unwell for sometime back with the Dr. attending her and as yet is only mending slowly.

On Saturday Father, Mother and Lizzie with the bairns went all over to Finnygaud. I was in the scuffle harrow all day.

On Sunday afternoon Uncle of Limestones came over with Uncle George of Aberdeen, Saturday being the tradesmen's holiday. He stopped all night and went over to catch the last train on Monday evening. Father and Lizzie went over with him to Limestones, while I running the swedes

I was over this evening at Kirkton getting the orchard in order for the Pic-nic. The weather is now more settled like, and everyone is expecting to get a nice day for our Annual gathering.

26th

During the past week the weather has been very changeable. Monday and Tuesday were cold and showery, the next three days were dry and warm with bright sunshine, while on Saturday we experienced a terrific thunder storm, accompanied by a perfect flood of rain. Yesterday and today have also been showery, but tonight it looks more settled again.

Tuesday morning being rather wet for the hoe, we went to Craibstone for two loads of lime for the purpose of mixing some earth for top-dressing. The afternoon was dry and we cut some of the hay.

On Wednesday morning I looked out rather eagerly to see if we were likely to get a good day for our Pic-nic when I was delighted to behold a clear sky, with the bright morning sun shedding a flood of light on all around. Going to the Smiddy and getting both the mares shod, was the most of my forenoon's work. I commenced to buckle as soon as I got my dinner as I had to go over to Newton for Miss E. Geddes whom I had presented with a ticket. The afternoon was all that could be desired. In fact it was a little too warm for dancing. By seven o'clock however, the tall trees on the top of the brae began to cast their shadows, over the orchard below, when after that it was nice and cool. Dancing became fast and furious and was kept up with great spirit until a late hour. Games were also heartily entered into by those who were not inclined to dance while Poor Aunt Sally received not a few sturdy whacks, as each in his turn tried to wean her from her smoking propensities.

Next morning I felt my legs very sore, but five hours in the scuffle harrow with the young mare put them all right.

Friday was Peter Fair when Father went over to it with Uncle of Limestones. Joan and I cut the seed hay.

We were second hoeing the swedes on Saturday morning. About one o'clock there came a few peals of thunder with a little rain, but nothing unusual until three. After that however, the thunder became very loud with a great deal of lightning, while the rain continued for two hours to fall in perfect torrents. The burns were soon all in flood and overflowing their banks and a great deal of damage has been done. Our turnips have been greatly spoiled by the burn breaking out and washing away a good strip along the side soil and altogether. I have heard of no damage done by the lightning except a few pailing posts being split at Skeith. We went to the moss this afternoon for two loads of peats but they are a good deal softer than they were.

1880 August
2nd

Showery weather still continues and turnips on wet land are being spoiled. Where the land is dry they are still holding out wonderful, but finger and toe is making its appearance.[27] There has been scarcely anything done at the hoe during the week.

We were binding up the seed hay on Tuesday. The spate on Saturday had spoiled a little of it as the burn was a good bit out over the haugh, some of the sheaves being washed down through the barley.

I went over to Kirktown in the evening to attend a meeting for the purpose of setting up the affairs of the Pic-nic. If we had not had a little money on hand we would have been some short of cash, there being a good deal more expenses than ordinary. At the close of the meeting a vote of thanks was proposed for the clerk Mr. Milne, and another for the chairman Mr. Duncan, followed by three hearty cheers for the Deskford Annual Pic-nic.

On Wednesday we went to the moss when Father and Joan stayed and wheeled out some of the driest of them.

---

[27] finger and toe, disease of turnips in which the tap root branches. The tap root is the strong main root stretching down vertically from the plant.

On Thursday, Friday and Saturday we managed to get home two loads each day, but the roads were getting very bad owing to the wet.

Today has been a good deal drier. I was scuffling the turnips in the forenoon, while in the afternoon we were turning the coles of hay.

9th

We have had a week of nice dry weather, and barley is beginning to change colour. Finger and toe however is doing sad havoc among the turnips especially the yellow ones and if dry weather with sunshine continue many a field will be spoiled.

On Tuesday I was busy running and furring up the swedes, while the others were at the hoe. In the evening I went over to Newton, when I had the pleasure of being introduced to a young lady—a Miss Morrison who is there on a visit. We were entertained by her and Miss E. Geddes, with some excellent music on the piano, accompanied by George Milton on the violin. We afterwards had a few reels and schottishes.

On both Wednesday and Thursday I was running and furring up amongst the turnips.

On Thursday morning Lizzie left this for Keith on her way home. Father and Mother went with her, and she is to leave for Cleland on Saturday morning.

On Friday we went to the moss where Joan, Annie and I stayed and took out all the dry peats setting up the wet ones. Mary Wilson and William Murray late of Ardiecow were in when we came home. He is a clerk at the Banff Brewery. After tea, and when I had got the peats built, Joan and I accompanyed them up the brae. We went in past Ardiecow when I was not a little surprised to find Miss Geddes and Miss Murray there, as also Mr. Simpson, Hillend. They had been amusing themselves before we went in, by playing on the piano, so we were now invited to take a dance. We had some nice schottishes. Don and Willie gave us some songs, and altogether we spent a very pleasant evening.

On Saturday and today we were busy driving peats.

16th

We have had a week of extraordinary warm weather with strong sunshine and everything is hastening on to maturity. The progress of the crops ripening, is each day perceptible and if this weather continue harvest will be here in no time.

1880 November
1st

This is a sad leap to take in the writing of my 'Journal' and very sorry I am that I was obliged to give it up so long, but the cause of my doing so will be soon explained. About the middle of August there appeared in The Banffshire Journal an intimation that prizes were to be given for the best solution of 'Doublets', three of which were to be given in each weeks Journal for twelve weeks. The said 'Doublets' consisted of two given words, which had to be joined together by other words called links, each link to be joined from the proceeding word by changing one letter only. Thus

More into Less

Lore)
Lose)   3
Loss)
Less

Those doing it with the least number of links being counted best. Well I commenced to try them, but found that they took up so much of my time that I had no time for writing my Journal, nor anything else. I dispatched the last of them today however, having succeeded in solving them all except four. Although I have no expectation of getting a prize, still I do not think I have lost my time, for I have perused more of the dictionary since I commenced, than ever I did all my life before.

Having taken up my pen once more however, I will endeavour to give a brief sketch of the principal affairs which have occurred since last I wrote.

The month of August was very dry and warm, with bright sunshine, being very favourable for the ripening of the grain crop. The turnips however, suffered rather severely from the drought, and before the rain came many of them had succumbed to the ever increasing disease of finger and toe.

There was a sale of wood in the Cotton Hill and Green Hill plantations on 14th August, and the week following we were busy driving brushwood.

Next week we were driving blinding for the Ardiecow road, which had been spoiled by the spate of 31st July.[28] We also grubbed, limed and furred up the fallow land on the Hill.

We commenced harvest on 27th August by cutting the lea corn in the 'Den'. The weather was then extremely warm, and working the sythe was no easy matter.

On Tuesday the 31st we were greatly surprised to hear, that Aunt of Limestones, had died the same morning at 1 o'clock. She had been very frail for sometime; and for a few days before had been seen to be

---

[28] blinding, gravel to put a smooth surface on a road.

sinking. She was buried in Fordyce churchyard on 3rd September when both Father and I were at the burial.

From the 1st to the 11th Sept we had Gordon Cameron assisting us with the harvest work, and as the weather was fine by that time we had got a good deal of it in the stack. On the 4th we got down to Ardiecow's reaper, when we cut the barley and a good bit corn. Next week I went up two days and gave them a 'yokin' with our horses in the machine. He had a splendid crop and having but the two horses they were unable to go all day. About the 16th the weather turned rather soft and it was the 22nd before we got it all in.

On the 27th Uncle George, Father and I went over to take a look at the farm of Cleanhill, which was then advertised for let. It is a very nice compact place. The land seems to be mostly good; the fields are finely laid off and everything about the houses in splendid trim. There had however been a great many people looking after it and although Father afterwards offered 25/-. the acre for it he was not successful. Mr. Munro, Keith, has become the tenant of it at £120 rental.

On 1st October we were up at Ardiecow assisting them with the steam mill. The day was rather rough and rain came on before we got it all through. We were made stay to supper however, after which Cultain and I stayed and had a dance. Next day we were over at Muttonbrae giving Uncle George a hand to thrash.

Next week the weather was very changeable and a good deal of rain fell. I was ploughing stubble when it was dry. On the following Monday I went over to Newton to see the Miss—I mean Johnny Geddes. We were busy that week lifting our potatoes, the weather being fine and dry. They were also an excellent crop, a few however, being diseased. I was down at Carestown on Thursday assisting them with the steam mill. His barley turned out very well and was well coloured.

On the 17th Oct. the weather turned stormy and during the following week we had a few inches of snow, the ploughing being thereby at a stand still. Next week however, the weather was fresh again and the plough was kept busily going.

On 4th and 5th Nov. I was at Ordens at the steam mill. The weather was rather rough and on the last day we had to give it up leaving a stack unthrashed. His barley was a fair out-turn, and weighed 56lbs per bushel.

The following week we ploughed all the stubbles for clearing and commenced to plough the 'Den'.

22nd

We are now experiencing our second snow storm of the season and (for this season of the year) it is proving a rather severe one. It commenced on Tuesday last with sleety showers from the N.E.

Wednesday was also showery but on Thursday morning there was a considerable fall. We have had occasional showers since and there is now about six inches all over.

The frost during some nights has also been intense. We have done little during the week but thrashed and pulled some turnips.

Today I was busy cleaning the horse harness.

On Thursday night I went over to the School Board Office Kirktown where I was met by Willie McWillie and Alex Milne for the purpose of arranging and classifying the Books in the Library. We wrought until ten o'clock but seeing that we were not likely to finish them we agreed to meet again on Wednesday first.

On Friday night Miss McIntosh, Ardiecow, came down to ask about Mother's back. She has been greatly troubled by her back for the past six weeks, being some days confined to her bed. It is now keeping better however, although this stormy weather is not the best for rheumatism.

29*th*

The snow has again disappeared and we are enjoying fine dry breezy days. The thaw set in on Wednesday morning and there being a good breeze of wind, the snow had soon to fly before it. I went over to the Library on Wednesday night to finish the classifying of the books. I was met by Willie McWillie, and besides putting them all in order, we managed to get all the new ones covered.

I was ploughing lea on Thursday all day and also on Friday forenoon. In the afternoon we were driving turnips. About two o'clock there arose a very strong gale of wind, which was like to do damage among the houses. We managed however, to keep everything down, although it was eight o'clock before it fell very much.

On Saturday I was over at Kirkton at the steam mill. The day was still rather blowy making it rather disagreeable to work, but on the whole we managed pretty well.

We had a good day's work it being pretty dark before we got through.

Father, Willie and I were at church on Sunday, and in the afternoon I went over to Limestones.

Today I was at the Manse assisting with the steam mill, and there being still a good breeze of wind you may be sure no one was singing in praise of 'the bearded barley'.

1880 December
6th

During the week we have enjoyed fine fresh weather, and everyone has been busy at the plough. Stubbles are now all ploughed, and on Tuesday and Wednesday I was ploughing lea.

On Thursday afternoon we were storing Swedes. We put them into a pit on the land as we had nothing to cover them at home.

On Friday we took in two loads of corn and thrashed them as we were expecting the steam mill in a few days. In the afternoon we winnowed up the corn. There is a very good out-turn of grain this year, nearly the double there was last year.

Next morning we had the corn over to Berryhillock Mills when it weighed 42 lbs per bushel. I was in the plough in the afternoon.

Joan, Willie and I were at Church on Sunday. The day was fine and there was a full church.

This forenoon I was in the plough while in the afternoon I was driving turnips. Father was at Hoggie at the steam mill. She is across and set up at Oathillock where they are to thrash tomorrow, while we are expecting to have her on Wednesday.

13th

We have had another week of fresh weather but it has been extremely blowy, indeed on several days the wind rose to a perfect hurricane and was like to drive everything before it.

On Tuesday Father and I were at Oathillock at the steam mill. Having started in the morning as soon as it was daylight, by twelve o'clock they had got it all thrashed and by half past one they were over and ready to commence with us. By three o'clock we had got the barley thrashed. The wind however, had been rising and by that time it was too rough for getting the straw properly managed. We therefore halted for about an hour, but the wind falling again we managed to get through one of the stacks of oats before it got dark.

Next morning it was still very rough but we started and by ten o'clock had it all thrashed, when the machine shifted down to Walter Gray's. Joan and I went down to assist them and we thrashed until three o'clock although it was very disagreeable. The wind however was now blowing nearly all the straw away, and so we gave it up for a bad job.

On Thursday morning as the wind was still very high; and not likely to be a thrashing day, we winnowed and filled up 7 quarters of Barley, which we had down to Glenglassaugh. We had not gone far when it commenced to rain, which it continued to do until we got home again. The barley however weighed very well, being 55½ lbs per bushel.

Friday was also a very windy day. Father had the remainder of the barley down to the Distillery, while I was pulling turnips. The Library had to be opened that night but John and I had been invited over to the Manse to our tea. Miss Annie McWillie and Willie, and Miss Barron were also there. After tea we had a game at Bagatelle until seven o'clock when we had to leave for the Library. After business was over we again returned with Mr. Ashley when Miss McWillie was also there.

On Saturday morning we rose at five o'clock and winnowed 8 quarters of corn and after getting the cattle sorted we yoked and set off with it to Portsoy. As they were loading a ship with grain we had also to carry it on board. It weighed 43½ pounds per bushel.

This forenoon I was in the plough but in the afternoon we went over to Berryhillock with some corn.

20*th*

Very stormy weather has prevailed during the week and out-door work is completely at a standstill.

On Tuesday there was an intense frost, with a slight coating of snow. I took home a few loads of turnips which had been pulled before. Mary Wilson, Limestones, came over in the afternoon. Snow fell on Wednesday all day and before night there was at least four inches. In the forenoon we took in three loads of barley straw, and in the afternoon I clipped the young mare.

On Thursday there was an additional fall of snow. We pulled and took home a few loads of turnips, but they were rather frozen.

On Saturday morning we received a letter from Edinburgh saying there was a basket at Portsoy station for us. As Joan had some errands to Portsoy, I yoked and about twelve o'clock we set off. There was however a stormy gale of wind blowing, and before we got past Cultain it was drifting so badly that we began to speak of turning back for fear the roads would be blocked up before we returned. We pushed on however until we reached Little Cultain where we had to leave the road for a little as it was too deep to get through, and on again returning to it we found it so deep that the mare almost stuck fast. The wind having risen a good deal it was now blowing almost blind drift, so we thought our best plan would be to return home, which we did.

On Sunday it was quiet but frosty.

Today Joan and I again set out for Portsoy and although we were not troubled with blowing, we met with a difficulty nearly as bad if not worse. Before we got the length of Fordyce the roads turned so slippery that it was with great difficulty I managed to keep the mare on her feet. We succeeded however in reaching the Smiddy at The Blacking where we at once unyoked and got the mare frosted. After that we managed nicely and got home about three o'clock. The basket you may be sure did not remain long un-opened, when everyone was highly delighted with their Xmas presents.

27th

We have received since last week a great addition to the fall of snow, and were it not that the hollows are drifted full I am certain these would be a depth all over of fifteen inches. Both road and rail are completely blocked and traffic since Friday has been totally suspended.

On Tuesday we took in two loads of oat straw for the horses and made it. I went over and spent a fore-night at Kirkton on Wednesday evening when we had a nice game of whist. Aleck and I were speaking of going into Aberdeen at the New Year, but I rather fear that the weather will now frighten us.

On Thursday sleet and rain fell the most of the day, and although toward night the snow sank a little I never thought it was to be a right thaw, there being always a white mist about the hills.

On Friday the wind changed from east to north and we had occasional showers of sleet and snow. The turnips however being bare and being quite fresh we took advantage of them and secured six loads. About four o'clock snow began to fall very thickly and there being at the same time a good breeze of wind it also commenced to blow. As night set in the wind increased and the snow thickened and at seven o'clock when I went out to supper the horses, it was a fearful night indeed. Thus had it continued to fall and drift throughout the night and next day until twelve o'clock when it cleared, but the wind still keeping strong, drifting continued until Sunday morning.

I went to church with Cultain, but there was a very thin attendance.

Today has been quiet but very frosty. In the forenoon we commenced to cast the snow in the road below the corn yard so as to get home some turnips. In the afternoon we took home six loads of Swedes.

29th

I went over to Kirkton on Wednesday to see what Aleck Duncan was always thinking about going to Aberdeen when I found that he had made up his mind to start on Friday providing no more snow fell. He was to have gone with the bus to Portsoy Station but we afterwards arranged both to go to Cornhill.

Thursday was a little soft, but went to the frost again at night. We took in four loads of straw and some turnips. I went over in the evening to the shoemakers for my boots which were being soled and went in past Muttonbrae.

31ˢᵗ

On Friday the 31ˢᵗ I rose and found it very frosty but looking rather black towards the North. On coming out after breakfast I found it beginning to snow with a stiff breeze blowing from the N.W. and in less than half an hour it was blowing blind drift. So bad was it that we could scarcely get the doors kept opened, and so; thinking of blocked railways and snowed up trains, soon all thoughts of going to Aberdeen were dismissed and I sat down to read Sir Walter Scott's 'Pirate', thinking how lucky it was I had not started and planning how I would yet go were it fair on the morrow. But as Robbie Burns says 'the best laid plans o'mice and men gang aft aglye' so mine were doomed to miscarry.

Looking out at the window about half past ten I was greatly surprised to see Aleck Duncan coming riding up the road along with George Duncan on another horse. Thinking however, that it was no use for me to make ready, as I would now be too late for the train, I waited until they came up. On going out I was greeted not too pleasantly with the words, 'Confound you, why are you not ready'. 'Ready', says I, 'Why you do not intend going to Aberdeen today'. 'Certainly come on' says he. 'But think if the train stick' says I. 'Come on' say he 'and make haste too, or we shall be late'. 'Well, well' says I 'if you go I'll no stick' and off I set to make ready. But little time did I get to dress. 'You need not be particular washing' he would say 'you can wash when you get to Aberdeen'. 'Never mind your hair, on with your hat and let us be off'. And in less than ten minutes I had on my hat and everything else, when we jumped on our horses and galloped off. On reaching Ardiecow however, the snow was so deep that the horses were unable to get through, so we were obliged to dismount and take to shanks mare. It was still blowing but the wind being in our backs we got on pretty well and being still afraid of missing the train we made all haste down the hill. On getting to the county road, by good luck we met Willie Morrison, coming up with a sledge, when we at once made him turn, and give us a help on the road. This he readily did, driving us as far as Brodiesord School, when we afterwards managed to be in time. On reaching Grange Station we found we had 30 minutes to wait, and as most of the people felt an inclination to slip down the way of the Inn, of course we also followed. A good many people here seemed to be bound for the Granite City, and the train was a considerable length. About Gartly the snow seemed to be getting deeper, not a black speck being visible all around. The rails however, were quite clear (although we saw some very deep cuttings) and we nearly kept up to time.

With such a dreary aspect however, as Old Mother Earth presents, when wrapt in her snowy mantle, we felt very little inclination to look from the carriage windows, but kept huddled close together; so as to keep as much warmth as possible.

Arrived in Aberdeen at four o'clock, we found George Duncan awaiting Aleck, while Uncle and Mira were looking for me. Before separating I arranged with George that I would call and see him at View Terrace on Sunday afternoon. We then made way for Craigie Street, where I was heartily welcomed and where I found them all well. My cousins being all at work, it was sometime before they all got home for supper. About nine o'clock we went out, going down to the Station to met an acquaintance of Jemmie's. We afterwards took a stroll about Market Street and Union Street (which were by this time a perfect steer) landing in the Castlegate about half past eleven. The Castlegate is a large square at the east-end of Union Street, on one side of which are situated The Town and County Buildings.

This is a splendid block of houses and like the rest of Union Street is built of granite. At one end of it there is a spire of great height with a clock illuminated from the inside. In the centre of the square there is a statue of The Duke of Gordon, and round about it there were now collected a great many sweetie stands with shooting stands, cheap Jacks and other vendors, who were haranguing the crowd on the extra quality and cheapness of their wares.

Here we stirred about (falling in with George Duncan and Aleck) until it was well on to twelve o'clock.

All faces were now eagerly turned towards the clock for the old year had but a few more minutes to live; and silence nearly prevailed.

The striking gear of the clock however, was either out of repair; or the officials had purposely stopped it for when the minute hand fairly pointed to twelve, silence still continued and no sound came to give the death knell to the dying year. Few more seconds however had time to pass, when a tremendous shout burst from a thousand throats, while hands clasped hands and friends wished friends a happy, bright New Year.

So ended with me the Year 1880
and so commenced 1881

And so I will again conclude my Journal writing for a Year.

At the close of last year I expressed a hope that 1880 might be brighter and more prosperous that its predecessor, and many reasons have we to be thankful that it has been so. A plentiful harvest has been reaped, both by sea and land and although things are not yet altogether what we might wish them to be, still they are on the turn, and as we commence a new year, we will again express the hope that things may go on to prosper. So that when it shall have run its course, we may have found the wishes of our friends prove true, when they wished for us.

A Happy New Year

A Journal of My Life and Every Day Doings

1881 January
1ˢᵗ

New Year morn in Aberdeen found every one rather dull and sleepy. I got up about half past eight o'clock and having got breakfast, Aleck and I went out to have a look about. We went down George Street, crossed Union Street and then down Market Street to the shore. We then went right across to have a look at the new bridge across the Dee.

It is a nice bridge of seven arches, but as the arches are very wide I think it would have looked better had it been higher.

We next took a stroll about the docks, but being a holiday everything was rather quiet. We saw the training ship 'The Clyde' a tremendous hulk, lying in the old course of the Dee. There were also in the harbour some very large steamers.

After dinner I went up to Gerrard Street to see Mrs. George Adam, and from there I was to go to Hutcheson Street to see old Mr. & Mrs. Adam. Maggie Biddie however, said that as they were also going there to spend the evening, I should wait and go with them. To this I agreed, but as they were not going until five o'clock, George would have me away out to see some of the town.

He took me across George Street and away West by Beechgrove Terrace, where there are very nice cottages, and which is I think by far the prettiest side of the town. We then turned to our left for Queens Cross, and again held West. There are here some splendid mansions, being the residence of most of the aristocracy in town, and the finest houses I saw in Aberdeen. By this time it was half past four, so we turned our take, took the tramway along Union Street and up George Street and arrived at Hutcheson Street at a little past five. Here I was a little surprised to find Swailend, never thinking that he was in Aberdeen. Walter Reid, John and Joseph Reid and Mr. Scott were also there but we were rather deficient for young ladies. Miss Adam being the only one present. We however spent a very pleasant evening and at half past ten I was very sorry I had to leave.

2ⁿᵈ

On Sunday forenoon I went to East Church, along with Jemmie, George and Aleck. They have not got a minister there just now, and it was the assistant that preached. After dinner I went up to 11 View Terrace to see George Duncan. As he and Aleck were intending going to the Catholic Chapel in the evening, I said I would also accompany them. To spend the afternoon we went out to have a look at the Victoria Park, which is close beside View Terrace. It is a good size of a place and although covered with snow at the time I thought it very pretty while in the summer I am sure it would be beautiful. In the centre of the Park there is a large fountain in course of construction, and a little to the West of that, a rockery is also being formed. At five o'clock we returned to tea, and then started for the Chapel. The entrance is from Huntly Street a little off Union Street. From the outside it looks a splendid building, but the inside is perfectly magnificent. At the far end is the altar lighted up with its thirty or forty different sized candles, while right above it is a circular stain glass window which but a few years ago cost no less than £1000. The walls also round about, with all the pillars supporting the arches, are all decorated and adorned with paintings and sculptor of such a style and in such a manner as the Church of Rome knows only too well how to execute. We got however, a fairly good address from the Revd. Mr. Stropani, while the music was first class, but for the rest of the service I could neither make head or tail of it.

3rd

On Monday morning I met Aleck Duncan and George at the Queens Statue, but as George had to be at work, the Bank being open, Aleck and I were therefore to have a day to ourselves.

We first went and had a look through the New Market, but being rather early the stalls were not all open. We next took a stroll round about the docks and a very busy scene they presented. Some of the steamers were unloading lime, some flour and others timber, while two or three were taking in cargoes of granite. We observed a rather novel looking engine, used for unloading lime, and standing on a platform nearly 20 ft high. We also saw another engine of curious construction employed in filling up the old channel of the Dee.

There being a show of dogs and cats in the gymnasium Queen Street, we now turned ourselves in that direction. There were not very many cats and we paid but little attention to them. The dogs however, were a good show, and some of them I greatly admired, especially those breeds: specimens of which I had never before seen, and among which were the Newfoundland, the St Bernard, the Blood Hound and Stag Hound.

After spending an hour among our Canine friends, we took our leave of them and as we were now going out to Sunnyside to see a young entire colt which Mr. McRobie had lately bought from Kirktown, we took the tramway up George Street to Kittybrewster Station. Sunnyside lies right between the station and the old town and we easily found it. We were also lucky in getting a sight of the horse, as the groom was airing him in a park, close by the roadside.

From this we held on to the Auldton intending to go as far as the brig of Balgownie. As neither of us knew the way however, we had frequently to inquire and as we always asked for the bridge of Don we at last found ourselves on the New instead of the Old Bridge.

We were not disappointed however, for the New Bridge is well worth seeing. It is composed of five large arches of great height and of the Roman style of Architecture, but looks to best advantage when seen from the old Bridge, which is about 300 yards farther up the river, and which we reached by a narrow footpath winding along by the Southern bank of the water. The Old Brig is a rather romantic sort of place, and has long been famed for its scenery. Its single arch is of the Gothic style and altogether the bridge bears the mark of being of no modern construction. A little above the bridge the river takes a quick turn, while behind it a steep brae rises, thickly covered with trees, which I am sure in the Summertime would be a pretty scene indeed. As everything just then however appearing in its winter garb looked rather dreary and being rather cold withal, we were not long in again turning our steps towards the town.

As we had to pass Old Machar Cathedral on our way back we determined to have a look at it and finding the sexton in the churchyard he very kindly showed us through it. It is a very ancient building with double walls and two massive towers in one of which there is a clock. The inside however, has been recently reseated and otherwise improved while there are also a great many stain glass windows. One of these attracted me particularly, being as I thought very beautiful. It was a representation of Faith, Hope and Charity. At one side Faith held the cup, at the other Hope stood with the anchor, while Charity in the centre held a child in her arms with others clinging to the skirts of her garments.

We now held away up through the old Town taking a look at King's College as we passed. It is a splendid block of buildings, but being the Xmas holidays it was closed so that we could not get a sight of the inside.

On getting back to Union Street we went into a coffee house and had a cup of coffee and something to eat. As I had often before been talking of buying a gun when I should come to Aberdeen, we now set off to see and make a purchase.

As we walked along Union Street, we kept a look out for gunmakers' shops and at last fixed on James Garden's close by the Union Bridge, where we would try to buy. He had a large stock of guns of every sort and after a little bargaining I at last purchased a single barrelled one for £2. I also bought a powder flask, and powder, with some shot and caps.

By this time it was nearly four o'clock and as George Duncan was free after that hour, Aleck went away to meet him, while I made for Craigie Street.

After tea Mina and I went and called on Maggie Murray (late of Ardiecow) who is in a place in Union Terrace. She likes the town very well, and she is greatly improved since she left Ardiecow.

From Union Terrace we were to go direct to see the Prince of Wales' Indian presents, which were then on exhibition in the Town and County Buildings. As Uncle was also going we met him at the Queen's Statue at the end of St Nicholas Street. I need never attempt however, to describe the numerous magnificent; rare and precious articles which we there beheld, the very sight of which was enough to dazzle one's eyes.

I will mention a few which particularly took my attention. There was a great variety of armour of every description. There were swords of all shapes, and spears of all sorts and sizes. There were daggers with rock crystal, and ivory handles, set with diamonds and rubies. There was a great number of guns of every description, many of them with the old flint lock, and all mounted with silver and gold. One was of solid gold while the stock was studded with emeralds and diamonds. There were battle guns and shields without number, besides a great many other weapons I had never before heard of.

I greatly admired two complete coats of mail. One was of the link, and the other of the scale pattern. The riding saddles were a great show. They were all covered with coloured velvet, and mounted with silver and gold, while the trappings for the horses were something gorgeous. There was also a Houdah or elephant's saddle, a Sedan Chair, and a Throne with footstool mounted with silver. Some models of temples, made of ivory, pith, and teak wood were very pretty. There was also a beautiful crown of great value, which of itself would have been a fortune, while the diamonds, pearls, emeralds, rubies and other precious stones with which it was set were dazzling to behold. There are a few, but only a very few of the many costly presents, with which H.R.H. The Prince of Wales was presented, while on his visit to India a few years ago.

We spent about two hours among them, and it was past nine o'clock before we got back to Craigie Street.

4th

Next morning I got up between eight and nine o'clock and by the time I had got dressed and breakfasted it was time to bid my friends goodbye. Uncle and Jemmie went with me to the station where we found George Duncan and Aleck awaiting us. It being within a few minutes of the time we took our seats and bidding them all adieu, the bell rang, the engine whistled, and away we started on our homeward journey soon leaving The Granite City, with all its smoke and din far in the rear. As we proceeded on our way we soon began to see that far more of the snow had disappeared than we expected, good pieces being altogether bare.

Having passed Buxburn and Woodside, where are a good many factories, we came alongside of the Don, and kept within sight of it all the way to Inverurie. The land here about seems to be all very good, but some of it at the waterside is rather level. The country altogether was looking a great deal better than when we came in, and it was very pretty to see the flocks of sheep by the waterside, and to watch how eagerly they nibbled the grass, looking as it did so fresh and green, when just newly relieved of its covering of snow. On looking out to our left after passing Oyne Station we saw the Gaudie, so famous in song as it runs at the foot of Benachie. A little on this side of Inch, but on the other side of the line, we saw another round hill called Dinnydeer on the top of which was what seemed to us some old ruins.

There was still a good deal of snow here, but on coming to Rothiemay we saw a few ploughs at work. On changing carriages at Grange, we went into an apartment in which were two young ladies, whom we afterwards learned had come all the way from Ballindalloch. Being rather talkative, and also very good looking withal, we soon got into conversation and all the way down kept up such a running fire of jokes that when Cornhill was reached we were very sorry to lose their company. The snow here, except where it had been blown into hollows was all gone.

24th

The drifting also has caused a great deal of inconvenience throughout the country. Blocking roads, stopping railways, delaying mails and newspapers and such like. The snowstorm also has not been confined to the North for I see that on Tuesday last London was visited with a tremendous hurricane of wind accompanied with sleet and snow, which fell until the streets were covered to a great depth whilst in some places wreathes were formed two and three feet deep.[29] Great damage has been done to the shipping on the Thames as many as 100 Barges being wrecked. The strong wind also blew back the water of the river and many of the low lying places were flooded to a depth of 10 feet, and it has been calculated that the loss to property about the Thames alone will amount to something like £2,000,000 sterling.

Thrashing straw for the cattle has been all our work during the week. We have still plenty of turnips, but they are frozen so hard, they can hardly eat them. We have been trying various plans to thaw them, one being to dig a hole and bury them among the horse dung.

31st

We have now got a good deal of the snow away having been fresh since Thursday, but I am still doubtful if it is to last long, there being a white mist always hanging about the hills.

On Wednesday and Thursday we were thrashing some corn to the people of Ardiecow, the frost having dried up all their water.

During these stormy days I have been getting some fine sport with my gun, having killed since I got it three pheasants and four 'cushies'.[30]

On Saturday we were busy pulling and driving home turnips but many of them seem to be spoiled with the frost. I went over on Sunday morning to ask for George Biddie who has been very bad with inflammation since Thursday. He was however a good deal better. Today we winnowed six quarter of corn and had it over to the mill.

Coming down from the stable tonight I beheld in all its beauty, that grand phenomenon of the North, The Aurora Borealis. It was the brightest and prettiest I ever saw and I could have stood and looked at it long enough. All along the northern horizon it was one blaze of light, while every now and then streaks and columns of light shot upwards towards the zenith shaking and quivering and assuming shapes innumerable.

1881 February
7th

The weather during the past week has been soft and the snow except where blown into wreathes has mostly disappeared. Yet it has never been a proper thaw, the frost not being more than two inches out of the ground, while yesterday it was again very hard and today it has just been as like the commencement of another snow storm as it possibly could be.

---

[29] wreathes (of snow), snow drifts.
[30] cushies, wood pigeons.

On Tuesday we were pulling and taking home turnips all day.

On Wednesday I was casting snow with the roadmen between this and Oathillock, while Father got one of the mares frosted and had a load of oats over to Berryhillock. I went over and spent the evening at Kirktown.

Thursday was a very bad day, snow and rain falling all day.

I was pulling turnips Friday all day, and would have driven them on Saturday, but it was very stormy with showers of snow and sleet from the North. I went over after dinnertime to the School Board Office and paid the Poor Rates.

Sunday was clear and frosty and Father, Joan, Willie and I were at Church. I saw Lizzie Gray, Hoggie, and Peter Rumbles, Tauchiehill Kirkit, they having been married on Saturday.

Today has been wild and stormy. The wind shifted from North to South and since dinnertime snow has been falling thickly while the wind was blowing a strong gale. We were thrashing in the forenoon but have done nothing else all day.

14th

> Stormy, stormy, wind and snow,
> Nothing else is on the go,
> Frost to freeze our thumbs and toes,
> One day calm, the next it blows

My surmises about the weather last week, have proved only too true, for during the past eight days, it has been more severe than any we have yet experienced in all this severe winter. True the frost has not been so bitter as in the first of January, but the weather has been more boisterous and there has been more drifting than in any one week before. As I stated last week Monday afternoon was a very bad night, but it had been felt far worse, in other places than here, because the wind being South put us in the shelter of the wood.

Tuesday was soft, but a nasty sleety day. I was driving turnips all day. Wednesday was frosty I was twice at the mill for meal. The roads were very slippery. I went up in the evening to Ardiecow when Miss MacKintosh was telling me she was going to Aberdeen for a few months to practice music, French and drawing.

We intended going to Cornhill market on Thursday, to sell the black cow, but it was such a terribly bad day, that we did not start. The whole day from morn till night, snow fell thickly while at the same time a strong wind was blowing from the East causing it to drift into every hollow and sheltered place, and blowing it into every nook and crevice where there was the least opening. The wind being right in the doors, we looked out as little as possible all day.

Next day the wind had shifted to the North and we had occasional showers of snow all day. I went over and opened the Library in the evening but being so bad a night very few attended.

Saturday was calm and frosty, but on Sunday it again snowed the whole day. It was a little soft however and did not drift much.

I was the only one at church from this side, and it was the most thinly attended I ever saw. I am sure there were not more than thirty.

Today it has been soft and a good deal of the snow has disappeared, but it is still very cold and white looking about the hills.

21st

Grim John Frost, seems determined to keep us as long as possible under this influence of his iron grasp, for although it has been some what fresh all the week, very few in Deskford have yet got the plough started. It has also been very blowy and extremely cold.

On Tuesday and Wednesday we were busy pulling and driving home turnips.

On Thursday I was casting snow off the wire fences in the 'Den' some of the wreathes being seven and eight feet deep.

I went over to Cornhill Station on Friday with a small box which was going to Cleland and when coming home went past Limestones. In the evening I went down to a concert at Fordyce, Don and Willie McIntosh accompanying me. It was a very nice affair and I was highly pleased with it. As Willie Mackintosh and I were to try who would give the best description of it, the following is my humble attempt.

Fordyce Concert

A grand amateur concert in connection with the Fordyce Poultry Association, was held in the Public School there, on the evening of Friday the 18th February. Doors were opened at seven o'clock, and by the time Mr. Innes M.A. head-master of the Public School was called to the chair, every available seat was occupied, while many were still crowding in.

Soon every corner was filled, and the standing room, even in the passes all taken up, while about the door and lobby, to use old John McBey's expression, they were 'completely suffocated and crammed to death'.

The programme which was both a lengthy and varied one commenced with a song by the Glee Party and which, led by Mr Chalmers, they rendered in excellent style.

Miss Evans, Glassaugh House then gave a solo on the piano. I am not going to attempt however to describe all the different songs, nor to enumerate all the performers as they followed each other in the programme, but will just notice a few of those which more particularly took my fancy.

Two nice songs were given by Angus McGilvary and Peter Stewart, two Fordyce 'loons' accompanied respectively by Miss Geddes, Newton, and Miss Thomson, Bogton, on the piano. Mr Stewart H.M.I.S. gave 'The Village Blacksmith' and 'My Nannie's Awa', Miss Stewart accompanying him on the piano.[31]

Although Mr. Stewart has got rather a weak voice his songs were rendered with great taste, and precision. 'Wait for the turn of the tide' was given by Mr. John Badenoch, with great approval, and was heartily applauded. Following it was a vocal duet by Mr. & Miss Johnstone, Rothmackenzie.

I was greatly taken with a song entitled 'Bygone Days' given by Mr. Wilson I.R.O., Glenglassaugh.[32] He was accompanied by Miss Thomson on the piano and truly he did render it most admirably, his fine, rich, deep mellow bass voice, making roof and rafters ring again. Mr. Stephen, Mill of Dunn and Mr. Elder, Cullen, gave some comic songs 'in character' both meeting with great approbation, Mr. Elder being encored. A few Strathspeys were given by Messrs. Geddes & Badenoch in their well known excellent style, their stirring strains causing so great a commotion among the lower extremities of the audience, as to elicit a remark from the Chair, almost the only one that worthy gentleman, ventured to make the whole evening. The Glee Party, consisting of four tenor, an alto, three treble, and four bass voices, followed next with 'My Mountain Home'.

'Bonaparte's Grand March' was also very creditably performed by Miss Geddes on the piano, and Mr. George Geddes on the violin; the measured beat of the music almost making you think, you heard the tramp of the red coats as they marched to battle array.

I must not forget to mention two recitations given by Miss Carry Grant, The Manse, entitled 'Lady Clair' and 'Somebody's Darling' in the rendering of which she showed both taste and elegance. With all these mentioned I was highly pleased, but I think, if any one, more than another deserved commendation I, for my part, would confer it on the the Misses Badenoch and McKay, two school girls who, accompanied by Mr. James Badenoch on the violin, sang 'Millie's on the dark blue sea' and whose young sweet tender voices, blended together in such perfect harmony, causing everyone to hearken with rapt attention.

[31] H.M.I.S., Her Majesty's Inspector of Schools.
[32] I.R.O., Inland Revenue Officer.

Another piece by The Glee Party finished the programme, thereafter the ordinary voles of thanks were proposed, the National Anthem was sung and the company dismissed.

We got back to Ardiecow about half past eleven, when we found Miss Mackintosh nearly asleep by the fireside but with also a nice tea awaiting us. Having done ample justice to the same, we commenced to try who was most expert at arithmetic, and so engrossed did we become, with our exertions, the one trying to excel the other, and all of us being so nearly a par, that it was four o'clock before any of us was aware.

Today we received an intimation of the death of Lord Seafield at Cullen House on Friday the 18th inst. He has been unwell since the first of January, but was thought to be recovering until Sunday last when he collapsed after which he never again rallied.

28th

Since Saturday we have again experienced the snow storm in all its severity. We have a fresh fall of snow to the depth of 3 inches or more, while the frost is also very severe. Last week although a little frosty at night the sun during the day gradually drew out the frost and on Friday afternoon I got a few hours in the plough.

The remains of the Earl of Seafield were conveyed on Friday from Cullen House by hearse to Keith Station passing through Deskford about half past eleven. From Keith they were taken by rail to Granton where they remained in the Castle all night, and on Saturday was conveyed to the mausoleum in Duthil churchyard (about seven miles above Granton). It was calculated that about 2000 people took part in the procession at Cullen and at Granton 1200 persons were supposed to be present. On Sunday Mr. Mackintosh in the course of his sermon referred in a very touching manner to the death of his Lordship.

1881 March
7th

The weather now is indeed becoming rather serious, for as yet there is no sign of fresh weather indeed the past week has been exceptionally stormy, and on some days tremendous blowing.

Let the fresh days come now as soon as they may, the Spring cannot be other than a late one, for many have scarcely any of the lea ploughed yet and none are more than half done.

Tuesday was Fastern-even, but I got neither the ring nor button among the brose.[33] I went over in the evening to Kirktown to my

---

[33] brose, dish of oatmeal mixed with hot water pease meal baked on a girdle.

bannocks and a jolly night we had. George Duncan getting the ring but the button was nowhere to be found. On Wednesday afternoon I went over to the poor's house with George Ewing for a load of peats for George Biddie.

On Thursday I was driving out dung all day. About dinner time the wind began to rise, and the snow on the ground being so loose, it soon began to drift. I unyoked at five o'clock as it was then getting rather close. Towards night the wind increased and drifting became furious and so it continued all night, all Friday, and all Saturday without intermission but without any more snow falling. At four o'clock on Saturday however, snow began to fall and the wind still blowing a strong gale from S.E. drifting soon became excessive. All night long and next day until three o'clock the snow fell and drifted forming into wreathes of tremendous size and so for the fourth or fifth time this winter blocking road and rail; and to a far greater extent than any before experienced. On Thursday the trains both on the Great North and Highland Railways were all stopped, three trains on the latter line being completely blown over. A tremendous wreathe was formed in our close, being at the deepest about 10 feet. It being such a bad day on Sunday none of use were at church. Towards evening it turned fresh and it has continued so. As Father has been very bad with rheumatism in his back for some days back, I got Geordie Ritchie today to assist me to cast the snow in the road and to pull some turnips. There was a meeting held in the School Board Office tonight, making arrangements for a lecture to be given in the Public School.

14th

We have had a week of fine fresh weather and everybody has been busy at the plough. The thaw which commenced on Sunday night has continued and a week of fine spring weather has been enjoyed. Large wreathes of snow however, are still to be seen, some of which it will take many a day to completely dissolve.

On Tuesday Geordie Ritchie and I carted 100 loads of snow out of the close, and I am sure we did not take the half of it.

On Wednesday forenoon I went to the Smiddy to get one of the mares shod and in the afternoon I went to the plough, it being 13 weeks since I was last in the yoke.

Thursday was Cornhill market day. Father was over at it. There was a large turn out of cattle owing no doubt to the turnips being so greatly spoiled with the frost.

A good many sales were effected but prices were rather low, 68/- and 70/- being the very highest.

A. Munro Buckie bought 2 queys from us as he was going home from market for £31.

The Library was open on Friday night and there was a large attendance. There was a meeting held afterwards when Miss Ker intimated that the Revd. Mr. Boyd, Portsoy, would give a lecture on the evening of Thursday next.

Saturday was a most delightful day. The wind so fresh and soft, the air so clear, and the sun so bright, the lapwing as it swiftly wheeled about seemingly enjoying them all to the full, with the little skylark as, springing from the dewy grass it mounted up into the azure vault all the while pouring forth its joyful notes of praise; all presented a very pleasing contrast to the frost, the snow, and the biting blast of only a few days ago.

Today I finished the piece of lea below the houses.

On Saturday Father was at the funeral of Mrs. Wood, Moss-side who died on Tuesday. She had been poorly for a long time back.

21st

The past week has been fresh, dry and windy on some days there being a very strong gale. Consequently the ground was getting very dry, and lea was growing rather hard to plough. We have got a week's work at the lea yet, but a few are finished and commenced to the clean land.

On Tuesday and Wednesday I ploughed the small park before the door, and a rather stiff job it was.

On Thursday we had our lecture in the School. It was a very blowy night and the audience was rather small, but we got a first class lecture. His subject was 'Eyes and Ears' and he handled it in a very masterly manner; his chief object being to show how to make the best use of these two very important organs. It proved both humorous and instructive, and was listened to with great attention by an appreciative audience.

The steam mill was to thrash at Kirkton on Friday but one stack was all that was got done as the wind rose to a perfect hurricane. In the afternoon I ploughed the end-rigs in the 'den'.

Next day was a little quieter and by three o'clock we had Kirton's cornyard all thrashed.

Sunday morning was frosty and some stormy like. George Stephen, Kate and the bairns arrived about ten o'clock from Keith. George went to church with Joan and I. The day grew very stormy and by the time we got home the ground was white. Geordie went home that night but Kate and the bairns are to stop some time.

Today we were winnowing corn and driving turnips in the forenoon and in the afternoon I was in the plough, there being however, a little too much snow.

28th

Nearly the whole of last week has been frosty with occasional showers of snow. Work has proceeded but slowly, it being generally too frosty for the plough in the mornings.

On Wednesday we had Mr. Imlah's steam thrashing machine and thrashed out the remainder of the crop. The day was rather windy but being frosty everything was fine and dry. There was a pretty fair out turn of grain of good quality.

On Thursday afternoon I was furring the clean land beside the wood but before six o'clock it was growing very hard.

Friday was fresh and I was busy all day turning over the lea. I went up to Ardiecow in the evening and had a round of arithmetic with Willie and Don.

On Saturday morning the frost was very hard. In the forenoon I was driving out dung, but in the afternoon I was at the plough.

I was not at church on Sunday. Willie Cowie, Finnygaud, was over, and when going home I went over to Muttonbrae.

Saturday was the day for letting the Farms of Knowiemoor, Wester Windy Hills and Bogside. This morning the ground was again covered with two inches of snow. By one o'clock however, the most of it had melted and I got to the plough, the afternoon however, was very rough and showery.

1881 April
4th

We have had another week of hard frosty weather. It was generally too hard for the plough in the forenoon and on some days I did not get yoked at all.

On Tuesday morning I tried the plough, but broke a thete when starting and so had to give it up.[34] We then filled up three quarters of potato oats and started for Portsoy to get an exchange for seed. We selected a sample of Sandwich oats, grown on Newton of Findochty, and weighing 42lbs per bushel our own however, weighed 44.

On Wednesday afternoon I again tried the plough. It was still very hard and I was only able to plough down hill.

---

[34] thete, the traces for attaching a horse to a farm implement via a swingletree.

Thursday was also very frosty. In the forenoon I went over to the Smiddy and got the filly shod. In the afternoon I was ploughing clean land.

On both Friday and Saturday I ploughed all day, although still rather hard in the mornings.

On Sunday afternoon Father went over to Newbigging to see Aleck Wilson who has lately returned from Demerara and is thought to be dying of consumption.

Mrs. Riddoch, Backies, and Miss Annie McWillie came over on a visit.

Today it has been fresh and warm and quite spring like, and I hope it may have long continuance. I had the filly in the plough a few hours in the forenoon, when she went very well.

I had finished my Journal writing for the week, and had my book put past, but after suppering my horses I beheld a scene which has compelled me again to resume my pen. The sun had been set for half an hour behind the hill of Maud and the curtain of night was drawing its folds of darkness over the earth. Scarcely a breath of wind stirred the air and as I stood on the old dyke beside the peat stack and gazed around me, I beheld what to my eyes seemed a most beautiful picture, and listened to what my ears reckoned the sweetest music. All along the hill side and wherever you turned your eyes, numbers of bonfires were shedding their ruddy glow and lighting up the gathering gloom, while above them the smoke was eddying and circling and rising in columns in the still evening air. Over the Clunehill could be seen the sea lying so calm and still like a glassy mirror, and instead of the deep blue, appearing under the darkness overhead, a bluish white; while far away in the distance the Sutherland hills could be dimly discerned their towering heads still capped with snow. Such was the scene on which my eyes did feast, while the treat provided for my ears was not a whit less worthy of notice. Many and varied were the sounds to be heard on this calm spring evening. Far and near could be heard the sharp 'pe-wit' of the lapwing, or 'pese weep' as we more commonly call it, great numbers of which are now preparing their nests in the fields around. The plaintive cry of the curlew could also be heard far away on the hillside ever and anon breaking forth into such a tumult of notes as is past my power of description. In the field close at hand I could hear the pleasant chirp of the partridge as it called its mate, while from the plantation behind me the little feathered minstrels were issuing quite a flood of music. The blackbird and the mavis, seemed to vie with one another which would produce the sweetest song, and all the other members of the sylvan choir, each in its own peculiar key yet all blending together in sweetest harmony, were pouring forth in joyful strains, their evening lay.[35]

Has the Revd. Mr. Boyd's recent lecture on 'Eyes and Ears' anything to do with these few remarks? Well, it may or it may not, I never thought of it until after I had penned them; but one thing I know, which is that of late I have paid more attention, and derived more pleasure than formerly from the many sights and sounds of Nature surrounding me.

11th

The past week has been a very busy one, the weather having been dry and windy, making the land in splendid working order. The two fine days however, in the first of the week had not many marrows for since then the weather has been extremely cold.[36] Not one vestige of growth is yet to be seen, although many no doubt are anxiously looking for some, their turnips being all done. We have still a few but they are nearly all rotten and are no use.

On Tuesday evening I went over to see the folks at the Newton. Johnny was away at Cornhill Station meeting Miss Lizzie, who had been at Keith. She has not got a situation yet but she has been applying for Grange, which is vacant just now.

On Friday we commenced to sow it being in splendid condition. We have still a great deal to plough but it will perhaps be got done when the harrows will not work.

Today I finished the lea on Ardiecow and in the afternoon was breaking in the other field.

18th

The weather still continues cold and dry, and work is progressing rapidly. During the week everyone has been busy, sowing and lea in most cases is finished. We were sowing on Tuesday and on Friday I sowed the Den. After finishing it on Saturday I went to the plough. Before sowing any more we are going to plough the clean land to get some barley sowed.

This morning it was very frosty and until ten o'clock there was a close mist. In the afternoon Joan and I were at the Steam Mill at Cultain. They were very short of hands and before it was finished we were like to be defeated altogether.

---

[35] mavis, song thrush.
[36] marrows, best parts.

25th

Cold frosty weather still prevails, and although rather backward for growth, the seed is being got in, in splendid condition.

On Tuesday I was at the plough.

On Wednesday Mrs. Bremner and I were at the steam mill at Ardiecow. We did a good days work, thrashing about sixty quarters.

On Thursday morning I sowed the Barley and some potato corn. As I never sowed any barley before I did not know about the thickness, and I am now afraid I have given it too little seed.

Friday was our fast day when we had Mr. Brown, Buckie, officiating. As there was to be no service in the evening, Joan and I went to Cullen for a few things. The grass about Cullen is little greener than it is here.

Saturday was a little warmer with a fine shower in the afternoon. I finished the ploughing of the clean land on Ardiecow. We have all the hill to plough yet.

Sunday was our Sacrament. In the afternoon we had Mr. Broochie, Cullen, who gave us a splendid discourse from Hebrews XII 1.2.3.

Today we sowed the clean land at the side of the wood and I have been busy in the harrows all day.

1881 May

2nd

The weather during the week has been a great deal warmer and we have also had some nice fresh showers. Vegetation is progressing rapidly and with warm weather grass might soon be expected for the cattle.

On Tuesday I was sowing all day having sown the grass seeds on the clean land and some tares in the parkie before the door.

On Wednesday forenoon I was harrowing at it, while Father was at the roller. In the afternoon I commenced to plough the hill and finished it yesterday at a quarter to five, having been 32 hours in ploughing 3½ acres.

Friday and Saturday were moist and warm with occasional showers. It was also very misty, but at times it would clear off when the fields so fresh and green were pleasant to look upon.

Sunday was showery but rather cold. It was the Sacrament at Fordyce and Mother went to attend when Father went with her. During the week I have been busy in the evenings working in the garden and have got my part, viz. the flowers all finished except the seeds sown.

9th

There has been no growth since last I wrote, indeed the grass is not nearly so green like as it was then.

On Tuesday Geordie Ritchie and I were putting up pailing while Father was grubbing a piece for the potatoes. In the evening I went over to Kirkton.

We were both in the roller on Wednesday forenoon, but the afternoon was showery and it would not work, so I drilled the potatoes. In the evening Willie and I had two queys down to Dytach, Willie Hay having bought them.

On Thursday we were putting out dung for the potatoes and cutting the seed. We got them set on Friday but the afternoon was very windy and we could not get the manure sowed. We went to the roller and got it finished.

Saturday was a fearful day of drought. The dust was flying in clouds all day. I was in the grubber. The turnip land is to be very easily made this year, so much frost has made it tender.

On Sunday afternoon Joan and I were over at Limestones.

Today has been quiet and warm and we got the potatoes covered in.

16th

The past week until Saturday was very dry, and everyone has been busy cleaning the turnips land. Work is now well advanced for the season a good few having commenced to drill, and even to sow, I believe in some places.

On Tuesday Father went to Portsoy for a load of manure, while I was harrowing with the other two.

Geordie Ritchie and I were turning the dung on Wednesday.

Thursday was Cornhill market. There was a large turn out of cattle, but a very stiff sale for all classes.

On Friday I was harrowing while Father took off the weeds, and rolled the piece, which is for Swedes. I was over at Kirkton in the evening opening the Library. The roup at Knowiemoor was on Saturday. Father and Mother were both at it, but bought nothing. I was grubbing and harrowing. At four o'clock I unyoked as I was intending going to Finnygaud. I started at half past five and arrived there at 7.40. The day was warm and showery and there was a little thunder in the afternoon.

Sunday was moist all day, the rain at times falling rather heavy. They have got three nice mare foals at Finnygaud and they have altogether only eleven horses about their place.

Today has been cold and stormy, the wind blowing from the North while, in the forenoon a good deal of rain fell. I have done nothing among the land all day. I was at the Smiddy in the forenoon and in the afternoon I was enclosing a small park for the calves.

23rd

During the past week we have had copious showers of rain and everything is looking fresh and green. The cattle have not a great bite yet but with warm weather grass would speedily improve. Braird is doing well and is thick and healthy looking. Owing to the rain, little has been done to the turnip land during the week.

On Tuesday forenoon I was in the drill plough but the afternoon was wet.

Wednesday was also showery and I did not yoke.

We went over to Cornhill Station on Thursday morning for a ton of Kynoch's turnip manure. In the afternoon I was in the drill plough.

Friday was Cullen market. I was making drills in the forenoon and in the afternoon was cross ploughing.

On Saturday we commenced to dung. The day was dry and warm. We covered them in, in the afternoon and got them sowed in the evening.

Today we have got a few more sowed and the land is now fine and dry.

30th

The past week has been a very busy one, and the most of the Swedish turnips are now sowed. The weather has been dry and for the month of May exceptionally warm. A good fresh shower would be very acceptable.

On Tuesday we sowed the remainder of the Swedes.

On Wednesday I was in the grubber. In the afternoon the belt of plantation between this and Cotton Hill took fire, when we had a rather hot job putting it out.

I was grubbing and harrowing on Thursday.

On Friday Mr. Mackintosh, Ardiecow, kindly lent me his machine when Mother and I went up to Keith. The day was fine and we had a splendid drive.

I was in the drill plough on Saturday.

Jessie Wilson, Limestones, was at Church with us on Sunday.

Today Father and Willie were at Keith for a calf which I bought on Friday, while the girl and I went to the moss and spread the peats.[37]

---

[37] 'the girl' may have referred to Mary Wilson, no relation, the domestic servant at Knowes.

1881 June
6th

The weather until Friday was excessively warm and dry, indeed I do not think I ever felt such a heat so early in the season. Since then however, it has been colder with slight showers. More moisture is still needed and if it do not come quickly crops will be spoiled. Oats are already turning yellow on wet land. Hay will also be very light if rain do not speedily come. The greatest complaint however is about the turnips. All the Swedes everywhere, have either been eaten by the fly or spoiled by frost, as not a single turnip is now to be seen. Some have sowed again but many have left them alone thinking a shower might still send them up.

We sowed the first of the yellow turnips on Tuesday.

On Wednesday we furred up and resowed a part of the Swedes, the rest we have not touched.

I was in the drill plough on Thursday all day.

On Friday we were putting out dung, covering it in and sowing the turnips in the afternoon. In the evening I went over to Kirkton.

On Saturday we went to the moss and set the peats. A few dry days would make them ready to drive.

I went over on Sunday afternoon to Newbigging to see Aleck Wilson. He is not improving any, and I would rather fear that he will never recover.

Today has been very cold with some showers. We have got another sowing of turnips done.

13th

The weather during the past week has been excessively cold and stormy on some days there being tremendous showers of hail. The cold and drought has stopped the growth of everything. Pasture is getting very bare. Oats are all turning brown, while not a turnip is yet to be seen above ground.

On Tuesday I went up to William MacBain's to cast a few loads of turf. There were a few terrible showers of hail, and I saw Ben Rinnes milk white.[38]

On Wednesday we sowed all the turnips except the endrigs.

Thursday was Cornhill market. Father was over at it but cattle met with a very stiff sale. I was ploughing and harrowing the endrigs.

On Friday morning I went up and set the turfs. In the afternoon I went over to Hoggie to plough Widow Gray's turnip land.

---

[38] Ben Rinnes, hill overlooking Aberlour on Speyside.

I also went back on Saturday when I ploughed it out and gave it a strip of the harrows.

On Sunday a drizzling rain fell the most of the day. Geordie Cowie was over from Finnygaud. David McBain and Annie were down in the afternoon. We went down to Sandend today for two loads of sand. In the afternoon I was at the Smiddy, while Father was at Craibstone for some lime.

20th

The weather during the week has continued dry but it has been warmer than the previous one, and there has been a little growth.

On Sunday however, the clouds which during the week had bedimmed the sky, and towards which many a weary look had been cast; at length released their treasure, and we enjoyed a most delightful shower.

Today we have also had some thunder showers and already the appearance of everything is greatly improved.

On Tuesday we took a survey of the Swedes and thinking they would do without re-sowing we finished off the end-rigs.

Wednesday was new Keith market. Father went up to it, getting a drive with Sandy McKay. There was a large turn out of cattle and horses but except for calves and sheep, a very, very stiff sale. I was oiling the harness and in the afternoon I went up to Ardiecow to get a sheep shear.

On Thursday we went up to the moss for two loads of peats, when we found them in first class trim for driving and for the next two days we kept busy at them.

On Friday and Saturday I stayed all day and wheeled out, and by six o'clock I had them all out and thrown up to defend a shower.

I set out on Sunday morning to visit Mr. and Mrs. Ross, Hillfolds. The morning was nice and warm and I had a delightful walk. Going in past Limestones I stayed a short time there, it being half past nine before I got over. I found them all well and I also found a great improvement on every thing about the place. They both went to church with me, when we got a very good sermon from Mr. McVicar. After dinner we went out to get a look at the crops but as it was raining we did not go very far. It continued to rain all afternoon and before I got home I was nearly wet through.

On Monday morning, today, we went to take another look at the Swedes, when we found they had nearly all disappeared. We yoked immediately Father putting one into the scuffle, while I put the other two into the drill plough and by six o'clock we had the most of them resowed.[39]

27th

We have had rather changeable weather during the past eight days, sometimes bright sunshine and at other times cold and cloudy, some days excessive drought, while others were warm and showery. Grass and cereals are growing fairly well, but turnips are scarcely moving out of the bit. In the first of the week everyone was busy resowing and I believe there will be some to do yet. We finished ours on Tuesday forenoon and in the afternoon I went to the moss.

On Wednesday Father and Mother went to Portsoy. I was cleaning some of the harness and then went up for a load of peats.

On Thursday we were driving peats.

We were driving lime and sand on both Friday and Saturday for the purpose of repairing the dyke between us and Ardiecow.

On Sunday afternoon Joan and I were up at William McBain's at our tea.

I have been twice in the moss today. The steam mill was at Ardiecow in the afternoon, when Father went up to give them a help. We have had a nice warm showery day and the evening looks so delightful that I can stay no longer indoors.

1881 July
4th

The weather during the past week has made a marked improvement on everything. We have had nice showers nearly every day and, 'were it only warmer', the farmers now say. Turnips have grown more the past week, than in any two before, and by the end of this one I believe we will be at the hoe.

We were driving peats all day on Tuesday.

On Wednesday I rose at 3 o'clock and started for the moss. It was the day of the Fordyce Pic-nic and Poultry Show and I intended going down to see them in the afternoon. One of the mares however had to go to the Smiddy and so after dinner I went up for a load of turfs. I then went up past Ardiecow for Don Mackintosh and we got down to Fordyce about six o'clock. There was an extraordinary turn out of people, the array of young ladies (I feel my heart beating yet when I think of them) being enough to turn one's head. The evening was delightful and I enjoyed myself thoroughly. I came home with Don Mackintosh and Willie. Miss Mackintosh had

---

[39] scuffle, horse drawn hoe.

arrived that night from Aberdeen and so I went in past a few minutes to have a chat.

On Thursday forenoon I was at the moss but the afternoon was rainy. I went over to Kirktown in the evening to a meeting held in the Public School for the purpose of making arrangements about our Annual Pic-nic. There were fewer of a committee than last year, but we had a strong debate before the day was fixed. At length the 27th July was agreed to, and George Proctor and I were sent off to ask the use of the Orchard from the Minister. This he readily granted us, and we were also successful in securing Mr. Smith as chairman.

On Friday we got home all the peats, having had 34 loads from 62 score.

I was scuffling the potatoes on Saturday morning while Father was at Craibstone for a load of lime. We got a swarm of bees that day and we got another splendid swarm on the Tuesday before.

On Sunday afternoon I went over to Newbigging to see Aleck Wilson. There is little difference on him yet, always very weak. I went down to the sermon at the School and went past Muttonbrae coming home.

This forenoon was wet, we took in a load of barley straw and was drawing it for thatch. Father was at the funeral of Elizabeth Gray, Hoggie, who died on Friday morning after a very painful illness. She was buried in Deskford churchyard.

11th

We have had little or no summer weather during the week, but cold rainy days instead. On some days we had also very high winds, and the wind and rain did great damage to the turnips, especially the small ones, washing the earth up on them, and driving them out of sight nearly altogether. Sowing turnips is not yet a thing of the past as I have heard of a few instances this week.

I was hoeing the potatoes on Tuesday. It was rent day and Father was at Cullen. I went up and spent the evening at Ardiecow. Miss McIntosh has made great improvement since she went to Aberdeen. She was practising music, French and drawing, but drawing is the subject in which she excells. She has some really first class drawings and she has also been trying to sketch a little.

On Wednesday morning I furred up the potatoes. In the afternoon I was driving some stones off the lea, but it turned wet and I had to drop them.

Thursday was a very stormy day. A strong N.W. wind driving the rain before it, shaking the crops, blackening the potatoes and almost burying the turnips. The afternoon cleared up a little and I went over to the shoemakers.

I went to Portsoy on Friday for two loads of coals for the blacksmith. The day was dry, but the roads rather soft, and so I came home past Tochineal.

Saturday was quiet and showery. Father and I were drawing straw all day.

Sunday afternoon was very warm. We got another swarm of bees.

Today we were going to thatch the mill. The morning was quiet and we commenced but by nine o'clock a good breeze of wind had sprung up which fairly put us to a standstill. We have been hoeing the rest of the day. The turnips are rather small, but a good many of them are about the same, so we will have to be working at them.

18th

A week of warm breezy days has been a great improvement on everything. Turnips are now doing well and hoeing is in full swing. We have good plants and are nearly half done with the singling. This afternoon I saw Walter Gray at the sowing, I think his turnips are the worst of any I see. Barley is now, full shot. Ours will be a fair crop. Oats will take fully a week yet. We have kept busy at the hoe all the week, doing nothing else.

On Wednesday evening I went over to Oathillock with Miss McKay's presentation ticket for the Pic-nic which she accepted.

On Friday evening Johnny Geddes came over from Newton, when we were putting the stone, shooting and other antics.

I went up to Ardiecow on Saturday evening with Miss McIntosh's Pic-nic ticket. She does not think however, she will be able to get as she is very busy.

25th

The weather during the past eight days has been very changeable. If one day was dry the next one was sure to be wet. We have now abundance of rain, indeed a little too much for the newly hoed turnips. Corn however, is still lengthening out, and will be in general a fair crop.

On Monday and Tuesday we had Mrs. Duncan at the hoe and we got a good piece singled.

We were hoeing at the Swedes on Wednesday. In the afternoon Joan and I went over to the Bogmuchal Pic-nic. The day was rough and showery but pretty dry like when we set out. We had not been there however, more than an hour when the rain came on, and of course the dancing had to be given up. It cleared a little about eight o'clock when a few reels were danced to the pipes, but the rain again coming on the company speedily dispersed. Coming out of the shelter of the wood we found the night far worse than we expected, the wind and rain being something fearful. I accompanied Miss Wyness home to Slackdale where I got myself dried. The people of the Newton came also in past and after getting tea from Mrs. Wyness we had a few nice reels and schottisches. The weather was now settled down a bit and I got home dry.

Next day was dry and we were at the hoe.

Friday was Peter Fair but it should have been Peter Foul for it was a spate nearly the whole day. Very few people went past this for it. Father was going but the day frightened him.

Saturday was a nice warm dry day. It being rather wet for the hoe we commenced to thatch the mill, and by half past five we had every thing finished off. Willie and I then went to Portsoy to get a pair of boots for him and it was eleven o'clock before we got home.

Sunday afternoon was rainy.

Monday was also soft, and it was afternoon before the hoe would work.

1881 August
1ˢᵗ

Since Tuesday the weather has been warmer but still very changeable, and the growth is anything but rapid yet. Everyone has been busy at the hoe during the week, and a few days will in general finish the singling.

On Tuesday morning I went over to the Smiddy for some new hoes. In the evening I went over to Kirkton to get the orchard in trim for our Annual Pic-nic. We cut the grass, set the seats, and put up a swing.

There were some doubts among the committee as to the success of the affair, very few tickets having been sold.

By three o'clock on Wednesday afternoon however, a goodly company of lads and lasses gay, all in holiday attire and bent on merry making, had assembled beneath the spreading boughs of the giant ash, that rears its towering head on the level haugh by the burnside. The afternoon was all that could be desired and the turnout was fully an average. By 3.30 our musicians viz. Messrs. Johnstone, Geddes, Duncan and Black had their fiddles tuned and we enjoyed a few reels and schottisches. About half past four Mr. Smith, Schoolmaster, was called to the Chair and after a new remarks by him, a sumptuous tea was served out by the stewards and stewardesses, who afterwards enjoyed their own cup by the dyke side.

Dancing was now entered into with great zest, all the Contra Dances—Rory O'More, Lochleven, Strip the Willow and others, being executed in excellent style while polkas and schottisches had full swing.

Those who were not inclined for dancing amused themselves with various games, while old Aunt Sally and the swing, was a source of great amusement to the youngsters. Many strangers and people from a distance, were present, but one and all, had seemingly said to dull care, 'begone', and were determined for one afternoon at least, to thoroughly enjoy themselves.

The most pleasant meeting however, must come to an end, and so the shades of evening, nay rather the gathering gloom at last reminded us that The Deskford Annual Pic-nic must once more be drawn to a close. Very reluctant were the dancers to leave off tripping the sward now no longer green, and had not the fiddlers slackened their pegs, and bagged their 'fickle friens'. I verily believe they would have danced until now. Mr. Smith having mounted the platform now proposed the usual votes of thanks, which were most heartily responded to. Our worthy Chairman also most deservingly received a lusty round of cheers. The whole company now joined in singing 'Auld Lang Syne', and as the last verse commencing with 'Now here's a han' my trusty frien' was pealed forth, hill and valley rang again. Thereafter, to use Mr. Smith's expression, like the members of parliament; all paired off to their respective homes.

On Thursday Geordie Ritchie and I cut the hay. We were hoeing on Friday forenoon and in the afternoon we bound up the hay.

I was scuffling turnips on Saturday, while Father was at the Smiddy.

On Sunday morning Jessie and Katie Cowie with a Miss Pirie from Keith came over from Finnygaud. In the afternoon Aleck and George Duncan and James Whytecross came in past, and so we had gentlemen to entertain our ladies.

Today we were busy at the hoe, and we have them all singled but one endrigs. We were all greatly delighted to hear tonight by a letter from Annie that she had got her holidays and would be home on Thursday first to spend a fortnight with us. We are also expecting Jessie in a short time. The family she is with were coming to Nairn today for two months and she was to get her holidays while there.

8th

Although the weather during the week has been warmer and the air fresher, we have had but little sunshine. We have had occasional showers, but always such a breeze of wind after them, that we never derived the full benefit. Turnips are growing wonderful and may yet be a better crop than was anticipated. Rumours are abroad already however, of finger and toe and I have seen a few among our own.

On Tuesday we went up for five loads of turfs, and set up the bottoms which were very wet. In the evening I went over to a meeting in the School to settle up the affairs of the Pic-nic.

I was in the scuffle harrow on Wednesday all day. I went eleven hours and was calculating I had walked nearly 20 miles.

Thursday forenoon was warm and showery. The afternoon was dry and I went a few hours in the scuffle. In the evening I went over to Cornhill Station to meet Annie. She arrived all right along with Minnie Stirling. The evening was nice and warm, being the finest I think we have had all summer and we got home a little before ten.

On Friday morning I went up to the moss for two loads of peats for Uncle George. In the afternoon we commenced to second hoe.

On Saturday we hoed all day.

On Sunday afternoon George and Jemmie Cowie came over from Finnygaud.

We have been busy today thrashing and building the hay. We had Uncle George and John over assisting us, and by five o'clock we had everything trig and trim. The out turn of seed however, is not nearly so good as last year.

15th

The weather continues changeable but generally it has been cold and cloudy. Barley is beginning to change colour, but is greatly in want of more sunshine.

We were hoeing and scuffling among the turnips on Tuesday.

On Wednesday I got Ardiecow's machine and Annie and I drove up to Keith for Jessie. She had come from Nairn to that the day before

.

Thursday was Cornhill Market and their flower show was also held that day. Father was over at the market, but it was a very dull one. I went in the afternoon with the people of Ardiecow to see the show. There was a grand display of everything, of course that includes the Ladies, and I enjoyed myself first class.

Friday was cold and stormy, with some showers and a boisterous wind from the N.W. Annie, Joan, Minnie and I were all over at Kirkton at our tea. A rather serious accident here happened to Aleck Duncan that day. Coming down from the loft, the stair which had been getting repairs and was unfastened at the top, gave way and he fell to the ground. He alighted on his side, cutting his cheek, and bruising and spraining his left arm. He had remained unconscious for sometime, and on Friday night his arm was extremely painful.

I went in past yesterday as I went to church when I was glad to find him recovering.

Saturday morning was wet and I was cutting thistles and other nic-nacks. It cleared up however, at twelve o'clock and I went up to Ardiecow with Rosie for the machine, when Miss MacIntosh, Jessie, Annie and I took a drive down to Cullen for the purpose of seeing the grounds of Cullen House. We unyoked at Mr. Michies and without more ado commenced our ramble amongst the romantic scenery that surrounds the ancient seat of the Grants.

On either side of the burn that flows past the House is a level haugh, covered with a sward of the richest green; all nicely cut and soft and thick as a carpet.[40]

Here the gigantic beech, the hardy pine and the beautiful sycamore, may be seen growing side by side; while beneath their spreading branches are shrubs and trees of some delicate growth. On our way to the garden we had to pass the pond, and here (to my mind) was the finest scenery of any we saw. The smooth surface of the water unruffled by the slightest breath of wind; and clean and bright as a mirror, the bushes and elders surrounding the pond, their drooping branches reflected in the water below; the wild ducks and water fowl coming flying over the treetops and alighting in the liquid element; the thickly covered islets with the swans houses peeping out from amongst the green verdure, along with the pure white swans themselves, gliding with arched neck so majestically about, all presented a scene so pleasing that I could have stood and gazed on it for hours with admiration and delight. We next proceeded to the gardens which are situated to the western side of the grounds on the slope towards the foot to the Bin Hill. They are finely sheltered, but have at the same time a good exposure. Mr. Berry, the head gardener, readily granted us permission to inspect the work he so masterly surveys and instructed the foreman to conduct us through the vinery and hothouses. There we saw the ripe grapes hanging from the roof in tempting clusters; while figs, dates, peaches and oranges were fast hastening to maturity. The flowers also, so finely trained and neatly arranged were quite a treat to see. The many varieties of ferns particularly took my attention. The 'Oak' the 'tree', and the beautiful 'maiden hair' contrasting finely with the richer colours of the geranium, balsam and pelargonium. The warmth of the temperature, the delicious odour of the fruit, and the sweet scent of the flowers would have tempted us to linger longer than propriety allowed, so thanking the gardener for the trouble we had given him, we took our leave. We now descended the brae that bounds the western side of the glen, where ferns and ivy grow in rich abundance.

---

[40] sward, the grassy surface of land.

We were disappointed however, in not getting a sight of the flower gardens, the gates being locked. Here we first caught sight of Cullen House, standing on its rocky eminence on the right bank of the stream. Lord Seafield and the Countess are at present travelling on the continent and a few female servants are the only occupants of the noble mansion. We leisurely surveyed the whole surroundings, taking notice of the great bridge that spans the burn first before the principal entrance, the established Church on the opposite side and the factor's residence a little beyond.

As we intended taking a stroll by the seashore we now made way for Cullen, passed through the town down by the harbour and away east between the rocks and the sea. The afternoon was all that could be desired and while occupied with gathering shells from the rocks, and collecting seaweed from the pools, the hours but too swiftly flitted past. The fresh sea air having whetted our appetites we retraced our steps towards the town to see and find some refreshments. The coffee-house, café, restaurant, or as the good folks of Cullen designate it the Harbour of Refuge, is in the outside a red tiled white washed rather modest looking cottage but the inside quality exceeded our expectations. A double row of tables and forms runs from end to end, around the walls are hung appropriate texts and other cheap prints while everything is scrupulously clean and in order.[41] A harmonium is also placed in the corner for the public use, and after finishing our repast Miss Mackintosh favoured us with a few airs on the same. It was now nearly seven o'clock and after some purchases made by the ladies in Smith's Warehouse, we started for home. The evening was quiet and warm. By the time we got to Milltown, the sun had gone down behind the western hills and the curtain of night was beginning to fold its wings of darkness over the land. On looking round as we came up the brae by Carestown, a most extensive and beautiful panorama met our view. The blue sea, lying so calm and peaceful; with the fishing boats scattered here and there and dotting its surface; could be seen stretching from shore to shore, while the rounded summits of the Caithness Hills, looking blue in the distance, yet clear and distinct in outline, formed a striking background. Nearer hand the Bin Hill (to me the hill of all hills) was sharply defined against the few lingering rays of the setting sun, while down in hollow by the burn side, the farmhouse and white walled cottages of Kirkton nestled so cosy among the trees. We got

[41] forms, benches.

home by half past eight not the least tired and all highly pleased with our afternoon's excursion.

On Sunday Willie Cowie and Sandy came over with the machine, and Annie went over with them to Finnygaud.

Today Father, Jessie and Joan went over with the cart, and as I write I hear them coming down the brae.

22nd

The weather is improving a good deal, but still very little sunshine. Oats are beginning to change colour. Turnips are growing and look fresh and green. Hoeing scuffling and furring up has been the most of the week's employment.

Tuesday was Keith Cattle Show. Joan was the only one at it from this.

Wednesday was the Cullen Flower Show. I went down to see it in the evening. There was a good show but very few people from Deskford.

On Friday afternoon we had a good shower which the turnips were greatly needing.

On Saturday morning Annie and Minnie Stirling left this for Edinburgh again. Jessie and I went with them to Portsoy. We were rather surprised when we came home to find Mary just newly arrived from Edinburgh. She had missed the train in Aberdeen and had to stop all night. The sale of wood in Cotton Hill was that day. Father bought a lot of trees and a lot of brushwood. I went over in the evening to Cornhill for Mary's luggage.

29th

We have had some very fine days & some very bad ones during the week.

Tuesday, Wednesday & Thursday were delightful days with bright sunshine and the ripening of the crops was daily perceptible.

On Tuesday morning Father, Mother, Jessie and Mary started in Ardiecow's machine for Keith. Jessie was on her way back to Nairn her holidays being ended and Mother was to accompany her and stay a few days. I was hoeing and furring among the turnips.

We finished the hoeing on Wednesday.

On Thursday afternoon I went up for some turfs. On coming home the rings of one of the wheels came off, and I had there and then to unyoke. On this day a grand Review of all the volunteers in Scotland was held in the Queen Park, Edinburgh, Her Majesty the Queen inspecting them in person at five o'clock in the afternoon.

Friday forenoon was a perfect hurricane of wind and rain, doing great damage to all the crops.

Saturday was also showery. Mary, Millie and I went up to Keith as Mother was to return from Nairn. Maggie Duguid arrived that day from Grantown, and as Mary was going to Finnygaud she came home with us. As it was past nine o'clock before we got home she stayed all night and went down to the Lintmill in the morning.

On Sunday afternoon a great quantity of rain again fell, but today it has been warm and bright. I was at the Smiddy in the forenoon and in the afternoon we were pulling out and driving brushwood.

1881 September
5ᵗʰ

We have had eight days of dull cloudy weather, the sun has scarcely been visible and the crops to appearance have made little or no progress towards ripening. Turnips however, are growing well and where thick enough are mostly covering the ground. Harvest is commenced on the coast side, but there will be no stooks in Deskford this week at least.

On Tuesday and Wednesday we were driving home brushwood. I was over at Kirkton on Tuesday evening when I got a grand eat of berries.

We were driving turfs on Thursday, but they were very wet.

On Friday Father accompanied the funeral of John Mackay, Cairdwells, to the churchyard of Fordyce. In the afternoon Maggie Duguid, Mary, Joan and I went all over to Limestones. We got home about half past eight, and I afterwards accompanied Miss Duguid home to the Lintmill.

On Sunday Joan and I went up from church to The Backies (Mrs. Riddoch's) Annie and Willie McWillie and Johnnie and Willie Robb from Keith were also there. They are getting up a new house at the other Backies, but the masons are not commenced to build yet.

12ᵗʰ

Another week of extremely dull weather. We have also had more or less rain every day, and harvest seems no nearer hand than when last I wrote. We have not been doing anything of much consequence during the week, but just any 'orra' needful job.⁴²

I went over on Wednesday night to see the folks of the Newton and spent a very enjoyable evening.

Thursday was Cornhill market day and I went over to see what was doing. It was a very dull market and little doing among anything

---

⁴² orra, odd.

except sheep. As I came home I went in past Muttonbrae to ask for John, who has been very unwell for the past ten days. I found him recovering but very weak and still unable to rise.

On Saturday while Father and I were putting in a bit-drain on the hill a heron flew past us and alighted in the burn at the tip of 'The Bogs'. I ran home for the gun, but never thought I would get within reach of it. I crept down by the side of the plantain however, and on turning up the burn in search of it, I heard a splash in a pool below me, I wheeled about and there I saw it through the trees mounting up into the air. I let it rise above the tops when I let fire at it, and brought it to the ground. It was young and not extra large, but thinking it might be many a day before I got another one, I went to Portsoy in the evening with it for Mr. Mortimer to preserve.

On Sunday I was unable to go to Church as I had a terrible dose of the cold.

19ᵗʰ

A great improvement in the weather. Although not much sunshine yet, it has been dry and corn has ripened more this week than during the previous fortnight. A good few have commenced harvest in Deskford and in eight days it will be quite general. On Tuesday I went up to the moss for two loads of peats for Uncle of Limetstones.

On Friday night I went over and opened the Library when there was a good attendance.

On Saturday we were cutting the sprotts, and a good crop they were. James Gray lost his grey horse that day, inflammation being the cause of his death. I went down this afternoon and gave him a 'yokin' in the machine with our horses.

On Saturday afternoon we cut a bit of corn in the Den, we are to commence tomorrow in downright earnest. The people of Ardiecow and us are to work together.

26ᵗʰ

We have had a week of harvest work, but it has not been a very forcy one. A good deal of corn however has been cut, a few at the end of the parish having clyach. Tuesday was a fine day, and we were cutting in the Den.

On Wednesday morning we were cutting roads, and by twelve o'clock we had the machine yoked. It went very well, but was rather stiff at the first.

Thursday was wet the whole day.

On Friday we finished the lea on Ardiecow and cut a bit below the houses.

We were at it by six o'clock on Saturday, and got on grand until dinner time when rain came on and nothing more was done that night. There had been a heavy rain on the night for next morning everything was very wet. This has been the best day we have had for a month, a good breeze of wind and bright sunshine. We cut out the lea in the morning, cut roads in the middle of the day, and got a yokin of the machine in the afternoon.

1881 October
3rd

A week of grand harvest weather, and a very busy one. There has been no stop except on Thursday afternoon which was wet. I have seldom seen so many stooks in Deskford, it being almost all cut, but very little in the cornyard yet. On Tuesday we cut about 5 ½ acres of the clean land.

We were at Ardiecow on Wednesday and did a good day's work.

We would have cut all his lea on Thursday had it kept dry.

On Friday morning we cut it out, made roads and got a yokin in the afternoon. We were all day on Saturday at his clean land. It is a splendid crop and we set up a great many stooks.

Sunday was a very breezy day, hard and dry. I went over to Newbigging in the afternoon to see Aleck Wilson. He is still unable to get up, but was a little livelier than when last I saw him. I afterwards went down past Limestones.

Today we were cutting at Ardiecow until ten o'clock. We then cut our bit clean land at the wood side, and also some on the Hill. In the afternoon I saw a good few at the leading.

10th

The past week has been very unfavourable for harvest work. We have not had one whole dry day. Everyone has been leading when the weather would permit. We have been cutting and leading both.

On Tuesday morning we only cut an hour when the rain came on. The afternoon however, was dry, and we cut the parkie before the door.

We finished the hill on Wednesday by 12 o'clock, when we afterwards went down to the Den where we took clyack. In the afternoon we were cutting some roads on Ardiecow. We took all the folk down with us to supper, which Mother had ready waiting us. We afterwards had a dance and some songs.

Thursday morning was rather soft but it got harder through the day and by four o'clock we started the leading. We led the lea on

Ardiecow and the Den. It was half past eight before we got finished, but it was a fine night with a full moon.

Friday was wet the whole day. We were thrashing and making rapes.

Saturday was dry until dinner time, when we were cutting at Ardiecow. A great deal of rain fell between Saturday and Sunday.

Sunday night however, had been dry with a good breeze of wind and we were at the cutting by half past six this morning.

This morning after dinner time we commenced to lead the barley and got it all in by seven o'clock.

17th

We have had a week of real October weather and no mistake, cold, blowy, stormy days. Some of them dry and forcy, others quite the reverse. There is still a good deal of the crop to secure about the hill sides, but many have now winter.

We took clyack at Ardiecow on Thursday by 12 o'clock. We then led our lea below the houses, which was in splendid condition. We got it all up by five o'clock, when we afterwards led two hours at Ardiecow.

On Wednesday morning we were started by five o'clock. The morning was very very cold. We led until half past ten when it grew showery and no more was done that day.

We got commenced by nine o'clock on Thursday morning and led all day at Ardiecow.

Friday morning was a perfect hurricane of wind and rain. The wind was N.E. but towards afternoon it veered round to the N. when we had showers of sleet and hail. I went over at night and opened the Library, but the attendance was very limited.

Saturday was cold and showery, we were setting up stooks all day. They were not so well as we expected, but the ground is something terrible. New grass will be greatly spoiled before the crop is got off.

Sunday was quiet, but dry.

Today has also been very quiet. We commenced to lead at 10 o'clock, and except a few loads on the hill and the haugh in the Den we have it all in the cornyard. What we did today however, was not in the best condition.

24th

The weather since Wednesday has been very unfavourable for harvest work. Cold wet days. Never much rain but always showery, with the wind in the east. A few stooks may yet be seen about the Greenhill, but a good many have now commenced the plough.

We were leading at Ardiecow on Tuesday and on Wednesday by 2 o'clock it was all in the coryard. He has got 18 stacks while we have sixteen.

Thursday was a dull wet day, we were making rapes the whole day! I was over that night (by special invitation) at Kirkton at tea, along with Mr. F. Mackintosh, medical student, Mr. and Mrs. Lorimer M.A. Schoolmaster, Glenlivet. We spent a very pleasant evening. We had various games at cards, and also some excellent music, Miss Duncan on the piano and George and Willie Duncan, Cottertown, on the fiddle.

On Friday we were at the rake it being too blowy to thatch.

Father was at Portsoy on Saturday with some corn, while I was at Ardiecow casting 'divots' to cover the potatoes. I went up for two loads of them this morning, we afterwards were thatching all day, and have got 11 of them covered.

31ˢᵗ

We have had good October weather during the week, it being always fresh. Farmers are getting their cattle kept out, thereby saving both turnips & straw. Turnip tops are still green, and you have not far to go for a load, but if severe frost were coming I fear the late ones could not stand out very well. For those who have stooks standing out however (and there are still some to be seen) the weather has been very bad, not a stook being in condition to lead during the whole week until today.

We were in the cornyard all day on Tuesday, and by five o'clock we had it finished.

I started the plough on Wednesday but the stubbles were exceedingly wet, and they always got worse towards the end of the week.

On Saturday morning the ground was white, and there was a little frost.

Sunday was a nice dry day.

This morning the frost had a good hold but it has been a splendid day. We have been busy lifting at the potatoes and we have got the half of them up. They are a good fair crop the Champions being the best.

1881 November
7ᵗʰ

For this season of the year the weather during the week has been good. Everyone was busy in the first of it lifting potatoes but Tuesday and Wednesday were cold windy days and not very suitable for the purpose.

We were working at them however on Tuesday and by dinner time on Wednesday we got through with them. We had 12 loads altogether.

I was in the plough on Thursday. In the afternoon I had the young mare when she went very well.

Friday was our fast day and also our thanksgiving day for the harvest. We had Mr. Wilson, Backside, officiating. In the evening I went over to The Newton, and was not a little surprised to find Mary Wilson, Limestones, and Mr. Raffan, Knowiemoor there before me. We spent a jolly night however. George played the fiddle and we danced—we got a grand tea—we had songs and Miss E. Geddes played the piano, and at half past ten we were very sorry to part.

We had a day of steam mills on Saturday. Father was at Carestown at one, while I was at Ordens at another. A shower in the middle of the day stopped us for three hours and we had back to go this morning. This has been a specially fine day. Quiet bright sunshiny and warm. I was in the plough in the afternoon with the young mare while Father was at the Smiddy. Willie Robb, Kirkton, was down seeing us this afternoon. They have given up the shop and Willie is going away south.

14th

Another week of excellent weather—fresh and warm. The grass is growing green again and cattle are out the half of the day. Work is progressing fast, stubbles in general being more than half ploughed. We have the piece below the house finished, also the parkie before the door and have commenced the Den's.

I was in the plough on Tuesday.

Wednesday was Hallow Fair, and I seldom saw it a better day. I took a 'yokin' at the plough in the forenoon. In the afternoon I went down to the market with the young mare for sell. There were not many horses at all. We managed to sell however, but at rather a low price £25 being all we could make. Mearns, beside the Bogmuchal School, being the buyer. I got home about 7 o'clock.

On Thursday I was at the steam mill at Kirkton. It was a nice quiet day and most suitable for thrashing. I was carrying barley all day. There was a good turn out, and of fair quality. After supper, George Duncan tuned his fiddle and we had a nice dance.

Next day I was at the Manse but we were through there by dinner time.

I was in the plough on Saturday forenoon. In the afternoon Father went to Cornhill Station for a box which was coming from Cleland, while I was driving some brushwood for Lizzie Ritchie.

Today I was in the plough.

21ˢᵗ

Although not so mild & warm as last week, the weather still continues very seasonable. Some days were showery and a little cold, but we had others—fine fresh dry blowy days.

Yesterday and today especially were very fine days. The stubbles are in splendid condition and are growing quite seed coloured after the plough.

On Tuesday we were thrashing, winnowing and taking in the remainder of the old straw.

I was ploughing on Wednesday forenoon. In the afternoon I went to the mill with a load of corn, and went up past the Smiddy.

On Thursday morning the ground was partly white, but it soon disappeared before the sun. Father was over at Alex Gordon's roup. They are all going to emigrate to New Zealand. I was driving top-dressing on to the lea. Joan and I were over at Ardens at our tea. James and Maggie Maitland were also there. We spent the evening playing at quartettes.

I was in the plough all day on Friday. I am ploughing the Den with one furrow.

On Saturday I was furring up turnips. The ground was fine and dry and I did 52 drills.

I was not at church on Sunday, but Father, Joan and Willie were.

I was in the plough today. Ardiecow's sheep has been 2 days on our grass this week.

28ᵗʰ

The past week has been characterised by strong gales of wind. On some days it increased in violence to such an extent as to do great damage— blowing down straw ricks, turring houses, and blowing down trees. It has been dry however, and ploughing is getting on briskly. A few have commenced the lea, but I think it would be rather dry.

On Tuesday forenoon we had a tremendous gale of wind. It did a good deal of damage among our houses, but none in the cornyard.

The thatched houses are a sad nuisance, especially in such an exposed place as this. I did not yoke in the forenoon, but was oiling some of the harness. I was in the plough in the afternoon. It was still very blowy with some terrible showers of hail.

On Wednesday Father, Joan and I were at Oathillock at the steam mill. It was very windy and rather disagreeable working. I was carrying barley along with David McBain. There was a good out turn of grain that is from the bulk of straw, and it appeared to be of fair quality. We were through by 2 o'clock, when we afterwards went down to Walter Gray's and thrashed 2 stack of barley which he had.

I was ploughing all day on Thursday. In the evening I went over to Kirkton to see 'Katie'—my own 'Katie'—my darling 'Katie'. After milking the cows, which I attended of course, we had a few games at whist.

Friday was a nice dry day, and the wind moderate. As soon as it was daylight I commenced to pull turnips for storing. They are a good fair crop and I kept very busy all day, but before night my back was getting very sore.

On Saturday Father and Willie gathered them into small pits and covered them. In the afternoon Father went to the mill and Smiddy. I was driving turnips.

Yesterday Father, Joan, Willie and I were at church. I went over to Limestones in the afternoon. Miss Helen Cowie, Hillside, was there. Mrs. Raffan, Knowiemoor, and the two Misses Raffan, were also over at tea. They are nice like girls, one of them being very pretty, tall and handsome.

I finished the Den this forenoon and commenced to plough the field on Ardiecow which we are to crop again. I was for back-furrowing it and not ploughing it until Spring. I think we would have been surer of a crop.

1881 December
5ᵗʰ

We have enjoyed 8 days of the finest of winter weather. Except Wednesday which was extremely windy and Sunday which was frosty the rest of the week was mild & warm. Ploughing and storing turnips has been the work of the week. Stubbles in general are done and lea is being turned over.

I was ploughing at the stubbles on Ardiecow on Tuesday and Wednesday forenoons.

On Tuesday afternoon we were taking in a stack and thrashing. I afterwards went to the Smiddy.

On Wednesday afternoon Father went to the plough while I went to the Smiddy with some swingletrees.

I was at the plough again on Thursday. The afternoon however was showery and I did not yoke.

Next morning I thought the stubbles some wet so I started the lea and have been ploughing at it since.

On Saturday afternoon we were thrashing and taking home some trees from the Cotton Hill. About 4.30 I set out for Finnygaud. The evening was quiet, fresh and warm and one would almost have thought it was the close of a Spring day instead of one in gloomy December. It was nice moonlight, but the roads were shocking bad. I got there before 7 o'clock and found them all well.

Sunday morning there was a white frost, and the ground hard. They were all at church except Willie and Jessie. Jemmie is always very busy. Mary was away at Banff. I started for home at half past five but I went in past Muttonbrae and it was 9 before I got home.

12th

Such fine weather as we were before enjoying, could not at this season of the year have been expected to last. The first of the week was fine, dry, fresh days, but since Friday we have had frost and snow.

On Tuesday I was ploughing at the 'yavals'.[43]

Father went to the plough on Wednesday, while Lizzie Ritchie & I were pulling turnips to store.

Thursday was Cornhill market. Father was over at it. Cattle of every kind were selling well. Fat at 78/- per cwt.

Friday morning was very frosty. I tried the plough, but it was too hard.

On Saturday morning I went to Portsoy and took the first train to Banff. My errand was to see the conditions of let of the farm of Netherton of Maryhill in the parish of Monquither which were to be seen with Mr. Bow, Merchant, Macduff; and also to see if I could get a young calf. I found two for sale, but they were too young, and the parties needing too much money.

I then went across to Macduff, where I got all the information about the place which Mr. Bow could give me. I found however, that it was a good bit farther from Turriff than I was thinking, being 9 miles, and 5 miles from Auchterless Railway Station. The office houses are new but the dwelling house is old and thatched. On consideration we do not think we will go and see it.

Today we were filling the mill and thrashing. In the evening I went over to Berryhillock I came down past Kirkton.

29th

The weather for the last week of December has been delightful. Everyone is busy at the plough while some are storing turnips.

I was ploughing on Tuesday forenoon. In the afternoon we took in a stack and also thrashed some.

Wednesday I ploughed all day also today. I am just newly come home from the Lintmill. I was down seeing Mrs. Duguid and got a small parcel for Maggie. Mother and Father were at Ardiecow at their tea. I am to go up to Keith tomorrow afternoon with the train. Uncle

---

[43] yavals, ground on which a crop of grain is grown on the same ground for the second year.

George is to take my basket down to the station as Father is going to the Manse.

And so, two more days and 1881 will be no more. It has been a year marked by many casualties especially in these last few months. As regards agriculture it has not been a very prosperous one. The seedtime was good, but the summer was cold and uncongenial.

VOLUME THREE
29 JUNE 1885-7 MAY 1888

1885 June[1]
29th

The summer days have come at last, and we have had a week of very
fine weather. We had some nice showers in the first of the week, and
then it turned extremely warm. Crops have improved considerably,
excepting turnips, which are not yet making very rapid progress. Our
yellow ones are doing best, I think some of them will hoe in a week.

Nobody has commenced the hoe in Deskford yet but I see some of
them cleaning the sides of the drills.

On Tuesday we went to the moss and set the peats. As there had
been a good deal of rain the previous night they were not very dry, but
it was a fine day and they were much better before we got through. I
went down past the Backies to ask for Willie McWillie as he has got a
very bad cut in the leg. He got it by falling on a scythe and the Dr. had
to be got to sow it. A large tendon has been cut, and he has to lie in
bed, and keep it in one position. I came down past the school, as there
was to be a meeting in connection with the Picnic. I was greatly on for
something new, and proposed that a flower show be held on the same
day. I did not get many supporters however, and so I expect it will just
be something the same as in former years.

On Wednesday forenoon I went down to Cullen for four bags of
cement. We were knocking down the old stable in the afternoon. In
the evening I went down to Fordyce to see their picnic. It was the
smallest gathering I ever saw at Fordyce, and there also seemed to be
very little spirit at the dancing.

We were putting cope stones on to the dyke beside the peat stack
on Thursday.

On Friday, Willie and I were at the moss driving gravel on to the
road.

---

[1] Volume 2 of the Journal covering the period 1882-1885 is missing.

We were putting in a drain on Saturday to take the water out of the close. I went down to Cullen in the afternoon for two loads of gravel. It was pay-day with the navvies and the town was swarming.

Father, Joan, Jessie and I were at church on Sunday. Father went up to the Backies.

Today, I was laying the floor of the joiner's shop with cement.

I took off a swarm of bees on Thursday, but I had failed to secure the Queen and by 8 o'clock they were all back again.

1885 July
6th

We have had nice warm days during the week, but it has been very, very dry and everything is suffering from the drought. Oats especially on clay land have lost much of their dark green colour and I fear some of the crops will be rather light. Barley has suffered less, and in general I think it will be a fair crop. The heat has greatly improved the potatoes, but I hear of them being blanky in many places. Ours are coming up well. Turnips have also advanced a good bit during the last eight days, and many are now at the hoe. There are some fields still however, far from being promising. I saw Ardoch re-sowing in the first of the week.

On Tuesday and Wednesday we were hoeing and furring up the potatoes.

On Thursday I scuffled the swedes, and we then commenced to cleaning the side of the drills.

I went to the moss on Friday to see the peats. They were pretty dry and I have been driving some since.

13th

On Tuesday morning Willie and I rose at 4 o'clock and went to the moss for two loads of peats. I have not been driving any since. We have been busy at the hoe. The turnips have greatly improved since last I wrote. We would finish the singling in three days I think.

On Tuesday and Saturday we had nice showers of rain but the wind always got up on the back of them, and dried them up too quickly.

Last night however, we had an hour and half of a good heavy rain, and today has been quiet and warm.

On Tuesday afternoon Father went over to Cornhill Station to meet Tom Stirling who was coming to spend a few weeks with us. He has not been very well for sometime, and the Dr. ordered him to go to the country for sometime. He arrived all right but was a little wet before getting home.

Him and I went over to Kirkton on Friday evening and opened the Library. There was but a small attendance, as this is scarcely the season for reading. It is intended to call in all the books belonging to the Library next month to have them all re-arranged and get a new catalogue printed.

James Lorimer, shoemaker, Kirkton died on Saturday at 2 o'clock. He has been laid up for about two months and has suffered greatly. He is to be buried tomorrow.

Mother, Jessie, Tom, Willie and I were all at church. In the afternoon Tom and I went up to Backies. We went in past to see Mrs Riddoch and got tea from her. We then went up to see Willie and Miss McWillie. Willie's leg is always keeping better and he is now able to walk a little with the help of a staff. There were two nice ladies there and being good singers we tried over some tunes. Miss McWillie accompanying us on the harmonium.

20th

We have had a week of exceptionally fine weather. Nice showers with warm sunshine. There is a marked improvement on everything. We have been busy all the week at the hoe, until Saturday when we finished the singling.

I was in the moss today, and the peats are now perfectly dry.

On Tuesday evening I went over to Kirkton to make the necessary arrangements for the Picnic.

Wednesday was a beautiful day. A better afternoon for the Picnic could not have been. The turn out, however, was scarcely up to an average, but at the same time everyone I think heartily enjoyed themselves. There was a fair competition at the games. Mr. Burnet, Drybridge carrying off the medal with 16 points; while our floormaster Mr. Bremner got the committee's special prize for dancing. Tea was served at five o'clock, and the dancing which before had been a little stiff was now heartily engaged in and kept up till the close. As I had presented Miss Mathieson with a ticket (a young lady from Aberdeen at present staying at Backies) I had the pleasure of escorting her home.

The bees have of course been engaging the greater part of my leisure time during the week. I have now got eight or nine swarms (more than I was wanting). I have on a good many sections but they are only commencing to fill them yet. As I had a swarm off today I will have to stop and go and see after it.

27th

Driving peats and cutting hay has been the most of my week's work. There was a meeting of the Picnic Committee on Tuesday evening. Had there not been a small sum in hand we would have been short of cash. As it was we just escaped with the skin of our teeth.

I was twice in the moss everyday until Thursday, when I took an afternoon at the hay. It was excessively warm.

Peter-Fair was held on Friday. It was a big market and fees on an average were down 10/.[2] There was also a large turn out of horses, but a very stiff sale. Father was at the market, and I was at the hay again.

We took home the last of the peats on Saturday, but there is not a very big stack. There were just 36 loads out of 73 score. I was furring up the potatoes in the afternoon.

We had late sermon on Sunday as the minister is away at Strathpeffer. It was a minister from Aberdeen who was preaching. When the church got out Uncle George and I went to up Swailand. Willie Bidie and Tom had gone over before.

I was running turnips this forenoon and in the afternoon we coled the hay.

The weather during the week has been dry and warm. The warmest we have yet had. The drought indeed is beginning to be rather severe and water everywhere is drying up fast. The Highland Society's Show is to be held at Aberdeen this year, on the four last days of the present month. I am thinking of going in to see it on Thursday and I will probably stay until Friday night. A good many are going from Deskford.

1885 August
3rd

Another week of dry weather, but not nearly so warm. The drought is beginning to tell however, especially on the pasture, which is burning up terribly. Turnips as yet are doing well. Some of ours are nearly meeting on the drills.

On Tuesday morning I went up to the moss for two loads of peats for Mr. Smith. In the afternoon we cut the seed hay. Some of it was a good crop, but I fear there will not be much seed, as the rye grass has got a very small stalk.

We were at the hoe on Wednesday. I went down in the evening to Fordyce and bought some honey. I am going to send it to a dealer in Edinburgh where I expect to make a small profit off it.

On Thursday morning I got up at four o'clock and started for Cornhill. I met Cultain and Clashendamer and we went down to the Station together.

A good many passengers went on at Cornhill and when changing at Grange we fell in with a good many Deskford people, the most of whom, had gone on at Tochineal.

---

[2] Wilson wrote 10/ for 10/-, or 10 shillings.

The morning was very misty and until we got to Inverurie we could see but little of the crops and country. The best oats I saw were on Bogie side. In general they are a light crop. Barley is much better and about Inverurie some fields are beginning to turn yellow. We arrived at Aberdeen at half past nine, just up to time. There were 24 carriages and two engines from Grange, but everyone had plenty room I think. After getting a cup of coffee and something to eat, we started direct for the Show, which is held on the Queen's Links. Twenty five acres were enclosed, and everything except the machinery in motion was under cover. I first inspected the horses which were a grand display. Among the cattle and sheep the Highland bulls, and blackfaced rams greatly excited my admiration. The implements were a show of themselves. I never saw such a collection in my life. There were machines for doing everything under the sun I think. I was greatly pleased with the Bee Show and spent two hours in the same. There was a great deal of Bee apparatus, which I had never seen before. I also saw some splendid big supers of honey. I noticed the words 'Aberdeen Show 1885' very ingeniously formed of honeycomb. I went in to see the drilling, which was in an adjoining tent. It was done with great expedition, and the performer succeeded in securing the Queen, which he placed in a glass tumbler, along with a drone and a worker bee and handed round for inspection.

I left the Show about six o'clock and went up to Uncles. I found them all quite well. After tea we went down to the Station with Mina who is engaged at the Free Manse of Cults.

Next morning I took a walk down the length of Union Street, and took a turn through the New Market. It was burned down a few years ago and has been all re-built and it is greatly improved from what it was formerly. Being market day it presented a very busy scene. The farmers' wives of the surrounding district all bring in their butter and eggs for sale, and as I saw them seated close beside each other round almost the entire circuit of the market it presented a sight the like of which I had never seen before.

After breakfast I started with Uncle and Jemmie to see the Duthie Park. It is situated on the South West side of the town, between the Dee-side railway and the river Dee and just adjoining the Allanvale Churchyard. It is the largest pleasure park I was ever in, covering 45 acres of ground and it certainly was a very handsome present for the lady whose name it bears, to present to the town of Aberdeen. It is beautifully laid out, and so nicely kept. There are two entrances with lodges for the gatekeepers. At one end there is an artificial mound of considerable height, from the top of which a splendid view is obtained of the lower valley of the Dee and on which is shortly to be erected a handsome monument to the memory of William Wallace. Near to the mound is a beautiful Fountain of Aberdeen granite, erected by the Good Templars of the Town and a drink of which is said to satisfy your thirst for all time. Lower down nearer the river are two or three ponds with a series of falls between. Tiny islets covered with the greenest verdure and the richest vegetation are dotted here and there over the surface of these, the Lotus and Victoria Lily display their rare and lovely flowers; while swans, ducks, water hens and other aquatic birds swim about among the reeds and bullrushes or plume themselves on the green banks. A large space in the centre has been levelled, but no shrubs nor trees planted. This is to be used as ground for playing cricket, lawn tennis, croquet and other outdoor recreations. A splendid rockery has also been erected, with wild flowers of every description looking out from its many nooks and crannies.

Truly the citizens of Bon-Accord are extremely fortunate in possessing a Park of such rare dimensions to which they can resort at anytime, for pleasure or pastime.

After dinner I went and called on Mr. Adam, also on George Bidie. Uncle and I then went and saw the Art Exhibition and took a turn through the Victoria Park. At 5.45 I was at the Station, where I met the most of my company and started for home.

10th

No more cry for rain I expect. The whole week has been moist and misty, and some days there was a lot of rain. The appearance of everything has been greatly improved especially the turnips. Ours are all close on the drills. We have hardly hoed any during the week, as they were always some wet. We were cleaning out the ditch in the den and casting some drains. We are going to put a big tile in the ditch and cover it in. It will require to be deepened a good bit down however, and until that be done we cannot get on as the water cannot get away.

Jessie and I were up at the Backies one afternoon at our tea. There was a good large company and we spent a very pleasant evening.

Willie and I went over to Finnygaud on Saturday afternoon and came home on Sunday. Jamie Cowie's wife has been very unwell for the last six weeks and is scarcely any better yet. It commenced like the rose in her face, but it is better now, and it is into her thigh. It is extremely painful and she can scarcely turn herself in her bed. Mary Cowie is also in a very bad way. For about a year back she has been in a desponding state of mind, and she seems to be always growing worse. I am really afraid that her reason is giving way.

17ᵗʰ

The whole week has been foggy, and we have scarcely got a blink of the sun at all. It has been bad weather for the bees and I fear there is to be little more honey got this season. It has not been very good weather for anything however, and on Thursday we had a tremendous hurricane of wind and rain which did a vast amount of damage both by sea and land. It has broken down the crops terribly, while the young turnips have been nearly buried with mud. I also see by the newspapers that great damage has been done to the fishing boats: many of them having been wrecked, and also some lives lost. We have not been doing anything of much consequence during the week, the water in the den preventing us from casting any more drains.

On Wednesday and Thursday I was driving tiles for the big drain, and I also took some loads of smaller ones.

24ᵗʰ

Little improvement on the weather yet. Cold, dull, misty days. The turnips are the only crop that has made any improvement. They have recovered from the hurricane of last week and are looking well.

On Tuesday we were cutting grass for bedding in the plantation, also some sprotts for rapes.

The Cullen Flower Show was held on Wednesday. Willie and I went down to Tochineal Station in the morning with some honey, which I was sending to Edinburgh. We went in to Cullen with a big super of honey for the Show. There was no competition for honey, but I thought I might have a chance of getting a merchant for it. Mr. Morrison, the Secretary, was to take charge of it for me. I went down in the evening. Several parties had been looking at it, but Mr. Morrison ultimately bought it himself. The Show was about an average of former years, but there were very few seeing it.

Mother and Jessie started that morning for Keith. Mother was going to Elgin to see Mary Wilson. She found her much better, but still very far from right. They came home again on Friday evening.

I have been busy in the evenings revising the catalogue of the books in the Library. The books were all taken in last night the Library was open. They have now been inspected, and numbered while a few have been sent off to be rebound.

31ˢᵗ

We have had a week of much brighter weather and consequently there has been a great improvement in the ripening of the crops. I hear that on several farms at the coast side they are to commence harvesting this week. It will be two weeks yet before we get any I think.

There was a sale of wood in Cottonhill plantation on Tuesday last. There was a good number of people and the wood sold well. Father bought two lots and a lot of brushwood. Driving the brushwood has been the most of our week's work.

On Tuesday afternoon Mother, Jessie and I were invited down to Cairntown to tea. After getting a sight through the offices (which have been all recently repaired) we went to have a look at the crops. They are all looking extremely well, his barley being a splendid crop. He is a very good farmer I think, however, I see he has two great heaps of earth for top-dressing for his lea. One mixed with dung and the other with lime. Mrs. Runcie, Bruntbrae, is staying there just now. She was inviting me to go down and see her, and so Cairnton and I were going down on Saturday first.

On Friday evening Miss Mackintosh, Ardiecow, came down to see us. She has got a school now at Glasnacardoch near Arasaig in the west of Invernessshire. Maggie also went to stay with her in the first of summer.

I went up with them on Sunday afternoon to the top of the hill of Summerton and had a fine view with the glass. We saw Bennachie, The Tap O' North, and also the Cairn O' Morven quite distinctly.

We were building the hay on Saturday and we got a very fine day. We have only two small stacks.

1885 September
7*th*

Another week of good weather and crops are hastening on to maturity. There are no stooks in the parish yet however, and I fear it will be the end of the week before there be many yet. During the week we have been tidying up and doing any odd jobs before beginning harvest.

On Thursday we were in the cornyard, cutting the grass, and cleaning it away from the stack 'foons'. Jessie, Joan and I went down at Miltown at tea that evening. There was a good large company. After tea we went out to see the garden and also took a walk at the burn side. It was a beautiful evening, and before going in we had a game at 'French taekery'. We then adjourned to the house, when the fiddle was tuned, and with songs and dancing a couple of hours were spent very pleasantly.

I was at the Smiddy on Friday. I went in past as I came home and paid J. Lorimer and A. Brander for the honey I got from them. We were in the 'Den' on Saturday casting a drain. After dinner I dressed and went down to Cairnton, as him and I were going down to Bruntbrae to see Mr. and Mrs. Runcie. It was a nice afternoon when I started but before I got down it had turned very black toward the west, and a few peals of thunder were heard. Before we started there were some tremendous loud peals and all the way into Portsoy the lightning flashed, and it rumbled away almost without stopping. On some parts of the road the rain had been in torrents, while at others it was quite dry. We escaped however, without a drop. We saw some stooks about Portsoy and two fields of very good barley were cut on Auchmore. They were also cutting on Kindrought the adjoining farm. We then passed on our left the farms of Smiddyboyne and Cairnton of Boyndie where we saw some splendid turnips (the best in all our travels). A little beyond Smiddyboyne we crossed the Burn of the Boyne with the wool mill close beside it. Ordens of Boyndie was the next farm we passed through. It seems to be very good land, while the cattle grazing in the parks were of very superior quality. We here left the Banff turnpike, crossed the railway and took to the hill passing the farms of Raggal and Baldavie on the one side, and the large farm of Blairshinnoch on the other. On looking back as we climbed the brae, we got a fine view of the hallow of the Boyne. The farms of Rettie were right opposite to us, lying so nicely to the sun, and some of the land of which is said to be the finest in Banffshire. The Lunatic Asylum is farther down, while the church and manse is a little nearer the sea. About a mile above Baldavie we passed the farm and school of Hilton also on our left the farms of Todholes and Denhead with Backhill on our right. The land here stands rather high and would be some exposed I should think to the north wind. Turning the summit of the hill we began to descend and soon came in sight of Strath of Brydoch. At Mill of Brydoch (which is right below the Strath and close beside the turnpike which leads from Banff to Aberchirder) we turned to our right and held up the road about half a mile. The land of Bruntbrae comes down to the road while the houses are a rig length up from it. The dwelling house is rather small and the office houses are old and thatched.

We were heartily welcomed by Mr. & Mrs. Runcie, and tea was ready waiting us. Mr. & Mrs. Hendry of Strath were also there, Mrs. Hendry being a sister of Mr. Runcie. After tea we went out to see the cattle which were being brought home. He has 8 good cows, and also some thriving three year olds. On returning to the house Mr. Runcie who is a great fiddler, produced his 'freen' and his sister accompanying him on the piano, they treated us to some excellent music. He is indeed a splendid fiddler, his whole soul seeming to take possession of his bow arm. Mr. Runcie is Inspector of Poor for the parish of Alvah and also Clerk to the School Board. He showed me all his books and gave me much information regarding both the offices. It was two o'clock in the morning before we went to bed.

Sunday morning was fine. We got up at half past eight and went out to have a look at Mr. Runcie's crops. His turnips had been very stiff to start and are still rather thin. His barley however is good and also his lea corn. He works on the 7 course shift and the land being soft his ayvels are rather dirty.[3] By the time we finished breakfast it was nearly time to start for church. Bruntbrae is about 2½ miles from the church of Alvah, but Mr. Runcie took his machine and we had a nice drive. We passed the farm of Firfolds and went through the slacks of Tipperty. We here got a sight on our left of the old castle of Inchdrewer, while right down before us we could see the top of Duff House peeping out among the trees. A little below the houses of Tipperty we turned off the Banff road and held to our right toward the Deveron and then opposite the farm of Mill of Alvah we got a grand sight of the far famed Brig of Alvah. It is indeed a very romantic spot and I would have liked greatly to get a closer inspection of it. Where the Bridge crosses the river, the water is confined between two high rocks and so narrow are those that tradition affirms that a man at one time leaped across to escape his pursuers. From the top of the bridge to the water is fifty feet, and it is said there is the same depth of water below. The Church of Alvah stands on an eminence overlooking the valley of the Deveron. It is surrounded by the churchyard while the manse is situated on one side and the school and school house on the other. It is a nice little church having been lately reseated, varnished, heated and otherwise improved. They have also got a harmonium and the congregation stand while singing and sit at prayers. In the afternoon we went across to Strath to tea, Mr. & Mrs. Runcie coming along with us. Old Mrs. Runcie is still alive but she is about four score I think. We started for home at six and I was home by nine.

Today we were draining in the den.

14th

The past week has not been a very good one. There has not been much sunshine, while there has been rather severe gales of wind and rain. Mixing top dressing for the lea has been the most of our week's work.

On Wednesday afternoon Jessie and I were over at Kirkton at tea. Messrs. G. & J. Smith Blairock were also there, and we spent a pleasant evening at the cards.

On Friday evening the Library was again re-opened. During the past month I have been inspecting and re-arranging all the books. I

---

[3] ayvels, same meaning as yavals, ground on which a crop of grain is grown for the second year running.

have now got them in good order, and have also got a new catalogue printed.

Saturday was a terrible day of wind and rain. I drummed a hive of bees in the forenoon and also took out some frames. It cleared in the afternoon, when I took them up to the Backies. Willie had got the loan of an extractor and so we tried our hand at extracting the honey. The frames wrought nicely, but the combs from the hive did not do so well. It would have been a sight for sore eyes to see us all at work with our coats off and our aprons on. Miss McWillie, Currie and I did the uncapping while Willie and the 'orra man' wrought the extractor.[4]

Sunday was a bright sunny day but there was a great gale of wind. Between twelve and two o'clock it rose to something like a hurricane and there is word of corn and barley in exposed places being shaken.

Today has been bright and breezy and we commenced the harvest by cutting some in the den. The braes are quite ripe, but I scarcely think we will get steady work. A great many in the parish have also begun today.

21st

It has not been very good harvest weather during the week. There has been some rain almost every day. We have not got many stooks yet, but it was needing all its ripeness and so we were never pushing.

We scarcely cut any on Tuesday it being wet.

On Wednesday afternoon we got a 'yokin' of the machine on the farthest 'Knowe'.

On Thursday we cut the hill and some more in the 'Den'.

We did not cut any on Friday and Saturday. We were gathering stones on the lea and driving them off.

Jessie, Joan, Willie and I were at church on Sunday. I saw Willie Stuart and his young wife in church. He was married on Friday. His wife is one of the Wrights of Netherton Grange. The Minister preached from John XIV. 6. 'I am the Way, the Truth and the Life'.

Father was at the funeral on Saturday of John Cowie, Inaltrie. He died on Wednesday last. He has been very poorly for the last three years, and has suffered a great deal. He was buried in the churchyard of Ordiquhill.

Last night there was a lot of rain, but today has been fine. We made roads round the barley, and in the afternoon we got four hours of the reaper. The crop is the best I ever saw on the same field.

During the week I have been reading in the evenings a book by Robert Chambers 'Vestiges of the Natural History of Creation'. The

---

[4] orra man, odd job man.

principal aim of the writer is to show, that the world was not created in six days, as the Bible would lead us to believe. Instead of this he affirms that the world must have been in existence countless ages, before man appeared on the scene. That it was inhabited by different species of animals and the sea by many varieties of fishes, both of them extremely different from that now to be found. He also asserts that these fishes, animals etc. have during these untold ages been undergoing a state of development, have been gradually progressing from the more simple forms of life which existed during the earliest ages, down to that state of perfection (if perfection it may yet be called) which exists at the present day. All these assertions are based on what he calls the testimony of the rocks. The crust of the earth he says, is formed of many layers of different substances, granite, Sandstone, Coal, etc. etc. These strata must undoubtedly have been formed and deposited by the action of water, and each of these also must have taken a considerable length of time to accumulate. The fossils of the fishes and animals living at the time of these formations are at the present day to be found in what is now the solid rock. Of course the farther down we go the older must be the formation. All this seems to be very natural, but how it can be reconciled to the testimony of revelation which tells us that the world with all the beasts and birds and creeping things were created in the space of six days, I cannot as yet perceive.

28th

Stormy weather has prevailed during the week. The proverbial equinoctial gales I expect. The wind has mostly blown from North and North-East, and there has been occasional showers every day. It has not been 'forcy' harvest weather at all, at all and only a few in Deskford have got clyack yet.

We were cutting at the barley on the Tuesday. We then went to the lea. It is a light crop. We cut it all today and commenced the yavels. Another day would cut the most of them I think. They are a fair crop. We have then only the hallow in the 'Den'. The most of it will be to cut with the scythe however, as it is badly twisted.

I went up to Ardiecow on Friday evening to pay the People's Friend. Mr. Wyness, Slackdale was there. They had commenced the harvest that day, and one of the 'hands' being a fiddler we went ben to the kitchen and had a dance.

1885 October
5th

A week of excellent harvest weather. Real October weather and no mistake. A great deal of work has been done since last I wrote. Except small patches about the hill sides no standing corn is to be seen, while a good few have got it all in the stackyard. It has been grand days for winning the stooks, cold hard winds, but at times a little too blowy perhaps.

We were cutting at the yavels on Tuesday and on Wednesday we cut them out. They are a fair crop.

On Thursday we led the barley in splendid condition.

We also led some on Friday forenoon but the afternoon was showery.

We took clyack in the 'Den' on Saturday. It was terribly laid and twisted and had to be all cut with the scythe. We were thankful to have it to cut however as it will always help the bulk a bit.

I was not in church on Sunday, but I went over to Muttonbrae in the afternoon. Uncle had also got in two stacks.

There was a rank dew this morning and there was no leading till afternoon. In the forenoon we were taking home turnips and tares and making rapes.

12th

The good weather which I reported last week has not had long continuance.

Tuesday was all that could be desired but since then it has been exceedingly stormy. A cold north wind with driving showers of sleet and hail. There has been no leading and scarcely any cutting during the week. There is still some to cut on Ardiecow and about the upper end of the parish. Cutting thatch and making rapes have been the most of our week's work. Some have been thatching their stacks, but they were always too wet I think.

Thursday was Cornhill market day. There were but few cattle went past this, but it was a fair size of a market. It was extremely stiff however, many a one never being offered money. Father bought a ram going past and he bought a ewe for me in the market.

I went over to Kirkton on Friday evening and opened the Library. The night was rainy and there was but few attended.

Sunday was a better day. The wind had gone round to the West, and it was quiet and sunshiny. Father, Mother, Jessie and I were at church. The minister preached from the text, 'Unto the upright there ariseth light in the darkness'. In the afternoon I went up to see my 'friends' at Backies. Willie has only a few stacks of barley in, but they have some to cut on Langlinburn. I was expecting it would be fit to lead this morning again, but there had been a good many showers throughout the night and I was disappointed. The wind has also gone back to the North, and since dinnertime it has increased to something like a gale, while the showers have been mixed with good hard hail.

19ᵗʰ

On Tuesday morning everyone commenced to lead, but the stooks were not very dry. Father went away to the Smiddy in the forenoon but after dinner we also started. By the time we had one stack in however, the rain was on, and there has been no more leading since. I went up to Ardiecow that evening. They took clyack that day, and they were having a dance. Miss Mackintosh was to leave for Glasnacardoch on Friday morning.

Between Tuesday and Wednesday there had been much rain, as the burns were all greatly swollen. I went down to Jemmie Gray's in the afternoon and got the wood sawn which I bought at Cotton Hill sale. I got the most of it sawn up to make bee hives.

On Thursday morning I yoked the plough and drew some furs for drains. I went down to Tochineal in the afternoon for some tiles.

Friday and Saturday were quiet warm days but there was very little drying. On Friday afternoon we started to thatch the stacks and as we had everything in readiness, we got them finished off on Saturday.

Sunday forenoon was showery, but the afternoon was hard and dry, and everyone was in the expectation of getting to the leading this morning. There had been no rain through the night and the stooks were in fair order, but they did not long continue so for soon the rain was on again. In the forenoon we were putting top dressing on to the lea (lime and earth). After dinner we began to cart up the stooks in the 'Den' so that they might get a little more chance of the drying. We had only up a few loads however, when it turned too wet. A good many have commenced the plough, some of them with the stooks standing along side.

26ᵗʰ

Turning heated stacks has been the only approach to harvest work done during the week. Ours are all keeping fine, but reports of them being otherwise are quite general.

We were driving up the remainder of the stooks in the Den on Tuesday, but they were very wet. There was a lecture in the School that evening, Mr. Benzie a blind lecturer from Banff. His subject was Matrimony and he gave us a very humorous but at the same time very instructive lecture. He commenced by reading a chapter from the New Testament. He then explained how the blind were taught to read and write and showed us samples of the different systems of writing— Moon's, Rails etc. A Blind person he said could correspond with another similarly afflicted but of course in doing so the letters had to be large and raised so that the receiver could feel them. This sort of writing was accomplished by placing thick paper between two brass plates, the upper one being full of small holes. A stole or style as he called it, was then used, and the letters were formed by piercing the paper through these small holes. The letters had something like this appearance Monday [written in dots by Wilson]. The paper being thick each hole was raised on the under side, and so a blind person could feel them. This was Moon's system. I did not understand the other as plainly. He related many humorous anecdotes, but he also gave us much sound advice. He said for instance that a young man should make sure that the woman who was to be his wife was a religious person, healthy, good tempered, cleanly, thrifty, etc, etc. After a lecture on Matrimony of course I had to see a young lady home.

On Wednesday I commenced to break fur the yavels.

I was also at it on Thursday. The ground that morning was white with snow, and it was midday before it melted.

On Friday there was a very serve frost, half an inch of ice on the watering trough. Father was at Fordyce for a cask of paraffin while I was driving dung onto a piece of stubbles for potatoes.

I was ploughing stubbles on Saturday but they were rather wet.

Sunday was a nice dry day, but rain came on in the evening, and it had rained all night I think. Willie and I were digging gravel in Carestons quarry in the forenoon, and in the afternoon we were driving turnips.

1885 November
2nd

There were three dry days during the past week, the others were wet. A good many stooks have disappeared, but a good few are still to be seen. One morning only was frosty.

On Tuesday and Wednesday I was ploughing stubbles, but they were rather wet.

I was in the yoke on Thursday morning but the steam mill was at Ordens, and they came over for me as they were very scarce of hands. It was a fine day and his barley was all thrashed except two stacks. Father and Willie managed to get in the last of our corn that day. I think the cornyard is just about the same size as last year.

Friday was the Fast Day, but it being a nice dry day everyone mostly was at the leading. The steam mill was at Hoggie and I went over in the morning to give him a hand. I was too late for church before we got through. I went up to Ardiecow in the afternoon and gave them a hand at the leading. They have the most of the clean land to take in yet.

Saturday was wet. In the forenoon we were driving turnips, thrashing and winnowing. In the afternoon we went down to the Den, and laid some tiles in the big drain.

Sunday was also a very wet day, a great deal of rain falling. We were all at church except Willie. It was not well filled however. The minister had no one assisting him, and he did not keep us long. It has been dry today. Father went to the plough in the forenoon, while I was casting divots to cover the potatoes.

9th

A great improvement on the weather. The harvest in this district in now quite finished except it be Bogetra.

They took it all in on Ardiecow on Wednesday.

Father and I were over at Muttonbrae on Tuesday giving Uncle a hand with the steam mill. He got a very nice day. The second meeting of the Mutual Improvement Association was held that evening. At the former meeting Mr. McWillie was elected President, Mr. Taylor Vice President, while Mr. Longmoor was re-elected Secretary.

I was at the plough on Wednesday.

On Thursday we commenced to lift the potatoes. It was frosty in the morning but was a very fine day. The potatoes are a very good crop, far better than I was expecting.

Friday was extremely frosty. It would not have been a good day for lifting potatoes at all, but I was intending going to Keith whatever. It was market day and I got a drive up with Willie McWillie. I was settling my account with Mr. Mitchell and doing other errands. I was also buying a marriage present for my sister Annie. She is coming home to be married in about a month to George Cowie, Cairdswell. It was a parlour lamp, which I bought for her.

We were at the potatoes again Saturday and today.

16th

We have had a week of very good weather, and everyone has been pushing forward the ploughing.

On Tuesday and Wednesday I was ploughing the potato land. Wednesday was Hallow Fair. It was a very nice day. Father was down for a short time. It was a very big market, but the fees were a little down.

We got a letter from Annie on Thursday, wanting Mother to go up to Edinburgh to help her to buy her things and then to come home with her.

She started on Friday morning. I was putting dung onto a piece for potatoes next year. We are also going to plough down the rest of the dung.

I was in the plough on Saturday. It was a cold windy day.

The minister intimated on Sunday that Wednesday would be observed as a Thanksgiving Day for the harvest.

The frost was very hard this morning. I went to the plough but had it not been for the dung I would not have managed at all.

I have been busy in the evenings during the week writing a paper for a debate against Disestablishment.[5] I have neglected to mention that Mr. Darling the Conservative candidate for Banffshire held a political meeting in the Schools on Tuesday evening. There was a good attendance, but a large proportion were strangers. Mr. Darling was received with cheers and hisses, and during his speech he was repeatedly interrupted. His speech was wholly taken up criticising the foreign policy of the Liberals, and defending the Church. He is a fluent speaker and a nice looking man, but I do not think his speech would have gained him any supporters.

23rd

We have had a very sharp frost, since last I wrote. Indeed I scarcely ever saw it so severe before Martinmas. Ploughing has been at a standstill and most people have been driving out dung.

We were at it on Tuesday. There was a meeting of the Mutual Improvement, that evening. A good few more became members. I managed to secure a majority of one on the debate.

Wednesday was the Thanksgiving Day. We had Mr. Macdonald from Cullen preaching and we got a very good sermon.

We were in the Den on Thursday putting the tiles into the drains, the water preventing us before, as Ardiecow would never clean out the ditch down below. The frost had the water dried up a good bit, but some of them are not very level. Jessie and I were up at Backies (Mrs. Riddoch's) that evening at a tea party. Mr. & Miss Duncan; Mr. & Miss Shepherd; Mr. & The Misses McWillie were the company. We had a lively discussion on politics, practical farming, matrimony and other interesting subjects.

On Friday I was at the steam mill at Ardiecow. The straw was very damp and the grain was also of inferior quality. I have heard since that it was only 37 lbs per bushel.

Mr. Duff the Liberal candidate for the county, held a meeting in the Schools that evening. There was an extraordinary turn out. The

[5] Printed in Appendix 2.

largest meeting except one I ever saw in the Schools. I had the honour of being introduced to Mr. Duff. He was very well received and he gave an excellent address. He considered the land laws, local government, disestablishment and free education, and many other subjects. At the end of his speech a host of questions were asked, which he answered very readily, although in some cases not very satisfactorily. A vote of confidence was proposed, and also a vote of no confidence, but while only a few supported the amendment the motion was carried with acclamation. The meeting dispersed, with cheers for Duff, Gladstone and Chamberlain.

The poll takes place on Friday first. The polling booth for Deskford is at Portsoy. On Saturday I was assisting at the steam mill at Kirkton. They thrashed their barley and also two stacks of oats. The barley was a fair sample, but badly coloured. The oats were scarcely up to his ordinary standard.

Jessie, Father and I were at church on Sunday.

Geordy Stephen and little Jim were down from Keith. It has been fresh today and I was in the plough. A good many people have been going today, it being the term.

30th

The past week has been a bad one. A great deal of rain fell in the end of the week, and the land is very wet.

On Tuesday I was ploughing. We commenced to pull turnips for storing on Wednesday. The yellow ones are a very good crop, but the swedes are rather small. Swedes in general are not a heavy crop this year. The summer was too cold I think.

Thursday was wet. We were thrashing, winnowing, and cleaning the harness.

Friday forenoon was also extremely wet, and there was also a strong gale of wind. This was the day of the poll for the representation of Parliament. Portsoy was the polling place for this district. I think the electors in Deskford had turned out very well, wet day and all. I was intending going to Portsoy with the cart for a load of coals, but the wet morning prevented me. Father got a hurl with James Wright. Everyone was quiet and decent at Portsoy, but at Buckie I believe they had been a little riotous.

The result of the poll was made known on Saturday, when it was found that Mr. Duff the Liberal candidate had come off victorious with a large majority. In Banffshire there are now 70018 [sic] electors. Of these 5748 recorded their vote, 3740 being in favour of Mr. Duff and 2008 in favour of Mr. Darling. Mr. Duff has therefore gained by a majority of 1732. A great many elections took place last week, and I see by the newspapers, that, although there is little doubt of a Liberal majority still it will not be so great, as was at one time anticipated.

The church question has been the cause of this a good deal in England but the main cause has been the manifesto issued by Mr. Parnell charging Irishmen on no account to vote for a Liberal.

Sunday morning was frosty but there was rain in the afternoon. It has been dry today. Willie and I were among the turnips. Father was at Portsoy for a load of coals. We had a letter in the end of the week saying that Mother and Annie were to be home tomorrow. They were to leave Edinburgh this morning but were to stay a night in Aberdeen.

1885 December
7ᵗʰ

We have had a week of very changeable weather. The first three days were good. The next two were rainy and now we have snow.

Father and I went over to Cornhill on Tuesday to meet Mother. Annie had gone on to Keith. Mother arrived all right, but only part of her luggage. We had both the carts, so Mother went home in one while I unyoked the other, and went up to Cairdswell to wait and see if the other things would come with the five train. I was fortunate enough to get them. It was half past seven before I got home. There was a meeting of the Mutual Improvement that evening, but of course I was a little late. We had a very good meeting however. Mr. McWillie read a excellent paper on 'Civility' and Mr. Longmore another on the Steam Engine. There were also new members joined.

I was in the plough on Wednesday forenoon, while Father and Willie were pulling turnips to store. We gathered them in the afternoon into a long pit. Annie arrived in the evening about seven o'clock. Geordy Cowie had gone to Keith to meet her, so he came home with her, and stayed all night. We were busy all the evening unpacking the boxes.

Thursday was frosty, but it was a nice day.

On Friday morning Father went to the mill and the Smiddy, while Willie and I were pulling and driving home turnips. It became very rainy however, before dinnertime, and by one o'clock it was a perfect hurricane of wind and rain, which continued for about two hours.

Saturday was stormy with hail showers. As the stubbles were too wet I started the lea.

On Sunday morning the ground was white, and there was a very sharp frost. Neither Mother, Jessie nor Annie attempted church. The minister preached from Ezekiel's version of the dry bones, and at the close of the service he intimated that the elders would collect the schemes of the church.

This morning there was another fall of snow and we have now three inches I believe. I was at Portsoy today with Mother and Annie, making some purchases. Father was at the funeral of James Lawrence, Tauchiehill. He was aged 71.

14th

During the past week we have experienced a very severe snow storm, but if it was sharp it has also been short.

On Tuesday it was blowing and snowing the whole day. I did little else but sported, but I did not get a heavy bag.

On Wednesday I went to Smiddy with bolts for a new barrow which the joiner is making for us.

I was making a barrel chair on Thursday and also a table for the Xmas dinner. This was a very frosty day.

On Friday Willie and I started the drains, they were nice and dry with the frost. I went over to Kirkton in the evening and opened the Library. It was the first month of the half year and there were more members joined than I ever saw in any one night before.

Saturday morning was fresh. After thrashing we started to pull turnips, and we managed them with the hand. We were driving them in the afternoon, but the land was terribly soft.

The roads being bad on Sunday none went to church but Willie and I. There was a strong fresh breeze of wind and it soon made the snow disappear. The steam mill was at Careston today and Willie and I were down assisting. We got a very nice day. They shifted up here when they were through, and they intend thrashing us and Oathillock tomorrow. I have been writing invitations tonight for Annie's marriage. It is to be on Xmas Day the 25th and there are to be about 80 guests.

21st

The weather during the past week has been quite a contrast to the previous one. I scarcely ever saw a week of such mild weather in December. It has also been so nice and dry, scarcely a drop falling all the week.

We got a very fine day for the thrashing on Tuesday. We started by screech o' day, and it was all through by eleven o'clock. We had plenty of hands. The barley was nice and dry, and turned out pretty well, about 4½ qrs. off the acre. The oats we thrashed was what grew in the Den and there was not much grain. The straw was also of bad quality. There was plenty time to thrash Sandy McKay's in the afternoon. His barley had been a very good crop.

I was at a meeting of the Mutual Improvement on Tuesday evening. The debate was 'Whether is married or single to be the happiest'. Mr. Muiry supported the married side, and Mr. Clarke the single. There was a very warm discussion, most of the numbers joining in the debate. On the vote being taken there was found to be a majority of one in favour of single life.

I was in the plough on Wednesday. Geordy Cowie came over in the afternoon, and after supper I went over with him to Mr. Smith's to put in the 'cries'.[6] He did not go home till next morning.

We had the barley down to Glenglassaugh Distillery on Thursday forenoon. It weighed 53½ lbs the bushel. I was furring up turnips in the afternoon. We have got the swedes nearly all pulled now, but I would like to get some yellow ones stored also. Jessie and Annie went down to Cullen in the afternoon and Willie and I followed in the evening. It was ten o'clock before we got home.

I was ploughing on Friday all day.

We were taking in straw on Saturday and driving turnips.

Willie, Joan and I were in church on Sunday. We were in plenty time to hear the proclamation. It has been misty today but very close and warm. I was ploughing the end-rigs of the stubbles.

28th

We have had some cold blowy days during the week, but it has been good December weather nevertheless. The great event of the week of course has been the wedding. Everyone was busy in the first of the week making preparations. Willie and I had to get the mill in order as we were going to dance in it. We had it nicely decorated with holly and other evergreens. At the farthest gable we had two large hearts joined together in this fashion ❤❤ with the motto underneath 'Union is Strength'.

On Thursday evening Geordy Stephen came down from Keith.

Friday morning was very blowy, and toward the afternoon it turned showery. In the forenoon I went up to Ardiecow for a table and also tidied up the close. The marriage was to be at 2 o'clock and everyone I think was up to time. There was 13 came with the bridegroom in four machines. 32 sat down to their dinner in the parlour, and there was just room for them all and nothing more. Jessie of course was cook and had everything up to the 'knocker'. Joan and Geordy Stephen carried the dishes to the door, while I waited the table. The first course was Albert soup, the next was a round of beef, a gigot of mutton, two turkeys, a rabbit pie, and boiled and roasted fowls. Then came the plum pudding with apple tart, prunes, custards, jellies, creams etc. etc. Last came the wine and the fruit—oranges,

---

[6] put in the cries, proclaiming the marriage banns.

apples, grapes, figs, nuts and raisins. About half past four we adjourned to the mill, and started the dancing. At six o'clock the people from Cairdswell had to leave, as there was to be some friends and neighbours waiting them when they went home. The wind had by this time softened down, and it was a clear starry night. Some of the horses were rather restless, but they all got seated at last, and drove off amid a shower of peas, rice etc. After tea, we again set to the dancing, and as we had now an excellent fiddler (a shoemaker from Muttonbrae) we did not allow the loss of our friends, in any way to mar our merry making. About half past eleven we finished up the dancing with 'Bob at the Bolster'. We then had supper, and before separating all joined in singing 'Auld Lang Syne'.

31st

On Tuesday morning the ground was white with snow while the frost was very hard. Snow fell all day and the wind being high it also blew a little.

On Wednesday forenoon there was another fall, and everyone was making sure we were in for a big snow storm. Towards evening however, it turned soft, and rain began to fall, and by next morning the most of the snow had disappeared. We had two loads of corn filled up so we started with it for Portsoy. It was the corn that grew in the Den and it only weighed 38 lbs per bushel, and we got only 15/2 the qr.

And, so we have seen the last, of the year 1885. I cannot say that it has been a prosperous one for the farmer, for indeed it has been the very reverse of that.

The Spring was cold and frosty. The month of July was the only summer weather we had, and it was too dry.

August was cold, dull and rainy and towards the end of it there were frosts that in low lying districts blackened the potatoes and also in some places frosted the corn.

In the upper end of Banffshire they say their potatoes are not eatable, while their corn will be of no use for seed. Fodder is everywhere, scarce, and has been selling at high prices. But if straw be dear, the grain has been as cheap. I never saw the barley so low in price. We got only 23/6 for ours. Yellow turnips are in general a good crop, but swedes are mostly small. Where the potatoes were not spoiled with frost, the crop was good, and has been selling at good prices. The greatest loss however, to the farmer will be the low price which he is getting for his cattle. Store cattle at some markets were almost unsaleable, while 68/ per cwt. is the highest offered for prime fat. With all these difficulties staring the farmer in the face it is evident that the rent of land must shortly be lowered. Landlords in many cases

have been granting concessions, giving 10.15.20, and in the case of
The Duke of Sutherland 50 per cent of reduction.

The postponement of the collecting of the rents till Candlemas
however, is all that is to be done on the Seafield Estates. The prospects
therefore, with which we enter on the New Year are far from being
bright, but be that as it may, I am going to close my Journal writing for
the year, as I did once before, with the good old motto.

> Hope for the best
> Be prepared for the worst
> And be content, whatever comes

A Journal of My Life and Everyday Doings

1886 January
1st

New Year's day was fresh and fair. As we had kept Xmas day I thought
we could scarcely afford a whole holiday. We thrashed in the morning
and then we were driving turnips. Geordy Cowie and Annie came
over about eleven o'clock. After dinner we packed her dishes and
other things which were not over before. As there was to be a
shooting match at Berryhillock Willie and I went over in the afternoon
to see it. They had two targets. One for balls and the other for small
shot, and there were plenty of competitors at both. The annual ball
was held at Raimore this year and was quite a success I hear.

Saturday was a nice day and I was at the plough. I was over at
Kirkton in the evening at a tea party. Mr. Ashley and the Misses
MacKintosh were there. We had a nice game at cards, and the ladies
gave us some excellent music.

We were all at Church on Sunday except Mother. The Minister
gave us a splendid New Year's sermon from the text 'there is a time to
be born, and a time to die'.

I was in the plough again to-day. It has been frosty however, and
also some showers of snow.

11th

We are having the third snow storm of the season, and it is seemingly
not to be so easily got rid of as the others. The whole week has been
very severe, and on some days there was a tremendous gale of wind.
Had there been more snow on the ground the blowing would have
been considerable. As it was roads have been partially blocked and I
hear also that the trains were greatly delayed.

On Monday evening, it being clear and frosty, Joan and I started
for Cairdswell to hold old Xmas. Willie and Sandy Cowie were there

when we arrived. We had a game at cards, and then the Sowens were cooked. Sandy got the button, while I had the good fortune to get the ring. After the Sowens, we had toddy with bread and cheese.

Next morning the frost was very hard, and it kept snowing and blowing all the forenoon. We got a grand dinner from Annie—soup—beef-roast fowl—plum pudding—apples and oranges. After dinner we all went over to Finnygaud, as there was to be a family gathering there,—George Milton, Isa Longmoor & Jessie Longmoor from the Bauds and Jemmie and his wife. There was eighteen I think at the tea table. We played at cards all the evening, and before we left we got a grand supper. It was snowing very thick as we went across to Cairdswell.

We were to be home on Wednesday morning, but as it was always stormy they got us persuaded to wait till afternoon. George Milton and the others came past on their way home. As Annie had got tiles for her parlour fireplace we commenced and laid them. They just fitted in where the stone came out, and we made a very nice job. We got home by six o'clock.

Thursday was very frosty and there was a tremendous gale of wind. We tried the drain twice, but was always driven home. Jessie and I were at a tea party at Oathillock. Mr. Peter Gordon and Mr. & Miss Barron were the company.

We got nothing done outside on Friday at all. It was blowing and snowing all day. I have been making an easy chair for Father in my spare time. I constructed it out of a barrel and I think it will be very comfortable. I have also got my first Bee Hive nearly finished. I went over to Kirkton on Friday evening, but very few attended the Library, the night being bad.

Saturday was quiet, but frosty. In the forenoon we were filling the mill and thrashing and in the afternoon we went to the drain.

There was very few at Church on Sunday. Willie, Joan and I attended. I went up to the Backies in the afternoon to ask for Willie McWillie. He was away at Strathpeffer for two weeks, and he has not been at all well for sometime. He is a little better now however. Mrs. Milne, Burnheads, has been very poorly lately. She is indeed very bad, and the Dr. has but faint hopes of her recovery.

The frost this morning relaxed a little and we took the opportunity of getting some turnips. It is not going to be a proper thaw however, for the wind is round to the North again and it is hard to the frost.

18ᵗʰ

After a thaw of three days the snow storm has again been renewed.

We were draining on Tuesday but it turned very dirty before night as the snow was melting.

On Wednesday morning the snow was all away expect the wreathes, and I got to the plough. It was a windy showery, disagreeable sort of day. Jessie and I had got an invitation from Miss Barron, to take tea with them that evening. Mr. & Miss McKay were all the company, but we had a very pleasant evening. We had a game of cards, saw her photos and Xmas cards, and got some songs and music.

Thursday & Friday were both good days and I kept busy at the plough.

Thursday was Cornhill market. Prices were not any advanced but the demand was a little keener. Father went over, and went up to Cairdswell, and stayed all night.

There was a ploughing match at Summerton on Friday. Willie went over to see it, and Father also came past. There were nineteen ploughs, and J. Robertson, Slogmahole, got the first prize.

On Friday evening it turned very frosty, and on Saturday morning the ground was once more white with snow. We winnowed up some corn in the morning and Father had it over to the mill while Willie and I were taking in some turnips. In the afternoon we were thrashing. I went out with my gun in the evening and shot a hare and two rabbits.

Father, Joan, Willie & I were at church on Sunday. There was a fair attendance. I went down to Cairnton in the afternoon. I was asking if they would take one of John Carmichael's books. He is thinking of printing a book of essays, stories, and poems, and I got a subscription sheet from him to see and get some subscribers. This has been a nice quiet frosty day. We were taking in straw in the morning, and we started then to drive out some dung.

25th

We have had a week of very changeable weather—sometimes fresh and sometimes frosty. On some days the snow melted a little, but yesterday. and during last night, we have had the heaviest fall of any all winter. There is now about six inches all over, and up the country I am sure there will be more.

On Tuesday we were driving out dung, and on Wednesday we emptied the court. We were driving gravel from Careston's quarry on Thursday forenoon, and in the afternoon we were draining.

We were also at the drain on Friday, and Saturday forenoon. In the afternoon I was over at the mill with a load of corn. I went down to Cullen in the evening for some errands. I was canvassing a little for John Carmichael's book, and I was fortunate in getting seven subscribers.

As Sunday was a snowy day only Willie and I went to Church. The minister preached from the text 'You hath he quickened who were dead in trespasses and in sins'.

We were taking home turnips this forenoon, and in the afternoon I was shooting and doing some joiner work.

1886 February
1ˢᵗ

The weather during the past week has been good for nothing. It was never fresh enough to let the plough work, and it was too wet for the drains. I have been sporting a good deal with my gun, and managed to shoot eight or ten rabbits. I had some of them down to Cullen on Friday evening and got nine pence for each.

On Wednesday we yoked the filly and went an hour or so with her drawing a stick. She was rather refractory at first, but next day she was going nicely. She is not going to be very big not nearly so strong as her mother.

I have also being doing some joiner work during the week. I have got one hive finished and commenced another.

A few in the end of the Parish got to the plough on Friday, but the frost was not out with us. We were pulling and driving turnips.

On Saturday it was frosty, and it has been very hard since. We went draining and it was nice and dry.

Willie and I were over at the Free Church on Sunday evening. The roads were very slippery. Mr. Walker intimated, that Principal Robertson from India would give an address next Sunday evening, on Indian Missions.

I see by the newspapers that we have got a change of Government again. The Conservatives were out voted on an amendment to the Queen's speech and have resigned.

8ᵗʰ

The frost has been very severe all the week, but there has been no snow but what fell on Monday and Tuesday. The turnips being nearly bare, I fear they will have suffered rather severely. The rabbits and hares have been cutting ours badly and I am always coming more and more to see the benefit of storing in the end of the year. Although frosty it has been nice quiet days, and we have been busy at the drains. We are commenced to the third one now. They are not very hard, and there is a good depth of mould.

On Thursday Father went over the hill a bit with Jessie as she was going to Cairdswell.

We had a meeting of the Mut. Imp. Assoc. on Tuesday evening.[7] There was a full attendance of members, and we had a very good meeting. Mr. McWillie gave a very interesting reading on Farmers and farming in Norway, while the subject for debate was, 'Should Farm servants have a weekly half holiday'. Mr. McBain ably supported the affirmative while Mr. Walker took up the negative side. The subject was discussed in all its bearings, the most of the members giving their opinions. The majority of the members expressed their sympathy with farm servants, and while considering that they are as justly entitled to a half holiday as other tradesmen, still it was thought that there were other privileges which would be of far more benefit to them. On the vote being taken only one voted for the holiday. There was some talk of the Social Meeting, and the debate for the same was fixed. The subject is to be 'Are we happier in youth or after attaining maturity'. Mr. Murray is to support the cause of youth, while I am to take maturity.

On Friday we received intimation of the death of Mrs Milne, Burnheads. She has been very poorly for the last two months, and it was not thought she would survive so long.

Father was at her funeral today. She was buried in Rathven Churchyard.

On Sunday morning it turned soft and it has been fresh since. Father, Willie, Joan and I were at church. Willie and I went over to the Free Church in the evening to hear Principal Robertson. He was a very able speaker and there was a full church. He spoke principally of the difficulties which missionaries had to overcome in persuading the heathen to accept the gospel. In India he said there were now 500,000 Christian Protestants but this, although seemingly a large number, was comparatively only a drop in the bucket, for the whole population of India amounted to 250 millions.

Willie and I were pulling and driving turnips this forenoon, and in the afternoon we were cleaning the harness. Before evening I went out with my gun and shot a rabbit.

15th

We have had a week of nice fresh days, and everyone has been busy ploughing. Other two days and I would have all the lea ploughed.

On Friday evening I went over and opened the Library. A large number attended. There was also a lecture in the Schools that night. Mr. Benzie from Banff. His subject was 'Hats Off'. The poor man I

---

[7] Mutual Improvement Association is occasionally abbreviated to Mut. Imp. Assoc. or Mut. Imp. by Wilson.

suppose tried to do his best, but I cannot say he was very brilliant. There was also a very poor audience.

Father and Willie were over at Cornhill market and sold a calving cow. It was very stiff, and the prices exceedingly small.

The good weather came to an end on Sunday and to all appearance we are in for another snow storm. On Sunday forenoon snow fell steadily until we had about three inches.

Today it has melted a little and I see them ploughing in the end of the parish. It is frosty tonight however again. We have been draining all day.

22nd

The whole week has been stormy, but it has not been very bad days. We have been draining every day, and we are now getting nearly through with them. They are always getting better to do I think.

We have a meeting of The Mut. Association on Tuesday evening. There was no debate but we had two essays instead. I read one on 'the employment of our Leisure Hours' and A. Currie another on 'Artificial Light'. We were also arranging about the Social meeting. It is to be held on 19th March, but the School Board is to allow no dancing this year.

On Friday afternoon I went down with the cart to Cullen with Mother and Joan. As we went into the town, an engine with two carriages was passing over the Railway Bridge. It was the Directors who had come all the way from Elgin. It will be open for goods traffic in a few weeks now. I went down and had a look at the embankment on the links. There is always parts of it slipping and about 40 men were working at it. I also took a stroll round the harbour. I saw more fish I believe then ever I did all my life before. The quantity of cod, ling, herrings, etc. which they are taking just now is something marvellous.

Mr. & Miss Barron and Mr. McWillie were up at tea on Saturday evening. We had a game at cards, and enjoyed ourselves very well.

I forgot to mention however that Jessie came home from Cairdswell on Thursday. Annie also came over with her but she went home the same night again. I went over that evening to Kirkton and spent the forenight.

Father was at a sale of wood at Park on Saturday and bought two lots. We are thinking of going for it tomorrow.

Father, Joan, Willie and I were at church on Sunday. The Minister preached from a text from Revelations, 'Whosoever overcommeth will I give to eat of the hidden and I will give him a white stone with a new name written'. On Sunday it turned a little soft, and it rained all this forenoon.

The most of the snow has now disappeared and a good many were in the plough in the afternoon.

1886 March
1st

The weather is indeed beginning to get a little serious. The month of March is here, and still there is no sign of the frost and snow disappearing. Indeed the last few days, it has been as like snow, as it has ever been all winter. It has been good weather for draining however, it having been frosty all the week. It was sometimes a little dirty in the afternoon, the sun softening the frost in the middle of the day. We got them all finished on Friday however, there being altogether 470 yds.

The great event of the week has been a Concert in the Public Schools given by the Church Choir on Friday. The evening was fine, and there was a good turn out, the School being quite crowded. The choir turned out in full force, and of course the ladies were in full dress. It being the first time that the greater part of them had appeared before a public audience I think they did remarkably well. The Programme consisted of solos, duets, trios, quartettes; and choruses and they finished up with 'Locke's music to Macbeth'. Among the choruses were, 'Bonnie Scotland', 'My Heather Hills', 'Loudon's Bonnie Woods and Braes', 'Away to the Meadows', 'All among the Barley', etc. etc. The ladies who gave solos were Miss E. Mackintosh, who gave 'Far Away', with taste and feeling. Miss Ingram, rendered 'Flora Macdonald's Lament' and 'Scottish Blue Bells' in grand style. Miss E. Morrison gave 'Wandering Willie' and Miss Reid 'The Ministrel Boy'. Miss Mackintosh played the accompaniment to the choruses on the piano, while Mr. Reid sat at the harmonium for the solos. Mr. Mackintosh at the close congratulated Mr. Reid on the success of the concert and proposed a most hearty vote of thanks to him and the choir.

On Saturday I went over to Cairnfield with James Grey for two loads of larch. It was a cold day and it was a very long road. We left the turnpike at Inchgower, kept right up to the Dry Bridge, then turned west, across the railway, past Thornybank and Farnuchty until we were nearly at the Chapel of Preshome. We again turned to the hill and into the wood. We had the trees to throw, and it was three hours before we got loaded. We came past the House of Cairnfield coming home, in the turnpike to Reinnes and through the grounds of Cullen House.

Father, Joan, Willie and I were at church on Sunday. The Minister gave us an excellent sermon from the text 'Thy testimonies O Lord are wonderful'. In the afternoon Willie and I went over to Limestones.

8ᵗʰ

We have experienced the most severe weather during the past week of any we have had all winter. There has been the most snow on the ground, and the frost has been very severe. We have also had two blowing days.

On Tuesday it never ceased from morning till night. I was doing joiner work in the shop all day. A meeting of the Mut. Imp. was held in the evening. After the ordinary business we were arranging about the Social Meeting. The Secretary had the invitations for the ladies, and they were divided among the members to deliver. There are to be far more this year than formerly.

We were putting in some draining posts on Wednesday.

On Thursday we were taking home some more from the Cottonhill.

There was a great fall of snow on Friday morning about 4 inches falling in the forenoon.

On Saturday forenoon it was blowing very hard but it quietened down by dinnertime. I went over in the afternoon to the Free Manse to ask if Mr. Walker would take one of John Carmichael's books. I then went up past the Backies to see my friends there. When I came home Miss Ingram was up from Milton. She stayed all night and went to church with us on Sunday.

Father was at Cullen today paying the rent while Willie and I were putting in more draining posts.

15ᵗʰ

Still the frost continues, and still no appearance of any change. Indeed it is far like a fall of snow tonight than anything else.

There has been no additional snow since last I wrote, and the strength of the sun has melted the most of what was, expect the wreathes. The frost however, has been very severe and on some days there was a cold piercing East wind. I am sure it must now be a good distance into the ground. We were taking in potatoes one day and I measured on the north side of the pit 7 inches. The most of our work during the week has been thrashing and winnowing. We thrashed out the greater part of one stack, and built it out, to be some straw when the mare foals. She will be at her time in two days now, and I hope we may soon get a thaw, that we may get the lea finished. I have been sporting a good deal during the week. Willie went to Cullen one evening with half a dozen rabbits and sold them. I have been busy in the evenings getting up my side of the debate for the Social Meeting.

I got it finished and took it over to Mr. Murray on Friday evening when I went over to open the Library. We were selecting some new books for the Library that evening.

As Willie went over to Cairdswell on Saturday afternoon, there was only Father, Joan and I at church on Sunday. We got a very nice sermon from the Minister. His text was Romans XV. 13.

I was over at Kirkton today at the steam mill. It was nice and quiet and everything was got tidy by half past five.

22ⁿᵈ

Since last I wrote there has been a change of weather more sudden, and more complete, than ever I remember witnessing. The first four days of the week were extremely bad. Cold, blowy days. Snow fell and drifted more or less every day.

On Friday it turned soft, but it was still very cold with a thick white mist.

By Saturday morning however a good deal of the snow had disappeared while it was nice and warm.

Yesterday and today have also been very fine days. More like the end of April than March. When I was out suppering the horses a little ago, I could scarcely realise that only four nights ago we were running to the house to get in from the snow drift, while tonight the birds were all merrily singing, the lapwings crying and the air so soft and warm.

Tuesday was Marnin Fair, but there were very few went from this side. It was a very cold day. Willie and I were at Ardiecow at the steam mill, but it was a bad day for the job. We had a meeting of the Mut. Imp. that evening, rehearsing the programme for the Social Meeting.

On Wednesday and Thursday we did little out of doors. I have now got three bar frame hives made and I am commenced to make some frames.

On Friday Willie Cowie and Sandy came over from Finnygaud. They were saying they had scarcely got any ploughed since Xmas. On Friday evening the Social Meeting of the Mutual Improvement Association was held. The roads were in terribly bad order, but I do not think they had prevented any one from attending. There was over 100 sat down to tea. As there was to be no dancing we made the programme a little longer. Mr. McWillie, President of the Assoc., occupied the chair. Mr. McIntyre, Portknockie, who was adjudicator on the prize essays, gave an address and also read the first prize essay, before the tea. The first prize fell to Mr. McWillie, I was second, while S. Walker and Mr. Currie were third. After tea the programme was commenced by the members and everyone I think did their part extremely well. The vote on the Debate was about a clear split. Mr. Murray obtaining just three of a majority. A special feature of attraction was a dialogue, acted in character, by Messrs. Walker, Longmore & Clark. It was the 'Pottinger-draucht' and a good deal of merriment was caused by their performance.

Everything passed off without a hitch, and votes of thanks to the ladies and others brought a very pleasant meeting to a close.

29th

If there was any reason for complaining about the weather before, there certainly is none now. Since last I wrote it has been all that anyone could desire—nice fresh, warm days. The ground is now in grand trim for ploughing, and everyone is busy turning it over. A few have commenced the clean land, a good many are ploughing ayvels while some are still at the lea. I finished our lea on Tuesday and since then I have been ploughing ayvels. The frost has them nice and tender. On Tuesday evening there was a meting of the Mut. Imp. Assoc. to settle up our finances. We left a balance of 10/- odds to carry to next year. There was some talk of having a pleasure trip or a flower show during the coming Summer, and a meting is to be held next week to consider the matter.

We were filling in the drains on Wednesday.

On Thursday I yoked the filly into the plough for the first time. I have her going on the land, but her shoulders are fired a little, and she goes some fast.

On Friday evening Revd. Mr. Porteous, Cullen, gave a lecture in the Schools on 'Burns', and I never heard a lecture which I enjoyed better. He is an excellent speaker and he treated his subject so fully and yet so pleasantly that it was quite a treat to listen to him. Another attraction was the presence of Mr. Reid and his choir, who rendered several of Burns' songs at intervals during the evening. It is the Free Church folk who have started the lectures to clear off a small debt lying on their church. There is to be one this week, and another the week following.

They were all at church on Sunday expect Joan and I. I had to stay at home as the mare, a cow, and a ewe, to all appearance will shortly increase the stock. The cow dropped a nice calf about an hour ago.

1886 April
5th

The weather since last I wrote has continued dry, but it has been cold and blowy. It is well that it turned cold however, for vegetation would soon have been too far forward. There being no break all the week, the work of the farm has been greatly advanced. Everyone is now ploughing clean land, while some have made a start at the sowing, the ground being in very good condition for the seed. I have just been two days at the clean land, and we are not to sow any for a few days yet.

The second of the course of lectures, was delivered in the Free Church on Wednesday evening. The lecturer was Mr. Soutor, F.C. Cullen, and his subject was 'Savonarola' the Florentine reformer. Willie went across to hear it, but there was not a very large attendance.

On Thursday evening I did not bed until past twelve o'clock as the mare seemed a little restless. She did not foal however, until two on Saturday morning. It is a good strong horse foal we have got.

On Saturday morning we lost one of the ewes, and although Willie looked for her far and near, he could find no trace of her. He started this morning again and found her in Edingight, but she had dropped two lambs in the hill, both of which were dead.

John Cowie, Finnygaud came over to visit us on Saturday evening.

Father, him and I were at church on Sunday. We got an excellent sermon from Mr. Mackintosh from the text, 'As we have borne the image of the earthly, so shall we also bear the image of the heavenly'. In comparing the earthly and heavenly images, he said that the former was characterised by sin, sorrow, and death, while the latter was attended with holiness, happiness, and life.

12th

The weather still continues seasonable, and the sowing is going on apace, the seed being deposited in an excellent seed bed. The lea in most cases is finished except it be Ardiecow and he has not commenced yet. I suppose he will have this week's work ploughing his ayvels yet.

The first of last week was showery, and so we did not start sowing until Friday.

We sowed the remainder of the lea on Saturday. It is very fine to harrow this year, having got so much frost.

On Friday evening the Library was open. After the ordinary business, a meeting was held to arrange about getting up something in place of the Annual Picnic. There was a fair attendance. It was considered that it would be very desirable to have a Flower Show, and the Public Schools are to be asked to hold it in.

On Sunday morning I went over to Newton, as I was going down with Johnny Geddes, to the meeting of the Young Men's Christian Association at Fordyce. There are not very many members, but I was greatly pleased with the manner in which the meeting was conducted. We afterwards got an excellent sermon from Mr. Grant.

We had a letter from Mary last week. Andrew and her are in Caithness just now visiting his folks. They are to be here in a fortnight, as they are thinking of starting for Australia in the month of May.

19th

Since the middle of the week the weather has been showery but never so much as to interrupt the sowing. We have got the clean land to sow yet, and I suppose we will have three days ploughing. It has been extremely cold during the week, and there is no growth whatever yet. Most people however have plenty of keep and so grass is not yet being looked for.

On Tuesday I finished the lea and was breaking in the yavels.

We sowed part of them on Wednesday morning and the remainder on Thursday. Willie McWillie came down that night and spent the evening.

On Friday and Saturday I was ploughing.

I was taking a look into some of my hives last week and cleaning the floorboards. They seemed to be in fair condition. It has been bad weather for inspecting however, being always so cold.

Jessie, Joan, Willie, Father and I were all at church on Sunday. The minister intimated that the Communion would be next Sunday, and the Fast day is on Thursday.

Willie and Father were driving home turnips today, while I have been ploughing.

26th

We have had some terribly frosty mornings during the week. Ice on the water at seven o'clock. Consequently there has been little or no growth.

Tuesday was a rainy sort of day, but since then it has been good weather for the sowing. The seed is mostly all in now in this district, excepting Ardiecow. He only commenced today to plough his clean land.

I was in the plough on Tuesday and Wednesday. On Tuesday evening I went over to Kirkton and gave the books in the Library an overhaul. I then went in past Kirkton for a short time. Miss Duncan is in great spirits about the Flower Show

Thursday was the Fast day and we had Mr. McVicar, Ordiquhill, preaching. He gave us a very good address from the text 'Thou desirest truth in the inward parts'. Jessie and I went down to Cullen in the afternoon, and we went up past the Free Church coming home.

We sowed the barley on Friday, but the harrows did not work very well, as it was some damp.

I finished the ploughing of the clean land on Saturday. I went up in the evening to see my friends at Backies. Willie and I were marking out some rules for the Flower Show.

We were all at church on Sunday except Mother. She has had a sore foot for sometime and cannot get on her boot. Mr. Mackintosh had no one assisting him. I know him failing a good bit now, still he speaks wonderful for such an old man. His text was Romans VIII 32. 'He that spared not his own Son, but delivered him up for us all, how shall he not with him also, freely give us all things'.

We sowed the lower half of the clean today. Willie was in the roller in the afternoon.

1886 May
3rd

Except Tuesday the weather during the week has been terribly cold, and there has been no growth whatever.

Tuesday was a nice dewy day, and had there come heat after it would have done an immense of good. I sowed the grass seed on the lower clean land and also some tares that day. George Cowie and Annie were across. They brought over some potatoes for a change of seed. I was giving Annie some flowers for her garden. She is going to have awfully nice flowers this year she says.

I was making the potato land on Wednesday, and we got them all set on Thursday. Miss Ingram came down from Keith that day as it was their Fast day. She was giving me some assistance in the afternoon among the flowers. She is always dressmaker to Mr. Gray.

On Saturday Jessie and I went over to Cornhill to meet Andrew and Mary. They came to Aberdeen from Caithness with the boat on Thursday night. They were both a little sick. They have got a nice strong healthy boy, nine months old. John Geddes Bremmer he is called after his Uncle in Australia. Their ship sails from London on the 9th of June.

10th

Finer weather than we have experienced since last I wrote, I never remember seeing in the first of the month of May. There has been some nice mild showers, and then it has been so fresh and warm. Grass has greatly improved and many cattle are now out the most of the day. I never saw the braird come so quickly I think. You could scarcely see it in the first of the week, and by the end of it, it was quite green. I have been working among the turnip land all the week, and it has been in excellent season. I have got a piece of swedes almost ready. There are a good many weeds on it, but the rest is cleaner I think. I have been among the flowers some little whiles during the week but I have not got them all finished yet.

There was a meeting on Tuesday evening in connection with the Flower Show. The School Board have granted the Schools to hold it in, and it is to be about the month of August. A. Morrison was appointed Treasurer of the Society while I am Secretary. We are to commence now and see to get members.

On Thursday evening Andrew, Mary, Jessie and I were invited over to Kirkton to tea. It was a showery afternoon but the evening was fine.

We got Sandy Lamb with his steam mill on Saturday evening, and thrashed out the remainder of the crop (two stacks). It was a nice quiet evening and we got everything tidy before it got dark.

On Sunday we were all at church except Joan and Willie. The Kirk was throng and we got an excellent sermon from Mr. Mackintosh. His text was I Peter IV 18. 'If the righteous scarcely be saved, where shall the ungodly and the sinner appear.' I went over to Limestones in the afternoon to ask for Uncle. He got a kick on the leg from one of the horses nearly two weeks ago, and has never been able to be up since. It is a little discoloured but I think it is just the rheumatism got into it more than anything else.

17th

We have been experiencing the 'Gab o' May' with a vengeance. Cold blowy days, with showers of sleet and hail. On several mornings the hills up the country were as white as a 'doo', and Saturday was just a fearful day. The wind was North and blew quite a hurricane, while the rain fell in torrents. There has been little or no growth during the week, indeed the grass is scarcely looking so well as it did ten days ago. We had the young cattle out for the first time this afternoon, but there are still a few turnips. Warm weather is greatly needed to make a full bite for them.

I have been working at the turnip land all the week, and until Saturday it was in good condition. I have got it nearly all cross ploughed.

The sale at Burnheads was on Tuesday. Father and I both were across at it, but we brought nothing. Considering the times I think it got on very well. There was an extra large attendance.

On Wednesday Father went across to Cairdswell with Andrew, Mary and Jessie. They have just arrived home again tonight.

Father was at Cornhill market on Thursday. Cattle were selling stiffly.

He also went over on Friday to a roup at Slogmahole, where he bought a turnip slicer.

We did nothing outside at all on Saturday. I was busy at a hive which has been lying unfinished since the busy season began.

24th

Lazy, lazy weather. We have got no turnips sowed yet. In the early part of the week there was some sowing but on Thursday night and Friday morning there was a tremendous lot of rain. The burns were all swollen, and the ground is quite saturated.

I was cross ploughing on Tuesday, and on Wednesday I was harrowing.

On Thursday Willie and I were gathering weed, while Father was in the harrows.

We did nothing at all among the land on Friday and Saturday it being too wet.

Friday was Cullen market. I was hearing that it was rather stiff, and fees had a downward tendency.

I was at the Brickwork on Saturday for some big tiles to finish our drain in the den.

We had a very large party of visitors on Sunday. Father, Mother, Mary and Andrew, Annie and Geordie Cowie and Jessie and I were all at church. Miss Ingram also came up with us from church and Uncle George was over in the afternoon. Miss Ingram I believe has left Mr. Gray and is thinking of starting dressmaking in Deskford on her own account. Sunday was a nice drying day and the land dried a lot, but today it has been close and misty and the ground is far from being in good condition for working. I was in the grubber, but was not at all pleased with it.

1886 June
1ˢᵗ
There was one good day last week and only one. It has been cold and wet, and there has been very little growth. The whole month of May however has been cold but now that we have seen the last of it, we might surely expect a favourable change.

Tuesday was a close misty day, and the sun did not once make his appearance. I was in the drill plough all day. Miss Elsie and Katie Duncan were up in the afternoon. Cultain and I accompanied them home in the evening. We were going to a meeting in connection with the Flower Show. The Flower Show is going to be a real success I think. About forty members have already joined and we have also got a good many special prizes. The date of the Show is fixed for 25ᵗʰ August.

On Wednesday there was some sunshine, but there were also some good showers of hail. We were putting out dung all day.

On Thursday I covered in the dung and got them sowed in the afternoon in good condition it being a nice dry day.

The following night however there had been a very heavy rainfall, and Friday was a soft day. Willie and I were in the 'Den' filling in the old ditch.

The land was too wet for getting anything done on Saturday. Mary and Andrew started that morning for Edinburgh en route for Australia. Father, Jessie and I went to the Station with them. They are to sail from Gravesend with the S. S. 'Austral' on 9th June but their luggage must be there four days before. We saw Uncle as we went past Muttonbrae when he was telling us that he thought old James Murdoch was just dying. Father and Jessie went in past as we came home and Mother was also across by that time. He was still living then, but he died at twelve o'clock. He was buried today in the churchyard at Deskford.

On Saturday afternoon Willie and I went down to the Lintmill for a young calf. We have a cow newly calved and we are going to put the two calves to suck.

Mother and I were town keepers on Sunday. It was a strange minister. There is a proposal just now of getting a harmonium or American organ for the church. Mr. Reid I expect has been the originator of the scheme but I hear that several of our principal ladies are going out to solicit subscriptions.

7th

There has been an improvement on the weather. It has been much warmer, but on some nights it has still been very frosty. It has been dry however, and the land is now in good workable order again.

On Wednesday I was grubbing and harrowing. We had Miss Ingram up that evening. She has left Mr. Gray now, and has come to Kirkton to start dressmaking on her own account.

Willie and I were gathering weeds on Thursday while Father was in the harrows.

On Friday I was in the drill plough in the forenoon, while in the afternoon we were putting out dung. I was over that evening at Kirkton among the books in the Library. John Carmichael's books arrived that day. They are much larger than his last one, and they are very nicely bound.

On Saturday we covered in the dung and got the seed in, in fine condition. In the evening I started for Cairdswell. Mother got a drive over with Jemmie Cowie on Tuesday, and was still there.

We were all at church on Sunday. After service I went up to Hillfolds with Mr. Books. Both Mr. & Mrs. Mackintosh were highly pleased with the appearance of the book. I received 33 copies of it, and I have disposed of 28 of them already. We were all at church on

Sunday except Father and Jessie. The new American Organ has been placed in the church and Miss Mackintosh is to be organist. It is a great improvement to the singing I think. This one is only on trial however, and as they have now over £25 of subscriptions, they are going to make an effort to get other £5 and so get a stronger instrument. I went up to The Backies in the afternoon. Mrs Riddoch is expecting her son William home from India in a week or so.

We would have finished the turnips today but the afternoon was rainy, and the land will be rather wet I fear. We had a letter from Mary today from off the Steamer at Gravesend. They were to sail at mid-day on Thursday. The name of the Steamer is the 'Austral' and their address in Australia will be c/o John Geddes, Stratford, Gipps Land, By Melbourne.

We have received word that Friday first, the 18th is to be Jane's wedding day.

21st

The weather during the week has been showery and excessively cold, not in the least like June weather at all. We have been driving earth up out of the Den, to mix lime for top dressing.

On Wednesday I was up at Keith market. I got a drive with my friend Backies, and Miss McWillie also went along with us. It was a very cold day, but there was a big market. There was pretty brisk sale among cattle, year olds bringing from £6 to £10 and two year olds £12 to £16. There was a good turn out of horses, but there seemed to be but little doing, and the prices offered were small. I was in past Mr. Mitchell's and looked over the proof sheets of Prize Schedule for Flower Show. I was also buying a book for a marriage present to Jane. The title of it is 'Heaven our Home'. We got a paper today, where we saw that the ceremony had taken place on Friday. They had been out at Cleland on Saturday.

Sunday was a little warmer day, but tonight it is as cold as ever.

28th

The cold weather still continues, and as there has been no moisture it is doing great damage to crops of every kind. Turnips are scarcely moving, grass has gone clean off, while oats which before were looking excellent have lost much of their dark green colour. We have also during the week had high Northerly winds and cattle as well as crops in exposed places have suffered greatly.

On Tuesday evening, there was a meeting of Farmers in the Public Schools, to give expression to their gratitude to Lady Seafield for giving a reduction of 10 per cent at last collection of rents. There was a fair attendance. Mr. Sim, Croftgloy, being Chairman and Mr. Smith Clerk of the meeting. A letter was drawn up be the Clerk and read, and unanimously approved of which is to be sent to Her Ladyship. There was also a meeting that evening of the Committee of Management of The Horticultural Society. The Prize Schedules were distributed and members tickets, also Judges appointed for the different sections.

We have been doing lots of odd jobs during the week, hoeing the potatoes, cutting thistles, painting the carts, cleaning harness etc. etc.

Willie and I were at the moss on Saturday spreading the peats. We had been rather long in going however, for they were badly stuck together. A grand excursion party of 60 went from Deskford that day to see Gordon Castle. They got a good day, but they had got further to walk I fear than they had bargained for, it being four miles from the Station. They had a fiddler and piper with them and were to have danced, but little of that amusement had sufficed, and they all came home rather tired.

Sunday was the warmest day we have had. Jessie and I were across at the Free Church in the evening.

1886 July
5ᵗʰ

We have had a week of very nice weather. Bright warm sunshine with soft showers. There has consequently been a marked improvement on all the crops. Grass has now turned plentiful, while turnips are coming up fast. Every-one mostly is now at the hoe. Some have got the swedes all singled.

We commenced on Saturday with some yellow ones, and we were at the swedes today but they are still rather small.

Wednesday last was the Fordyce Pic-nic. They got a splendid afternoon but I did not get down. I saw several Deskford ladies and gentlemen go past. Willie and I were laying down stones for a dyke alongside the cornyard.

On Thursday we were at the moss setting the peats. Father went up with us with the cart and took home a few peats. There was only Joan, Willie and I but we set them all except a few that had been later cast.

On Saturday evening a Mrs Smith from Portsoy came up to see us. She has but lately come to Portsoy, and she has opened a baker's shop and refreshment rooms. She brought her gig and pony and dog along with her. She has a very nice manner but is not particularly good looking.

We were all at church on Sunday except Willie and Joan. We got an excellent sermon from Mr. Mackintosh. His text was 'Unto you therefore which believe He is precious'. 'Christ' he said 'was most precious to believers in his capacity as mediator; but he was also precious as their Prophet, Priest and King. As a Prophet, in that he revealed more fully the will of God. As A Priest in that he offered up himself a sacrifice for our sins. As a King in that he over-rules all things for the good of those who love him.'

12th

We have been busy at the hoe all the week, but it has not been nearly such a nice week as the previous one. We are sorely in need of rain now, and we had two awfully cold days Wednesday and Thursday. It is still bad weather for the bees. I hear of a few swarms in Deskford but they are but few I doubt. I do not think any of mine are ready for swarming yet. I put sections on four of them more than a week ago, and they are just commenced to fill a little.

Wednesday was the day of the polling. Mr. Duff was opposed by a Sir Charles Grant, who calls himself a Liberal Unionist, and who is therefore opposed to granting Home Rule to the Irish. He has completely failed in his attempt however, to unseat our old member who has again come off victorious with a majority of 1180. From the elections that are past however, I fear that the Conservatives are this time going to get into power.

We hoed all the turnips on Friday that were ready.

On Saturday Willie and I started for the moss. The peats were far drier than I expected. I went over to the Smiddy in the afternoon and got hind shoes on to the young mare, as we intend driving peats with her. James Gray came up in the evening and we put her into the cart. She made no disturbance in the least.

We were twice at the moss today again and we had her in the afternoon.

19th

No more cry for rain. There is now abundance of moisture, but it has turned cold after it. We have been very busy hoeing all the week, and we have now excellent plants.

Tuesday was a very nice day but Wednesday forenoon was a perfect spate. We did nothing outside all day. I was making some fancy supers for my bees.

It was the day of the Bogmuchal Picnic, but the bad night had spoiled it a good bit.

Thursday was St. Swithins day, and it was cold and showery. The old saying is, that when rain falls that day, we will have rain more or less every day for six weeks. I do hope it will not prove true on this occasion.

Friday and Saturday were both good days and we kept busy at the hoe. We finished the singling today by dinnertime. I was furring up the potatoes in the afternoon. I got a swarm of bees today, the first of the season.

26th

We have had a week of rather better weather. It has not been very warm but it has been dry. We have been driving peats for most part during the week, and they are in good condition. We took the mare with the foal in the morning and the young one in the afternoon. She is making a grand carter.

On Tuesday and Wednesday afternoons Father and Willie went to the moss while I was cutting the hay. It is a wonderful good crop for the land.

Friday was Peter Fair but none of us was over at it. We were coling the hay in the afternoon and it was nice and quiet. We got a letter that day from Lizzie, saying she would be to see us on Saturday.

Jessie and I went to the Station to meet her at three o'clock but she did not put in her appearance. Thinking she might come with the last train we went up to Cairdswell and when we came back again she was there all right. It had been a very wet morning and she had not started with the morning train. She brought John and Charlie with her. They are both grown a good bit. John is never very strong but Charlie is a nice hardy boy.

Sunday was a wet, misty sort of day and neither Mother, Lizzie, nor Jessie went to church. Mr. Mackintosh is away at Strathpeffer just now, and it was the assistant from Keith that we had. He is quite a young man but he is an excellent preacher.

We were second hoeing today.

I got another swarm of bees on Thursday, but I put them into the hive beside the other one.

1886 August
2nd

We have seen the last of the month of July and I do not remember ever seeing it such a cold month. It is keeping everything back terribly, and the harvest must now be a late one. Barely is about full shot, but oats are not nearly at their length. The moisture which we have had lately has helped to improve them however, and in this district there will be an average crop I think. Early turnips are doing fairly well, but the late ones are scarcely moving. Ours are all looking very well. The past week has been showery and also extremely cold. We have done no hoeing at all, the land being always too wet.

On Thursday evening Willie and I went down to Cullen for an iron bed which Father had bought. There was a grand menagerie in the town so we unyoked and went into see it. There was a good many people down from Deskford and it was well worth seeing. There was lots of animals I had never seen before. The lion tamer was a dark man, a big strong fellow, and he was daring in the extreme. He went in among the wolves, bears, and lions and made them jump over his head, and he fed the lions with raw flesh from his naked hand. He also went in among the tigers, opened their mouths and put his head between their jaws. I went up to the post office to ask for letters and received a telegram for Lizzie from John, telling her to come home on Saturday, as they had got orders to leave their house directly. They are going to take coals out below it and the Rly. Co. will not buy it.[8]

On Friday morning Mr. & Mrs. Bidie arrived with the six train. Jessie and Uncle George went over and met them. They got a very wet morning to come from the Station. After getting breakfast, they all came across the hill, as Lizzie was to start for home in the afternoon. I yoked the cart and drove her over to Cairdswell after dinner.

We were all at church on Sunday except Willie and Joan. Jane & Willie, Father and Mother were all over at Muttonbrae in the afternoon.

9th

We have had a week of rather better weather and there has been a marked improvement on everything. We kept busy at the hoe in the first of the week, and they were working fine. We also cut the seed hay.

There was a meeting of the committee of management of Desk. Hort. Soc. on Wednesday evening.[9] We were making arrangements for the Show.

On Friday we started to drive peats again but the moss was not very dry.

I was not at church on Sunday. George Stephen was over seeing us, and I went over with him in the evening to the Free Church.

Geordie Cowie and Annie were over from Cairdswell today. Willie and I were twice at the moss. I am thinking of going to the Keith Show tomorrow.

16th

Rain, rain, and nothing else but rain. We have had a sad week of soft weather. Every second day we have had a fall of rain. Crops have

---

[8] Rly. Co., Railway Company.
[9] Desk. Hort. Soc., Deskford Horticultural Society.

scarcely advanced any during the week while the last touch has been given to the late turnips. The moss has also been locked all the week, and I fear it will not be very dry this year again. There are lots of peats to be driven yet however.

On Tuesday I went up to see the Keith Show. I got a drive with the folks of Oathillock. It was a nice day until five o'clock, but we got a big shower coming home. The Show was scarcely up to former years I think, and until one o'clock there were very few spectators. The Flower Show was held in a marquee within the Show Yard. There was an excellent display of flowers, far better than ever I saw at Cullen. The vegetables were fair, but apples and pears were almost a failure. The Show of honey was also poor, Mr. Donald Mains of Grange being the only competitor. He had some well finished sections however, considering the season.

On Wednesday forenoon a lot of rain fell. We were turning the heap of earth and lime in the afternoon. Jessie, Jane and I were over at Kirkton at tea. We went out to have a look at the garden of course. Everything is looking extremely well I think, and I was congratulating Miss Duncan on the honours she was sure to gain at the Show.

Thursday was the Banff market and Cornhill Flower and Poultry Shows. Jessie & Jane went over to Cairdswell and Father and Willie were at the market. I was mixing the top-dressing.

Friday was a wet misty day.

Saturday was a little drier. I was cutting grass in the 'den'.

I was driving stones this forenoon for a bridge that is to be built over the burn at Midskeith. In the afternoon we took in and built the hay.

23rd

A great improvement on the weather. We have had nice bright sunny days all the week. Barley is changing colour fast, and will be ready a week at least before oats.

On Tuesday morning June left us for Edinburgh again. Father and Joan went with her to the Station. We have heard since that she arrived all safe.

Wednesday was the day of Cullen Flower Show. I went down to see it in the evening. There was a large turn of people but there was athletic games and dancing in a park beside Cathy House, and most of the folks seemed to be taken up with them. There was a very poor show of pot plants, and fruit, but cut flowers and vegetables were good. I had the good fortune of falling in with a young lady, and had the pleasure of seeing her home.

We were driving peats in the end of the week, and we got them all home on Saturday morning. We went up for two loads for Mr. Smith in the afternoon.

I was kept very busy on Friday and Saturday evening's taking in entries for the Flower Show. There was quite a bundle of letters on Saturday, and in the evening there was sometimes quite a throng. There has been over 400 entries made in all the classes, so, if all come forward, we will have a grand Show on Wednesday.

On Sunday Jessie and I went up from Church to Backies (Mrs. Riddoch's), Dr. James Robb was there and him and Mr. Riddoch were both in Church. He is speaking of starting for India again in about three weeks.

We were in the 'Den' on Monday forenoon taking home the grass that I cut. We went down to Tochineal in the afternoon for two loads of tiles. We would like to get in the drains before harvest.

30th

The great event of the week has been the Annual Picnic and Flower Show. They were held on Wednesday last, the Show in the Public Schools, and the Picnic on the playground, and they were both attended with a success far beyond my most sanguine expectations. The morning was bright and sunny, with a light breeze of wind, and by nine o'clock the road was quite throng with carts, gigs etc. each bringing its load of stuff for the Exhibition, while occasionaly might be seen, some one tenderly carrying a flower and sheltering it from the wind with a large umbrella. For a couple of hours we had quite a busy scene within the Schools but by half past ten we had everything in order; the tables being filled to overflowing. We did not only have a large number of entries, but a good proportion of the exhibits were of excellent quality. The Judges were for Flowers, Fruit and Vegetables Mr. Webster, Park; for Dairy Produce, Mr. Brown, Fordyce; for Honey, Mr. Morrison, Cullen; for Scholastic, Mr. Lorimer M.A., Forglen; and for Industrial Work the Misses Duncan and Mackintosh. The Show was to be opened at 12 noon but it was nearly one before the judging was through. The Judges and one or two of the committee afterwards went down and got dinner, Mrs. Lorimer being our hostess. I had the good fortune to get three prizes. First for a Pelargonium, second for Annuals, first for Floral Device and an extra for the best Geranium in Show. The dancing commenced about three o'clock, and was carried on briskly until day light faded. There was a great many strangers, but the people of the parish also turned out remarkably well, more so than ever I saw at any Deskford gathering. Between five and six hundred it is calculated visited the Show during the day. I had Ardiecow's gig taking over my flowers, and Willie came over for them about half past seven. We danced till nine, when everyone paired off and went home.

On Thursday morning I went to the moss for two loads of peats for Willie Innes, and on Friday morning two loads for Mrs. Milton.

On Sunday they were all at Church except Joan and I. I had a very bad cold. I got infected I think by conveying a young lady home one evening. Mr. Riddoch and Willie came up from Church and spent the afternoon.

1886 September
6th

The past week has been exceptionally fine. Warm with bright sunshine. Crops have advanced very rapidly, and some patches of barley are almost ready for the reaper. The turnips however would be greatly benefited by a shower. A good many complaints are heard of finger and toe. Ours are scarcely thriving as I should like them. It has been splendid weather for the bees however and they have been busy gathering honey from the heather.

There was a meeting on Wednesday evening to settle up the affairs of the Picnic and Flower Show. We had a very large income, nearly £30 and after paying all expenses we had over £10 to carry forward to another year. Driving wood has been the most of our week's work. The sale was on Saturday last. Father brought two lots of larch and one of fir, and James Gray and us had a lot of brushwood between us.

Willie and I were at Portsoy on Saturday for two loads of coals for the blacksmith. After dinner I saddled the young mare and set out for Finnygaud. It was the day of the Sillyearn Flower Show, and as I had never been round the back of the Knock I thought I might go that way and see both the Show, and the country. I put in the mare at Knockbog which is not far from the Schools. The Show of pot plants was far behind Deskford, but some things were fully up with us. On going back to Knockbog I had to go in and get tea. There was a large company of ladies and gentlemen. I arrived at Cairdswell about seven o'clock and stayed there all night.

I went over to Finnygaud on Sunday morning. Sandy was town keeper, and after the others went away to church we had a look at the crops and stock. Their turnips are looking remarkably well, but some of their oats seem light. There is never any difference on Mary. She was only up for about an hour on Sunday.

13th

The weather has been duller since last I wrote. There was scarcely any sunshine until Friday. Although dull there has been but little rain, but I hear of good falls in some districts. There are some stooks now to be seen in the Parish, the furthest up being Kirkton, who commenced on Thursday. It is only barley however, and it will be the end of the week before there be much oats. I scarcely think we will get any this week yet.

We sold the black horse on Wednesday to a carter in Portsoy. I think the young mare will manage now nicely. We had a call of Mr. Harper from Wishaw the day. In the afternoon I went over to Muttonbrae with Willie Riddoch.

Thursday was Cornhill market day. Father and I were both across. He was going to sell two ewes, so I had them over while he followed with the cart. He sold his ewes and I bought one from Sandy Cowie for £1.10. There was but a small market. After it was over, we went up to Park with the Gardener to see his flowers. He has a large garden, nicely laid off, and well kept. The hot house is not large, but he has some nice plants. I got two ferns from him, a double geranium, a gymnogramma   and some slips of sedums.

I was over opening the Library on Friday evening, but there were not many attended.

We commenced on Saturday to cast our drains in the den. We drew some furrows with the plough which will help us greatly.

On Sunday morning, George Cowie and Annie with Sandy and Willie came over with the machine. Sandy and Willie went over to Swailend. The rest of us were all at church. Annie is going to stay with us all the week, so Jessie went over to keep house at Cairdswell. We were getting wood cut today for soles to our drains. I had it down to the sawmill in the afternoon. After we came home, Willie and I started to drum a hive. It was a very large hive and was well filled with honey. Willie McWillie came down and spent the evening with us.

20th

We commenced harvest today, just a week later than last year. The most of the barley is now cut in the Parish and in general I think it is a better crop than oats on clean land. Some of them have stopped a few days after cutting their barley as the oats were not ripe. It has not been 'forcy' harvest weather during the past week, being rather quiet.

There was a very sharp frost on Friday and Saturday mornings, real white, while in Grange they say there was ice on the water. The potatoes up there have been all blackened in the stems. We have been in the 'Den' casting drains for the most part during the week. They do not take long to cast as we get them little over two feet, and they are quite soft, no sign of a hard bottom. We have two hundred yards to put in yet.

I went over to Kirkton on Wednesday and spent the evening.

We had a letter from Mary on Thursday. It had been written on 2nd August and had scarcely been six weeks on the way after being posted. She seems to be greatly taken up with the new country, people, place and everything. One of Andrew's Uncles had built a cottage for them and Andrew was working fitting it up. The houses are all built of wood she says. I have been thinking for some time back, that I might do worse than start for Australia myself by another year. Willie will soon be able to do the work, and there will be no use for us both at home. And then farming here is such a poor job. It is hard work and little pay, with the prospect that very soon there will be no pay at all.

We had Willie Riddoch down on Thursday afternoon bidding us good-bye as he was to leave for India again today.

On Friday Mother and Annie set out for Portsoy and Mother went up with her to Cairdswell, and came home with Jessie last night.

Only Father and Willie were at church on Sunday. I went down in the afternoon to have a sight of the Bogs before the leaves begin to fall. I met Miss K. Duncan who was telling me that George was very unwell and was to be home whenever he was able to be removed. I went to the Free Church in the evening, and saw Mrs. Walker in church. She is a very tall lady, but seems to be rather indifferent looking. We got an excellent sermon from Mr. Walker.

26th

Harvest operations are now in full swing, and a good many stooks are to be seen in the Parish. I scarcely think that yesterday will be stookie Sunday however. The last three days have been dry, but before that it was showery.

We did not cut any on Tuesday forenoon, and the afternoon being showery also, we left the barely, and cut roads round the lea.

We got seven hours of the reaper on Wednesday.

Thursday was a wet day out and out. We were making rapes.

Friday and Saturday were both dry days.

On Friday we finished the lea and also the most of the barley. They are both a better crop than I was thinking.

We cut roads round the ayvels on Saturday and got the machine yoked in the afternoon. About five o'clock we were greatly disappointed at the reaper breaking down, part of the framing giving way. The blacksmith came over and took part of it with him, but it was dinnertime today before he brought it back. We yoked however and were getting on nicely when another bolt broke and Willie had to go off to the Smiddy while I took the scythe. It has been extremely blowy today, quite a gale at times. I was sometimes fearing that it would shake the corn, but I did not see any out.

Father, Jessie and I were at church yesterday. It was a very nice day but the church was rather thin. We got a very good sermon from Mr. Mackintosh from the text 'Ye know the truth, and the truth shall make you free'. In the afternoon Mr. & Mrs. Hendry, Cairnton, and old Mrs. Hendry came up to see us. They have a day and a half's cutting yet.

1886 October
11ᵗʰ

A very bad week of harvest weather. Except Friday afternoon and today there has been no leading whatever. There has never been much wet, but it has been close misty days, very bad for heating stacks. I hear of there being some and we had one which was a little.

In the first of the week we were making rapes. I went up to Backies in the evening to see my friends there. Mrs. Riddoch has been rather lonely since Willie left, but she has Miss Robb staying with her just now. Willie was to sail from London on the 30ᵗʰ Sept. I was sorry to find that Miss McWillie had been unwell, and the Dr. attending her. It is inflammation in her shoulder but it is keeping better. Willie and I spent a very pleasant evening discussing the various topics of interest—agriculture, beekeeping, The Flower Show—The Mutual Improvement Society—etc. etc.

As we had plenty of rapes made I went down on Wednesday and gave James Gray a hand, as he was not done with the cutting. He has got a very good crop this year.

On Friday afternoon we took in two stacks but I was not greatly pleased with it.

I went to the brick work on Saturday forenoon for two loads of tiles and in the afternoon we were at the drain in the 'Den'.

Sunday was a nice dry day. Joan and I were town keeping. There being a late sermon at Fordyce we went down there. We got an excellent sermon from Mr. Gibson, Portsoy, from the text 'As long as the earth remaineth, seed time and harvest shall not cease'. We came up with the folks of Little Cultain and they made us go in past and have tea.

This has been a good day. We were thatching in the forenoon and the in the afternoon we got in two stacks in good condition. There has been some rain since evening however.

18ᵗʰ

We got finished with the harvest tonight, having been four weeks and one day. There has been more than a week of bad weather out of that however. We have a bigger cornyard than last year. One stack more, and they are a little bigger I think. The extra quantity will not make up for the lowness in price however. Grain I fear is to be very cheap this winter. At present Barley is 20/- and oats 15/- per quarter. We have not thrashed very much yet, but I think it is appearing to turn out pretty fair, and it also looks well bodied grain. The past week, has been a good harvest week, and the greater bulk of the stooks have now disappeared, excepting our neighbour Ardiecow, who has only got the half of it cut. His corn is very very green this year.

We got other two stacks in on Tuesday afternoon.

Wednesday was a grand day. We turned over the clean land stooks in the morning and by dinnertime they were in very good order. We got it all in by six o'clock. We have 18 stacks in all.

Thursday was Cornhill market day. Willie and I went to the rake in the morning for two hours, but I then went over to the market. There was a very small turn out, being harvest time, but there seemed to be a pretty ready sale, especially among sheep. I was going to buy a ewe but they were too dear.

On Friday we were tidying up the stacks. Ordens came over in the afternoon to get two loads of corn thrashed, as he had no water.

Saturday was a wet day. A lot of rain had fallen during the night. I was cutting thatch in the afternoon to cover the potatoes.

Father, Mother, Joan and I were at church on Sunday. We had the assistant from Keith preaching as Mr Mackintosh is ailing.

I was down at Cullen House today trying to make a new bargain with 'The Laird'. There is a break in the Lease next Whitsunday, and the times have so greatly altered since five years ago, that we think it absolutely necessary that there should be some reduction in the rent. I did not get great encouragement however, Mr. Bryson was very civil, but he could not see his way at all to let down the rent. The land was too dear perhaps, but it was not dearer than our neighbours he said. The only concession I could get was that they might give money to drain for 5 per cent interest. I did not agree to accept of it however, as I intend going back to try them again.

25ᵗʰ

It has been a weary, weary week for those who are still harvesting. There has been no leading at all since last I wrote. The days have been warm, quiet, and showery, on some nights a good deal of rain falling. There are still a good many stooks about the hill sides, and Ardiecow managed to get clyack tonight. It has also been bad weather for the stacks that are in, and I hear of a good many needing to thrash out. Ours are all keeping as yet I think.

On Tuesday morning I went up for Backies chilled plow as I was to get a trial of it for a few days. Instead of break-furring the ayvels I have given them a light fur 4½ inches. I think it will clean the land and also let in the frost better. It is Oliver's Patent Chilled Plow and I am greatly pleased with it. It is much easier held, and I am sure it is also easier drawn than the common plough. It also comes more speed. I have been ploughing at the rate of an acre in eight hours.

We had a meeting of the Mutual Improvement Society on Tuesday evening. The rules and regulations were all revised and a good many alterations made. Office bearers were also elected for the coming session. Mr. McWillie resigned the office of President and I have been elected instead. It has fallen upon me to write an essay for next meeting, and so I will have to stop and set my wits to work.

1886 November
1ˢᵗ

Assisting at the steam mill and lifting the potatoes has been the most of our week's work. It has been good weather for both these purposes.

I was in the chilled plow on Tuesday.

The steam mill was at Careston on Wednesday, and Willie and I were down giving them a hand. Father took a few hours of the plow in the forenoon. In the afternoon he had it up to the Backies.

On Thursday we commenced to lift the potatoes. We had William Innes and Lizzie Ritchie helping us. We kept very busy all day and we managed to take up ten loads. As we had to go to Hoggie next day to the mill we had to let the potatoes alone.

We were at them on Saturday again and got a very nice day. We had other six loads.

I was town keeper on Sunday. Alex Duncan and George were up in the afternoon. George is looking a little better I think, but he has still a very bad cough. He is speaking of going to Bridge of Allan for some time.

Today Jessie has left us for Edinburgh again. Father went over with her to Cairdswell, she is not leaving however until tomorrow morning. We will miss her I am sure for some time. Willie and I were driving turnips in the forenoon. I went up in the afternoon and gave Ardiecow a help with the leading. His corn was not in the best condition.

8ᵗʰ

We have had a week of excellent weather. Grand blowy days with bright sunshine. It will do a vast amount of good, but it was sorely needed. There is scarcely anyone but has had some warm stacks.

On Tuesday we were putting out dung on to the stubbles. We had a meeting of the Mut. Imp. that evening. There were eight or nine new members. Willie has joined this winter. I read a paper on 'Time'.[10] We were speaking about getting up a course of lectures during the winter.

Thursday was our fast day. We had Mr. Grant, Fordyce, preaching. I went down to Fordyce in the evening and came in past Cairnton. He has got an extra large cornyard this year. Willie and I were at Muttonbrae on Friday forenoon at the steam mill. He thrashed 6 ricks and he had a very good out turn of grain. The day was quiet and warm.

Saturday was quite a change however, it being cold and stormy.

Sunday was also very cold. We were all at church except Willie. The minister had no one assisting him but he gave us a very touching address at the close.

Today I went down again to the office at Cullen House to see if I could get the Factor to reduce the rent any. Mr. Michie is to be sent up to see what draining we require and to report.

15th

A week of very wet weather. A great deal of rain has fallen, and the earth is now quite saturated. The stubbles are too wet for ploughing and I have started the lea in the Den. I think two days would finish the stubbles. The past week has been one of sudden deaths. Mr. Pirie, watchmaker, died on Monday of heart disease after 12 hours illness. Mr. Smith, Nether Blairock was up and going about on Sunday. In the evening they had gone out with some friends and on returning they found him dead in his chair. He was buried in Deskford Churchyard on Thursday. Peter Murray, Banker, Portsoy also died rather suddenly on Monday.

Wednesday was Hallow Fair. It was a terribly bad day. Rain fell in torrents nearly all day. Father was down but he did not stay long. Wages are a little down, but many are not engaged.

I went over on Friday night and opened the Library. It was the Annual Meeting but very few attended. The members of Committee were all re-elected.

On Sunday morning I put the saddle on the young mare and started for Puttingbrae. The morning was nice and clear and it was a very fine day. There had been rain through the night however and the roads were very wet, especially about the Shielburn. It is a rather bleak looking country over there, and they have got none of their stacks thatched yet. On gaining the top of the hill a splendid view is obtained. Far away to the

---

[10] Printed in Appendix 2.

west, as far as the eye can reach, stretches a fine level cultivated country, while the sandy beach winds out and in till lost in the hazy distance. The fishing villages could be easily seen all along the coast while the town of Buckie seems almost to lie at your feet. As the morning sun was shining clearly the Sutherland hills could also be seen quite distinctly stretching along the coast, some of their number being topped with snow.

I found them all well at Puttingbrae, and having got in the mare and rested a little Geordie and I went away to have a sight of the House and grounds of Letterfourie. It is a sadly neglected place. The walks are all full of rabbit burrows, the fences broken down and the fields uncultivated. It is a very large house however, and would have been a pretty place if kept in order. The gardens lie down in the brae and are finely sheltered. They are let to a man who makes market of everything. There is a great extent of hothouses full of vines and figs. After getting a sight of them we kept down the burn side past the 'Craigie' well. It is a very pretty place here, fine level haughs with large spreading beech trees. Further down the burn winds through a deep ravine, with ivy climbing up the sides and ferns still green nestling in the nooks and crannies. A very romantic bridge here spans the burn called 'Craigmin'. It is a bridge above a bridge there being one arch below and two above. Looking over from the top the height is tremendous. We then went past Puttingbrae to give the horses meal and Mrs. Davidson took us in and gave us a 'dram'. I started for home at half past four but it was quite dark before I got home.

I was in the plough this forenoon again.

22nd

I was over at Kirkton assisting at the steam mill on Tuesday. It was a very fine day, the stuff was in good order, and so we did a big day's work. We were thinking there was nearly 60 quarters of barley, and 7 of oats. The barley is 57 lbs per bushel I hear. There was an entertainment in the Schools that evening. Mr. Ross, photographer from Cullen, with a 'magic lantern'. There was also a meeting of the Mut. Imp. Society. We had a debate and a very animated discussion it was. The subject was 'whether is there more pleasure in the pursuit, or in the attainment of an object.' Mr. A. Geddes led for the pursuit and Mr. R. Duncan for the attainment. Both gentlemen had excellent papers, and did full justice to their respective sides. The most of the members also took part in the discussion. At the close 8 voted for the attainment and 4 for the pursuit.

Wednesday was the thanksgiving day for the harvest. We had Mr. Macdonald from Cullen preaching. Joan and Willie went over to Cairdswell.

I was ploughing lea on Thursday forenoon. In the afternoon I went to the Smiddy and got one of the mares shod.

Friday morning was very wet, and I did not go to the yoke. We were winnowing corn.

On Saturday Father had it to Portsoy. The price which was up to 16/6 last week, is down again to 15/ and only that for good corn. His weighed 42lbs. Willie and I were filling the mill.

They were all at church on Sunday but myself. Willie and I went to the Free Church in the evening. Mr. Walker gave us an excellent sermon from the text, 'your sorrow shall be turned into joy.'

Willie was ploughing stubbles this forenoon, while Father and I were at the drains in the Den. They are almost finished now.

I have been reading during the week a very interesting book on New Zealand by William Dalishe Hay. He gives a glowing description of the country, its climate and its people, but it is not the bright side only which he pictures. He tells of the hard work which must be undergone before the forest can be subdued and rendered cultivated land, but he also tells with what certainty well directed, persevering labour always gains a competency.

29th

I hardly ever remember a week of such fine dry weather in November, as the past one has been. It has also been extremely free of frost. Every one has been busy at the plough and a good breadth has been turned over. I have been in the 'den' but I am only ploughing down hill. The storing of turnips has also been commenced by some. I furred up about two acres in the end of the week.

On Friday evening the first of a course of Lectures, under the auspices of the Mutual Improvement Society, was delivered by Rev. And. Black, Keith. His subject was General Gordon. He gave us a good lengthy lecture, but he had a very bad cold, and consequently did not deliver it so well as he might have done. The audience was not very large.

We were all at church on Sunday except Willie. In the afternoon I went up to Backies to see my friends there. Willie has not been very well for sometime, and is looking very thin.

Father went to the mill this forenoon with a load of corn while Willie and I have been pulling turnips to store. They are not nearly such a good crop as last year and there is a lot of canker among them.

1886 December
6th

We have experienced the first snow-storm of the season and it has been rather a severe one.

Tuesday was excessively cold and blowy, and we were saying it was surely blowing through snow. I was in the plough in the forenoon, but in the afternoon we gathered and covered the turnips we pulled the day before.

Next morning the ground was white. We took in a load of corn, thrashed and winnowed it, as we were expecting the steam mill. In the afternoon we went to Tochineal for two loads of tiles. The proprietor is going to put in some drains to us this winter and they are to be let tomorrow. As we were loading at the Brickwork it began to snow and it kept falling very thickly all the way home. About five o'clock the wind rose, and there being now about four inches of snow it commenced to drift. It had kept blowing the whole night I think for in the morning there were some tremendous wreathes.

It also drifted some on Thursday all day while the frost was intense. Willie and I were cleaning at the harness.

Friday was quiet and a little soft. We took in the remainder of the stack, thrashed and took home some turnips. I went over to the singing in the Schools that evening. I am going to attend this winter I think.

Saturday and Sunday were both soft and a good deal of the snow disappeared.

Joan, Willie and I were at church. It was very thin, the roads being very bad. I went over to see the folks at Muttonbrae in the afternoon. I was telling Uncle that I was thinking of going out to Australia next year and he did not seem to be greatly against it at all.

It has been nice and fresh today and except the wreathes, most of the snow has disappeared. I have been ploughing all day.

13th

We had a meeting of the Mutual Imp. Soc. on the evening of Tuesday last. Most of the members were present. Mr. Geo. Taylor read an essay on Happiness. Our drains were let that day. There were twenty people on the ground, and 10 offers were given in. James Cameron, Cullen was the lowest, his offer being 11/11½ for the minors and 13/6 for the leaders. They are to be 3½ feet deep.

Ten of them made a start today. We have been driving tiles the last three days. The past week has been very soft, rain or snow almost every day.

Sandy Lamb got his thrashing machine into the Cornyard on Saturday evening.

We were to thrash today, but there had been rain through the night and the stacks were very wet. I hope it may go to the frost and dry up the dubs by tomorrow.

On the evening of Friday last the second of the Course of Lectures was delivered by Rev. A. M. Porteous B.D., Cullen. His subject was 'John Knox and Mary Queen of Scots'. The lecturer handled his subject in a very masterly manner. It was exceedingly interesting and altogether it was quite a literary treat. Mr. Walker occupied the chair.

20th

We have had two weeks of rather stormy kind of weather, but we have now got a proper fall of snow. I have not measured it but I am sure there is from ten to twelve inches all over. There has also been a little blowing and some roads are partly blocked. Out door work of all kind is quite at a stand still, and they may be very thankful who have got a good supply of turnips.

We got a very good day for the thrashing on Tuesday. It was quiet and frosty, and we commenced betimes in the morning. We were done by twelve o'clock, and he went down and thrashed James Gray in the afternoon.

We were twice at the brickwork on Wednesday.

On Thursday morning we winnowed up two loads of barley but it looked showery and so we went for tiles. We had it down to Glenglassaugh in the afternoon.

We were also back on Friday. It scarcely turned out so well as we were expecting there being but 14 qrs./bu. It weighed 55½ and 56 lbs however. The snow came on on Friday afternoon and by Saturday morning there was 6½ inches. It kept snowing and blowing the most of the day. Something strange at this season of the year is so much thunder and lightning. Several loud peals of thunder have been heard during the past week, and the lightning in some places has done great damage.

On Sunday morning there was another large addition to the snow. I was the only one at church from this side, and the attendance was very small. It has been quiet today and extremely frosty. We were taking in straw and turnips.

As I was tidying up my desk the other evening I came upon some verses which Annie sent me more than a year ago. I returned an answer to her and as I would like to preserve them both I will copy them into my 'Diary'.

The following is my Sister's production:-

The Hardest Time of All
There are days of silent sorrow, in the season of our life,

There are wild despairing moments, there are hours of mental strife,
There are times of strong anguish, when the tears refuse to fall,
But the waiting time my Brother, is the hardest time of all.

Youth and love are oft impatient, seeking things beyond their reach,
And the heart grows sick of hoping, ere it learns what life can teach,
For before the fruit be gathered, we must see the blossoms fall,
And the waiting time my Brother, is the hardest time of all.

We can beat the heat of conflict, though the sudden crushing blow,
Beating back our gathered forces, for a moment lays us low,
We may rise again beneath it, move the weakest for the fall,
But the waiting time my Brother, is the hardest time of all.

For it wears the eager spirit, as the salt waves wear the stone,
And the garb of Hope grows thread-bare, till its brightest tints are flown
Then amidst Youth's raven tresses, silver streaks begin to fall,
Oh! the waiting time my Brother, is the hardest time of all.

But at last we learn the lesson that God knoweth what is best,
For with wisdom cometh patience, and with patience cometh rest,
Yea a golden thread is shining through the tangled woof of fate,
And with our hearts we thank God meekly, that he taught us how to wait.

The Sweetest Time of All

There are days of sweetest gladness, in the course of every life,
There are seasons when all sadness, seem quite banished from the strife,
There are times of strong emotion, when the tears of joy do fall,
But the waiting time my Sister, is the sweetest time of all.

Love and Youth may be impatient, but impatience is no crime,
For it properly directed, oft leads to heights sublime
And the greatest zest of pleasure, in anticipation's found,
In pursuit more pleasure is than in possession safe and sound,
Although'fore the fruit be gathered we must see the blossoms fall,
Sure the waiting time my Sister is the sweetest time of all.

Love and Youth they are twin sisters, and their pleasures none may name;
'Tween the gloamin' and the mirk, when the kye come lowin' hame,
Or when at the trysting tree, the shades of evening sweetly fa',
Oh! the waiting time my Sister is the sweetest time o' a'

27ᵗʰ

The snow-storm still continues, but there has been no addition to the
fall since last I wrote. I see by the newspapers however, that over all
the north of Scotland it is extremely heavy, two feet being mentioned
in some places. The powdery condition of the snow in the first of the

week would have rendered it very liable to drift had the wind risen in the least.

On Tuesday morning there was a slight breeze, and in exposed places there was a little blowing, but towards night it softened, and it had been quite fresh throughout the night. Frost however, again set in on Wednesday and since then has continued very hard.

On Tuesday I went down past Glenglassaugh and got money for the barley and went in to Portsoy. I then took the train and came out to Cullen. There was a meeting of the Mut. Imp. in the evening. The Debate was 'Should Scotland have Home Rule'. Mr. Bain led for the affirmative, while Mr. McWillie sent a paper supporting the negative. The Debate was rather tame, very few of the members taking part in it. On the vote being taken there was found to be a majority of five in favour of Home Rule. My friend Mr. McWillie has been in bad health for some time, and I fear his is not seeming to make much better. I was writing him a long letter the other evening and sending him a Christmas card.

I got two Xmas cards on Saturday, one from Mrs. Bidie and one from Jessie. Jessie has got a situation now. She is going to be cook and housekeeper to some engineers at the Forth Bridge Works, and is getting £35 a year.

On Saturday Father was at the funeral of James Inglis, Muir of Glassaugh. He has been confined to bed for the past three or four months and he died on Wednesday morning.

I was not in church on Sunday forenoon, but Willie and I went to the Free Church in the evening. Mr. Walker in the course of his sermon made reference to the close of the year, and spoke very touchingly on the fleeting nature of time, and how we ought to strive to make a proper use of the same.

We have been employed during the week trenching a piece in the Den, but we got it finished tonight.

31ˢᵗ

The month of December has been a very stormy one throughout. The bad weather coming on so suddenly found farmers but badly prepared for it. Turnips have not been stored to any great extent, but the great depth of snow has protected them from the frost and as yet little damage has been done. During the past week the frost has not been extreme, and had it not been for the snow, it would have been fine winter weather. There is some appearance of a thaw tonight.

Yesterday we commenced to drive out dung, and today we have been pulling turnips, managing seven loads as our day's work.

This morning Father set out for Aberdeen. Uncle has not been well at all for some time, and Father thought he would like to see him. Uncle George was thinking of going with him, but the cold weather frightened him.

And so another year has run its course, and we have seen the last of 1886. I cannot say it has been a bright year, nor yet a prosperous one, for it has been and still is dull in the extreme. The season during the early spring was fairly good for sowing the seeds. During the turnip sowing it was rather wet. This has probably been the cause of so much finger and toe among the turnips. The summer time was extremely cold with strong frosts until the end of June. With such weather it seems surprising that there could have been such good crops, for good crops there were; cereals I am sure being above an average in this district at least. If crops have been good however, prices have been very low. Oats at present are selling from 14/ to 15/ per quarter. Barley which at one time was almost unsaleable, took a great start about the end of November and rose 4/ per quarter. This was caused I believe by the barley being all spoiled in the south, and also by the Brewers in the south requiring an extra supply from the fact that the other grains from which they have been malting for some years proving unremunerative they have again turned to the barley. The cheapness of beef however is the farmer's greatest grievance. Six or seven years ago he was getting £4 the cwt. At present 58/ Is about the highest while 40/ is quoted for second quality. Manure has this year been a little cheaper, but other things are about the same.

The prospects therefore with which we enter on a new year are not particularly bright. I have been turning my attention lately to some of our other colonies, especially those in Australia. I have got handbooks and circulars from the Emigrants' Information Office on the colonies of Victoria, New South Wales and Queensland. I am convinced that any one with good health and willing to work, could do far better there than in this country. New South Wales seems to me to offer the best prospects of any. I have been talking the matter over with Father a little, but he does not seem to be very fond of me going at all. He is failing he says and will soon be unable to manage things. Now this is very true and for his sake I would be easily persuaded to remain and think it was my duty to do so; but when I think of Willie who is now a strong boy going sixteen years of age and who in a few years will be quite a man, I cannot see that there is any real difficulty in my way. For my own part I would make no hesitation, but it is hard to decide when others are concerned.

A Journal of My Life and Everyday Doings

1887 January
3rd

What a short time it appears since I was sitting writing the first week of my 'Diary' for 1886. And yet a whole year has gone since then, carrying with it such a host of incidents, marking such a number of changes, and yet leaving us seemingly so little improved, from what we were at its commencement. How quickly time flies past, and what a strange thing time is when we consider it seriously. Never for a moment does it stay its course. While we are speaking it flies past and is gone forever, never more to be recalled again. Tennyson's lines in reference to the brook, are strictly true as regards time

Men may come, and men may go
But I go on forever.

May the consideration of the fleeting nature of time,—the consideration of its immense value, stir us up, to be more earnest in its improvement. May the words of Job be in engraven upon our minds, and written on the table of our hearts, so as to influence our lives; 'Whatsoever thy hand findeth to do, do it with all thy might'.

I have finished reading Smiles' book on 'Self Help' and a better book I never read in my life. It is a book which all young men ought to read and study. It contains so many practical lessons, and so many illustrious examples, of what other have done, by their perseverance; courage; industry; economy; honesty; energy; application; decision of character; truthfulness; accuracy and punctuality; that beyond any other book I have ever read, it ought to be the means of stimulating us to diligence in business; to self improvement; and to an earnest striving to follow those, who have left such well defined footprints, on the sands of time.

New Year's day was fresh, and a good deal of the snow disappeared during the day. George Cowie and Annie came over from Cairdswell in the forenoon. Uncle George also came over before dinnertime. The Annual Ploughman's Ball was held at Raemore this year. The Shooting Match was held at Berryhillock as in former years.

Joan and I were at church on Sunday. We had a young minister preaching, and we got an excellent sermon from him. His text was, the raising of Jarius' daughter, and more especially the words 'Trouble not the Master'.

I went to the Smiddy this morning and got both the mares frosted, as the roads will be as clear of snow now, as will let me get tiles driven.

10th

I have been busy all the week driving tiles, and since last I wrote I have lifted from the Tilework over 7000. The road to Milton is good, and I get on full loads, but I take nearly the half off, before coming up the brae. I had Joseph McKay with me two days, and we were greatly obliged to him for such a friendly lift.

There is going to be a ploughing match at Oathillock the first fresh Friday. They lost one of their horses about a month ago. We had a meeting of the Mut. Imp. on Tuesday evening. It was a hat night and most of the members had very good papers. Father came home from Aberdeen that evening. Uncle 'Limes' had also been in, and came home with him. He was telling us that George had got married about two weeks ago and he thinks a good deal of his wife.

I was up at Backies on Saturday evening seeing my friends there. Willie is now keeping much better and is able to go about and do something again. The weather which has been frosty all the week, has turned a little soft today. I hope it may continue as we are needing turnips.

17ᵗʰ

I have had a busy week again among the tiles, but other two loads now, and I would have plenty I think. There are five or six thousand of them at Milton yet however. The roads have been extraordinary slippery all the week, in fact I never saw them so bad, but the horses were holding quite well.

There were two pairs from Kirkton on Friday giving us a lift, for which we were very thankful.

On Thursday evening the third of the Course of Lectures, was delivered by Mr. McIntyre, Seafield. His subject was 'The Talmud and its humourous Lore'. He first explained what the Talmud was stating that it was a Jewish book of 12 large quarto volumes containing traditions, fables, proverbs etc, supposed to be handed down from Moses and the other Judges of Israel. He then gave a large number of extracts, chiefly of a humourous character, but many of which were also very instructive. There was about the usual attendance, and Mr. Mackintosh occupied the chair.

The Library was open on Friday evening, when there was a good attendance.

Willie, Joan and I were at church on Sunday. Mr. Mackintosh preached from Romans I, 14. We had a letter today from Jessie. She went home to her new place a week ago. She is cook and housekeeper to six young gentlemen (engineers and contractors) out at South Queensferry, where the Forth Bridge is being built.

24ᵗʰ

We have got rid of the frost and snow at last, and thankful we are to see the green grass again. In the first of the week we were driving tiles up from Milton and except eight loads or so they are now all home.

We had a meeting of The Mut. Imp. on Tuesday evening. Mr. Mitchell read an excellent paper on the Life of Gladstone. It was agreed to have a Social Meeting this year again.

On Thursday afternoon the thaw set in, but it was Saturday before I got to the plough.

I was town keeper on Sunday, but I went over to the Free Church in the evening. I commenced today to plough the haugh in the Den, but it is going to be a very stiff job. I had a letter from Andrew Bremner today. He is liking Victoria remarkably well, and getting on grand. He is getting all the work he can manage and gets 10/ in the day and his dinner. I will have to stop writing however, and go and clean the harness as I expect the ploughing match will came off on Friday.

31ˢᵗ

A week of excellent weather, with the plough going merrily again. It is a little too good to last long I fear. There has been very high winds during the week, and the land is quite seed coloured. The drainers are getting on with their work, and are more than half done I think.

We got a very good day for the ploughing match on Friday and there was a grand turnout, there being 29 ploughs. The Judges were Mr. Duncan, Muirpark and Mr. Ingram, Joukstone. They awarded me three prizes but the committee said I broke the rules and only gave me one. I did not hear the regulations read but it seems there was no leading allowed except at the furring. I had a leader taking out my mids until the Committee told me it was against the regulations, when I put him away and finished myself. The Judges placed me ninth for ploughing; the best finish, and the neatest ends. The Committee however only gave me the prize for the neatest ends. Several of the other competitors broke the rules but they were taken no notice of. Such bungling could scarcely be let pass without being taken notice of. I am going to send a few lines to the Banffshire Journal next week to expose them. Geo. Taylor was first for ploughing. J. Maitland for harness and G. McCombie for grooming.

I went over to see the folks at Cairdswell on Saturday afternoon and came home on Sunday.

I went to church when we got a very good sermon from Mr. McVicar.

We have been ploughing in the den today.

Although little outdoor work has been done during the month of January still the weather has not been extra severe. Except last week it was always frosty, still the frost was never excessive, and the wind was generally quiet. The most noteworthy feature in connection with the past month has been the slippery condition of the roads. I never remember such a time of ice. The slipperiness has been the cause of a great many accidents, two of our own parishioners getting broken bones. James Rumbles, Senior, fell in Cullen and broke his thigh, while Mrs. Barron fell at her own door and broke her arm. Since the thaw we have had several gales of wind. I have not heard of much damage being done on the land, but considerable loss has been caused at sea. A Portsoy boat was run down by a trawler off Fraserburgh and the whole crew of eight men drowned. An emigrant ship going to Australia also foundered and nearly 300 lives were lost.

1887 February
7th

Another week of ploughing weather, and every-body is taking advantage of it. As it continues dry, those who have ayvels have been ploughing at them. There is still a good breadth of lea to plough. We were several days in the 'Den' but we have now got it all finished. I was two days in the little park beside the wood.

There was a meeting of the Mut. Imp. Society on Tuesday evening. The debate was 'Whether is Nature or Art the most beautiful to the eye'. It fell to me to support Nature, while Mr. Clarke upheld Art. Most of the members took part in the debate, and the discussion was very lively. On a vote being taken, there was a majority of one in favour of Nature.[11]

On Friday evening we had a lecture—the last of the Course, delivered by Mr. Walker F.C. His subject was 'Something in everybody's mouth', and he made out the something to be language. There was a large attendance and the Rev. gentleman got a very patient hearing. He could not tell us however what was the first language spoken. It used to be thought that it was Hebrew, but that idea was now relinquished. One thing he said seemed to be obvious- that man did not have a language ready made to his hand. He then explained the different theories, that have been set forth as to how language had been formed viz. the bow-wow theory; the ding dong theory, and the phoo phoo theory. Mr. Smith performed the duties of the Chair in his usual able manner.

[11] Printed in Appendix 2.

On Sunday Joan, Willie and I were at church. It was well filled. The minister gave us a very impressive sermon from Acts XXIV, 24. Paul reasoning with Felix and his wife, on righteousness, temperance and the judgement to come.

I commenced today to plough the ayvels. Father was down with Craibstone seeing James Cowie of Drakemires, and is newly come home. Mrs. Gray, Knowes, got twins last week; a son and a daughter. John Reid, Squaredoch, died last week. He was aged 87.

14th

I was in the plough all day on Tuesday. The land is in the best of season for ploughing. There was a meeting of Committee that evening making arrangements for the Social Meeting.

There was a hard frost on Wednesday. We were filling the mill, and driving off the stones that came out of the drains. I went down in the evening to a Soiree in the Lintmill. A great many Deskford people were down and I was quite delighted with the whole affair. The best speaker I think was Mr. Stockdale from Grange. An excellent choir under leadership of Mr. Buchanan, Teacher, gave a number of hymns and songs in excellent style.

Thursday was Cornhill market day. Father and I went over with three of the cattle. There was a good turn out of beasts, and a fair demand for keepers. Fat however brought but a very low figure. We were reckoning we had 13 cwts. and we just got £35. There has been several outbreaks of Pleuro Pneumonia in this district lately. At Mill of Buckie 60 cows have been killed and about 20 in Buckie. Geo. Benzie, Blackhillock, has all his killed, also Geo. Ewing, Summerton. I also hear that it has broken out at Breach. Calves coming from the Dairies about Buckie have been the means of spreading it a good deal. Willie McWillie came home with us from the market, and stayed the evening. His is never very strong yet.

It was soft again on Friday but I could not manage the plough. There was a large attendance in the evening at the Library.

I was in the plough all day on Saturday.

I was town keeper on Sunday, but I went over to the Free Church in the evening.

21st

There was a meeting of the Mutual Improvement Society on Tuesday evening. Mr. Longmore read a paper on Hypocrisy. Some further arrangements were made as to the Social Meeting.

Father went to the Tilework on Wednesday afternoon for a load of tiles, while I was at the mill and Smiddy. I had over a load of corn, but the miller is stopping buying. I hear that they will scarcely buy it anywhere. The drainers are now commenced to the new grass. The contractor has made a new bargain, and got two shillings more for them. We also drew two furrows for him.

I was writing to Andrew Bremner in the end of the week. I was asking a great many questions about Victoria. I have now made up my mind that I shall go out there in the end of summer, probably in the month of August. Jessie seems always inclined to go too. She is going to give me a loan of £30 to take me out.

We had a letter from Jane today, and she was saying that Tom Stirling was confined to his bed altogether now, and that the Doctor had no hopes of his recovery. Poor Maggie, she will be sorely tried with so many little ones.

We were all at church on Sunday except Mother and Willie. The minister in his sermon directed our attention to the sin of unbelief. We were all extremely liable, he said, of falling into the sin of unbelief. We disbelieved, not only God's threatenings, but also His promises. The chief causes of this were, ignorance, and the want of a true conception of God's power and greatness. The subject of his discourse was the unbelieving lord, who, when the city of Samaria was besieged by the Syrians, and with famine staring them in the face, scoffed at the words of Elijah the Prophet, when he said, that 'a measure of fine flour for a shekel, and two measures of barley for a shekel shall be sold tomorrow in the gate of Samaria'.

The weather continues good. Slight frosts. A little rain.

28th

I never remember such fine dry weather in the month of February. The whole month has indeed been excellent, but the past week has been exceptional. There has been very little rain all the month, and last week there was none. The ground is perfectly dry, and would be in grand trim for sowing, but it is a little too early yet. I hear that they have commenced on Tochineal. Every one is now ploughing clean land.

I finished the yavels on Thursday. We were taking up some turnips today that were furred up. They are not nearly so much spoiled with the frost as the others.

I was over on Tuesday evening, giving the books in the Library an overhaul. I went in past to ask if Miss Barron was to give us any assistance at the Social Meeting, but she would neither sing nor play. Mr. Barron is going away back to America, in a week or so. He has bought a farm of his own now.

I see there has been a very severe earthquake in Italy, Switzerland and France and about 15000 lives lost.

Father was over at a sale of wood at Park on Saturday. He came home last night. I was town keeper yesterday. I went up in the afternoon to see Mrs. Riddoch.

1887 March
7th

Better weather at this season of the year I never remember seeing, indeed the oldest people say there has not been the like since 1826. There has been frost on two mornings only, and not a drop of rain all the week. The earth is now getting exceedingly dry, and every-one is complaining of it being hard to plough. Sowing has been commenced in some districts, but there is none in Deskford yet. Ploughing except where turnips are, is now nearly through, and if the good weather continues sowing will be begun shortly I should think. Small patches of lea are still to be ploughed. We have about 3 acres.

A meeting of the Mut. Imp. Soc. was held on Tuesday evening. The subject of Debate was 'Whether is moderation, or total abstinence, the most worthy of support. Mr. Walker, Teacher, supported moderation and Mr. Mitchell total abstinence. Both had excellent papers. A warm discussion ensured. Total abstinence carried by a majority of one.

A meeting was held on Thursday evening for the purpose of forming a Temperance Society. There was a fair attendance. Mr. Walker occupied the Chair. Mr. Michie gave an address also Mr John Scott. At the close about 32 put down their names as willing to join the Society. I was appointed one of a Committee to draw up rules for the same.

I went over to Park on Saturday for the wood which Father bought, at the sale. After I unyoked at Cairdswell I went down to see the gardener at Park and got some flowers from him.

Father, Joan and I were at church on Sunday. Mrs. Riddoch and Miss McWillie were down in the afternoon.

I was up at Ardiecow today at the steam mill. Every-one is needing thrashing for want of water. I have been making out an application tonight for a situation as working grieve which I see in the newspapers. It is for a place beside Ellon.

14th

I have very important news for my Diary this week. Something which may have a very important bearing on my after life. Since last I wrote, I have engaged to act as Working Grieve on a farm on Speyside above Aberlour. I saw the advertisement in the Banffshire Journal, so I got testimonials from Willie McWillie and Aleck Duncan and went up on

Saturday and made application. The name of the place is Balliemulloch, and the nearest railway Station would be Carron I think. On getting to Craigellachie however, I found I would have two hours to wait for a train up Speyside, and so I resolved to tramp it. I got company for three miles with two men, who told me the names of the places, and directed me on my way. They also told me what sort of a place it was I was going to, and what kind of people they were. It is a beautiful road between Craigellachie and Aberlour. It keeps close by the river side, and passes right up through the village. Balliemulloch is 2½ miles above Aberlour. The farmer died about a year ago. The widow is still alive but the farm belongs to two daughters. Richardson is the name. There are 170 acres of arable land, and there must be a good bit pasture as they keep 200 sheep. They have three pairs of horses just now. Besides the grieve there are three men and a cattleman. None of them are to be kept, and I have to engage men for myself. I am engaged for one year, but there is a mutual break at six months end, with two months notice. I am to have £30 of wages.

On Thursday we had a coating of snow, and there has been additions every day since. We have now six or seven inches.

On Friday evening after the ordinary business of Library, there was a meeting about the Flower Show. I of course resigned the Secretaryship and Wm. Milne was appointed in my room. A. Morrison was re-elected Treasurer.

21st

Farm work has been completely stopped during the week. On Tuesday forenoon there was a great fall of snow and also some blowing. It was the day of Marnin Fair, but I saw no one from this side.

I went down to Portsoy on Wednesday and bought a young calf for £2.10. I took the cart to Fordyce as mother went with me.

On Thursday and Friday we were driving sand from Cultain. It is to mix lime for the dyke by the cornyard. The Social Meeting of the Mutual Improvement Society was held on Friday evening. It was a nice evening but bad roads. Being President of the Society I had to perform the duties of the Chair. There was no debate this year, but we had instead a good supply of vocal and instrumental music. We had Mr. Duffus' piano on hire, and Miss Duncan and The Misses Mackintosh were the pianists. We also had Mr. Mackay and Mr. Taylor as singers. Rev. A. Walker also gave an address on 'The benefit of Mutual Improvement'. The Programme was in two parts with the tea in the middle and altogether there were 29 pieces. The members of the Society did all their parts remarkably well I think. There was a dance for two hours after the programme was finished. The musicians were Miss Duncan on the piano and Messrs J. & W. Stephen & Mr. Duncan on the violin. Everyone seemed to be highly pleased.

I was town keeper on Sunday, but I went to the Free Church in the evening. Mr. Walker preached from Job XXII. 21. 'Acquaint now thyself with him and be at peace.' The snow has gradually been going away and I got to the plough this afternoon. Sandy Lamb got his thrashing machine into the cornyard tonight, and we are going to thrash out the crop tomorrow. We had a letter last week from Jane saying that Maggie had got a daughter. We also had a letter from Cleland, and they have got a ship to a station between Port Glasgow and Greenock. I forget the name.

28th

We were greatly startled on Sunday afternoon, by hearing that Mrs. Taylor, Cultain, had died very suddenly. She had been ailing a little on Friday, and on Saturday they had called the Doctor, but he had not thought there was anything very serious.

On Sunday afternoon however, when they were putting a poultice to her breast she fell back and never spoke again. Oh! how uncertain is life. How little may be required to quench the vital spark! How near we may be living to the external world. 'Help us O God so to live; as we would wish we had done when we come to die.'

Mrs Taylor is to be buried on Thursday in Deskford Churchyard.

George Stephen came over to see us on Sunday. Father, Mother, him and I were at church. The minister preached from the text 'My people shall never be ashamed.'

The snow has now entirely disappeared and we are again enjoying fine spring weather. Except where there are turnips, ploughing is almost done, and sowing will likely be commenced as soon as the land is in condition. We are thinking of sowing the little parkie tomorrow.

There was a meeting on Thursday evening settling up the affairs to the Mut. Imp. Soc. The expenses were rather heavy, but we managed to carry a small balance forward. There was also a meeting of ladies that evening, making arrangements for collecting subscriptions for the 'Women's Jubilee Offering' to the Queen.

I had a letter last week from Miss Richardson, Balliemulloch, asking me to send some samples of sandy oats for seed.

1887 April
4th

The proverbial phrase, that March should go out like a lamb has certainly this year not been fulfilled. The last night of March was a perfect hurricane of wind, and much damage has been done both by land and sea. It has been very changeable weather during the week.

Wednesday was a very fine day. We sowed the little parkie in front of the houses and on Thursday we sowed other two quarters. About dinnertime however, the wind rose greatly and there was a tremendous shower of rain and hail. There was no harrowing in the afternoon. Mrs. Taylor's funeral was at one clock. She was the first to be buried in the new part of the Churchyard. A meeting in connection with the Temperance Society was held in the schools that evening. I was to take part in the programme but the wind being so boisterous I did not think it would be safe to leave the horses. I hear there was but a small attendance. Mr. Walker was elected President, Mr. Longmore Secretary and Mr. Mitchell Treasurer.

On Friday the storm was a little subsided but still very blowy. I went over to Cornhill in the afternoon for some manure. I got word from Miss Richardson that day that she wanted 12 qrs. of Kirkton's corn for seed. They had it over on Saturday to Cornhill station. I was 12/3 for carriage to Aberlour at the rate of 6/6 per ton. We got railway bags to hold it in at ½d each. There was a great deal of drying that day and Willie was in the harrows.

We were all at church on Sunday except Father and Mother. The minister's text was 'Who giveth songs in the night.' These words he said were not to be understood literally only. By 'the night' was represented seasons of distress, sickness and sorrow, and by 'songs' we were to understand exemption from care, and peace of conscience.

It has been showery today and there has been no more sowing. I was down at Cullen. I have been thinking for some time back of insuring my life, and I have been making inquiries regarding the different Societies.

11th

Since last I wrote we have experienced a very sharp snow storm.

On Tuesday morning I was greatly surprised to find four inches of snow. Of course it soon began to subside, but the next three days were very frosty and had it been at Xmas, the snow would have all remained.

By Saturday the most of it had disappeared and the ploughs were going.

I went over and opened the Library on Friday evening. There was a meeting of Committee of Management to appoint another Librarian as I had sent in my resignation. Mr. John Longmore was appointed to the office. Mr. Ross, Cullen, gave an entertainment in the Schools that evening. He was exhibiting views by means of a Lime Light Lantern. He took us a tour through Scotland, showing us all the principle places of interest, Castles, Cathedrals, Caves, Lochs, Falls etc. They were indeed splendid views.

Father and Willie only were at church on Sunday. Mother is at Cairdswell just now. Geordie came over for her on Thursday.

Yesterday and today have been splendid days. The weather seems to be quite settled. Everyone was at the sowing this morning. We sowed the Den.

18th

The past week has been a very busy one. It has been very dry, and the seed has been deposited in a good bed. It has been very cold however, and some mornings it was very frosty. Consequently there has been no growth.

We sowed the haugh in the Den on Tuesday. It was a bad job to harrow and you could almost count the furrows yet.

I went down to Cullen on Tuesday evening. I was arranging with Mr. Fortune as to assuring my life in the 'National Provident Institution.' I have agreed to take out a policy for £100 payable at 55 years of age. The yearly premium I will have to pay is to be £3. 13.4.[12]

I had the Dr. inspecting me on Friday.

Father and I were at Cornhill market with two stots on Thursday. There was a large market but trade was dull. We sold them at £22.10. I engaged a man for Balliemulloch in the market, William Currie who used to be in Backies I feed him for second horseman at £11.15.

On Friday we sowed the ayvels.

There was a meeting about the Flower Show on Saturday evening. The Prize Schedules were distributed. There are more extra prizes than last year I think.

Willie Cowie and Sandy came over from Finnygaud on Sunday morning. Sandy went with Father and me to church.

We were driving home the last of the turnips today. We had a letter from Lizzie saying they were liking their new place fine. Bogston is the name, between Port Glasgow and Greenock. We also had a letter from Edinburgh saying that Jane had got a daughter.

25th

I was ploughing on Tuesday and on Wednesday I finished the endrigs of the clean land. Father went over that afternoon to the sale at Bogetra, and bought an iron scuffle harrow.

---

[12] Wilson used this experience of life insurance in his short story, 'Rustic Courtship'. See Appendix 3.

Thursday was the fast day. It snowed and rained the whole day from morn till night. We had Mr. Ledingham from Boyndie, but the attendance was small owing to the bad day.

Friday was also very showery. I went up to the Backies in the afternoon. Miss McWillie was not at home, so Willie and I had the evening all to ourselves.

We went to Portsoy on Saturday with two loads of corn. It weighed 44lbs per bushel, but we only got 15/8 for the quarter. We were rolling down the drains in the new grass, in the afternoon. We had the road roller and put both the horses into it.

Sunday was dry but cold. Father, Joan and I were at church. We had Mr. McVicar, Ordiquhill, officiating, and Mr. Mackintosh only served the tables himself. Mr. McVicar took for his text, the parable of the barren fig tree, which he said was a fitting type of all unfruitful workers. They not only bore no fruit themselves but they prevented others from doing so.

It has been dry and blowy today. We sowed all the clean land but it was very frosty in the morning and it was eight o'clock before the harrows would work.

1887 May
2ⁿᵈ

A week of backward weather. There has been much rain during the week, and work has been greatly hindered. In the first of the week there was also very hard frosts, there being a quarter of an inch of ice several mornings. There has been no growth as yet, what grass there is looking quite brown. The month of April has been very cold throughout. Indeed I scarcely think there has been one fresh day from beginning to end of it. Sowing is now finished in this district, and land is being prepared for the potatoes.

On Tuesday we received intimation that Mrs. Cowie, Cairdswell, had got a son on Monday evening. Joan was over on Friday when both were doing well.

On Wednesday we were at Portsoy with two loads of corn.

We were casting a drain on Thursday to take the water into the Den park.

The steam mill was at Cultain on Friday afternoon and at Knowes Saturday forenoon. I was giving them a hand. I sowed all the grass seeds on Saturday.

Joan and I were town keepers on Sunday. We went down to see the folks of Cairnton in the afternoon.

We have been in the roller today all day. Father was over in the afternoon at William Innes' roup. Everything sold remarkably well. He is going away to America. I got a two hours among the flowers.

9th

The weather has greatly improved since last I wrote. The whole week has been dry and last few days have been nice and warm. There is a marked improvement on everything. Grass although short is now looking grand. Very few cattle are out yet, the winter keep not being done. Braird is coming up thick and strong. Potato planting was engaging attention in the first of last week. We got ours in on Wednesday.

On Thursday we finished the rolling. Since then Willie has been ploughing among the turnip land. Father and I have been at the paling.[13]

I went over to Finnygaud on Saturday evening. I went past Cairdswell to see the folks there. Annie is always keeping a little stronger. She got up for the first time on Friday but on Sunday she was going through the house. It is a very little baby, and is very quiet I think. I got over to Finnygaud about eight o'clock. Mary is never improving any. She scarcely every gets up at all now. I do think they should try a change for her.

It was their Communion Sunday and they were all at church except Katie and John. I came up to Jemmies with them as they went to church. Him nor Isa were not going as they had a mare like to foal. The little shalt has a foal this year again.[14] After getting dinner I came over to Cairdswell. Geordy was not come home from church so I got dinner there again. About five o'clock I left and came over past Hillfolds. Miss Katie Duncan was there and after having tea, and seeing Mr. Ross's cattle we started for home. The evening was fine and of course we had a very pleasant walk.

16th

Excellent weather for clearing turnip land. A few have commenced to sow today. Last two days have been warm and grass and braird have improved considerably. Cattle are now part of the day in the fields.

On Wednesday afternoon I went up to Aberlour as the feeing market was next day. I got a bed from Maggie Murray and went up to Balliemulloch in the morning. What a difference there is on everything

---

[13] paling, fencing.
[14] shalt, working horse, smaller than a Clydesadale, often used to pull a gig.

since last I was up. It is indeed a very pretty place about Aberlour, and at the water side fully as early as Deskford I think. They are very well on with the work at Balliemulloch. Fourteen acres for turnips being almost ready. The feeing market was considered stiff and wages were a little down. I engaged two. John Grant, foreman for £13 and James Macdonald for third, at £7.15. I left the market at 12 o'clock and walked from Keith. I came past Backies, got tea and spent two hours. I also called on Mrs. Riddoch.

I attended the Library on Friday night, and handed over the books I believe for the last time. There was a large attendance, and after the ordinary business was over Mr. Smith, in name of a number of friends and well wishers, presented me with a very handsome and valuable present, in the form of 'Chambers Encyclopaedia'. It is in ten volumes, and there is also a smaller book on Agriculture. I was deeply touched by their kindness and thanked them as best I could. I am sure if the good wishes of kind friends were to be of any service to me, it need be with no doubts and no misgivings that I enter upon my new duties.

Balliemulloch
Aberlour
1887 May
30th

Away from home, among strangers in a strange country. Home! what emotions does the very name call forth. After all, there certainly is no place like home. I have slipped a week in my diary writing, but I was so busy preparing for leaving home that I could find no time. The week before last we had good weather until Friday. It was Cullen Market, and was a fearful day of cold. Father and I were both down. Father engaged Sandy Donald as man for the half year at £10 of wages. It was a very small market but feeing was rather brisk. I was home by one o'clock and got a yokin' in the grubber.

We commenced to dung on Saturday morning but about ten o'clock it began to snow. The afternoon was fearful bad, the hills being quite white. I scarcely ever saw a worse day in May I think. We were fitting up the joiner's shop as a sleeping place for the man.

Sunday was a good deal better. Willie McWillie came up with me from church and stayed the afternoon. He was telling me to send up some of my hives and he would take charge of them. I was very glad to accept of his kind offer.

We got our turnips covered in and sown on Monday in fine condition. I went over to Kirkton that evening to bid my friends there goodbye.

On Tuesday morning Willie and I went up to Craibstone for two loads of lime, as the masons are to be in a few days to build the dyke by the cornyard. We took up the hives with us to Backies.

I packed my trunk on Wednesday afternoon, and at six o'clock I bade goodbye to them all, and for the first time in my life, I set out to try my fortune alone, in 'the wide wide world'. May the blessing of Almighty God go with me! May his presence be ever near me to guard me from evil; and to lead me in the narrow way that leadeth unto life. Willie came over with my box to Cornhill Station and I went up to Cairdswell all night. Annie's baby was rather weakly, but is now much stronger.

I left Cornhill with the first train in the morning, and came up to Keith. Having some messages there I waited until the one o'clock train. I arrived at Craigellachie about two, only to find that there was no train to Aberlour until six thirty. I resolved to walk, and got to Balliemulloch about four. After getting some tea I went down to the Station for my box. Next day was dewy, and as the straw was all done, one of the sisters and I took in a stack and thrashed. In the afternoon I took a look round the place. I must say that the first night I felt a good deal home sick.

I went down and met Mrs. Currie on Friday evening. The foreman also came that night. I may as well here describe the family. First there is the old woman, about 70 or there about I suppose, but hale and hearty yet. Then there are three sisters Jessie being oldest; Mary Ann next, and Maggie youngest. Their brother Andrew is also at home, but he has nothing to do with the farm at all. He had been almost through for being a Dr. I believe, but being a great prodigal, he took to drinking; and at last enlisted in the army. He was among the soldiers nine years, and had been out in the West Indies and a great many ways. He looks after the sheep and does a good many odd jobs. Then there is Stewart Richardson, a boy of sixteen and a nephew. He is here to learn farming and he puts out and in the cows.

The work of the farm is pretty well advanced, the turnip land, except some small pieces being all made. To all appearance it is a good farm I think but some of it is rather steep. A good part of it is fenced with substantial stone dykes, and it is also well watered.

On Saturday one of the men was ploughing while the other went to the mill with a load of oats.

I went to church on Sunday. They always take the machine, and I have to drive them down. It is three miles I believe to Aberlour. They attend the Established Church. Mr. Sloss is minister, but he is at the General Assembly just now, and it was Mr. Rees, Boharn, who preached. He seems a very easy going man. The church has been newly repaired, and is the prettiest country church I was ever in.

1887 June
7*th*

I have now spent a week in my new quarters and things are now beginning to get a little home like.

I find that I will have plenty of scope here, both for my mental and physical abilities, but energy perseverance and a brave heart, can overcome many difficulties.

We have had a week of very good weather, and the work has been going on a pace. We sowed an acre of red top swedes in the first of the week, and we have also laid down two acres of yellow. The third man came home on Monday but he grew unwell and only stayed a day.

I went to Elgin market on Friday and engaged another. There was any amount of servants to be got, but I am frightened the one I have got is not to stay long yet. He is complaining of the little wages and is speaking of enlisting. I do hope he will stay however. The others were at the moss on Friday cutting peats and we were also back Saturday and today. I shortly got into the set of it and could cut nicely. We got grand days.

I had a letter from Mother on Friday. She was saying that Sandy Donald was away with a sore back. I hope he may soon be able for his work again. She enclosed a letter which had come from Andrew Bremner to me. In my last letter to him, I was saying that Jessie and I would perhaps be out in the end of Summer. He was giving me a great many instructions for the voyage, only that is all out of head in the meantime.

I was at church again on Sunday and had the pleasure of hearing Mr. Sloss preach. His personal appearance is not very prepossessing, being dark and sallow coloured, but I must say he is an excellent preacher. I never heard a finer voice, and he speaks so plainly that not a syllable is lost. His text was Eccles. XI 4. 'He that regardeth the clouds shall not reap.' It was useless, he said to spend our time, speculating upon those things which are entirely beyond our control. There were two classes of people in the world, with whose views of life he did not agree. Those who only looked at the bright side of things, who would not believe that there was any suffering, or want, or misery in the world at all; and when their attention was called to such, would shut their doors and windows to keep out the unwelcome sight. The other class are those who look only at the dark side. They never see a cloud, but they are sure it will be a deluge, they are certain there never was the like of the present evil times, and when no troubles in reality beset them, they are busy speculating on those which may befall them. Neither of these views of life, were in accordance with the Word of God, Mr. Sloss said. There certainly was a dark side to the picture and it was our duty to look it straight in the face, but there were also many bright and beautiful things in this world, and we would be the losers, if we allowed them to escape our notice.

13th

After a week of excessive drought we have got some refreshing showers. If warm weather continues crops of every kind will be greatly benefited by the same. Turnips were sorely needing rain. We have three acres which I believe will need to be re-sown again. It had been bad seed seemingly.

On Tuesday we were sowing turnips in 'The Brackens', a small field up at the foot of the hills. It was extremely rough having only been ploughed out of lea last year. We put the weeds into the drills as there was no dung. I thought I would be defeated sowing the manure, as the wind was almost at hurricane pitch.

Next day we were in 'Paradise' another small field; but Currie says it is scarcely up to his expectations of that place.

On Thursday morning the man I engaged in Elgin decamped, but I have engaged another, and I do hope he may remain with us. His name is John Strachan and his wages is £8.5.

I was not at church on Sunday. In the afternoon Currie and I went down to Speyside, past the distillery of Carron and up as far as the Station. There are very pretty haughs about the water side. A two year old quey had dropped a calf when I came home. We had a young horse with a very sore eye. Andrew called it ophthalmyd. We burned it with caustic, and washed it with sulphate of zinc. A penny worth mixed in half a bottle of water. He was better in a few days.

I had a long letter from Jessie today. She is always troubled with her back at times. She would be ready to go to Australia in a month's notice she says.

20th

We have now got through with the turnip sowing. We would have finished on Monday but the afternoon was rainy.

On Tuesday morning I took a look through the turnips when I saw that we would have to re-sow nearly four acres. In the afternoon they were harrowing down and furring up again, while we also gathered the weeds. Andrew sowed them in the evening.

We finished off the endrigs on Wednesday. They were driving out some dung which we left in the afternoon, and on Thursday forenoon they washed the carts. We went to the moss in the afternoon and cut some more peats.

We were also back on Friday, when we set those which were cast before. They were in grand trim and will soon be fit to drive.

We had a busy day on Saturday at the sheep shearing. Being all green hands we were all rather awkward. The sheep were all driven into the fold, and we shore them in the turnip shed. A shepherd was to have come and given us a hand but he did not turn up. There were three pairs of shears going in the forenoon and four in the afternoon and we turned out 67 sheep.

I was at church on Sunday. Mr. Sloss preached from the text 'Bear ye one anothers burdens and so fulfil the law of Christ' Gal. VI 2. He was intimating that Mr. Findlay of Aberlour House had presented the church with an American organ. Also that the Scottish Hymnal was now to be used and also that the congregation in future would stand at praise and sit at prayer.

We were at the shearing today again, but in the afternoon three of them were hoeing the potatoes.

27ᵗʰ

The celebration of the Queen's Jubilee has been the great event of the week. Never in the history of Great Britain I believe, was there such universal rejoicing, as was witnessed on Tuesday last. Throughout the entire length and breadth of the land, not only at home, but also in our vast and extensive colonies abroad; the whole body of the people united together to honour Queen Victoria, who for the long period of fifty years, has reigned over us, so wisely and so well. The manner of celebrating the Jubilee has of course been different in different places. Treating the children and giving donations to the poor were popular ways of commemorating the event. Processions; addresses; picnics; games, balls etc. were also means whereby the people gave expression to their feelings, while at night large bonfires were lit on almost every hill and eminence throughout the land. It was a general holiday in Aberlour. We got the afternoon and all went down to the village. At every farm mostly, a flag was displayed while Charlestown was completely arrayed in holiday attire. Every chimney nearly had its banner waving in the breeze, lines of bunting crossed and re-crossed they street, while several of the large windows had festoons of evergreens surrounding them, with various mottoes between.

The E.C. and F.C. ministers were addressing the people in the square when we went down. A prayer was also offered by Mr. Sloss. The scholars numbering 700 were then got into order, and headed by the Keith Brass Band and followed by a large concourse of grown up people, marched to the grounds of Aberlour House. Through the kindness of Mr. Findlay, the proprietor, the grounds and gardens were all thrown open. At the top of the gardens a halt was made, and the children seated on a croquet lawn were treated to milk and biscuits. Returning past the big house, some speeches were made and 'God save the Queen' sung. The company then adjourned to the grounds of the Orphanage, the whole place being thrown open to the public. It is an extensive building having over 200 inmates. I saw more than twenty babies in the nursery, none of them more than three years old. At five o'clock tea was served in the dining room, being laid out on three tables running from end to end. A grand ball was held in the evening but I did not stay to it.

We have been at various jobs during the week—repairing the road to the moss—making a foundation for the peat stack—cutting thistles – driving peats etc. etc. It has been a week of excessive heat. I am sure I never felt it warmer. Everything is greatly in want of rain. I saw a stalk of barley coming into ear today. I never remember seeing the same in the month of June.

On Sunday the minister gave us a sermon a little out of the ordinary run. It was a short sketch of the reign of Queen Victoria, and he put it in a very interesting manner. This has been the Aberlour holiday and everyone was away but myself.

1887 July
4th

The merry month of June has come and gone, mid-summer is past, and again the day is on the turn. A warmer or drier month of June I never remember. There has just been one shower I think during the whole of it. Oats are now coming into ear, and in many places will be but a short crop I fear. The crop on Balliemulloch is still looking well and if rain come shortly it would still improve greatly. Rain has offered to come several times during the week, but has always worn off. It has been very cloudy today, and we have had slight showers.

On Tuesday and Wednesday forenoon we were driving peats, and we got home forty four loads. They are in grand condition. Since then we have been busy at the hoe. The swedes are extremely dirty, and being rather small we only cleaned the sides of the drills of one half of them. We have got the other half singled and also a few yellows.

We were sheep shearing on Friday. We had John Sharp, Ballinteam, assisting us and we were through by four o'clock.

I was at church on Sunday. The subject of the minister's discourse was Deborah's Song. In the afternoon Currie, Mary, Elsie and I went to the top of Ben Rinnes. It took us two hours to make the ascent. It was extremely blowy on the top but we got a grand view. I had a pair of Mr. Calder's glasses and I managed to pick up Ardiecow and Knowes quite distinctly.

11ᵗʰ

The dry weather has come to an end at last. We had four hours yesterday of a warm refreshing rain. The benefits to the crops will be immense. I see by the newspapers that the drought has been telling severely in some places, and oats in many cases will be but a very short crop. Turnips however it would seem are in general looking well, and this rain is just what they were needing. Except one day we have been hoeing all the week, and we have now excellent plants.

The three men were driving John Grant's peats on Tuesday while the women and I were at the hoe in 'Paradise'. The foreman had a man in his place on Tuesday. He had got word that his mother (who has been ailing for sometime) was very poorly.

On Friday morning we all went to the moss as the turnips were rather small. We took them all home in the afternoon in excellent condition. There was fifty-six loads in all.

I had a letter from Willie last week, when he was saying that the bees had been doing remarkably well with him. They had also a good lot of the peats driven but not many turnips hoed.

On Sunday morning I set out with the foreman to see Glenlivet. The morning was misty and there had been some rain on the night but I did not expect more. When only half way it came on however, and rained the whole road. We had twelve miles of a walk I believe. The nearest way is over the hill, but everything being wet we had to keep the road. We left the turnpike and went up past the distillery of GlenFarclas over the shoulder of a small hill, down past the farm of Tomfarclas, and on to the main road again at the shop of Belliehiggles. Coming over the hill we got a grand view of the valley of the Spey, and also of the Avon which here joins the Spey. The Castle of Ballindalloch lay down beneath us, while the distillery of Cragganmore could be seen further up Speyside. After catching the turnpike we kept up Avonside, passing the policies of Ballindalloch Castle, and the inn of Dalnashaugh on the one hand, and the farms of Marionburgh and Tommore on the other, both of which farms are at present in the hands of the Proprietor. There is a good deal of wood on Avonside, mostly birch, and for the first time I saw the etnach bush, an everygreen prickly shrub, which grows here in great profusion. The arable land which consists of little more than small haughs along the waterside, appears to be light sharp sort of soil, much of the crops being burned up with the drought. There is just a row of farms on each side the water, on the left bank being Castletown, Craigroy, Haugh and Finnachlie while on the other are Aldoch, Dalmenach, Craggan and Drumin. The farm of Drumin is occupied at present by Mr. Skinner, Factor to the Duke of Richmond. His mansion house, as well as the ruins of an old Castle, stands upon a natural mound, right in the angle between the Livet and the Avon. There are here some very fine trees, and altogether it is a very pretty place. We have left the Avon and turned up Glenlivet. The turnpike road keeps along the east side of the Livet, but on coming to the churchyard at Bridgend we crossed the water, and up past the school of Croftness. The Teacher here is a Mr. MacConnachie, a nephew of the Misses Richardson, Balliemulloch. A little down this we came in sight of the Distillery of Minmore, belonging to Major Smith.[15] It is by far the largest Distillery I have yet seen in this district. As we went past I paced the width of one of their bonded stores. It was forty two yards wide and I am sure it was twice as long. There is also a very large farm, requiring five or six pairs of horses to work it. I must say that the appearance of Glenlivet fairly astonished me. I had always pictured it in my own mind, as a narrow highland glen, with the heather more than half way down the hill sides and with only small patches of arable land on each side the water. Judge of my surprise then, when I looked upon a fine valley of seemingly excellent soil, stretching from the water almost a mile, in some parts on either side. The farms here, are also very large; three and four pairs of horses, being about the average strength on each. The parks are also large, and well laid off, being for most part enclosed with substantial stone dykes, or fenced with hedges. As I said before, the main road leading to Tomintoul keeps along the east side of the water, passing through the farms of Deskie, Tomnabreckachie, Auchorachan and Nevie. On the other side and above Minmore are Blairfindy and The Laggan. On looking back as we went up the Glen we got a fine view of Morange. This is a district lying at the foot of Ben Rinnes, the farms in it being mostly of the smaller size. Nearer hand and close at the road side, could be seen the Established Church and manse of Glenlivet, the minister being a Mr. Calder, who was assistant a few years ago to Dr. Henderson in Cullen. I forgot to mention that we passed the Free Church and manse of Inveravon, below Drumin, beside the farm of Craggan. Having arrived at John's Mother's, the rain which had been rather heavy at times, now turned far worse, and we felt very thankful that we were under cover. We found Mrs. Grant a little better, but still very weakly and confined to her bed. It is a cancer I believe which is the matter with her. She was very pleased of course

---

[15] Now Glenlivet Distillery.

to see her son. A daughter is at home attending to her, and she has also another son and daughter. About three o'clock the rain cleared off, and we went out to have a look about us, but everything being wet, we could not get up the hill very far. A little farther up the Glen is the school and schoolhouse, where William Lorimer was sometimes Schoolmaster, while across the water is the Roman Catholic Chapel. The road to Tomintoul here crosses the Livet, and winds away among the hills towards the South West. We could here see part of the Braes of Glenlivet, a remote glen far up among the hills. At seven o'clock we started for home. We came past an Uncle of John Grant's, who has a small croft above Minmore, and who gave us a drive down the road a bit. It was a grand evening, and the roads being now quite dry again, we had a nice walk home. We arrived at Balliemulloch about eleven o'clock.

18th

In the first part of the week, we were very busy singling turnips, the plants being very large. We finished them all on Thursday. Our turnips are now all doing well. There has been several good showers during the week and some mornings were rather cold. In the end of the week we were drill harrowing the swedes again and cutting the thistles in the parks. We also cut the hay. There is only about 1¼ acre of it and I made them put it into sheaves as we will take some of the seed out of it.

This forenoon three of us went to the wood above Belnakyle for brushwood. I was assisting Andrew in the afternoon to shear a few sheep and to pack the wool. They send their wool to Glasgow and it is packed in large bags, each holding between two and three cwts.

I had a letter from Jane the past week and she was saying that Tom Stirling is always getting weaker.

I was down with the ladies at church on Sunday and we got a very good sermon from Mr. Sloss. His subject was Jacob's dream, when he saw the ladder reaching from the earth up to Heaven with the angels ascending and descending upon it. We could learn from this he said, 'that the inhabitants of Heaven, took a far warmer interest in the dwellers on the earth than was generally supposed and might often be much nearer to us than we fancied. We could also learn, that although God was the Almighty Creator and upholder of the Universe, of the tremendous extent of which we could form no adequate conception, still he was the God and Father of individuals protecting them from harm, and over-ruling all things for the good of those who love him'.

I saw an advertisement in the newspapers sometime ago, wanting a precentor for Aberlour Church. I was expecting we would have new ones every Sunday on trial, but there has been word of none as yet.

Mr. Hill, Supervisor of Inland Revenue, has been officiating since Mr. Watt resigned. A salary of £50 was offered.

One day last week Mr. Young, the farmer of Bogenduie, was coming down the road, and met Stewart as he was putting out his cows. He was asking about me and said he would like to see me as he belonged to near by Deskford. I went over on Sunday afternoon.

Bogenduie is in the Edinville district, below the distillery of Ben Rinnes. It would appear to be a farm of about 140 acres, and there is a very good dwelling house on it and excellent offices. I found that Mr. Young belonged to Slatehaugh, his brother John having still a small place there. He has also another brother in Cunningholes beside Buckie. He had been fee'd in several places about Deskford in his younger days and had also been a grieve on several large farms. It is only five years since they came to Bogenduie, having shifted from Glen Muick beside Ballater. Mr. Young is a very talkative man and took me through all his houses, and also to see his stock and crops. He has some very good black cattle. Mrs. Young is a big stout woman, but is seemingly a very nice person. They have some family but none of them were at home, so I just got tea with the old folks.

25th

Except a shower on Sunday morning, the past week has been very dry. Turnips have not grown much and are sorely needing rain. Pasture grass is also getting very bare. Oats are now full shot I think, and barley is changing colour. With a continuance of such weather, we would get harvest I believe by the end of August.

I had a letter from Edinburgh last night, telling me that Tom Stirling died on Saturday morning (the 23rd) at twenty minutes past eight. Poor Tom he has had a long sore time of it. It was consumption that was the matter with him, and it is years since he turned badly. He was always able for his work however until about eight months ago, and for the last three months he has been confined to his bed. He did not suffer much pain latterly but he was worn to a mere shadow. He is to be buried tomorrow (Tuesday). I am truly sorry for Maggie in her great bereavement. She will have a hard struggle to bring up her little ones. Jeannie and Andrew are dead, but she has four yet Jamie, Minnie, Tommy and the baby. I have never heard what it is called yet. I was just writing to Maggie tonight.

Driving brushwood and second hoeing was our last week's work. We got the 'hag' in the wood above Belnakyle and it just took us the five hours to drive the 'raike'.

The foreman and I were down at Aberlour one day with a load of corn and a load of wool. They send their wool to McLeod wool broker Glasgow. They had about seven cwts. of it. The corn is 13/ for 40 lbs, but it weighed 44 lbs per bushel.

I was at church on Sunday. The minister preached from Philippians II. 21. 'For all seek their own, not the things which are Jesus Christ's'. 'How little' he said 'could we call our own, when we seriously considered it. Our life even was not our own and the talents which we have were but lent us from the Lord'. What a different world would it be, were all selfishness to be laid aside, and the glory of God and the good of our fellow men, made the great aim of our existence.

1887 August
1ˢᵗ

We have been hoeing all the week and have now got finished. The yellow ones were not at all dirty. It has been a week of excessive drought on some days there being terrible gales of wind. Turnips on thin lands are now suffering greatly. The most of ours are standing out well. Barley is fast changing colour. They say that on the farm of Rutherie will be ripe in two weeks.

I had letter from Jessie and Willie last week, also one from Miss Katie Duncan. Willie was telling me they had Uncle George and Jeannie from Aberdeen visiting them.

On Saturday we led and built the hay. There is only a small stack of it. I cannot say that I am liking Balliemulloch very well yet. There are too many mistresses, and they take by far too much interference. The tools and implements about the place are also all completely done, and to speak of new ones would be out of the question. We are also very poorly feed, it being nothing uncommon to get porridge three times a day and always twice.

11ᵗʰ

I am behind with my diary writing, because I have been holding my holidays. I got away on Saturday at eleven o'clock and came back on Tuesday evening. I saw some of the barley at the water side almost ripe. The crops about Keith and Grange are far heavier than they are here, and with few exceptions the turnips are also looking well. I did not take the train farther than Keith as I intended calling at Backies as I went down. I arrived there about four o'clock and found Willie and Annie both well. Willie is looking a little better than he was I think, but it is still very thin. After getting tea, we went out to inspect the bees. They have been doing well this summer. The two large supers of mine are both filled, the 'JW.' being very neatly finished. There was some brood in the other one, which spoiled it a little. He had also got fourteen full sections from my hives. From one of his own he had taken twenty four. He has scarcely such a heavy crop of oats this year, but his barley is good. His cattle are also in grand thriving condition, only he has been given them cotton cake all summer. I called on Mrs. Riddoch as I came down past and I arrived at home about half past seven. Mother and Joan were in the road meeting me. I never thought the house looked so well before, neither inside nor outside. The kitchen seemed so large and airy, and clean and tidy. The garden also seemed far prettier than ever it appeared to me before.

Uncle from Aberdeen has been staying at Knowes for the last two weeks. He is getting very frail, and is sorely troubled with rheumatism in his leg. He has been pointing all the tiles since he came.

I went to church on Sunday with Father and Willie. Mr. Mackintosh is away at Strathpeffer just now, and it was a young man who preached but the church was very thin.

Willie and I were taking a look at the crops in the afternoon. I am almost sure there is a better crop than last year. The haugh in the den is beautiful crop, and the parkie beside the wood is also good. It is not so well mixed however as up this way. Everyone down there has had abundance of pasture during the summer, and although it has turned dry now it is still plentiful. The natural grass in the braes in the den is better than I ever saw it and McKenzie has been cutting a lot on the hill. It is a great pity that the hill is not fenced for I am sure it would help half a score of ewes with lambs very well. The swedes were nearly all re-sowed again, but the yellow ones are looking very well.

On Monday forenoon I went over to see Cultain. He has been re-roofing his dwelling house and otherwise repairing it. From that I went over to Muttonbrae. Uncle's crop is light besides last year he says, but he has a lot of hay. As he was going to the Backies he dressed and came over the hill with me. Annie and George Cowie had come across only a little before us. The baby is now thriving fine and is a keen little fellow. We took out the reaper after dinnertime and put it together. It is going to be sent to the Smiddy to be cleaned, and get some little repairs . I went over about five o'clock to see the folks at Kirkton. They are not finished with the hoe yet but Aleck came home when he saw me. They have splendid swedes on the Kirkhill. The old man is getting very frail now, scarcely able to go further than the houses. After tea we went out to see the garden. The vegetables are far back besides last year, the summer being too dry. There is a grand crop of gooseberries however, and being quite ripe I did take a proper feast. Katie is over at Hillfolds just now, their youngest lassie having got itself terribly burned a few days ago.

On Tuesday morning I bade them all good bye and intended going up with Willie McWillie to see the Keith Show. The Show is falling back every year I think, the display of horses and cattle not being nearly up to some former years. I saw lots of Deskford folks, and every one was asking how I was liking my new place. I met Currie in the Show Yard and we came home together.

15th

The weather during the past week has been dull, cold and stormy with slight showers. The moisture has helped to freshen the turnips a little, but it has never got farther than the leaves yet. Cereals have not made much progress in ripening, owing to the want of sunshine, never-the-less they will be better I think. In early districts they are harvesting. A field of barley is cut on Rutherie, and some small patches by the water side. It will be the most of two weeks before we get any yet.

On Wednesday we were driving stones off the old lea.

We were cleaning out the ditch which takes the water for the house, on Thursday. Since then we have been casting drains to take the water from the roans of the houses. They are extremely hard. I have made them take in the horses for the past few nights it has been so cold. They are getting nothing to their suppers but old straw.

I was in church on Sunday. Mr. Sloss preached from the parable of the Good Samaritan. There were still many, he said, among professing Christians, like the priest and the Levite; who on seeing their brother in trouble passed by on the other side. The question is not so much 'who is our neighbour' as 'to whom can we be a neighbour', and we should strive to act a neighbour's part to every one with whom we come in contact.

22nd

We have been doing a great many odd jobs during the week. We finished our drains on Tuesday.

On Wednesday two of the men were driving wood for cornyard purposes. The trees were by far too large however, the half of them being of no use for the cornyard at all. We had one load to the sawmill, but there would be other two I believe.

On Thursday and Friday we were driving blinding for the road, and cleaning out the side ditch. The foreman was at Rothes Show on Thursday but he had a man in his place.

On Saturday morning Andrew and I started to gather the sheep as we were going to dip the lambs. We went round the whole of Ben Rinnes. When near the top we were caught in a dense fog, and for sometime we thought we would have to give up our search. It was piercing cold but in half an hour it cleared off and we again proceeded. We got the most of them we thought and were home by twelve o'clock. The dip was made up in a washing tub half a gallon to each sheep. A ladder was placed between two barrows. The lamb was laid on its back on the ladder and the dip poured on. Then turned it and did the same. It was a lazy process and would never do with a large flock. The regular way is to have a dipping trough with dripper attached. The sheep are plunged in for a minute or so then lifted on to the dripper, where they remain for twenty minutes or so to allow the drip to run back into the trough. In this way hundreds can be dipped in a few hours.

I was at church on Sunday but Currie was driving. We had Mr. McLachlan, Inveravon, preaching. He really is a grand preacher, and we got an excellent sermon from him. His text was Proverbs XI. 30. 'The fruit of the righteous is a tree of life'. 'We ought to learn from this', he said, 'that everyone bore fruit of some sort, either good or bad. Without Christianity however it was impossible to bear such fruit as that described in the text. Civilization and culture might do a great deal but without the influence of Christianity civilization was but savagery silverized'. He also entreated us to remember that the fruit which we bore viz our words and actions not only affected ourselves, but had also a great influence for good or bad on our neighbours. The simplest action of our lives might therefore possess a train of consequences, something awful to contemplate'.

From church I went over to Aberlour Mains. I got acquainted with the orra man there at the Keith Show, and promised to go and see him sometime. He is married and has a house on the farm. His name is Roy. He has been in good places, being grieve on several farms in Morayshire. After getting some dinner we went to have a look about the place. It is really a fine farm and the office houses are the best finished I ever saw. Except the cow byre it is all loose boxes for the cattle, and the whole of the court is covered. There is an acre of slates on the roof it is said. He has some very good horses, a good few of them being prize takers. It is all polled cattle that he keeps, and except a few the cows are all suckling their calves. The crop is not very heavy on it this year, and they are to begin the harvest about the middle of the week. It is a Mr. Robertson who is tenant of it just now. I left about five o'clock and as I came down past the English Chapel the folk were gathering for evening service. Never having been in an English place of worship I went in. The Chapel was richly decorated with corn, berries and evergreens, being an offering of the first fruits unto God, after the Jewish custom. The service differs greatly from the Presbyterian form of worship, the liturgy forming the principal part of it. The singing and music was first class. Twenty four boys all dressed in white, formed the choir, and twice they marched round the Chapel headed by one carrying a large cross. There is also a splendid organ.

29th

We commenced the harvest on Saturday afternoon by cutting roads round the clean land. It was excessively warm and quiet. The barley (of which there are four acres) is a fair crop, but the oats are very light. We were stopped today at three o'clock with a tremendous thunder shower.

During the week we have been doing lots of odd jobs,—repairing the fences, tidying up the cornyard—mending the wind-kilns etc. etc.

I had a note from Willie Milne, Burns, on Friday saying that he was coming up to Drumuir on Sunday and asking if I would come down and meet him. It is a brother-in-law of his George Anderson, who is grieve there, and being anxious to see the place, I took the road at seven o'clock. It is far nearer across the hill than past Craigellachie, and being well directed I thought I would try it. I went past Rutherie up past Birkenbush, right over the hill and down upon Dufftown Station. I then kept the railway all the way to Drumuir. It was a long walk taking me fully three hours, and the morning being very warm, I was a little tired before I got there. The Grieve has got a very nice cottage beside the office houses, and the square is the finest looking I have yet seen. Having got some refreshments and rested a little we set out for church, which is close by. It is the parish Church of Botriphne and Mr. Mackay is minister. He is but a very sober preacher however, and the singing is the poorest I have almost ever heard. After dinner we went out to have a look at the cattle and horses. It is all black polled cattle and some splendid animals he has. He has five mares with foals all after one sire, Mr. Riddle's horse Arnacraig. Two of the mares are perfect dandies, one of them having never been beaten at any of the Shows round about. It is a far prettier place about Drumuir than I had any idea of. The parks are finely sheltered with trees and hedges, and many of them have been in grass for a long time. The house is a three storey building built on an eminence overlooking the railway. I was telling Mr. Anderson that I did not think I would stay here all winter. He said he might help me to get another situation if I was thinking of leaving, only there are not so many vacancies at Martinmas. I have quite made up my mind not to stay here longer than the term. I really could never put up with them at all.

1887 September
5th

It has been a very bad week for harvest work, having just got one whole day.

On Tuesday we were cutting at the clean land and did a good day's work. We cut on three sides.

We were cutting roads round the yavels on Wednesday forenoon but it was not nearly dry. In the afternoon we were at the barley.

Thursday morning was also soft. We cut some roads round the lea before dinnertime and got a yokin' at the barley again in the afternoon. Friday forenoon was a perfect spate. Two of the men were at Aberlour for coals. The harvest man and I were at the rapes. We got two hours at the machine in the afternoon.

We had only two hours on Saturday forenoon, but the afternoon was fine. We finished the barley and went to the yavels.

I was at church on Sunday, or at Chapel rather. The others were all going to the English Chapel, so I went also. It enters half an hour earlier. Mr. Jipp the minister gave us a very good sermon, but the congregation was very small. In the afternoon and evening a tremendous lot of rain fell. I see by the newspapers that in some places it has done a great deal of damage, washing away part of the crop etc. etc. There has been no cutting at all today. We have been at the rapes.

12th

There has been plenty of rain now and there will be no more cry for moisture this season. We got none cut till Wednesday afternoon. We were sometimes picking stones, and sometimes making rapes.

Thursday was a good day, and we were cutting at the yavels.

We finished them on Friday what would cut with the reaper but there will be a day's cutting with the scythes in the braes.

On Friday afternoon there was a strong gale of wind, and on Saturday it was also very blowy. I saw a good deal of the corn shaking in the lea. It is very ripe now, and the wet has made it tender. There is some of it a very good crop.

I was not at church on Sunday. The day was showery and today has been the same. No cutting done. We went over all the stooks, made some rapes, and mended some fences. The cattle are getting very bad to keep in, the parks being completely bare.

I went down to Aberlour one evening last week and got measure of a new suit of clothes. They are to be £2.17 cash or £2.19 credit.

19th

Another week of wet weather. It is really getting serious. I hear of barley and corn sprouting in sheltered places. The colour of the grain must now be a good bit spoiled.

On Tuesday morning the corn was rather wet but we started and cut till three o'clock when a big shower drove us home.

Wednesday forenoon was very wet. We were all at the rapes. The afternoon was showery and there was no cutting.

On Thursday forenoon we were cutting green thatch in the 'brackens'. We got a yokin' of the reaper in the afternoon. We cut all day on Friday in 'Knock-a-har', but there were several showers.

Saturday forenoon was wet again, but the afternoon was good. We were cutting in the braes with the scythes. I went down to Aberlour to have my coat fitted on in the evening, and called on James Murray.

Yesterday was a nice dry day. I was at church. Mr. Sloss gave a lecture on the unjust steward.

This has been a grand day. We finished the braes in the forenoon and in the afternoon we led the barely in good condition. There is scarcely two stacks of it.

25th

There is an improvement on the weather, but it is still far from 'forcy'. There has not been so much rain during the past week but it has been quiet and never much drying. I hear of stacks heating, and the steam mills have been busy the last few days.

We were cutting all day on Tuesday in Knockiehow when we finished it.

On Wednesday forenoon we cut a bit in the 'brackens' with the scythes. We were leading from the 'soccoth' in the afternoon, in good condition.

We led all day on Thursday but I was not well pleased with the clean land at all, only we put wood into it.

On Friday rain came on at ten o'clock and there was no more leading that day. We were cutting green thatch and driving it home in the afternoon.

We led all day on Saturday going to the lea in the afternoon. There was a strong dew in the morning however.

Sunday afternoon turned blowy, and in the evening a strong gale sprung up, and I was in the expectation that by this morning the stuff would be in grand order. A heavy shower however wakened me at three o'clock and between five and six a lot of rain fell. The folk were making rapes, setting up stooks and thatching.

I was at church on Sunday. I got my new clothes from the tailor last week. They fit me very well. It is a black coat and vest, and striped trousers. The suit cost me £2.17.

1887 October
3ʳᵈ

Another day and we will finish the harvest, only it must be a good day and so I may be speaking too fast.

This has been as good a day as we have had all harvest. We cut one of the bits in the Brackens, and led the other piece. We also thatched and dressed some stacks, and took home horse rakings.

Yesterday was a dry day but it was dull and cloudy. Currie and I were at church. Mr. Sloss chose for the subject of his discourse, the temptation of Pilate when Christ was brought before him to be tried. Pilate's conscience told him that Jesus was innocent, but he feared the people and had not the courage to say no to them. When we came home from church we found James Grant waiting us, him who used to be in Raemore and Burnheads. He is foreman now in Tommore, one of Sir George McPherson Grant's farms, but he is leaving at Martinmas and going home.

On Saturday forenoon I put the mare to the plough, as it was wet, but we got thatched in the afternoon.

Thursday and Friday were both wet days, and little was done at the harvest work.

Tuesday and Wednesday were dry and we were busy leading. There is not to be a large cornyard off the acreage. 76 acres in crop and 24 stacks and they might average about 9 quarters in each.

I had a letter from Willie last week. They had it all in 19½ stacks.

10ᵗʰ

The first four days of the week were exceptionally fine.

We did not have the like of them all harvest. Since Thursday however it has been very stormy, indeed I scarcely ever remember such bad weather so early in October, only I was never so far from the sea before.

We were busy in the cornyard on Tuesday but we did not finish until Wednesday at dinnertime having been five weeks, three days and a half. The men were ploughing in the afternoon and also on Thursday.

Friday was a very wet day, a great deal of rain falling in the forenoon. We did no outside work. We were dressing corn, cleaning harness, hacking fir etc. etc. I went down to Aberlour in the evening with two of the young ladies. They were going to a Social Meeting in connection with the Lawn Tennis Club. I went in to the druggists to get something for a sore ear which I have. It looks like 'scaw' or ringworm, and I expect I have got it off the calves. They have been affected with it all summer. I got a box of Iodine ointment to rub it with, and it is getting a little better.

On Saturday morning I sent one of the men down to Aberlour with six quarters of oats. It weighed 41½ lbs but the price was only 11/9. It is proverbial that farmers are a grumbling set, but truly they have got something to cry out about in the meantime. Barley they say is almost un-saleable, and with beef at 54/- the cwt. the outlook is truly not very bright.

I was not at church on Sunday as I had to keep my ear covered up. Currie was coachman. I forgot to mention that on Saturday morning the top of Ben Rinnes was white with snow which did not melt until midday.

On Sunday morning it was white almost to the door and today on the hill top not a black speck is to be seen.

17th

The past week has been remarkably stormy. A cold North wind, with showers of rain sleet and snow. Ben Rinnes has been completely covered all the week. Andrew was up one day looking for the goats, and he said there was five or six inches on the top, and it had also been blowing in several places to a considerable depth.

On Saturday there was a little improvement and yesterday and today have been splendid days. The men have been always at the plough and there is now a good breadth turned over. We have never taken but one yokin' in the day of the young horse as his shoulders are a little fired. The grey horse was very bad with colic one day. The damp straw had been the cause I believe. We were driving out some dung in the first of the week, but the road got too soft, and we gave it up.

I had letters from Jane and Mother in the end of the week. I was telling Jane in my last letter to her, that I was thinking of coming up to Edinburgh all winter. She was asking what I thought I would do, and said that Willie would do all he could for me. Mother was telling me that they were getting more drains this year again and I was very glad to hear it.

On Sunday morning Currie and I set out for Inveravon Church. We were to meet James Grant and go up with him to Tommore. We turned off the turnpike at the shop of Bellihagglis, the church being about a quarter of a mile down nearer Spey. It is a very pretty place about the church and manse, and is finely sheltered. It is rather a small church, but it was very well filled. The pews run right across, with a pass at either side. There is a small gallery, the choir and harmonium being placed in it. Mr. McLachlan preached himself and gave us a very good sermon from the text 'let every man wherein he is called therein abide with God' I. Cor. VII. 24. 'We were to learn from this', he said, that everyone was responsible for the situation in which he was placed, and also, 'that however lowly might be our position in life we could still abide with God'. Or in other words, we could always strive to show by our conduct and conversation that we were the servants of God and not of Mammon.

Tommore is about a mile and a half from the church. There is just a grieve upon it, and the men are in a bothy. It is an old thatched house, rather miserable looking outside but very comfortable seemingly inside. Having got some dinner we went to have a look round the place. There is a good steading and the cattle of course are all black polls. There were thirteen bull calves just newly weaned, two year old bulls, and an aged sire. There were also some very large cows. It is a mid aged man who is bailie and he was extremely willing to tell us the pedigree of all his cattle. It seems to be good land, but a great many big stones. We took a walk down past the inn on Dalnashaugh, across the bridge, past Swiss Cottage and Lady Grant's schools until we were opposite the farm of Lagmore. We then went down the water side a little and got a sight of the Castle. It looks a little like Cullen House only not so large. It is a very pretty place here, the changing colour of the leaves adding greatly to the beauty of the landscape at this season. I saw some splendid larches. Having returned and got some tea we started for home, arriving about nine o'clock.

24ᵗʰ

After a week of excellent weather, we are (for this season of the year) experiencing a most severe snow storm. The whole week was fine and potato lifting has been engaging attention the land being in grand condition.

We were among them on Thursday and Friday forenoon and got fine days. We have about twelve loads I suppose. They were a good crop. The cattle have always been getting out to the grass but there will be no more grazing now I fear. They have a fashion here of putting turnips on to the stubbles for the cattle but I do not approve of it at all. The cows got turnips today for the first time, but there are still a good few tares.

On Sunday morning a good deal of rain fell and it was showery throughout the day, turning to sleet at night.

This morning everything was white, while it has kept showering all day, and I believe we have now three inches all over. I did not put the men to the plough today, but I did see some ploughs going. There is too much snow now however. Andrew and Strachan went away to the hill in the afternoon to bring home the goats but they returned about five o'clock without getting a sight of them. It was blowing terribly on the top of the hill, and the cold was most intense.

31st

The last day of October. How quickly time flies. I have just been reading the entries in my Diary about the time I came here, and it would only seem like yesterday.

If the snow storm in the first of last week was severe it was of short duration. It turned fresh on Wednesday and by evening the snow had mostly disappeared. Since then we have had very fine days. Those who had not their potatoes lifted, have been among them. We have been ploughing beside the houses with one furrow. Strachan, Andrew and I were pulling turnips in the 'Brackens' and 'Paradise'. They store the whole of the turnips here, to be out of the sheep's way. It would be rather early yet I fear to store many. We filled one of the sheds, and emptied the others in the cornyard covering them with rashes.

Wednesday was the Thanksgiving Day for the harvest. Instead of going to church I went down to Drumuir to see Mr. Anderson. My errand was to see if he could assist me in getting a good place. I do not think I will take a situation as grieve again just now. I would be better to have a little more experience, and be learning something first. I would take a second pair as I think it would be better even than a first. I would have nothing to do but follow. Mr. Anderson showed me every kindness and promised to do all in his power for me.

I have just received a letter from him tonight telling me to go up to Ballindalloch. He had seen Mr. Stewart the manager there and had recommended me to him. I think I will go up tomorrow night, as I am sure it would be a place where I would get a good deal of insight.

I had a long letter from Willie McWillie last week, on Wednesday I think, and then I had a short note from him on Saturday. I was asking his advice about going to Queensland, but he thought I should rather look for another situation here. In his note however, he said he had been at Knowes and Father or Mother had apparently asked him to write and see if I would not come home. I have quite made up my mind however that I will not go home to be on the same footing as I left. I think I could manage things fully better than Father now, and if he cannot see his way to make ends meet, and is willing to give me the management, for his and Mother's sake I might go home, but when once I am away I would be better to take another half year whatever. One is always learning something.

1887 November
7th

Since I last wrote I have engaged to go to Georgetown, Inveravon as second horseman.

I went up on Wednesday evening and saw Mr. Stewart the manager. I would have preferred getting in at Marionburgh but he had no opening there. I was rather unwilling to accept the small wages, £11.10 being all he would give me, but I believe it will be a place where I will learn a good deal. The grieve and foreman are married and have houses, but the rest of us meal in a bothy. There are other two besides me, and there is a woman to make our meal. We get 3 bolls and a firlot of meal; three pints of warm milk a day and as many potatoes as we can use.

Tuesday last was a wet day a lot of rain falling in the afternoon.

Wednesday was dry and they were all in the plough. They have been ploughing yavels all the week. I was cutting thorns about the burn and the roadside.

On Thursday afternoon a telegram came to the foreman that his Mother was very poorly. I went to the plough and he set off for Glenlivet. He has not yet returned, and I fear that his Mother will be gone.

We were dipping the sheep on Friday and a very dirty job it was. It was half past nine before we got a start and we had them finished 240 in all, by four o'clock.

14th

A good deal of rain has fallen during the past week. The men have not been in the plough the stubbles being too wet. We have been storing turnips when the weather would permit and we have now about sixty loads. We were stopped today however as there is a good coating of snow, and it looks very like more tonight.

Thursday was Aberlour feeing market, and we were all down. They made us work till eight o'clock in the morning. It was a large market and fees were down considerably. A large number were not engaged. Neither Currie nor Strachan got the chance of feeing. I met James Murray in the market, and he made me come down and get some dinner. We then went down and saw the houses at Fishertown. They are very neatly finished and it is a tidy little place altogether. I saw Mr. Stewart in the market, also Mr. Finnie the grieve of Georgetown. I am going home the term night and am getting two days afterwards.

Friday was the fast day for the sacrament. Currie and I were both at church. It was Mr. McLachlan, Inveravon, who preached. In the afternoon Currie and I went over to John Grant's for three loads of corn to thrash.

We were pulling and driving home turnips out of the Brackens on Saturday.

On Sunday Mr. Sloss had Mr. Pirrie, Knockando assisting him. He is a very good speaker. There were two tables. The side seats being only covered half way back.

The foreman who has been away all the week returned this morning. His Mother is still alive, but getting very weak. The ground this morning was white, and there has been showers of snow all day. One of the men was at Aberlour with two loads of corn. It weighed 41 lbs and the price was 11/6.

21ˢᵗ

The snow storm which commenced in the first of last week has been of short continuance.

On Tuesday there was a couple of inches of snow and the frost was most intense, but a thaw set in on Wednesday morning and by mid day it was all away. Since then the weather has been good.

The men were driving out dung on Tuesday and Wednesday forenoon. Since then we have been at the turnips.

On Thursday evening I asked for Currie's wages as he was going to Keith market on Friday and was not coming back. They kept 2/- off for every day he wanted. They had no right I think to keep off so much as his wages only ran to 1/6 a day but they are the meanest greediest folk I ever saw.

Sunday morning was wet but I went to church, but I was not driving. Dr. Richardson a brother is at home from India just now and he drove them down. I went over in the evening to see John Grant.

The foreman went to the mill this afternoon for meal, while Strachan and I were gathering turnips.

Georgetown
Inveravon
1887 November
28ᵗʰ

I have been nearly a week in my new quarters and I should now have some idea how I shall like them. I must say that I feel a great change from Balliemulloch but then it is a change for the better in every respect. I can keep my mind so easy now and then when work is well done it is known to be so. I am also liking the bothy far better than I expected. The woman keeps everything clean and tidy and seems to be a good cook. We have brose in the morning, potatoes for dinner and porridge for supper, but of course she would cook anything we like to give her.

The sleeping place is right above the bothy, and will be fairly comfortable I think. There are three pairs of horses on the farm. The first pair are young strong horses. Mine are a brown mare 12 years old, and a grey horse 8. The mare is a little lame on a fore leg when going on the hard road, but she has grand legs, and is well proportioned. When four years old she cost 110 guineas. There is also good harness, and good tools of every kind to work with. The Grieve and foreman are both married, and have houses at a little distance from the steading. William Younie is the Grieve's name and the foreman is Peter Hepburn. The third horseman is a quiet young lad Peter Thomson by name, while the orra 'loon' comes from Glenlivet and is called Lamb. 'Bothy Jean', and last but not least Sandy Grant the cattleman and you have the entire working strength of the farm.

There is a steading of excellent houses. A complete square with a 'Pen' for entry. A causeway about 8 feet broad runs right round while the centre is occupied with a covered court.

A herd of over 40 Aberdeen Angus cattle comprises the stock, nearly all of them being pedigreed. Of course they are kept in grand order, and it seems to be the cattleman's hobby to tell of the noble blood of his 'black skins'.

The most of our week's work has been gathering and covering turnips. The pulling of them was set to contractors and the crop of swedes I never saw equalled.

The foreman was away on Saturday seeing some relations in Dufftown, and so I was townkeeper on Sunday.

I had a letter from Currie on Saturday. He had been in all the markets but was still unengaged.

I find they have got a Mutual Improvement Society in Inveravon. The meetings are held in the Schools on the evening of every second Thursday. The foreman and I went across and joined as members. The debate was 'Whether is the gossip or the flirt the greatest nuisance to Society.' A Mr. McKenzie supported the flirt but the member who was to take up the other side was absent. The gossip never-the-less gained by a majority of five.

1887 December
5th

I have been at Deskford since last I wrote seeing all my friends there. I went down with the 5 train on Thursday evening. It was seven when I got to Keith and having some messages it was eight before I left it. They were all to bed of course before I reached Knowes it being past eleven o'clock. I found them all well and everything getting on nicely. Willie has got more than half the lea ploughed and they have also been storing turnips. A good many drains are going in this winter but they have nearly all the tiles driven.

I went up to see the folks at Backies on Friday evening. Willie was away at Keith market, and it was nearly seven o'clock before he came home. He has been buying a great many Irish stirks this fall, and this year he is feeding with oats and oilcake. He has over forty head of cattle I believe.

I went over to Limestones and Cairdswell on Saturday. Annie's baby has a sad broken out face, but is otherwise thriving fine. George was telling me he had got down his rent £9. It will help a good bit but it is too dear yet. He has sold two stots just now coming three year old, for £36.

I got a very wet night to come home, but I had the little mare and I was home by eight o'clock.

I went to church on Sunday with Father and Joan. The church was very 'thin' and I thought the singing very poor. There is scarcely one sings through the church at all. Uncle George came over and went to church with us, and George Stephen was also across. When he was going home I went over to Kirkton with him to see the folks there. The old man is always failing, but is just now in good spirits.

As I had to be at Keith by half past nine, we had to start on Monday morning rather early. As Father and Joan were going to Keith, they took a cart and came up with me. It was good moon-light and a fine morning. By the time I made some small purchases, it was train time and I got home by half past eleven. They had commenced to plough lea when I was away and we were both in the yoke in the afternoon.

12th

The fresh weather has not continued long.

We were in the plough on Tuesday but Wednesday was frosty and since then it has been fresh and frosty alternately, but we have never got back to the plough again. Driving out dung has been the most of our work. The dung in the fold is excellent quality and we cart over it.

I was at Ballindalloch Station one afternoon for a ton of oilcake, and I went past Marionburgh with part of it.

On Saturday afternoon we were thrashing a small stack to the blacksmith and taking in a stack of our own. We are using more than a stack in the week just now.

I went to church on Sunday. They have got a splendid organ, and there is also good singing throughout the church. I went up to Marionburgh in the afternoon to see their cattle and houses. They have good houses but I think the cattle at Georgetown are fully best.

Today we went to the Smiddy and got two of our horses sharped, and in the afternoon we were driving firewood.

There was a meeting of the Mut. Imp. Society on Thursday evening. The subject of debate was 'Whether does the mind gain the more knowledge from reading or from observation'. Mr. Brown read a very able paper in support of Reading, while Mr. McKenzie upheld observation. Most of the members seemed to be in favour of the latter and so I spoke a few words in behalf of Reading. Observation gained by a majority of two votes.

19th

Good winter weather but no ploughing. We have got the dung all out, and have been doing some other odd jobs.

On Saturday we were pulling and driving turnips, it being a fresh day.

It was very hard on Sunday morning again however, and about nine o'clock it commenced to snow and there was three inches I believe before it ceased.

The foreman was town keeper and I went to church. Mr. McLachlan preached from Philippians I. 23, and gave us a very good practical sermon. 'We should all strive to live' he said 'so that our conduct and conversation might have a good and not an evil influence on those around us.'

We were thrashing and dressing corn this forenoon, and in the afternoon we were leaving the cattle in the fold to lead.

26th

Christmas falling upon Sunday, it has for most part been held today. In this district Xmas is far more generally observed than down with us. The Laird's people get both Xmas and the New Year. We also got a few pounds of mutton from Sir George for our Xmas dinner.

I was townkeeper both yesterday and today. I was at Ballindalloch Station this forenoon with Aleck Grant's trunk. He along with other six from this district is away to Glasgow. In the afternoon I was over at George Reid's seeing them kill a fat stot. He was not two year old, and he weighed a little above seven cwts. He was a black polled stot.

There was a meeting of the Mut. Imp. Society on Saturday evening. Very few of the members attended, but there was a very spirited debate on Home Rule, I gave 'Mary Queen of Scots' as a recitation, and I took in hand the side of a debate for next meeting.

The subject is 'Are large or small farms most beneficial to the community', it falling to my lot to support the large farms.[16]

On Friday evening I was at a Concert in the School. It was in aid of the School fund and the scholars, under the leadership of Mr. Myron and Miss Ledie, teachers, supplied the larger part of the Programme. A little girl, only four years old, sang 'Poor Old Jeff' in a most astonishing manner. Several ladies and gentlemen gave solos, and a few trios and duets were also sung. Among the songs were 'The Auld House', 'The Wishing Cup', 'Two Hearts', 'My Wife Has Taen The Gee', 'Willie Brewed a Peck O' Maut', 'Sailing' etc. etc. Sir George occupied the chair and they had the platform nicely decorated.

On Tuesday evening a fresh snow storm came on and on Wednesday morning there was five inches. Since then it has been fresh and frosty alternately, it never being twenty four hours on the way.

We have done very little outside work all the week. Driving in turnips, filling the mill, thrashing and dressing corn etc. being the most of it. I have been hearing that Sir George has granted his tenantry 25 per cent reduction for three years.

1888 January

2nd

The weather still continues changeable, frosty one day and soft the next. There has been no more snow, but the roads have been very slippery. We have been driving gravel on to the low road, from a pit close at hand.

I was at church on Sunday. Mr. McLachlan gave us an excellent New Year's Sermon. His text was 'How long have I to live'. 'The New Year', he said, 'was a season which induced us to look back on our past life, and it also led us to look forward to what might be before us'. People were sometimes asked how old they were but it was very seldom we asked ourselves how long we could have to live. In the evening I went over to hear the sermon at the Brig. O' Avon. It was Mr. Grant F.C. Manse, Boharn who preached. He was not a very fluent speaker but he was very earnest. His text was from Revelation XX 12. 'And the Books were opened.' The School at the Brig O' Avon is called Lady Grant's School, and it is a very nice building.

I went down today to pay the shoemaker for my boots, and I went up to see John Grant. McLean the merchant had a shooting match down in the burn, and we went down to it for a little. The prizes consisted of clocks, horse-clippers, pipes, cakes, fish, tobacco etc. etc. but I was not fortunate enough to get any of them.

---

[16] Printed in Appendix 2.

The past summer has been remarkable for its heat and dryness, very little rain having fallen until September. Much of the cereal crops were exceedingly short and a deficiency both in grain and straw is the result. Turnips and potatoes are both a good crop in general. Prices of all kinds of produce are exceedingly cheap, but there is a slight prospect of a rise both in grain and beef. Best oats are at 14/ and barley 20/ while beef, top quality is 60/ per cwt. There is great word of farmers failing in every direction, and large meetings have been held to petition the proprietors for a reduction of rent.

Unlike the summer months the autumn was exceedingly wet. Consequently much of the grain was damaged in colour and doubtless also the straw was lessened in value. Since harvest the weather has been remarkably changeable. The past year will always be memorable to me, as the one in which I left home. After having seven months to consider it I must say that I have never yet repented taking that step. Whether I will have to go home again or no, I am sure I will be much the better of it. When I was down Father was saying that I would need to come home at Whitsunday again, as he was getting unable to manage things. He would be willing to hand over everything to me, and give me the management. Although I am sure I would soon get an opportunity of bettering myself here still for Father and Mother's sake I believe I will have to go home.

A Journal of My Life and Everyday Doings

1888 January
9th

Once more have we passed through the golden gate of the New Year. Once more have we seen the old year die, and the New Year spring to life. How little do we know what will befall us during the year that is to come. How appropriate for us would be the prayer of Jabez, which Mr. McLachlan took for his text yesterday. 'And Jabez prayed unto the Lord God of Israel and said, 'O that those wouldst bless me indeed, and enlarge my coast, and that thine hand might be upon me and that thou would keep me from evil, that it might not grieve me'.

The snow storm has now entirely disappeared and we have had some very fine days.

We were pulling turnips on Wednesday afternoon and driving them on Thursday. In the afternoon they were all at the steam mill at Burnside, while I was at the Station for a ton and a half of oilcake. Since then we have been at the plough.

There was a meeting of the Mutual Imp. Soc. on Thursday evening. Most of the members took part in the debate and on the vote being taken there was a majority of four in favour of small farms. The minister was up and presided at the meeting.

On Saturday evening I went over and got a book out of the Library. The School Master is librarian and the books are kept in the School. There are about 400 volumes. I have taken out one of Dickens' 'Sketches by Boz'. The subscription is 1/ in the half year.

16th

We have been at the plough all the week and have turned over a good breadth. The half of the lea would now be ploughed I think. The first of the week was fine fresh days and very warm.

Since Thursday it has been frosty some mornings being hard enough for the plough.

I was at church on Sunday. The minister preached from Eccles. XI. 1. 'Cast thy bread upon the water for thou shalt find it after many days.' In the afternoon I went up to see George Brown. He has a small croft above Burnside and he is a very quiet well-read man. His mother is still alive. I found that a son whom she had before she was married, to the farmer of Phones, is Mr. Burgess a Banker in Wishaw, who is married to Ann Fraser, daughter of Mr. Fraser late Forester at Cullen House. Lizzie was very well acquainted with them, when they were at Cleland.

I see by the newspapers that two or three of the arches of the Cullen viaduct have fallen. The foundation seems to have slipped but it was observed giving way and of course the trains were stopped. It will no doubt be a great expense repairing it again. I also see that there is great agitation among the Lewis crofters just now. They seem to be in extremely destitute circumstances, and much of their land having been taken from them and converted into deer forests, they proposed making a raid and killing the deer to satisfy their hunger. This they did killing a large number and driving others into the sea. Of course a number of them were arrested and taken to Edinburgh but I see tonight that they have been acquitted.

23rd

We have ploughed none since I wrote last. The frost has been very severe and there being no snow, it has gone in a good bit. Five or six inches I believe. Turnips that are not stored must be much spoiled.

In the first of the week we were driving gravel on to the low road. We were then driving out dung up to the fields above the road. We cart over all the dung.

On Saturday the frost relaxed and since then it has been fine and fresh.

I was at church on Sunday and went up to the loft, to see the organ. It is a large instrument with an excellent tone. Miss Myron teacher, Brig O' Avon, is organist. Mr. McLachlan's text was 'Wherefore leaving the principle of the doctrine of Christ, let us go on unto perfection'. 'It was but the law of nature', he said, that every thing in the world should be progressing. Art seemed to be the only thing that was not advancing. Where now could a Raphael, a Rubens, or a Vandyke be found? As regards religious life we must be always progressing, always striving to attain to perfection, which is only to be found in our great example.

We have been pulling and driving turnips today. There is a strong breeze of wind tonight and I expect we will get to the plough tomorrow.

30*th*

After six days of fresh weather, John Frost has again laid his icy grasp on old Mother earth. We kept busy at the plough until Saturday.

Friday however, was very frosty, and in the afternoon it was blowing blind drift. We have been a day and a half down beside the big house. It is very dry land, some of the hillocks being inclined to sand.

On Saturday we were driving Swedish turnips all day. It was quiet and frosty.

I was town keeper on Sunday.

Today we were at the dung in the forenoon, in the afternoon we were taking in hay. We shook the seed out at the foot of the stack.

I had a letter from Jessie on Friday saying that Maggie's baby was dead. She has never been very healthy and Tommy and her took the measles about the New Year. She died on the 22*nd*.

I saw in the newspaper that Mrs. Gray of Hoggie was dead. I also see that the farm of Ardiecow is for let again. I wonder where Donald will be going or if he will take another farm again.

1888 February
6*th*

Fresh weather again. It is really very changeable weather. We were driving out dung until Friday when we emptied the fold.

We were driving home a stack of corn and straw from Tommore on Friday.

Saturday and today we were at the plough. I suppose the furrow is nearly 500 yds. long. It is very good land I am sure but dry and stony.

There was a meeting of the Mutual Imp. Soc. on Thursday evening but the attendance was thin. It was a 'hat' night, and the subject which fell to me was 'Courtship'.

I was at a prayer meeting in the vestry on Friday evening. The minister took the principal part himself and explained two portions of scripture very well.

We got to the plough on Saturday. In the evening James McKenzie, Alec Smith and I went to the Manse (by invitation) to consider what might be done to put more life into the Mutual Imp. Soc. I proposed that the members should give readings and recitations by turn, and that they should write letters to each other. Mr. McLachlan thought that these proposals would be improvements. We were also speaking of how we should finish the Session.

I was at church on Sunday. We got a very impressive sermon from the text 'How dreadful is this place, surely this is none other than the house of God and this is the gate of Heaven.' Mr. McLachlan said 'that the ladder which Jacob saw shows us that Heaven may be much nearer to us than we think, and the even in the most desolate places, God's eye is ever upon us.' In the afternoon Peter and I went over to see their cattle and horses, at Lagmore and Cragganmore. They had the disease among their cattle last year and the stock, which is a mixed one, have all been bought in. The Distillery at Cragganmore is close beside the farm, and they do a good business at it I believe.

13th

Before the New Year we had frost and thaw alternately almost every twenty four hours. Since then it has been week about. After six days of fine fresh weather, we are experiencing the sixth snow storm of the season.

In the first of the week we kept busy ploughing, and except the turning rig, the lea is now all turned over.

I had a long letter from Willie McWillie on Thursday. He was telling me that the School Board had refused the School for a Concert in aid of the Library. I see a letter in the Banffshire Journal this week giving the School Board a rub anent the same. There will be an election of members in April again I believe.

On Friday morning there was two inches of snow, and a sharp frost. We were planting seed turnips in the forenoon and driving firewood in the afternoon, from above Marionburgh.

On Saturday we were driving oats to Ballindalloch Station. This is the first which has been sold off the farm this season. It was 'fine fellow' oats, and weighed 43 lbs the bushel.

On Sunday Mr. McLachlan took up the life of Jacob, where he left off the previous Sabbath. James McKenzie came down to see me in the afternoon. I went up and had tea with him, and then went to the Service at the Brig o' Avon. It was Mr. Robertson's assistant who preached. He seems to be a very earnest man, but has a bad delivery and is terribly confined to the paper. The subject of his sermon was, the seven sayings on the cross.

On Saturday afternoon Sandy Grant lost one of his cows. She has had a sore foot for several weeks, but the bursting of a blood vessel was the cause of death. She was not a very high pedigreed animal, but of course there was great lamentation over her.

I forgot to mention that on the morning of the 2nd Feb. a slight shock of earthquake was felt over the North of Scotland. A few persons in this locality experienced a slight shaking, but it was felt most severely to the West. I saw snowdrops in full bloom at Ballindalloch Castle on 5th Feb.

20th

We have had a good few snow storms during the winter, but we are now experiencing a proper one. Snow commenced to fall on Tuesday evening and by Wednesday morning there was fully 10 inches. It was dry as powder and had the wind risen would have drifted terribly. Since then five or six inches has fallen, but on some days it sadded down a bit. There would now be about a foot all over.

I went up on Tuesday evening to see Willie Tulloch the blacksmith. He is a very serious thinking young man and being well read and intelligent he is very good company. His master's name is Fraser. He is a widower and has just a housekeeper, but no family. Tuesday being 'Fastereven' of course we had brose. Peter stayed to sup with us, and there was a good deal of excitement. The 'Boy Lamb' managed to get both the ring and button.

On Thursday the frost was most excessive. I heard that the thermometer had not been so low for seven years. There was a meeting of the Mut. Imp. Soc. that evening. Geo. Brown read a very good paper on the 'Advantages of Libraries.' Any criticism that was, was favourable to the same.

There was great regret over the loss of a calf on Friday. It was a three year old quey and she was rather bad in calving, requiring five of us on the rack.

I was town keeper on Sunday and was not at church.

We have done nothing all the week except driven in some turnips, thrashed and winnowed.

We were driving the snow out of the square today.

I see by the newspapers that Ordens has signed his trust deed. If Miss Steinson had been told that this would happen a few years ago, she would have thought you were crazy I believe.

27ᵗʰ

Other two days and February will be done. It has fairly fulfilled this year the old proverb that 'February should fill the dyke'. Last year it was an exceptionally fine month, there being scarcely a broken day during the whole of it. This year we have just had five ploughing days. There has been no addition to the snow since last I wrote, it having been mostly quiet frosty days. We were driving in turnips for the most of two days last week. The yellow ones are pretty well through, but there is a great quantity of swedes yet.

On Saturday we filled up 32 qrs. of providence oats. It weighed 43 lbs the bushel.

We were driving it away today to Ballindalloch Station. When filling up we were all having ourselves weighed on the bisomer. I was 12 stone and 12 lbs.

We got a good sermon from Mr. McLachlan on Sunday from the text, 'Let us arise and go up to Bethel.' I went up to Marionburgh in the afternoon, and got a sight of all the cattle. I was also down at the old square seeing the colts. There are four yearlings and a two year old.

1888 March
6ᵗʰ

March should come in like a lion, and so it has certainly. The snow storm still continues but the snow is gradually sinking. Beside the ordinary routine of providing food for the cattle, we have been shaking and dressing grass seeds. We just spread a sail at the foot of the stack and then built up the hay again.

We are thrashing barley just now. The mill has a beater and makes a very good job of it. There was a Show of roots and grain at Aberlour on Tuesday last. Mr. Stewart bought several quarters of grain for seed.

A meeting of the Mut. Imp. Soc. was held on Tuesday. Mr. Wilson read an old ballad 'The battle of Harlaw' and then were several readings and recitations. It was proposed that there should be a Social Meeting to finish the Session with, and a committee was appointed to carry it out.

There were very few at the prayer meeting on Friday. I read the XC psalm and made a few remarks.

The Kirk was also very thin on Sunday. The minister gave a short but impressive sermon on forgiveness. James McKenzie came down in the afternoon, and stopped to take a cup of tea with me.

I was writing Mother and Willie McWillie today.

12ᵗʰ

We had a very bad afternoon on Wednesday and we kept the mill. Sleet fell thickly, and towards night it turned to snow. Everyone was sure that we were in for a fresh snow storm, but next day a thaw set in.

I went over to the Smiddy on Wednesday evening to ask the blacksmith's daughter, Jessie Ann, to give a song at the Social Meeting. She was willing to help us as far as she could. Petrie is their name and there are three daughters at home—nice like girls. They have a son who went out to Australia about a year ago, and of course we were all interested in speaking about that country. Jessie Ann also gave us some music on the piano.

We were driving out dung on Thursday and Friday, and emptied the fold. It was very soft only we had but a few yards off the road to go.

I saw some ploughs going on Friday the snow being nearly all out of sight.

On Saturday and today we were driving up swedes and emptying them at the back of the byres.

Mr. Anderson, Drumin, was in past today. He was going up to Tommore to try and buy a bull.

19th

The weather during the week has been the coldest we have experienced all winter. A strong Easterly gale prevailed for two days, and it was piercingly cold.

I see by the newspapers that much snow had fallen in Aberdeenshire. We were driving up turnips in the first of the week but the frost was a good bit into the pits. The snow is now all away but the frost has been very severe. Grass I fear will be injured and turnips which are not stored, will be little use I doubt.

We had a meeting of the Mutual Improvement on Thursday and some more arrangements were made about the Social Meeting. The debate is to be 'Whether is it better to have loved and lost, or never to have loved at all.' James McKenzie and I are to take the respective sides. The meeting is to be almost the same as what we had in Deskford, only the School Board will allow no dancing.

I had a letter from Mother on Friday. She was saying that Willie McWillie was seriously ill. I was writing him yesterday forenoon. I rather fear that Willie is not going to be a long liver. If this frosty weather continue I will perhaps take a run down to Deskford on Saturday first.

26th

The Social Meeting of the Mutual Improvement Association which was held on Friday evening has been the great event of the week.

There having never been a meeting of the same nature in Inveravon before a very warm interest was taken in the same. The night was stormy but about eighty ladies and gentlemen sat down to tea. The tables were presided over by seven ladies, who had all put themselves to a great deal of trouble in assisting us with the tea and each having her table beautifully decorated with flowers and evergreens. Mr. McLachlan, President of the Association occupied the chair, and tea having been finished a lengthy and varied Programme was gone through. There were two readings, two recitations, the debate, and several songs and duets. Miss Elsie Reid sang with much taste and expression 'The Farmer's Boy' while the same lady and Mr. Stuart gave as a duet 'When ye gang awa' Johnnie'. Another duet was sung by the Misses Begg and Petrie entitled 'The Cousins' which they sung very sweetly. Mr. Tulloch gave 'Rothesay Bay' and Miss J. A. Petrie 'Take me back to Switzerland.'

The debate caused a good deal of excitement. My opponent had a very able paper, and of course I did my best to oppose him. On the vote being taken there was found to be a majority of 18 in his favour. I would indeed have been surprised had it gone otherwise. After singing 'Auld Lang Syne' the company dispersed, highly delighted with their evening's entertainment.

At mid-day on Saturday I got leave of absence and set out for Deskford. Snow had begun to fall on Friday afternoon and before I left Georgetown there was at least 4 inches. This was the worst day we have had all winter. From morn to night it never faired. The roads about Keith were in a fearful state, nothing but slush, but by good luck I was not at the Railway bridge, when John Longmore came up with me in Ardoch's phaeton. He had come up to meet his brother, but did not get him. I was very thankful to get a drive in such a bad night, and of course I was also anxious to hear all the Deskford news. I came off and went past the Backies. I found Willie a little better from what he had been, but still very, very weak. His lungs I fear are much wasted and he is so thin, but he is quite cheerful and contented, and he has got the best of nurses. It was about six o'clock when I got home.

Mother has not been very well for sometime but always going about. Father was away at Portsoy at a sale of manure. No tenant has been got for the Mills as yet and the stock of manure was being sold by auction. Father bought 24 cwts. of bone dust at £6.15 the ton, and 10 cwts. turnip manure at £2.13. They were telling me that Ardiecow has been let to a Mr. Jenkins from Portsoy at an yearly rent of £80. I believe that the minister has given up his land, and the gowely haugh is going to Ordens. A tenant has not been selected for it yet. Mr. and Miss Steinson are going to Glasgow I hear.

They had a great day in Deskford two weeks ago at the ordination of their Free Church minister. He is a Mr. Morrison, a son of Loanheads, below Cornhill. He was assistant at Forres.

Sunday was also a bad day and none but Willie went to church. Father is complaining greatly on his loss of sight, and about not being able to go the markets, and he is sorely put about as to how the seed is to be got in. I was sorry to see him troubling himself so much, and he got me to promise that I would come home at Whitsunday again. He is to go down to Cullen House and get my name put in to the tack, and Willie is going to be put to learn a trade. I will be much benefited however by the year I have been away from home. I have seen and learned much which I would not have done otherwise.

1888 April
2nd

And still the stormy weather continues. The seedtime must inevitably be a late one now.

On Monday last fifteen inches of snow was measured in this district. It has gradually subsided, but there is not much of the black ground visible yet. Filling the Mill, thrashing, winnowing, and taking in turnips has been the most of our week's work.

I was over at Ballindalloch Station with a young bull today in the cattle cart. He was 5 ft. 4ins in girth. Some of the yearling heifers are 5 ft. 10. We were trying the girth of the horses one day. The five year old horse was 7 ft 4 in another was 7 ft. 1 in. and my grey horse's girths 6 ft. 10 in.

The last meeting of the Session of the Mut. Imp. Assoc. was held on Thursday evening. A balance of 10/- was carried forward to next year's account.

I was town keeper on Sunday but went to church. Mr. McLachlan took for his text the parable of the two sons, the elder of which refused to go and work in his Father's vineyard, but afterwards repented and went. The younger said 'I go Sir but went not.' The appliction of the text was, 'to which class do we belong.' I am reading at present George McDonald's novel 'Sir Gibbie'. There are many passages in it well worth remembering.

9th

On Tuesday evening I went over and called on Mr. McLachlan, as he had asked me a week ago to do so. He soon let me know what he wanted. He rather suspected he said that I had some object in view in coming to drive a pair at Georgetown. He had his own idea, and it was that I wanted to get insight about the polled herd, and so prepare myself for a farm manager. If such was my object he said I might depend on him giving me every assistance in his power and more than that, he would speak to Sir George about me, and he was sure he would be able to do something for me. I was greatly touched by the interest he took in me, and thanked him kindly for the same, but of course I told him that I would be obliged to go home I feared. On explaining this he said it was certainly my first duty to assist my Father. We then discussed a good many topics of interest, and before leaving Mrs. McLachlan gave me several books to read.

The strength of the sun and the length of the day has forced the snow away on the low grounds, but back from the water side it is still lying in patches, while Ben Rinnes is scarcely broken.

We ploughed the endrig of the lea on Saturday and filled in the furs, and today we were at the clean land. It was in fair condition for ploughing.

I went down to Aberlour on Saturday evening to see James Murray.

I went to church with Maggie and him on Sunday. We got an excellent sermon from Dr. Scott. He is not a very fluent speaker, but seems to be a very learned man.

16ᵗʰ

Commenced sowing today. We put 9 qrs. potato oats into a 12 acre field. The land is in grand condition only the park was an exceptionally dry one.

It has been good weather since Saturday, but until then it was never fresh. Only small patches of snow can now be seen on the hill sides, and the top of Ben Rinnes is well broken.

We were twice from home for fodder last week.

On Tuesday we were over the water for corn and straw at Tomintuigle. We had to go round by Carron Bridge and up through Knockando. About the distillery of Cardow and the Manse of Knockando it is rather a pretty place, but farther up the land, seems very cold and wet. A good deal of lea is to plough in that district yet. We were nearly four hours going and it was half past six when we got home. 26/- the qr. is the price I believe.

We took home the last of the yellow turnips on Wednesday. More than half of them were rotten.

On Thursday we were at Bogs of Advie for hay. It would be about 8 miles farther up than this I believe. We passed the farms of Lagmore and Garland on the one hand, and Cragganmore, Tormore, Achavoctie and Mains of Advie on the other. We also passed the church and manse of Advie, both seemingly new buildings, the manse garden being at present reclaimed from the heather. A little further on we left the turnpike and turned down past the Schools and railway station. Bogs is on a level haugh beside the Spey. Across the water we could see the farm of Knockinbuie, and a little farther up Tulchan Lodge.

We were ploughing clean land on Saturday.

On Sunday 'Dod' Kemp, Westertown, came up and went to church with me. We went up to Marionburgh in the afternoon and got a sight of their cattle, horses and sheep. The ewes are nearly all lambed now, most of them having a pair.

I had a note from Annie McWillie last week saying that Willie has taken another bad turn, and was in a very critical condition. I was extremely sorry to hear it, as I was expecting to hear of his partial recovery.

23rd

Having been ploughing endrigs this afternoon my hand is in bad condition for yielding the pen. Again we have had a break in the weather with considerable rainfall. The two first days of the week were exceptionally fine and grass was springing beautifully.

Wednesday and Thursday were dull. We sowed the remainder of the lea on the latter day. A great deal of rain fell the following night and Friday forenoon.

It was Saturday afternoon before we got to the plough, and not very dry then. A cold Northerly wind has prevailed since with occasional hail showers.

I had a letter from Deskford written on Tuesday night and there was no sowing done at that time. I was greatly astonished at the same.

30th

A very busy week. The clean land above the road is all ploughed and sown. We ploughed a 10½ acre park in 61 hours of one plough. Weather cold and showery.

I had a letter from home saying that Mother was very bad, and Willie McWillie I fear is dying.

1888 May
7th

I have been off work for four days and I am just going away to pack up my box as I intend leaving for home tomorrow. I took a bad cold in the first of last week, sore head—sore bones and all the other usual accompanyments, but being very busy and the third man laid up at the same time I strove my utmost to keep going.

Thursday was the Communion fast day, and I thought it might put me all right, but no! I have been able to work none since. I have got

John Grant who was with me in Balliemulloch to work for me until the term. He is to be ready for work tomorrow morning. The other lad is home to his folks and is not better yet either.

I had three of them down from Marionburgh tonight bidding me good-bye. Robert Macdonald is leaving at Whitsunday. He is going to Texas, America to a large cattle ranch. He has a brother there already. Another brother is proprietor of the 'The Farming World' and his eldest brother who died six months ago was editor of 'The North British Agriculturist'. They belong to Glen Rinnes. The married men are all staying on, but they have had to submit to a small reduction of wages.

VOLUME FOUR
14 MAY 1888-26 JANUARY 1892

A Journal of My Life and Everyday Doings

Knowes
1888 May
14ᵗʰ

After nearly twelve months absence I am home again. I left Georgetown on Tuesday at eleven o'clock. The man who was to come in my place, had not turned up when I left, and I was greatly disappointed. It was one o'clock when I got to Keith, and having some errands there I waited until five. I was making some inquiries of tradesmen about getting Willie home as an apprentice. Mr Pirie Saddler is in want of one, and I believe Willie and I may go up this week again. As I had written home telling them to met me at Cornhill on Wednesday. I went up to Cairdswelll on Tuesday evening. The baby's face is now almost better, and he seems to be thriving fine. George had bought a grey mare with a foal at foot the day before at sale at Allacardoch. She cost him £19.10.

I met Father at Cornhill Station on Wednesday at ten o'clock. I was very sorry to find Mother so weak when I got home. She is scarcely able to come out over her bed yet, and she can take but very little food. She has just been a little better however for the last few days.

I was up seeing Willie McWillie on Wednesday evening. He was keener that I expected to find him, but oh so thin and worn. 'I am always here you see Jamie' were his first words to me on entering his bedroom. He has no expectations of ever recovering, but his is quite resigned, and so contented. He was telling me, that he had appointed Mr. Michie and me as his executors in his will.

I have been working in the garden since I came home, but Father had everything done except the flowers. Him and I were putting up wire netting today to keep the rabbits from the corn in the Den.

They planted the potatoes in the first of last week and since then Willie has been working among the turnip land. The weather is extremely cold and stormy, the wind being due north. Vegetation makes no progress, but cattle are being turned out to the fields the winter keep being done.

Of course there has been changes in Deskford since I left it. Mr. Walker the Free Church minister had gone to Glasgow. A Mr. Morrison from Forres, has been appointed in his place. His father has the farm of Loanhead beside Cornhill. A heating apparatus has been introduced into the Established Church during the winter and considered to be a great improvement.

Ardiecow and Ordens are both getting new tenants at Whitsunday. Donald has taken a small place in the Bauels and a Mr. Jenkins from Portsoy is to be his successor. Ordens failed, and Miss Stevenson and him have gone to Glasgow it is said. What he is to do I have never heard. A Mr. James Watt Marnoch is to be tenant of Ordens.

During the past winter Father got in a great few hundred yards of more drains. All is drained now that is in the least wet, and I would expect a great improvement from the same. They also limed about an acre and a half.

21st

There is very little improvement on Mother yet, and I am becoming rather anxious about her. She can take a little food, but she does not seem to derive much benefit from the same. The Dr. changed her medicine last time he was seeing her, and Willie was for it yesterday. Perhaps it may do her some more good.

I was up seeing Willie McWillie on Saturday but there is not much difference on him either. He can take scarcely any solid food, but except a slight cough at times, he has no pain, and he also sleeps a good deal.

Father and I were at the sale at Ordens on Wednesday. Everything sold well I think. The cattle and horses did not come to much money, some of them being rather inferior quality, still I think they were rather above market value.

I was in the drill plough on Thursday and drilled as many as we are to sow in swedes.

On Friday I went to the sale at Black Culphin, for the purpose of buying a roller. There were two metal ones, and I bade £3.4 for one of them but did not get it. The cattle and horses were of very superior quality and bought handsome prices. I see by the newspapers that cattle are selling well at all the sales and grass parks are also up in value this year. I might be informed from this I think that things are on the turn, and the outlook for farmers therefore appears a little brighter.

On Saturday Willie and I took a cart and went up to Keith. We were taking home some wire and wire netting as I am thinking of enclosing the hill and putting some sheep on to it. We called on the saddler, and Willie is to go and start with him in two weeks. He is to be bound four years, and is to have 3/6 in the week for the first year, with a rise of 2 shilling each years. He is to lodge with a Mrs. Burgess on Land Street and is to be 1/9 in the week.

We were putting out dung this forenoon and I sowed about an acre and half in the evening. The weather has been dry all the week and therefore most suitable for cleaning the turnip land.

Until Friday however it was cold, with no growth. Since then it has been warm and genial. Grass has greatly improved, while braird has made rapid progress.

28*th*

I sowed another acre of Swedish turnips on Tuesday and we are not going to seek more. I have been giving them 5 of manure to the acre in the proportion of two bags of Bone dust to one of turnip manure. We gave them a fair allowance of dung three good loads to four drills. The weather still continues dry. In the first of the week it was very warm and everything was growing fine.

Since Thursday it has been cold again with a northerly wind. The ground this morning was white with hail.

The cattle have been out in the afternoon since Friday.

I was taking home my hives from the Backies in the end of the week. Willie was very low on Saturday. The Dr. has warned them that he may be taken at any time. Annie has also been laid up with rheumatism, but is keeping better. Willie is away up to ask for them tonight.

Mother was improving a little until Friday and was twice at the kitchen fireside. Since then however she has been rather worse, on two days being unable to get up at all.

We got news on Wednesday that Jane's baby had died on the 21*st*. Janet Black was her name and she has been ailing for sometime. Spinal disease I believe was the cause of her death. She was about fourteen months old I think.

1888 June
5*th*

It is with deep and heartfelt sorrow, that I have to record the death of my very dear friend William McWillie. We have been friends I may say since ever we left school, but for the past five years we have been very intimate—confiding freely in each other, and always consulting about everything as to which we were in any doubt. Although his death was not unexpected still I must say it was a blow to me. We were so near each other's ages; were always interested in the same plans and speculations; and were so warmly interested in each others welfare that his death has come home to me very forcibly. How mysterious are the ways of Providence. How many are there, who being long past the allotted span of life, and whose time of usefulness is past and gone who are still preserved from year to year, while one in the very prime of life—in the hey day of youth, whose life is brimful of hope and promise, is cut down as the early grave. What an uncertainly hangs over life and how near may any of us be to an eternal world?

Oh! That God would deeply impress upon my mind, the most solemn lesson taught by the death of my friend; so that by leading a holy and devoted life, I may be able from my heart to say, 'Let me die the death of the righteous, and let my last end be like his.' Ever since he left school, Willie I believe has not been strong but about three years ago he had rather a bad limb and since then he has gradually been sinking. He was always able to go about however, and do a little work until the beginning of March when he was confined to his bed, and I believe he was scarcely ever up again. Towards the end the Dr. told them, that his lungs were almost entirely wasted and that he could hold out no hopes of his recovery. Willie was quite sensible of this himself however but he was quite resigned to his fate, and I never saw anyone more contented and cheerful. What a blessed thing it is to have a sure ground of hope, and to trust implicitly in the finished work of our Redeemer.

I saw him on Saturday the 26th, but he was not able to speak much. In the beginning of the week Willie went up and asked for him, when he was a little better.

On Wednesday afternoon however a change was seen to come over him and Annie sent over for his Father and sister. All through the night he spoke but little but still seemed quite sensible, and at four o'clock he quietly fell asleep.

I went up to see his remains on Friday evening. He was terribly worn but his face was peaceful, and there was no sign of a struggle.

He was interred in Deskford Churchyard on Monday 4th June and his funeral was very largely attended. Being one of the Trustees I had to go back to Backies after the funeral to hear the will read. It was Mr. Stephen the lawyer from Keith who had made it out, and of course he was then to read it. After we got tea the important document was proclaimed, when it was found that except £20 to his brother George, and a like sum to his Nephew (John's eldest son) everything was to be divided equally between his sisters, Jane and Annie. The lease of the Backies was also left to Annie, if the proprietor agree to accept her as tenant. He had also requested his sisters to give his watch to me, and although I am sure I would have required nothing to keep the memory of my friend fresh in my mind, still I shall ever value Willie's watch very highly.

Since last I wrote we have experienced weather the like of which was never remembered by the oldest person living.

We had thirty six hours of rainfall, commencing on Saturday night, and on Sunday morning it turned to snow, continuing the most of the day. By afternoon there was two inches all over, there being also a strong gale of wind, and having all the appearance of a day in March. I have read of some one saying 'the summer had set in with its usual severity' and I am sure that the leafy month of June has commenced severe enough this year whatever. I see by the newspapers that in the upland districts a considerable depth of snow fell; which wreathes in some cases two feet deep were formed. From four to nine inches was reported from different places. Cattle in parks must have suffered severely and I heard of a case of one dying from exposure. I do not think that the turnips will be injured as there was not much frost with it.

One morning in the first of the week was extremely frosty however, there being ice on the water. With such weather, much vegetation could not be expected.

We have the turnip land all drilled but only one sowing of yellows done yet. I was up at Keith with Willie today, and saw him started work before I left. I brought home a load of manure with me. I have been giving the turnips five cwts to the acre in the proportion of 3 Bones to 2 turnip manure.

11th

What a variable climate we do have. The first of the week was cold and stormy, Friday and Saturday were mild and warm, while yesterday was very cold again. We have been sowing turnips since Wednesday but the land was never in good condition. Swedes are coming up very well however. Pasture in many instances is getting bare, and more heat is greatly needed. Lord Seafield and the Emperor of Germany have both died during the past week. The latter was a son-in-law of The Queens, and was much beloved of his people.

19th

The anniversary of my birth has once more come round. I was only reminded of the same by receiving a most beautiful card, from some kind, although unknown friend. (Not altogether unknown perhaps). May the commencement of another year of my life, find me more firmly resolved than ever, to do all the good in my power, for truly our days are short and fleeting. Mother has been a little better for the last three days, and I truly hope that the improvement may be permanent.

We have had eight days of very good weather, and the appearance of everything has greatly altered for the better. Crops are still two weeks behind however, but otherwise they have a promising appearance. Turnip sowing is being brought to a close, and they too under favourable conditions. We finished on Friday. Swedes are doing fairly well, but the early yellows are showing signs of eating off.

On Saturday we washed the carts also washed and dried the harness. Willie came down from Keith. He seems to be taking to his trade remarkably well.

Father and I were at church on Sunday. Mr. Mackintosh gave us a very able and touching sermon from the text. 'Can the Ethiopian change his skin or the leopard his spots, then might those do good who are accustomed to do evil.'

Father and I were down yesterday at Cullen House getting my name put into the tack. We were taken 'ben' and introduced to Mr. Campbell the new Factor. He is a middle aged man tall and dark, but I liked his appearance and manner remarkably well.

I went down to see some sheep of James Gray's but did not find him at home. I bought a ewe and two lambs at Cornhill market on Thursday. We are enclosing the 'hill' to keep in sheep.

We were away at Millighan today for posts.

25th

The longest day of summer has come and gone and once more the 'days are drawn in.' How quickly the first half of summer always seems to go past, but indeed we may say that summer is only commencing yet. We have truly got some summer weather now however, but it was only yesterday that the wind shifted round from the North and turned soft and warm.

We went to the moss on Wednesday and set the peat. Isa Reid, Cullen, who has been with us for the last three weeks, went with us and gave John and I a hand. The moss was not in very good condition, and we did not manage to finish them. John went back on Thursday. I was up at Ardiecow that day, giving Mr. Jenkins a help to finish his turnips. His land is in very bad condition, it being wet when they ploughed it. He is intending to build some this summer I believe. They have no family, but she seems to be a very managing wife.

We were fencing at the hill on Friday. I sent word to James Hay that I would take his ewes and lambs so he sent them up. Four ewes and five lambs for £10.

I was cleaning out all my hives on Saturday and putting on some sections, and I must stop and go and prepare more.

John Cowie was over on Sunday and we also had a visit from Willie Wilson. He is always cattleman at Connycleugh beside Huntly.

I am glad to be able to mention that Mother is always improving, although slowly. She was trying to sow a little today.

1888 July
2nd

I had letters both from Jane and Jessie last week. Jessie was anxious to know when I was coming to see the Glasgow Exhibition, and to pay her a visit. I see that the Railway Companies are offering great inducements in the form of cheap fairs. There is a Keith holiday on Wednesday first, when tickets available for three days are to be issued for 8/9. I would not think of going however for less than a week but I fear it will be the month of August before I can get time to get away.

In the Glasgow Herald which Jessie sent me, I saw an account of the progress they were making with the Forth Bridge. It is truly a most gigantic undertaking and would be as well worth seeing I believe as the Glasgow Exhibition. At the sides where the water is shallow, the piers are comparatively near each other, but in the centre where the water is deep, they are a tremendous, and to those unacquainted with the system of bridge building, almost an incredible distance apart. In the centre of the Firth there is a small island it seems, and a pier is built upon it, while the spans at either side are over 1500 feet. The rails are to be 150 feet above high water mark to allow of large vessels sailing underneath, but some of the piers are carried to a height of more than 300 feet. Over 6000 men are at present employed in the construction of the Bridge, working night and day and it is supposed that it will be finished in about fifteen months.

In the first of the week we had nice warm days; Thursday was dewy and everything looked beautiful, bt it turned cold after the rain and Friday and Saturday were very stormy. Grass and corn have some progress, but turnips very little. Some of our yellow ones are eating off yet I think, and the clay bits are extremely hard. A few have commenced hoeing. Cutting thistles and mixing top-dressing has been our week's work.

George Cowie and Annie were over on Wednesday. Mother has scarcely been so well for the last three days.

I was over on Sunday evening hearing Mr. Morrison preach. The subject of his discourse was the account of Beltshazzar seeing the writing on the wall. He spoke of the great evil of intemperance and profanity, and said that both generally went hand in hand. He seems to be an earnest preacher, and has also a good delivery. A few of the members of The Vale of Deskford Temperance Society are going to the Temperance Demonstration on Wednesday at Duff House.

I was at the moss today and found the peats in good condition.

9ᵗʰ

I do not think we are to get any summer weather this year at all. The past week has been dull and cold, and on Tuesday a lot of rain fell. With the absence of heat, there has of course been but little growth. Hoeing is now pretty general, but many plants are rather small yet.

We did nothing outside on Tuesday rain falling all day.

On Wednesday morning we were repairing the road in the cornyard. This was the day of the Temperance Demonstration in Banff. The morning was cloudy and the appearance of the day had doubtless prevented some from being present. The Deskford folks met at the Public Schools where carts were awaiting to convey us to Cullen. There were just thirty of us in all. We arrived at Banff at half past one, and at once marched, by the low shore to Duff House grounds. The programme for the afternoon was from 2 to 4 Athletic Games, from 4 to 5 Tea, and then the speeches. Not being greatly interested in the games, a few of us returned to the town for the purposes of inspecting the Museum. It is situated at the south end of High Street, and had at some former time been a School I believe. A good many fossil remains, and geological specimens have been collected, which we gave a very close inspection. There were several cases of preserved butterflies and other insects, some of those from foreign countries being of immense size and of very gaudy colours. The stuffed birds and animals were not a large collection but some of them were rather noteworthy. A Persian Pheasant Cock and hen, presented by the late Lord Seafield were beautiful specimens, the male bird having a tail at least 5 feet long. A collie dog lying below the lobby table was really lifelike. There was also the head of a farmers black polled cow to which belonged to Mr. Henry, Gavenwood. Several pieces of coral from the South Sea Islands were very beautiful. We also saw a brick found in Egypt, and supposed to have been made by the Israelites.

We were just in time for tea when we returned, which was served on the lawn right in front of Duff House, a company of 1400 partaking of the same. Mr. Summers, Portsoy, was Chairman, and there were other four speakers. A Mr. Smith, from Aberdeen gave a rather humorous address, but the publicans received from him many a hard blow.

After we returned to Cullen the Deskford company treated themselves to a cup of coffee and biscuits when (the carts being waiting us) we took our way home.

We commenced hoeing on Thursday afternoon.

On Friday I went up to Keith market with James Gray, and bought a calf four months old for £4.10. Cattle were selling well.

16th

Cold rainy weather still continues, and hoeing is only progressing slowly. We have seen the sun only for a few hours all the week. Barley is coming into ear, but I would fear it will be deficient in grain, the weather having been so cold when the ear was forming. Turnips in many instances are still very backward, and none of them have been making much progress. We have the first sowing of yellows hoed.

I was at the Station on Friday evening meeting Lizzie. She is only going to stay a week with us. I cannot say that Mother is getting any stronger yet indeed I fear she is rather getting weaker. I think we should get another Dr. to see her.

We sold a fat quey on Saturday about 4½ cwts for £13.15. Beef and mutton are both getting up in price, and in America it has risen about 40 per cent.

Father was at the merchants of Berryhillock roup today. They are going away to America it is said.

George Stephen was over on Sunday and went to church with us. We got a very good address from Mr. Mackintosh from the subject of Elijah being fed with ravens.

Willie was down from Keith but I doubt he is not going to take to his trade very well. His hands are very sore.

… have scarcely, seen the sun at all [page missing from Journal]

We finished the singling of the turnips on Friday, but there were some days we did nothing at them. We were turning our top-dressing.

I was up at Langlanburn on Tuesday evening. There were some things about the valuations they were not altogether agreed about. The crop and grass were not valued for the Queen's dues, but of course everything ought to be valued for the division.

I went over to Peter Fair on Friday with Uncle Limes. The supply of harvest hands was fully equal to the demand. Men to cut and build were getting £4.10. Bandsters from £3.10 to £4 and women from £2.10 to £3. There were not many cattle nor sheep, but a brisk business was doing among the latter. There was a very large horse market in the afternoon, and a considerable number changed hands. £55 was the highest price I heard of. George Cowie sold a ten year old mare for £26.

On Sunday I got James Gray's machine and drove Maggie over to Cairdswell. I went to church with George. Mr. McVicar's sermon was intended to illustrate the insufficiency of faith without works. There were three kinds of faith he said, temporary faith—speculative faith—and true living faith. Faith was the life of the soul, and might be compared to the life of the body in several respects. Intelligence, activity and progression, were characteristics of life both in soul and body. We were to judge from this, whether ours was a true and living faith.

We commenced today to hoe the second time. This was the Deskford holiday and return fares were issued to Glasgow for 8/9 and Aberdeen for 3/. Mother has been awfully bad with pains in her legs last week. She has got a lotion to rub them with now, and I hope it may give her some relief.

1888 August
6th

There is a great difference on Mother since the first of last week. Her strength is visibly failing, and her voice is altering. She is always greatly tormented with pain in her legs, and she has also had several bad turns of wretching which must be very sore on her, being so weak. I am very glad that Maggie is here to assist Joan in nursing her.

Little or no improvement on the weather yet. Wednesday and Thursday were just a little warmer, but yesterday was extremely stormy again, with a strong northerly gale. There has been a good deal of thunder during the week, and rain every day.

It has been bad weather for hay making, but everyone has been ploughing it nevertheless. We have little more than two acres in hay this year, and the crop is fair, far better than at one time I expected. The nitrate of soda has paid itself very well, there being more than double the hay. I have a small piece for seed yet to cut, but I fear the outturn of seed is to be poor.

We were twice at the moss last week, but the peats had not dried much.

I was up one evening at tea at Ardiecow. His turnips are far from looking well. He has some of them to single yet, and the rabbits are eating those at the wood side terribly. He is going to get the other half of the square built, this summer but they are not commenced yet.

13th

Since last I wrote Jessie and Jane have both come to see Mother.

Jessie came to Cairdswell on Tuesday evening and George Cowie and Annie came over with her on Wednesday. Jessie is not looking strong at all. Troubled with rheumatism in her back at times.

Jane came over on Friday night and I know little difference on her.

Mother was awfully bad on Tuesday with a pain in her side, and we had to send for the Dr. He injected some morphia into her side, which eased her for a time, but it has to be done at intervals yet. He has been every day since. She is very weak now, and her back has turned very sore with lying. The Dr. thought today that she was just a little better. The pain is out of her legs now since her side grew bad. We had some nice warm days last week, but always super abundance of moisture.

Turnips have improved however a good bit.

We got the hay coled on Wednesday.

Thursday was Cornhill market. I sold five lambs to J. Green in the morning. Four at 27/- And one at 30/-. Had I taken them to the market however I am sure I would have got 30/- for them all. We also took a cow to the market—the one that leaped the fences. We sold her for £12.10. There seemed to be a demand for cows, and every other class was also selling well. I would have liked to buy two stirks, but could not get any I thought worth the money.[1] We have plenty of grass, and I am afraid the corn in the den will not ripen well this year. I have been thinking it might be a good plan to buy some cattle and feed them on it.

On Friday and Saturday we were putting out lime and earth for top-dressing. We had eighty loads and there were twenty four bolls of lime. It would have taken some more lime however. We spread it over three acres.

Father, Jane, Maggie and I were at church on Sunday.

I saw Miss Mackintosh's marriage present on Friday evening. It was a gold bracelet set with diamonds, and cost fourteen guineas.

20th

We have experienced excessive cold weather during the past week and have scarcely seen the sun. Great word of canker among the turnips. I see none among ours as yet.

Mother is always getting weak and the pain has returned to her legs again.

The Dr. brought his son with him on Sunday, and they were to consult together about her case.

---

[1] stirk, a yearling or young cow.

Jessie went away on Wednesday and Jane on Friday. Maggie is to stay sometime yet. We could not manage without her now for someone must always be beside Mother.

We put out other twenty loads of top-dressing in the first of the week and went over it all with the link harrows. We have been driving peats since, and have now home thirty loads. They are not getting much drier yet.

I went to Cullen on Sunday afternoon for some mixture for Mother, and went up past Burns. I intended going to the Free Church, but they would let me no further.

All their crops are looking remarkably well, also their cattle. I see by the newspapers that oats have taken a great start in the price 20/- being truly offered.

27th

The Deskford Horticultural Society held their annual Show and Picnic on Wednesday last. There was a great thunder shower about midday, but the afternoon was fairly good. I expected a good show of flowers, the late season having rather favoured them, but vegetables were far beyond my expectations. Some of them were really first class especially James Lorimer's leeks and James Maitland's onions. The fruit was the only section in which the backward character of the season was noticeable. There was an excellent display of black currants, but the rest of the fruit was small and unripe. Bouquets were a show of themselves, the entries for the seven different classes being numerous, and the specimens very good. I had fourteen entries and got two prizes, one for a wreath of garden flowers and one for a picture frame. James Maitland got one of the medals with 48 points and Miss Duncan got the other and the silver brooch. They were scarcely so many visitors as the first year.

We have been driving peats for most part during the week, but neither them nor the road so bad for many years. There are forty loads home, and a good many to come yet.

There is a difference on Mother every week,—always getting weaker, but she has scarcely been so bad with pain for the last few days.

We got a beautiful sermon from Mr. Mackintosh on Sunday from the text 'O! taste and see that the Lord is good. Blessed is the man that trusteth in him.' Willie was down from Keith and I accompanied him the length of the Backies when he was going home. He seems to be taking to his trade far better now.

The following are some verses, of which I would like to preserve a copy.

Rules for Daily Life
Begin the day with God; kneel down to Him in prayer;

Lift up they heart to His abode; and seek His love to share.

Open the Book of God; and read a portion there;
That it may hallow all thy thoughts, and sweeten all thy care.

Go through the day with God; whatever thy work may be;
Wherever thou art—at home abroad, He still is near to thee.

Converse in mind with God, thy spirit heavenward raise;
Acknowledge every good bestowed, and offer grateful praise.

Conclude the day with God, thy sins to Him confess;
Trust in the Lords atoning blood, and plead His righteousness.

Lie down at night with God, who gives His servants sleep;
And when thou tread'st the vale of death, He will thee guard and keep.

1888 September
3ʳᵈ

Every week—almost every day there is a difference on Mother. Her
strength is evidently failing. She can always manage to take a wonderful
bit of food, also some stimulants; but then she is so tormented with pain,
that it can do her little good. Pain in her legs, in her side, and in her
bowels. She gets morphia injected, which eases it for a time; but it is
only for a time. How humbling it is to see, how decrepit the human
body becomes with age and sickness,—racked with pain and suffering,
and bent almost two fold, and all because of sin. How imperative with us
ought the injunction of Solomon to be 'Remember now thy Creator in
the days of they youth, when the evil days come not, nor the years draw
nigh when thou shalt say I have no pleasure in them.'

When Mother was first laid down, she seemed to be much troubled
about her condition, but now she is far more content, and has more
peace in her mind. She often repeats to herself some of the psalms or
phrases and her mind seems to have been well stored with the same.

John and I have been driving peats nearly all the week but they are
not getting much drier. We have 56 loads home and I believe there
will be other six yet.

We thrashed the seed hay on Tuesday afternoon. We had only two
loads of hay, and the outturn of seed was not very great.

The weather has been much warmer during the past week, and
there has also been more sunshine, but there has also been a good deal
of rain. Turnips have improved considerably, and barley is now
changing colour. Oats in many cases are still lengthening.

We were trying the potatoes last week, and found them better than
our expectations.

Miss Mackintosh was married on Thursday last. Her husband is a Mr. Emslie a first cousin of her own, and he is a stock broker in London. There was nobody at the marriage but relations as the bridegroom's brother is lying very unwell. They started immediately after the marriage on their wedding tour, and are to visit Paris, and other places of interest in the Continent.

10th

Picking and driving gravel, building the hay, and driving peats has been our week's work. The gravel is from Caveston's pit, and we are putting it on to the road in the cornyard.

We took home the last of the peats on Saturday and had 64 loads out of 73 score. The first of the week was fine days with some sunshine, but Friday and Saturday were very cold.

Mother took a very bad turn on Tuesday. The pain seated in her breast and for two hours we were doubtful if she would rally again. We were very glad when the Dr. came, but he could do little for her. The pain has been going through her since then and some nights she is very bad. She has scarcely taken anything for the last week except some bay tea and a little wine.

16th

Sunday—Not being at church, I was going to write a few lines but only got on the date and now here is half past nine on Monday evening.

Maggie and I have just prepared to watch beside Mother for the first half of the night. Joan takes the morning. We have done so for the last six nights. Mother is always with us, but she is little more than just alive. It will be two weeks tomorrow since she tasted any solid meat. A little port wine, and some beef or chicken tea, and today she has scarcely tasted any of these. The skin of her back is now broken and must be very painful, but the pain in the rest of her body is scarcely so bad as it was. She gets the morphia injected twice or three times a day. Some days she was wandering in her mind greatly and talked a great deal, at other times she lies almost motionless. All her doubts, and fears, about the salvation of her soul, and her future state, seem to be gone now; and she appears to have perfect trust in the Lord. When she is conscious she is constantly repeating some of the gracious promises of Scripture, and there is one verse of the Psalms of David very often upon her lips. 'The Lord my God's a son and child, He'll grace and glory give, and will without no good from them, that uprightly do live.' How comforting to those about her, to see her so resigned and so well prepared for that great change, which sooner or later must come to us all. Oh God help me so to live now, as I shall wish I had done when I come to die, and although thy afflicting hand has been laid long and heavy on Dear Mother, may thine everlasting arms be round about her, and thy presence near to comfort her, when she is called upon to cross the swellings of Jordan.

What beautiful weather we are now enjoying. Clean, bright, glorious sunshine, with sometimes a shower to refresh. The fruits of the earth are beginning to mellow and ripen. Old Mother Earth is thinking of downing her golden garb of autumn. How calm and peaceful are the days with their dreamy sunshine. Peace and plenty seems to be the burden of the song of all animate and inanimate Creation. Spring used to be my favourite season, but I rather doubt she will feel jealous, on hearing me sounding so sweetly the praises of her elder Sister.

Every season has it own aspect, and truly there is super abundance of beauty in every season, (would our dull eyes but only see it) to fill us with wonder at, and admiration of, that Great Being, who in the beginning made all things very good, and who still in a no less remarkable manner, is sustaining and upholding all things by His Almighty power.

How astonishing is the mystery of Food, and how little do we think of it as a mystery. What an enormous quantity of food is required to sustain the human family for one day, and when we consider the countless myriads of beasts, and birds, and fishes, and creeping things, all needing daily to be provided for, we must confess that nothing less than a miracle is constantly being performed in our midst by 'Him who giveth food to all flesh.'

We have got the cornyard finished now all the road gravelled and the stack 'fours' cleaned. I also thatched the hay one day.

Cornhill market was on Thursday I bought a ewe and a ram lamb. I sold four ewes and three lambs in the first of the week. Sheep are still very dear.

The sale of wood in Cottonhill plantation was on Saturday. I bought four lots, but no brushwood. It was selling as high as 17/- the lot. The other was six to eight shillings.

26ᵗʰ

Wednesday—morning—today at one o'clock is Dear Mother going to be laid in her last resting place. Poor Mother, she is now at rest and peace, and much reason have we to feel thankful that she is so. How mysterious are the wonder working ways of Providence. What a long and sore struggle she has had. More than five months, and then such extreme pain she suffered all the time. I have often remarked that those who have been weak and delicate all their life time, are generally called upon to suffer much before they are called away, while those who are healthy and robust are often very quickly cut off.

Thursday night—on the night of Friday the 21st Maggie and I were sitting with Mother as usual. She was very, very restless, and wanted lifting every ten minutes or so. I am sure her back must have been very painful, lying so long upon it, and there was a good round piece of it broken skin. Her thirst was also something terrible. She could not get enough to drink and indeed we were afraid always to give her when she asked. Sometimes she would take a drop of wine among the water, sometimes ginger beer and she also drank a little tea. About one o'clock I went to bed, and shortly after a great change came over her. Her breathing turned extremely heavy, her mouth was open, and her breast was heaving. She continued in this state until eleven o'clock on Saturday, and although she never spoke I am sure she was always quite conscious. Annie and Aunt came over about that time and she knew Annie quite well and spoke some words. After that she never spoke again but gradually sank, and at seven o'clock she breathed her last. A good and a kind Mother she ever was to us all and although I rather doubt she had a very hard struggle in bringing us all up, still I am glad to think that she enjoyed a few more comforts in her latter days.

On Sunday morning I went down to Portsoy and told the Dr. and also ordered the burial letters. There were 90 sent out, and except those at a distance nearly all attended.

Willie came down on Saturday night and I wrote a few lines to his master saying he would not be up till after the funeral. John Whyntie made the coffin and he brought it up on Monday afternoon. A great many wreathes of flowers were brought, one from Mrs Riddoch and Miss McWillie and one brought by Annie being very pretty.

On Tuesday afternoon Father and I went over and took off new ground in the churchyard. We had plenty of old ground but there has been a great many other Wilson's buried in it lately so we thought we would like a new bit when there was plenty to be got. They sell the new ground now, the price of what we have fixed upon being 12/6 for the first lair and 7/6 for each additional one.

On Wednesday morning Lizzie arrived about eight o'clock having travelled all night. Mrs Riddoch and Mrs McKay were also over when the corpse was lifted. In the evening Maggie, Lizzie and I went over to the churchyard. They were anxious to see it and as Maggie was leaving today she had not much time. Father went over to Cairdswell with her today.

Last week we enjoyed exceptionally fine weather. A clear sky with bright warm sunshine. Crops made rapid advances to maturity, and all along the coast harvest is quite general. A few have also commenced in the lower end of Deskford. A good deal of rain fell on Monday and since then it has been duller. The rain will benefit the turnips which were needing it. Late turnips have improved considerably, but there is a tending among early ones to run to seed.

1888 October
1st

Cauld Jocktober, shakes his tail, in angry showers o'sleet and hail, so says the old rhyme, and we are experiencing the truth of it to the letter.

Saturday afternoon turned a little stormy, but yesterday and today was exceedingly cold. There has been a strong northerly wind sometimes amounting almost to a gale with driving showers of hail and sleet.

On Sunday morning it was lying white at the dyke sides. I have not seen any corn shaken yet, but it would be rather afraid of it where it was ripe.

In the end of the week we were driving some, brushwood. I bought the remainder of James Jordan's lot at 6d the load.

On Sunday Geordy Cowie came over. Willie Sandy and Annie were at Swailend, so he came with them. Father him and I went to church. We got a beautiful sermon from Mr. Mackintosh from the text, 'Those will keep him in perfect peace whose mind is stayed on thee; because he trusteth in thee' Isaiah XXVI and 3rd. We could scarcely conceive he said, 'how much was contained in the time "perfect peace".' It was a blessing which no earthly riches could buy, and of which nothing could deprive us. It was also a blessing which all might possess, if we had only strong enough faith—if we would only follow the injunction of Solomon—'trust in the Lord with all thine heart, and lean not to thine own understanding.'

8th

Such a week of stormy weather in the first of October I never remember. Had the crops been all secured it would not have been so much thought of. With the great bulk of cereals still on the stalk the injury and loss will be immense.

On Wednesday the storm subsided a little, only to be resumed on Thursday with redoubled fury.

The frost on Thursday and Friday was most intense. I saw icicles hanging at the corn two inches long.

On Friday morning a complete covering of snow lay on all around, and it was well through the afternoon before it melted. It being mostly hail however, and then being a strong breeze of wind at the time, it did not flatten the corn so much as if the snow had been softer. Much of the crop however is now terribly twisted, and a good proportion of it I believe will have to be cut with the scythe.

In a report of the storm in the newspapers, it is said that it is impossible for the grain to ripen more, and that much of the corn even in lower Banffshire will be unfit for seed. With this I do not at all agree. With good weather a great improvement might yet be expected, although there can be no doubt but that the ripening must now be slow. It is quite different however in the upper districts where four and five inches of snow was lying all over for days. In these places no seed nor braird is expected, and there can be no doubt but that the straw must also be injured, while great labour must be incurred before it can be got off the ground. Little cutting has been done during the week but everyone will now be anxious.

We commenced on Saturday by cutting some oats in the 'den' but the day was showery.

This afternoon we were cutting barley. It is a splendid crop, but none of it will cut with the reaper. We have Willie Wright with us.

15th

Never since I commenced to write my 'Diary' have I found it necessary to study so much, how I ought to commit to writing the event I am about to relate. Seeing it will doubtless be one, if not the most important even of my life, there may be some excuse however. I must go straight to the point at once.

On the evening of Monday last I went over to Kirkton for the express purpose, of asking Katie Duncan to be my wife. For sometime back I had decided upon this course, finding that she had completely gained my affections, and believing at the same time that I was esteemed and respected, if not also loved by her in return. I did not intend speaking to her for sometime yet however, had not the disgraceful conduct of Joan forced me to do so. Of the shame and disgrace caused by the conduct of her, whom I shall never henceforth countenance as a Sister, I shall make no more mention here. This account of my daily life in intended to be something which I peruse in after years with pleasure and profit, and were I to go into minute details of this case, it would most assuredly be the means of producing neither of these effects.

With what different feelings and emotions, do I turn to speak of the other subject already hinted at. How I broached the subject, what I all said, and what was said by her in return, I could not now relate were I ever so willing. I felt very keenly, that the circumstances, in which I was placed, were very far from being favourable to my suit, as it might appear that it was entirely from stress of circumstances that I had appealed to her. I was open, straightforward and candid with her, as to every particular and great was my happiness when I heard her say that she thoroughly believed me, and trusted me. Of course I was impetuous and wanted an answer there and then; but no—I must wait. She must have time to consider my proposal, but on Friday evening she would let me know her decision.

With this I was entirely satisfied. She reminded me that in some of my letters to her, I had expressed the hope that we might ever be true friends to each other, and she hinted that friendship was all which she ever thought existed between us, but had any one surprised us at that very moment, I rather doubt that her behaviour would in their eyes, have altogether believed her words.

Revd. E. P. Roe says that 'love can gather hope from a marvellously little thing' still it was with a beating heart that I knocked at the door at Kirkton on Friday evening.[2] Katie herself answered my call, came out and shut the door. This with her warm hand clasp somewhat reassured me. The night being chilly I threw my overcoat round her shoulders, and led her into the garden, and there at the upper end, with her head reclining on my shoulders,— with the October wind singing among the trees, and the crescent moon with her pale silvery light looking down upon us, as if to witness our plighted troth, she whispered in my ear that her heart was a' my ain. God bless the dear lassie and may his best blessing ever rest upon both of us. May we never forget his gracious promise, but with increasing faith put our trust in it. 'I will instruct thee and teach thee in the way which thou shall go I will guide thee with mine eye.'

The weather during the past week has been fairly good for harvest work, and the corn has also ripened a little. We had Willie Wright the two first days of the week and scythed the barley. It was an excellent crop.

On Wednesday and Thursday we were cutting thatch and making rapes.

We had John Wright on Friday and Saturday and cut the clean land and some in the den. They were rather stormy days.

Sunday was a most beautiful day, bright sunshine and a moderate breeze of wind. Father and I were both at church. I went over in the afternoon to see George Duncan, and had a short walk with Kate before I went in. I know a very great difference on George since last I saw him. He is greatly troubled with his throat now and has great difficulty—in swallowing. The quantity of matter he spits up is also something incredible, but he seems to be far more resigned now, and is

---

[2] For further information on E.P.Roe see www.freepages.books.rootsweb.com/~bobsc/.

very grateful for the attention given him. He is only able to be up for the half of the day.

We cut the lea beside the house today and made a very good job with the reaper.

22ⁿᵈ

Except Saturday and yesterday the weather has not been to complain of. We would have taken more sunshine however, for much of the corn is yet very green. There are a lot of stooks in Deskford now there being none to cut below Kirkton. The greater part of the barley has been secured.

We took in the last of ours on Friday, in good condition. The only cutting we have done was about an acre in the den, thinking it too green.

I went to Portsoy on Tuesday evening and bought a ring for the finger of my lady-love, and on Friday night I went over and fitted it on. We had a long and very pleasant talk, sitting on the washing stool in the meal-house. Owing to George's illness Katie says our marriage cannot be earlier than June, and seeing how fast George seems to be sinking I said I could not press her.

I do not know if Joan will stay on all winter or not. I would never have asked her if it had not been for Father's sake.

I was in church on Sunday when we got a beautiful sermon from Mr. Mackintosh from the text, 'Casting all your care upon Him, for he careth for you.' 'It was very strange', he said, 'how unwilling we often were to cast all our care upon the Lord, and how we would persist in carrying our heavy burdens of sin and grief, when we had his own gracious invitation, 'Come unto me all ye that labour and are heavy laden and I will give you rest.' The great cause of this unwillingness he said was pride. We must have no confidence in ourselves, but thoroughly believe that he was able and willing to carry our burdens, and then unto we very soon feel them tumble off our backs.

29ᵗʰ

We have been busy at the leading from dawn to dark today, and I do not feel inclined to write much this evening.

We got a man and a woman from Ardiecow on Tuesday and cut the den.

We cut the little parkie of yavels on Wednesday with the reaper. I went over to see Katie that evening, and the washing stool in the meal-house had again to bear the weight of two for a good long hour.

Thursday was wet. We thatched the barley in the afternoon.

Friday was a grand day. We got a boy from James Gray and a woman from Kirkton and cut the lea on Ardiecow. It was very green, but an excellent crop.

We got some leading on Saturday afternoon, and today we were at it again. There is nine stacks now in the cornyard.

Ardiecow only commenced to cut on Friday. Donald and him came to an understanding themselves about the crop. He is to give him £200 and harvest it. I rather think he would have required it to be insured.

1888 November
5th

Lazy, lazy harvest weather. We led on Tuesday the most of the day, but there has been none since. The day is getting so short now, that there is very little drying.

On Thursday we making rapes and cutting thatch. Willie was down from Keith it being their fast day.

Friday morning being wet I set out for Keith market. I went past Backies and got a drive with Miss McWillie. She was wanting me to buy Irish calves for her but there were none in the market. I bought two queys for ourselves one at £7.5 the other at £8.5. I do not think they were too dear. It was a small market and little business doing.

We were thatching all day on Saturday, and managed to cover them all.

Father and I were both at church on Sunday. The minister intimated that the Communion would be in two weeks. It was postponed owing to the late harvest. We were turning the stacks today. I see by the newspapers that new grain is now freely offered in the market, but the price is coming down every week. Before harvest oats were 22/-. They are now at 15/-. I am in the expectation however that in a month or so it will rise again.

We were greatly shocked to hear on Sunday morning that a man named Eddie, who is engaged at James Gordon's, Broadrushes, had during the previous night attempted to commit suicide. His strength had seemingly been giving way, and feeling that he would no longer be able to work, he had taken a very gloomy view of the matter. He had first tried to cut his throat, and then to hang himself, but neither attempt had succeeded. He was removed to Grange where his wife resides and placed under the charge of the Inspector of Poor.

12th

Father and I were at George Duncan's funeral today. He was buried in Deskford Churchyard. He sank very rapidly toward the end, being down stairs about a week before he died. The pain was all in his throat, and to speak or swallow anything, was extremely painful for him.

On Thursday it was quite evident he was sinking, and he also seemed to realise it himself. He lingered on all day until ten o'clock at night, when without any struggle he breathed his last.

I went over to se his remains on Sunday afternoon and I never saw anyone so worn as he was. How mysterious the working of Providence, the think of one being cut off in the prime of life. But God's ways are not our ways, nor his thoughts our thoughts. His work had been done, and He called him away. God grant that the lesson may be deeply impressed upon our hearts, and the words ever ringing in our ears, 'Be ye also ready, for in such an hour as ye think not the Son of man cometh.'

We had some excellent days in the end of the week for harvest purposes.

We led all day on Tuesday last but the stuff was only in fair condition.

It was showery on Wednesday, and we were putting out dung.

On Thursday forenoon we started to lift the potatoes but the afternoon being dry we were at the leading.

We took in the last of it on Friday in grand order. I never saw so much bulk in the cornyard before. There are 22 stacks only some of them are rather small.

We were at the potatoes all day on Saturday. They are a fair crop. Far above expectations, the greatest deficiency being in size.

We thatched the last of the stacks today. Five weeks a day and a half since we commenced harvest. It is the latest I ever saw.

19ᵗʰ

A week of splendid fresh weather but terrific gales of wind.

I commenced the plough on Tuesday among the potatoes land.

Wednesday was Hallow Fair, and an excellent day. I engaged a boy William McBeth for the winter half year at £2 of wages. I also engaged a second horseman for the Backies. Boys were rather in demand but a good few men left unengaged. Wages were—little alteration. A good deal of business seemed to be going on in the selling of grain. Both oats and barley are seemingly tending upwards, 25/- for 54 lb barley and 16/- for 40 lb oats. Steam mills are in great request just now, scarcity of money and water being chief causes I believe.

Thursday was our Fast day, but being a dry day John and I went to the Greenhill to lead.

I was ploughing on Friday. About one o'clock the wind rose to a perfect hurricane, and continued so all the afternoon. It did little damage to us, but I hear of many stacks being blown over, and it lifted the zinc roof clean off Ardiecow cart shed, one half of it being a total wreck.

John and I were at the steam mill at Careston on Saturday. The day was very blowy, and we did not make a good job.

It was to be thrashing oats today, but did not get a start with the wind. I was at Ardiecow in the forenoon assisting them to lead. A big shower at twelve o'clock put an end to it. We would have a stack or so to take in yet.

Mr. McIntosh had Mr Grant, Fordyce, assisting him on Sunday. I scarcely ever remember seeing the church so thin on a Sacrament Sunday.

27th

The last week of November and stooks still to be seen. Truly the year of the three eights will become long held in remembrance. It was extremely blowy all last week, and also a good deal of rain fell.

On Tuesday morning the ground was white, but it soon melted.

I have been ploughing when the weather would permit. We also put out some dung in the first of the week. We are going to drive all we have over to the braes and plough it down.

The stubbles being too wet on Saturday morning, I commenced to plough lea. I was down at Careston in the afternoon at the steam mill. They could get no thrashing all the week for wind.

Yesterday they were at Ardiecow.

We have a hard frost this morning and Ardiecow folk were leading all day. At Greens of Blairock they only took clyack in the term day and on Barnyard of Benuchers they have a large park to cut yet.

Father was at the mill today with a load of corn but it only weighed 39 lbs per bushel. The price was 14/6.

1888 December
3rd

We commenced today to store turnips.

I went over to the smiddy on Saturday evening, and got tailers made and also spoke to two men for a few days.[3] I would like to store four acres at least.

The yellow ones we were pulling today were a fair crop.

Father and I were both at church yesterday. We got a very impressive sermon from the text, 'I have learned in whatsoever state I am therewith to be content.' 'True contentment', he said, 'was a

---

[3] tailers, tail chains by which a horse hauls a wagon.

blessing which very, very few possessed.' We were apt to think if we could only attain to a certain position, or gain some desired object, we should be content, but experience had shown that although our every wish were gratified, true contentment seldom followed. It was only by living the life of a Christian—by having an implicit trust in an over-ruling Providence—by believing that God was ordering and directing our every step in life — and by placing ourselves entirely in his hands, that any degree of contentment was attainable. The minister intimated at the close that Thursday first had been appointed by the Synod of Aberdeen as a day of thanksgiving to Almighty God for the bounties of the recent harvest. I was a little surprised to hear the banns of marriage published between Robert Cruickshank and Jessie Legg. Mrs Riddoch was down seeing us in the afternoon. She was telling me that Robert Duncan and Miss McWillie, Langlinburn, are to be married in a very short time.

I was up at the Backies one evening last week. The new stable is almost finished now and the cattle are all thriving well. There is an extra cornyard but the grain is very light. I was busy ploughing most of last week, and half of the 'Back Den' is now turned over. I had letters both from Jessie and Maggie in the end of the week. Jessie is always sorely needing me up to see the Forth Bridge.

10th

I was at the steam mill at Kirkton today. The barley was a fair sample, but deficient in quantity. We also thrashed three stacks of oats. The day was all that could have been desired. Indeed the weather during the past week has been exceptionally fine for this season of the year. I have not been in the plough all the week, as we have been storing turnips. The yellow ones are a fair crop and good quality but the Swedes are small and a good many of them going to seed. We had two boys pulling at 5/- an acre. We have 50 loads of yellows and 17 of swedes lifted. I would have liked another acre or so but Father is afraid they will not keep.

On Wednesday morning I went down for two loads of tiles for Uncle George. He is getting 300 yards of drains put in. Father was at Tochineal Station in the afternoon for oilcake. I am giving the calves a pound each in the day and a quey that is feeding two pounds.

Thursday was observed as a thanksgiving day for the harvest. It was Mr. McIntyre, Portknockie, who officiated, and an excellent address he gave us. I went over to Limestones in the afternoon. The masons are commenced to build a new dwelling house there.

After filling the mill and thrashing on Saturday, I went into Banff for the purpose of buying chilled plow. I fixed on a Ransomes which I purchased for £2.10. I came up to Cornhill Station and went over to Finnygaud. There is never any improvement on Mary and although she may rise twenty times in the day she can never be induced to put on her clothes.

I came over to Cairdswell on Sunday middle of day and called in past Little Greendykes as I came past. Little George is now learning to speak a little, but his face is never perfectly whole.

17th

Fine weather in the month of December I never remember seeing. There was frost one day, and only one shower all last week. Everything is as dry as though it was the month of May, and those who have water mills have great difficultly in getting straw.

We were putting out dung on Tuesday.

On Wednesday I was furring up turnips. I also furred up the drills that we lifted to store. I think the covering of the tops will be a great advantage.

Thursday was Cornhill market. Father went over and went up to Cairdswell and stayed all night. Fat was selling at from 65/- to 68/-. Calving cows were in demand, and keepers were also selling well. I see that there were more fat cattle at Smithfield shows than were ever seen before. I had the chiller plow in the yoke on Thursday in the Den, and was highly pleased with her work. It is very light on the horses and easily held.

I went over to the Library and got my books exchanged on Friday. I took out 'A short History of our own Times' by Justine McCarthy M.P., and 'Adam Bede' by George Elliot. I went a little out of my way coming home, and had a very pleasant hour with Katie. Robert Duncan had been down from Langlinburn that evening, inviting me to his marriage with Miss McWillie. It is to be on Friday first at four o'clock.

George Stephen was over on Sunday and went to church with Father. I went over to the Free Church with him in the evening. It was Mr. Cowie, Forglen who was preaching, and it was an address to young men and women he gave us. His text was 'The glory to young men is their strength.' He is a very plain speaker, and scarcely came up to my expectations, but his prayers were very earnest and touching. The church was well filled.

I have been plowing down dung today, and the chiller plow is just the implement for the purpose.

24th

Christmas Eve—On this night 1888 years ago; in the manger of the stable at Bethlehem, was our Saviour supposed to have been born. The stars no doubt were twinkling brightly in the firmament, just as they are doing tonight, when the angel of the Lord appeared to the Shepherd of the plain and intimated to them that a Saviour had been born in the city of David.

With what overflowing gratitude should our hearts be filled, when we think of the great love wherewith The Father loved us, in sending his only begotten Son into this world of sin and misery to suffer and die for us sinners. May our hearts this night be filled with the sentiment expressed by the heavenly host, when they praised God and sang, 'Glory to God in the highest, and on earth peace, good will toward men.'

It is not every week that I have an account of a marriage to give. The wedding at Langlinburn on Friday evening was a very nice affair indeed. There was just a company of twelve in all. We had tea and supper and it was home by eleven o'clock. But the most important matter was that I had to act as best man, as I never heard any word of the service until the minister was at the door. The cutting of the bride's cake was the only duty of importance, which fell to my lot. It was the largest and most beautiful cake I ever saw. The bride and bridegroom both looked remarkably well I think.

We had beautiful days in the first of last week and it was ploughing dung in the den, the ground being fine and dry.

On Thursday afternoon I went to Portsoy for some coals as we were expecting Mr. Lamb with his steam mill. He arrived about six o'clock in the evening.

Friday morning was fine but about ten o'clock it turned dull, and a drizzling rain fell. It did not do much damage I suppose, but we would rather it had been dry. We thrashed for 4½ hours and was through by half past two. There will be about 26 qrs of grain.

Saturday was wet all day. We winnowed and measured up the barely in the forenoon and in the afternoon I went down to Glenglassaugh with a sample. They are not taking in any more there however until the month of March. I therefore went in to Portsoy and sold it to Mr. Smith for 25/. for 54 lbs. We had down two loads of it today when it weighed 54½. There is 13 qrs in all, but we have a small stack to thrash yet.

Father did not try to church on Sunday as the roads were awfully bad. I had an invitation to tea at Kirkton, and went over in the afternoon. Before going in I went with Aleck and had a look at the cattle and horses. They have got three young calves already and two fat cattle are sold. At the great Xmas markets held in London last week very poor prices were realised. The supply being greater than the demand, much of it remained unsold. The consequence doubtless will be dull trade for some time to come.

31ˢᵗ

The year 1888 will be one which I will never forget. It has been a year of many changes, and sad bereavements. How little did I think at the beginning of the year just closed, that I should be called upon to mourn the loss of so many dear friends. Within the past, seven months I have seen the grave close over the remains of a very dear friend, a fond Mother, and one who had he been spared I should have expected soon to call a brother. How true are the words of the hymn 'Friend after friend departs, who hath not lost a friend?' 'There is no union here of hearts, that knows not here an end.' How short signed we are. What a short distance we can penetrate into the future, and yet what a wise Providence that keeps the future from our ken. Many a one would entirely succumb, were it revealed to them, how much they would be called upon to suffer during the years that are to come. But it has been wisely ordered otherwise. A kind and loving Father, knowing well the weakness of his children, only sends troubles as we are able to bear them. True indeed is the proverb 'the back is always made for the burden', and these are the words of Him who cannot lie, 'As thy days, so shall thy strength be.' God grant that our trials and bereavements may be the means, not of souring our tempers and dispositions, but of sweetening and refining them,—not of making us sorrow as those who have no hope, but of leading us to say, 'The Lord gave and the Lord taketh away, blessed be the name of the Lord.'

The year of the three eights will for many reasons, be one long into in remembrance, there being snow in summer, and snow in autumn and in none of those seasons is it very acceptable. The months of January and February were seasonable, with about their average amount of frost and snow. A very heavy snow storm occurred in the end of March and the beginning of April. The seed time was consequently late, and much of the clean land was ploughed in bad condition. The month of May was dry and cold, and although unfavourable for vegetation, it allowed swedes and early yellow turnips to be sowed in good condition.

A most unusual, and almost unprecedented snow storm occurred in the first of June, and indeed neither June, July, nor August were in the least like summer months. September was the best month of all the year, and helped immensely towards ripening the grain.

We had another snow storm in the beginning of October on one morning there being a complete covering of snow all over. The crops were in consequence greatly flattened, and the ripening process therefore much retarded. Except in very late districts, the harvest (taking into account the lateness of the season) was a very good one. Crops in general were harvested in fine condition, and although there is a great deficiently both in quantity and quality of grain there is an abundance of straw.

I never remember seeing finer weather in November and December. Turnips are not a full crop. Yellow ones are fair, but Swedes are small and many of them have run to seed. The fresh open weather has greatly helped to make them stand out, the tops being still green. Potatoes are not nearly an average crop, in many cases being almost a failure. They are going up in price 2/- per bushel being freely offered. Grain is bringing far more money than at this date last year. In the end of harvest it was 15/- for 40 lbs. Now it is at 16/- for common oats, but potato oats 42 lbs the bushel would bring 20/- or more. Barley is 25/- for 54 lbs. Beef is also selling at a fair price from 65/- to 67/- per cwt. The live stock Xmas market however was completely glutted, and many butchers lost heavily. With brisk trade and cold weather we may soon expect it back to its old figure. I am rather inclined to think that by the month of May beef will get dearer, as turnips being a short crop, farmers will feed off as quickly as possible. Taking everything into account, the outlook for farmers at this New Year if not particularly bright is at least improving.

Let us hope that the dull times are past—that the reaction has set in, and that the sun of prosperity may again shine forth, throw his kindly beams over dear old Scotland, and to cheer the hearts of her weary 'farmers'.

We were at Portsoy with barley again on Tuesday.

On Wednesday I was ploughing stubbles all day.

We were at Oathillock and Knowes on Thursday at the steam mill. Lamb was at Ardiecow for two days, and I was over at Uncles on Saturday.

I was at a meeting on Friday night of the Library Committee arranging to have an Entertainment on Burns' Anniversary. A good number of local ladies and gentlemen have consented to take part in the programme. I had another meeting also the same evening, and although the attendance was rather <u>limited</u> and we had neither fire not light (there were several degrees of heat perhaps) still it was a <u>very</u> <u>pleasant</u> meeting and we were quite unanimous.

A Journal of My Life and Everyday Doings

1889 January
7th

Uncle George came over and went to church with us yesterday and we got a very impressive New Year's sermon from Mr Mackintosh from the text, 'How long will ye be slack to go up and possess the land.' These words were spoken by Joshua to the Children of Israel, and the same question might with equal force, be put to the children of men at the present day. However eager men might be in the pursuit of pleasure, wealth, honour or fame still it was a lamentable fact that they were but very slack to put themselves in possession of that inheritance which is incompatible, undefiled and that faileth not anew.

Mr. Mackintosh is failing greatly, only he is getting to be a very old man now. I believe he is over eighty. He is speaking of getting an assistant and successor, but I fear it will be some time before one could be fixed.

Uncle of Limestones and George came up past from the church. Uncle is sadly troubled with the rheumatics always. I have had to touch of them myself for the last ten days, in my back and top of my thigh.

New Year's Day was quiet and frosty: — a most beautiful day. I went down to Inaltrie in the forenoon and paid Mr. Cowie for the cows we got served. He was showing me his young polled bull which he bought from Cullen House. He is a lengthy animal and big of his age, but otherwise rather plain. He has an excellent stock of cattle on the farm, several three year olds being ready for the butcher. George Cowie and Annie came over in time for their dinner and stayed the afternoon. We also had Willie and Jamie Stephen.

Wednesday was also frosty. I went over to the Station in the afternoon with a boll of meal and a bag of potatoes which we were sending as a New Years present to Maggie.

It was fresh on Thursday and we were pulling and driving turnips. Since then I have been in the plough.

I finished the stubbles for cleaning tonight and commenced the yards.

14th

During the past week I have been ploughing yavels and they are in excellent condition. The field on Ardiecow is all turned over, having just been 30 hours in doing the same. I was over at Cornhill market on Thursday. It was about the average size. Fat might be quoted at 65/- I think, but keepers were in very keen demand. The few calving cows that were realised good prices. I would have bought a keeper, as I think we will have plenty of turnips, but I thought the prices too high. We have got some corn mashed now, and I am giving the two stots 3 lbs of grain and 1lb cotton cake each while the queys got 2 lb grain and ¾ linseed cake.

I was the only one in church on Sunday. I had an invitation from Mrs Riddoch to go up to dinner along with Aleck Duncan and Miss A. McWillie. After enjoying Mrs Riddoch's hospitality we went up to see 'Annie's Stock', her cattle being indeed well worth inspection. She has got other 12 Irish calves but they are far dearer this year each costing close on £7 while last year they were bought at 5 guineas. She has only sold one fat quey yet but the other will soon be ready. Miss Duncan and Miss Elsie came up to tea in the evening.

The frost was too hard for the plough today and I was putting out top dressing.

21st

There was scarcely any frost all last week. I was ploughing at the yavels beside the house two days, and since then I have been at the lea at the back of the byres. It is very hard and stony—sorely needing a good dose of lime. We yoked the coll into the chiller plow one day and he went very well.

On Friday afternoon we had a tremendous gale of wind. I could scarely get the horses to go in the plough. About half past two it lifted two stacks of straw almost bodily and dashed them over to the ground. No doubt some of it was blown away but being just at hand we held on sticks to keep it down. We do not get it rebuilt until today.

On Friday evening I went over to Kirkton, to tell old Mr. Duncan that I was wanting Katie for my wife and to ask if he was willing to entrust her into my care. I should have liked a rather more direct answer, but from what he said viz 'that it was time I was taking a wife now, and that it was sure Katie would be very well with me.' I inferred that he had no objections.

Katie and I had arranged to go over to Hillfolds on Sunday.

She went over on Saturday morning while I went over to Cairdswell on Saturday evening. I met Mr. & Mrs. Ross at the church, and went up past with them. Katie and Cathy were coming to meet us so we went through the garden. After dinner we went to have a look at the cattle and horses. He has four strong young cows, one of them being at the drop of calving. His year olds, and two year olds (five of each) however are rather small. He has four horses in the meantime— two work mares, a three year old filly and a foal. They are all nice compact animals but not very big. We started for home at five o'clock, but the roads being very bad, walking was not over pleasant. Otherwise we had a nice walk, the evening being clear although there was no moon. During the past week I have been reading a book which I intend giving to Katie on her Birthday. It is entitled 'A Woman's thoughts about Women' by the author of John Halifax, Gentleman. I have a favour for Mrs Craik's writings and this one has in no degree lessened my estimation of their sterling worth. It is brimful of useful and practical suggestions not only for women but also for men. The chapters I liked being those on 'Female Servant' 'The Mistress of a Family' 'Happy and Unhappy Women' and 'Growing Old'.

28th

Friday last was the anniversary of Burns' birth, and for the first time in my remembrance it was celebrated in Deskford. It was the outcome of a suggestion of mine, made at a meeting of the Library Committee some two months ago, for the purpose of augmenting the funds of the same. The night was showery, but notwithstanding there was a full house. Of course the songs, readings, recitations were all from Burns, and the performers were all local ladies and gentlemen. Mr. Reid had a large choir which gave several choruses at intervals. 'Duncan Gray', 'Green grow the rashes O', 'The Lea Rig', 'There was a lad was born in Kyle', 'Ye banks and braes' etc. Several ladies and gentlemen also gave solos, Mr. Reid accompanying on the harmonium. Miss Wood gave, 'Braw braw lads', Miss Mackenzie, 'My Nanie's awa', Miss Morrison, 'I whistle and I'll come to you my lad', Miss Milne, 'Ca the Yowes to the Knowes', Miss H. J. Morrison, 'Last May a braw wooer', Mr. J. Morrison 'Nannie O', A. Morris, 'Willie brewed a peck o' maut', J. Maitland, 'The lass O' Ballochmyle' etc. etc. Several readings and recitations were also given. Mr. Smith occupied the chair, and gave the history of the different persons mentioned in the songs. Altogether it was a most enjoyable meeting and finished off by the whole audience singing 'Auld Lange Syne'.

We have had another week of most excellent weather. There was some frost yesterday but it was all away today again. We would be far better of more frost to check the growth of things. I have got the yavel finished now and also the lea at the back of the houses. I ploughed about an acre of lea with the chilled plow but I was not altogether satisfied with her work.

There are some indications of grain falling in price, a great amount of foreign stuff being brought in. Beef is also a little back. 65/- being the very tops for prime.

1889 February
4th

'If Candlesmas day be fair and clear, the half of the winter to gang and muir'. 'If Candlemas day be wet and foul, the half of the winter's gang at yule.'

If there be any truth in this old proverb we are going to have a very early spring, for it was scarcely fair all day on Saturday. It was frosty, a strong breeze of wind and snow showers off and on all day. I did not go to the yoke, but was cleaning my harness and doing other odd jobs about the houses.

Towards night the wind rose to a perfect hurricane, blowing the snow with blinding fury—a perfect blizzard. Before morning however it had blown fresh, and I was in the plow today again. I was plowing all last week at the 'Knowes'. I have been increasing the quantity of feeding stuff for the cattle since last week. The six calves are getting 1¼ lbs each oil cake, and two stots 3 lbs of corn and ½ lb oil cake, 1 lb cotton cake, the three queys and the cow that is calved 2 lbs corn and ½ lb both of oil and cotton cake each.

As I have taken in hand to speak at a Temperance meeting on Friday, I cannot spare time to write more, as I will need to set my wits on edge and get something strung together.

12th

I did not get written last night as I had to go to Portsoy on rather a painful errand. I was at Tochineal in the afternoon for some oil cake, and afternoon I came home, Willie and I were taking down some turnips from the pit. I was filling with a graip, with my back to the cart, and didn't he stupidly come across close to my elbow and on coming round my graip stuck him below the eye.[4] It did not bleed much, but being so near they eye I was afraid the ball might be touched, and so I went down for James Gray's gig and had him down to Portsoy. I had a few lines from him today, saying that it was likely soon to be better.

The fine open weather which we have been enjoying all winter, suddenly came to an end on Friday. Thursday was frosty and we were driving out dung.

There was a slight coating of snow on Friday morning. About ten o'clock the wind turned due north, and increased to the violence of a gale. When the showers which were frequent came, it blew a perfect hurricane, and the snow being dry and powdery roads and railway have been partly blocked. Saturday was much about the same, and I see by the newspapers that much damage has been done at sea, and some loss of life.

Sunday and yesterday were quiet, and there is some sign of a change tonight. There was to have been a meeting in the schools on Friday evening under the auspices of the Temperance Society, but owing to the very bad night only a few turned up and it was therefore postponed.

On Wednesday a ploughing match was held at Ordens. As the horses had the cold I did not go. Thirty five ploughs turned out and

---

[4] graip, a four pronged fork.

the work was good. John Morrison, Clunehill was undoubtedly champion, carrying off four first prizes. George Taylor came in second.

18th

The snow storm has been short and sharp. The most of the week was quiet and frosty, but on Saturday forenoon we had three hours of a regular blow out. It blew fresh however at twelve o'clock and by Sunday morning a few wreathes only were to be seen.

I was in the plough all day today. In the first of last week we were dressing and driving away grain. We were keeping it to give to the cattle but Father does not think it will pay to give them more so he has sold it all out. It only weighed 39 lbs and the price was 14/6. I am decidedly of opinion that it would pay to make beef of it. We had 4 qrs off the clean land newly thrashed, which weighed 40 lbs and for which we got 16/-.

Mr Mackintosh was up on Friday afternoon. He has been making out a Will for Father I believe, and Cultain came over and signed it. For some time past I have been thinking that he was going to make a settlement, but he never said anything to me about it, but on Friday I asked him. He said he was to leave the stock and subject to me and what money there was to be divided among the others, but I do not know in what proportion. I have certainly no reason to be displeased with the settlement. Father and I can never come to an understanding however about little Joan. Of course he wants her to be left here, and for his sake I might have made no objection, but then I cannot forget that she is Joan's bairn, and she has never so much as asked if I would allow her to be left here, but on the contrary she has told me that I am doing everything I possibly can to put her out of a home. How could I ever ask anyone to take charge of her bairn after such conduct. I do not think anything ever gave me so much trouble but I really cannot see that I can give in to Father in the circumstances, more especially as Katie is not inclined to take charge of her.

Sunday was Katie's birthday and on Saturday evening I took a run over with a book as a small present for her. I did not wait to see her but left it on the girnal in the meal house.[5]

I had a letter from her tonight, saying what a pleasant surprise she got when she found it, and thanking me kindly for the same. There was also a nice bouquet of snowdrops enclosed.

24th

---

[5] girnal, meal chest.

Very good weather. I have only been taking one yoking in the day during the past week, and doing some odd jobs in the afternoons. There is just one yoking of lea to plough and the clean land will take some time before it be in trim, as there has been much rain today. I was over at Kirkton on Tuesday evening and Katie and I had a long talk about little Joan again. We are so grieved to think, that we cannot comply with Father's wish respecting her. The understanding we came to was, since Father was so unwilling to part with Joan, and seeing that we could not think of taking charge of her, we would be quite willing to wait. I told Father this next day, but he would not hear of that either and so he said that the lassie must just go, but it cost him a good deal to say so. I am sorry for Father, but perhaps he will soon forget her, and I am sure we will strive to do everything in our power to make him happy and comfortable. He was saying that he would be willing to give over everything to us at Whitsunday and let us make the best of it we could.

On Saturday Father and I went over to the Bauds to see George Milton about a stone for Mother. He had several of them in stock, but we did not fix on one. Willie was down from Keith when we came home. He was saying that Mr Pirie was leaving Keith and going to Aberdeen, and that his jouneyman had taken the shop. He had been asking if he would stop on with him, but he had not made a bargain yet. Father and I were at church on Sunday. We got a very touching sermon from the text, 'Jesus Christ of whom the whole family in Heaven and earth is named'.

1889 March
4th

The old proverb says that March should come in like an adder's head, and go out like a peacock's tail. If this means that it should come in sharp, it has verified the truth of the proverb to a 'T'.

The ground was white every morning all last week, but by noon it had generally disappeared. The frost has been more severe the last few days however, and we have two inches of snow.

We had George Cowie and Aunt over from Finnygaud on Wednesday, but they did not stay very long as they were going in past Muttonbrae. I had two hours with Katie that evening. I have been casting off the bank at the side of the Ardiecow road, and driving it into a heap.

On Thursday we had a forenoon at the dung.

I was at Keith market on Friday. Got a drive up with Aleck Duncan. There was a very stiff sale for fat cattle, 60/- only offered for prime. Calvers however were in demand. There was a meeting in connection with the Temperance Society in the evening and so after getting tea, Aleck and I went up to it. There was a crowded house, Mr. Morrison being chairman. The programme consisted of choruses, duets and solos and they had me down for an address. I made a few remarks as to the origin of the Temperance movement. A very pleasant evening was spent.

I was at the steam mill at Ardiecow on Saturday. His stuff is in very bad condition, the stacks being by far too large.

11th

Father and I were at Portsoy today with two loads of oats, and brought home coals. We are going to thrash out the remainder of the crop in a week or so. The corn weighed 41 lbs and we got 17/-. I was making inquiry about a servant. Joan has got word that Jane has got a place for her in Edinburgh and she has to go up about the middle of April. She also had a letter from Gordon last week. He had never gone farther than Aberdeen. He sent a man all the way with the letter, acknowledging that the bairn was his and sending some money.

We also had a letter on Saturday saying that Annie had got a daughter, on the morning of the 7th and that both were doing well.

Geordy Stephen was over on Sunday but I was the only one at church. The minister preached from the text 'But they made light of it'. 'Those who refused the offers of salvation', he said, 'did not merely make light of the invitation of an inferior or an equal, but of a superior, of a King, yea of the King of Kings'. They made light of God and of God's well beloved Son,—they made light of the soul, and they made light of eternity.

We were driving out dung last week in the forenoons. By afternoon the frost was generally slackened. We were also driving some spruce trees from the Cotton hill. We had them down to James Gray and got them sawn into posts.

18th

It has snowed all day today and is still like more. Thrashing and winnowing has been our days work.

The past week however was dry, and I was ploughing clean land for three days in the end of the week it being in good condition.

Thursday was Cornhill market. We were intending to go over with the black cow but I sold her to William Hay the day before for £13.15. Father was across but everything was a very stiff sale.

The ploughing match at Limestones came off on Wednesday. I got Father to go over and see it so I did not go. It was a success however there being thirty six ploughs. James McLennan, Stonedykes, was champion.

When I was in Portsoy last week I called on the painter to see about painting and papering some of the house. He sent up his pattern book and I took it over to Kirkton one evening when we were selecting some papers.

He came up himself today but we did not make a final bargain. Father and I can never come to an understanding about the management of things. He is willing to give over the half of everything to me, and I would be quite satisfied with that, but I do not think he is capable of managing things now and I want him to hand it over to me. This however he is not at all willing to do. I have asked the advice of Uncle George and he says I am only asking what is reasonable. Father has been taking too many people's advice however and he will not hearken to Uncle. It as gone from one thing to another until Father has said that unless Katie is willing to come here and be under him he will keep Joan, and I have said that I will never take Katie here under such conditions. Shakespeare says, 'The course of true love never did run smooth', and I am certainly finding his saying true from experience.

25th

There was no ploughing last week, but the weather now seems to be settled. We were putting up some fences, and preparing for the steam mill.

Willie and I were at Cultain at the thrashing today. It was very blowy and disagreeable working. The mill is over into our cornyard ready to begin tomorrow. Father was telling me last night, that he had a letter from Gordon a few days ago, and he is going to marry Joan yet. He is still thinking of going to America I believe if Joan would go with him.

1889 April
1st

We got no thrashing done on Tuesday, it being a very windy day, and bitterly cold I was ploughing all day.

Wednesday was quite a contrast, quiet and warm with bright sunshine. A better day for thrashing I could not have wished. It was half past two before we got finished and I never saw so much straw in the cornyard at this time of the year. Uncle George stayed and gave us a hand to tidy up the cornyard and after tea Father and I signed the agreement which I had drawn out and Uncle signed it as witness. Everything except the things in the house is to be valued and one half is to belong to each respectively, but Father's half is to be maintained. After Whitsunday I am to get the management and should Father wish at any time to reside anywhere else I am bound to pay him £15 in the year.

Father seems to be quite pleased with this arrangement now. I wrote to Jessie about two weeks ago asking her mind on the subject. She wrote Father himself and urged him strongly to give me the management and I believe she has been the means of making him consent. I earnestly hope that neither Katie nor I may ever be the means of making him repent his decision. I went over to Kirkton that evening to let Katie know of the arrangement and matters being now somewhat settled of course we had much to talk about.

I had the coll in the plough in the end of the week, while Father was driving home turnips.

A few commenced sowing about Friday but there was rain on Saturday and today has been stormy with hail showers.

I went down to Fordyce on Friday evening and engaged a woman to the term.

On Saturday afternoon I went in to Portsoy. I went past Burn and saw old Mrs Seivwright. She is to come and keep house for a few weeks after the term. I also called on the painter and brought home some paint for the doors. He is to come up and paper the two rooms, and paint the doors in the parlour.

It being showery today instead of going to the plough I went to Craibstone for some lime. I should like to lime four acres at least.

8th

Cold, dull, showery, weather. There has never been a great deal of rain, but always showers and no drying. Of course there has been no sowing. We have the turnips all home and two days would finish the ploughing. I was driving lime when the plough would not work. There are thirty two bolls driven. I took two hours in the middle of the day at the painting. The sitting room doors are finished and the lobby ones have got one coat.

There was a political meeting in the schools on Thursday evening, but I did not get the length, the meeting in the meal-house having more attractions. It was a Mr. McAllister from Glasgow who was speaking.

On Friday evening there was a meeting in connection with the Temperance Society. Mr. Porteous from Cullen gave an excellent address on the Bible aspect of the temperance question. Total Abstinence he said was not only permitted by Scripture, but it was commended.

I was the only one at church on Sunday. We had a young man preaching and I hear it is an assistant that Mr. Mackintosh has got.

15th

What sad and tragic events, do happen in this life. We have heard today that Mrs Mackintosh, The Manse has put an end to her life this morning by throwing herself from her bedroom window. About eight o'clock in the morning, Mrs Strachan (who has been attending her for sometime) had occasion to leave her for a short time. On returning she was surprised to find that the toilet table in front of the window had been set aside, and that the window was drawn. Finding the room empty she ran to the window and there was Mrs Mackintosh lying on the gravel below. Frank, the Doctor, was fortunately staying at the Manse, and Mr. & Mrs. Ernslie were also paying them a visit. It is said that she survived an hour, but never regained consciousness. It is rumoured that she was very restless during the night, but none of the particulars have as yet transpired. Of course everyone would be fair to believe that her reason had been gone, but on consideration we must confess, that it does look extremely like a premeditated affair. The funeral I believe to be on Thursday and is to be public.

A week of extremely bad weather and little appearance of it settling yet. The seedtime must now inevitably be late.

Rain commenced to fall on Wednesday afternoon and continued more or less for three days.

Father and I were both at the market on Thursday. There was a large turnout of cattle, and one year olds were selling at very high prices, from £8 to £12. Fat however was extremely stiff 58/- per cwt being the highest I believe. I bought two small ewes from J. Green and I then went down to Portsoy and bought other four ewes and five lambs for £9.15.

I went down for them today and was surprised to find one of the lambs dead. I do not know on whom the loss should fall when I had never taken possession of them, but we just made a new bargain leaving out the ewe that lost the lamb. I gave seven shillings more however, than what I considered the value of them, the price being £7.12. The maiden at Cairdswell was christened last week I believe, Annie Bidie Cowie being the name.

22nd

We have lost a young calf since I wrote last, and another one has taken badly. It commences like rheumatism in their legs. I rubbed the knee joints with oil and turpentine, and also blistered it on the lungs, as the farrier said they seemed to be affected. It took its milk until the last day. I hope this one may soon recover.

The particulars as to Mrs. Mackintosh death have now transpired. During the early morning the little dog had been annoying her barking outside, and when Mrs. Strachan left her bedroom its is conjectured that she had risen, drawn the window and looked out, and that one of the fits to which she was subject, coming on her at the time, she had fallen out the window being very low. Much sympathy is felt for Mr. Mackintosh poor old man and I rather doubt he will never preach again.

I was ploughing land for the potatoes in the first of the week.

We commenced sowing on Thursday on the Knowes. The day was beautiful and the land in very good condition.

Friday forenoon was dull. We sowed some at the back of the byres in the afternoon but by four o'clock it was raining heavily and I had to unyoke.

A good deal of rain fell during the night, and there was nothing done among the land on Saturday. I went over to Limestones in the afternoon to get two quarters of seed corn changed. Their new house has got one coat of plaster. It will be a very nice looking house I think and there will be ample accommodation.

We had the new assistant preaching again on Sunday. He is a very small man, but has a good voice, and we got a very able sermon from him. His text was, 'Fight the good fight of faith, and lay hold of eternal life'. 'A better rendering of these words', he said, 'was to found in the revised version, which had it, 'fight the good fight of the faith, lay hold on the life eternal'. There was a great difference he said between faith, and the faith and he defined the two in a very plain and explicit manner. He further remarked, that it was a good thing for us that we had to fight and to strive against many circumstances and conditions, both in the natural and the spiritual life. The fight also was a good fight, and the prize was well worth fighting for viz. the life eternal.

Today has been dry and we resumed sowing.

29th

Yesterday was Communion Sunday and it was Mr. McDonald, Cullen, who officiated. I scarcely liked him so well as Mr. Mackintosh. We had Mr. McVicar on Thursday and got a very earnest address from him on Christian work. We ought to work he said with a will, with perseverance and with diligence.

On Tuesday we sowed the little bit of yavels beside the house. Wednesday was wet.

We sowed the yavels on Ardiecow on Friday and on Saturday I went over for Cultain's brake harrow and went over the clean land.

This forenoon I sowed all the clean land. It was in good order. I am afraid I have given the oats too little seed.

1889 May
6th

Sowing I believe is not altogether finished yet, the past week having been most unsuitable.

On Tuesday morning I commenced early to put out lime, but about nine o'clock a severe rheumatism came into my back and I had to give it up. For two days it was very painful but is now much better.

Wednesday and Thursday were both wet days, much rain having fallen, and nothing was got done among the land.

I went over on Wednesday afternoon to see the folks at Cairdswell. Annie is looking remarkably well I think and the baby is very quiet but quite healthy.

We put out the lime on Friday but the land was still wet.

It kept dry however and we got in the grass seeds on Saturday. I went up to the Backies that evening at Miss McWillie's request, to send the lawyer some particulars as to the valuations.

I was town keeper yesterday. Robert Gordon was calling. Joan and him are to be married I believe in a few weeks but I am told no particulars and I ask none.

I have always been doing a little at the painting when I can get time. The painter's boy was in the end of the week and gave the parlour doors two coats.

The oldest calf has now grown stiff on its legs and the younger one is never quite better. I saw the Cullen farrier one day, and he gave me some ether for the young one a teaspoonful among its milk, and bade me rub its joints with cream.

Father bought another one last week for £2.17.6.

13th

Seldom do we experience such a week of fine weather in the beginning of May as we have had since I wrote last. It has been dry and warm, and grass and braird have made great progress in growth. I never remember the corn lying so short time in the ground I think. We sowed the barley two weeks ago, and only finished the harrowing of it a week past at Saturday and the braird I am sure is an inch long already.

We planted the potatoes on Tuesday and got a very fine day. Since then I have been preparing the turnip land in the den and another yoking would have it all ready. It was very tender and free of weeds and so I grubbed it.

On Wednesday George Cowie and Annie and Aunt from Finnygaud came over. They were over at the churchyard seeing Mother's grave.

Thursday was Cornhill market Father was over. Fat was a very stiff sale, and keepers were also cheaper. I see that grass however is letting dearer than last year. Father and I were at church on Sunday. Mr.Lamb preached from the text, 'Abraham, the Father of all them that believe'. Willie was down from Keith. He is speaking of giving up his trade at the term yet.

Father was telling me today that Joan is to be married on Saturday the 25th of May.

20th

Beautiful weather. Dry and warm. The last two days have been particularly mild. Grass and braird looking well. Clay land would take a shower. We have not the cattle out yet, more than a weeks turnips. I sowed the first of the swedes today in splendid condition.

Was at Cullen market on Friday but did not engage a boy. Wages were up especially boys. I must go and do something in the garden as I have not touched the flowers yet.

27th

Weather continues exceptionally good. Swedes are now mostly sown, and the rest of the land is being prepared.

We had a tremendous thunder shower on Tuesday last, which will do an immense of good as it has continued warm. After the shower on Tuesday Mr. Kitchin, Clune, and Uncle George came over and valued the cattle, dung, grass and other effects. We have not got the fences measured yet, but I think the whole will come to something like £340. Of course the crop has to be added to this.

On Wednesday forenoon we were down at Glassaugh Station with Joan 'providing'. It was an easy matter for her to provide when she could take as she had a mind. The marriage was on Saturday.

On Friday night I saw that preparations were being made for a large company but as I was never told who any of the guests were to be, and considering it entirely out of place to have a large party after the manner they have conducted themselves, I did not attend but just went to the yoke as usual.

Mary Ritchie comes up and milks the cows and the woman is to be home tomorrow evening.

I engaged a boy Joseph Ewing in Keith market on Friday for £6. Got a drive up with Miss McWillie and assisted her to buy a new machine.

1889 June
3rd

From the beginning to end the month of May has been remarkably fine. I never remember seeing it so good. To have been a late seedtime cereals have an excellent appearance, and grass is abundant. Swedes are coming up strong and healthy and the remainder of the turnips land is being prepared in excellent condition.

We sowed the haugh in the 'Den' on Wednesday – the first of the yellows. It got no dung but I gave it 9 cwts. of a special mixture of manure, 4 cwts. bone meal, 2 cwts. No. 2 turnip manure and 2 cwts. phosphate slag mixed and I have tried some slag by itself at the rate of about 10 cwt. to the acre. I had 1¼ cwt. and I sowed 11 short drills in the corner. About 50 yards at the lower end of the 13th drill got no manure.

On Thursday I was ploughing and harrowing at the little parkie beside the houses. The turnips land is now all made.

On Friday and Saturday we were at the brae in the Den.

I was over at Kirkton on Thursday evening and had a very pleasant walk and talk with Katie in the 'bogs'. Our marriage is to be within the last week of June or the first of July.

Katie was going over to Hillfolds on Friday and was to go to Huntly on Saturday to buy some of her things. Father has refused point blank either to give or lend me any money, but I am to get a loan of £14 from Jessie, and I hope I may never forget her kindness.

We had a great thunderstorm yesterday afternoon with much rain. The lightning was extremely vivid and some of the peals of thunder awfully near.

There was also more thunder and rain today.

We were dividing the new grass today as we do not think we can eat what was allotted for pasture.

10th

We have been very busy sowing turnips all the week, and we have just the calves parkie beside the houses to do now.

We finished the 'Den' on Wednesday and yesterday I saw them all coming. I expected a fine mould beside the wood, but it was very firm with the thundershowers. I should have liked a half more dung for it. It got 5 cwts. manure per acre, 3 cwts. bone meal, and 2 of No. 1 turnip manure. I had a tryst with Katie on Friday evening. Our marriage has been fixed for Friday the 28th. We were speaking at one time of taking a trip to Edinburgh, and Jessie and Jane have both been pressing us hard to come, but we do not think we can see our way to go in the meantime. We may perhaps take a two days, but we have not finally settled where we shall go yet.

On Saturday evening I went down to Cullen for some patterns of carpets which were coming from Edinburgh.

I went over to tea at Kirkton on Sunday afternoon. They have got two foals, but none of them are very old. Cultain and Jessie Geddes were proclaimed in chuch, also William Legg and Mary Calder.

Today Helen, Joseph and I went to the moss, spread the peats and set part of them. They were in fair condition, but are by far too thick on the lair.

17th

Weather warm and dry. Greatly in need of rain. Hoeing is commenced in several places, but there are still some to sow. We finished sowing on Thursday.

We were oiling the harness and cutting thistles on Friday. Father went to Cornhill market, went over to Finnyguad and stayed all night at Cairdwell.

I went over on Saturday and gave the folks at Limestones a day among their turnips. They will have the most of this week's work yet. Their new house is now almost finished and both outside and inside it is as nice a new house as I have seen yet.

Willie was down on Sunday and went to church with us.

We were in the moss today and set the remainder of the peats.

1889 July
2nd

This is rather a big leap to make in my diary writing, but I was too busy last two weeks to think of such a thing.

The week before last I was doing a good many odd jobs, washing and painting the carts, tidying up the garden etc. etc. There was no rain all the week.

On Saturday I went in to Banff to make some purchases. I went up past Cairdswell as I came home, and Father was at the station meeting me.

I got over a Marriage Notice from Mr. Smith on Wednesday and after Katie and I had signed it with two witnesses we sent it back, with instructions to put it on the 'Board'.

I was in church on Sunday but Katie was not.

I was over at Kirkton on Monday evening when everything was arranged about the marriage. I was getting a sight of the bride's presents. There are over twenty I believe and some of them are very pretty. My one was an olivewood work box, with her name on a silver plate on the lid.

Friday morning dawned bright and clear, not a cloud to be seen. I was whitewashing the houses in the forenoon. About two o'clock Father and I commenced to dress and before we were well begun George Cowie and Annie and Mr. Ross had arrived. Uncle George came shortly afterwards and Miss McWillie also came down past with her 'Tilbury Car'. We were at Kirkton punctually at four o'clock. George Smith was the only other guest, as Willie did not come. Mr. Mackintosh was very shaky during the ceremony. I never felt the marriage ceremony to be so solemn and impressive. Katie seemed to be quite firm and when we joined hands it was with a warm and 'Siccar grip'. May God grant that our hearts as well as our hands may ever be united with the silken cords of Love. After tea we went out to see the garden. The evening was most lovely, and as we sauntered down the bogs, Katie and I fell somewhat behind. A holy quiet seemed to spread over Nature, our hearts were too full for much converse, and when a sharp bend in the path hid the others from our view, I slipped the ring on to her finger and it was only then that I seemed fully to realise that she was my own dear wife. We had supper at eight, and at nine we started for Hillfolds, amid a most tremendous shower of rice, old shoes and 'beesoms'. I never saw Miss McWillie in such spirits, as she was that evening. George Smith and her were quite a treat. We arrived at Hillfolds at half past ten Mr. Ross meeting us at the garden gate with a hearty welcome.

Next morning I took good care to rise first in case Katie should 'don the breeks'. Having got breakfast I went out to have a look at Mr Ross' stock and crops. His pasture is excellent, and his hay good. He is also to have a fair crop of barley and oats, and his turnips are looking well. As we had arranged to take a run up Speyside, and spend a few days, Mr. Ross drove us down to met the nine train. The morning was warm but not bright. We got an apartment to ourselves mostly all the way and we had a very pleasant ride. I was much interested as we passed through Botriphnie in learning from Katie the names of all the places we passed. On our left we saw Mossend where her Uncle Peter Shearer resides. A little farther up Fenrovel was passed where her Mother was born and where she was also wooed and won. About Drumonian Castle everything was looking beautiful, but the charming appearance of the loch was completely spoiled by it being drained off in the meantime, for the purpose I believe of cleaning out the weeds, and repairing the islands. Aberlour was to be our destination and we arrived there between ten and eleven o'clock. We at once went to the Aberlour Hotel and arranged with Mr. Henderson about staying for a few days. Harry got some refreshments and wishing that Katie should get a sight of Ballindalloch Castle and the country round about we got a hire, and at twelve o'clock took the road up Spey. At the top of the Brae o' the Briars a splendid view is got of the valley of the Spey. The road is still close by the water side but some hundred feet higher. Away down the water, the white walls of Arndilly House may be seen peeping forth from its green surroundings the hill of Benaigan forming a striking background. At several places we got a peep of the river and the dry weather having greatly narrowed its breadth, two lines of white shingle, contrasted very beautifully with the darker colour of the water. The river here takes a sharp bend to the west. We look right down upon it and the railway. A boat is seen drawn up on the beach beside the boathouse, on a green haugh by the water side the sheep and lambs are quietly grazing. Up the brae the House and farm steading of Wester Elchies are to be seen, and all together a more lovely view is rarely met with. Seeing it for the first time, with everything dressed in its full, fresh summer attire Katie was fairly enraptured. On the farm of Kinermony we saw the first oats in ear. The crop on Balliemulloch was looking remarkably well but their turnips very backward. On turning the gradient and coming down through the farm of Marypark one of the best views of Inveravon is obtained. This parish has always been famed for its scenery and it certainly is a bonny spot. A beautiful sight is got when opposite the Public Schools. Both them and the Schoolhouse are of welcome construction while close beside them is the shop and croft of Belliehiggles all new, neat erections. Down in a sheltered hollow about two hundred yards from Spey, are the manse, church and churchyard, all nestling close together. Across the water the pretty shooting Lodge of Pitcroy can be seen, with a wooded hill for a background. Further down, but on this side is the perfect square of Georgetown with Georgetown House standing on a bare knoll, and looking as if placed there to keep sentry over the valley, but the gem of the whole picture is always the silver thread, which winding between its peebly beaches and birch bushes, seems to give life and animation to the whole scene. At the gatehouse opposite the smiddy at The Slack we alighted, and telling the driver to go on to the inn at Dalnashaugh and there await us, we entered the grounds of Ballindalloch Castle. They are not very extensive, neither are they particularly well kept still there are some pretty spots to be found. One thing which took our attention was the great number of splendid larches. I never saw such magnificent trees, so large, so straight and so tall. At the end of a park called 'The Bow' we saw a monument or rather a tomb in which one of the late lairds of Ballindalloch lies in a stone coffin above ground. The castle stands on a level haugh, about a quarter of a mile from the Spey and perhaps two hundred yards from the Avon. The style of architecture resembles a good deal that of Cullen House, and except one of the wings, it appears to have seen a good many summers. There being no one residing in the castle in the meantime, we took a good look round it. The principal entrance is from the Brig O'Avon, but before leaving the grounds we took a rest for a short time on a mossy bank, by the side of the clear winding Avon. This stream is proverbial for its clearness and in this dry weather when its volume is so perceptibly lessened it certainly did appear like crystal.

On regaining the public highway we crossed the water, and passing Swiss Cottage we went as far as Lady Grant's Schools. It was four o'clock when we got up to the inn at 'The Haugh' and as we did not want to be back to Aberlour before six, we decided to have a drive up Avon side a few miles. I never saw such a quantity of dust on a road before, caused doubtless by the long continued drought and the extraordinary traffic from Minimore Distillery. A more pitiful effect of the drought however was to be seen in the parched and scorched fields. I never saw such a miserable appearance all my life. The soil seems to be light and gravely, the oats scarcely the length of your finger and all turning red, the hay scarcely worth the name, and the pasture dry and burned. Not one good field did we see from Tommore to Drumin. At the latter place which is the residence of Mr. Skinner factor for the Duke of Richmond we turned and again took down the water. On arriving at Aberlour we refreshed ourselves with a good wash and a cup of tea, and after going out and making some purchases we retired to rest.

The Sabbath morning was quiet and warm. Plenty of clouds but no rain. We breakfasted at eight o'clock, and was much pleased with the size of the Aberlour eggs, and the sweetness of its honey. Remembering the maxim that 'A Sabbath well spent, brings a week of content, and health for the toils of the morrow', we spent the forenoon in reading the Scriptures, meditation and prayer. At twelve o'clock we repaired to the Established Church to hear Mr. Sloss. I thought he had improved in preaching since last I heard him. He gave us a very practical sermon on the training and up-bringing of children from the text, 'If any provide not for his own and especially for those of his own household he hath denied the faith and is worse than an infidel.'

'The general idea of providing', he remarked, 'was simply to supply food and clothing, but he said that it was as much the duty of parents to provide for the support and growth of the mind as the body.' One of the Miss Richardson's of Balliemulloch was in church, and twice I caught her eye looking intently down upon us. Having dined we went down and called on James Murray and Maggie. James went down to Fisherton with us and showed us his byres and dairy. Katie was quite delighted with the clean and tidy appearance of the whole premises, more especially the diary the like of which she had never seen before. The floor and walls were laid with enamelled tiles, smooth, clean and spotless. There were metal stands for holding the milk basins, each resting on a revolving foot, while all the other dairy utensils were of the most recent improvement.

We then took a walk round past Aberlour Mains. The Proprietor, Mr. Findlay, has now taken this fine farm into his own hands. The farm steading is one of the finest in the north of Scotland, and I have heard it remarked that there was an acre of slates on the roofs. Coming down above Aberlour we got a grand view of the parish of Knockando across the water. As Katie was desirous of witnessing the Episcopal form of worship, we resolved to go and hear Mr. Jupp in the evening. The Chapel is a neat little building, the inside being particularly beautiful. We had no difficulty in getting a seat, for had it not been the inmates of the orphanage, the congregation was extremely meagre. We were disappointed in not having Mr. Jupp himself, but his assistant gave us a very good discourse from Mathew VI. 24, 'No man can serve two masters.' His principal aim was to illustrate what was the true meaning of the word 'serve'. The general meaning attached to the term is simply to be a servant to but this was not the meaning in the passage referred to. It was to be a slave or bond servant, and he there pointed out to us the striking difference between a slave and a servant. 'The latter part of his text', he said, 'reminded us that everyone in this world must belong to one of two parties. We must either be the bond servants of God or Mammon.'

After service we took a look round the orphanage. A large addition has lately been made to it, and at present it is a refuge to over 200 orphans. Before retiring we took a look through the churchyard. A splendid mausoleum stands in the centre, erected for Miss Macpherson Grant of Aberlour and there are a great number of beautiful tombstones. We were greatly astonished however at the churchyard and being kept in such bad order. The folks of Aberlour generally like to see things neat and tidy, but there certainly is room for much improvement here.

On Monday forenoon we went to see Aberlour House, gardens and grounds. It has the reputation of being one of the prettiest residences on the banks of the Spey. The house is of modern construction and everything surrounding it is in the most perfect order. Mr. Bisset with great kindness showed us over his gardens and green houses. His flowers at present being in full bloom the display was most gorgeous. I need never attempt to describe them for any pen is quite inadequate. It would require the flowery zeal and enthusiasm of Miss Duncan to do anything like justice to them. The only regret that Katie had was that she was not with us to enjoy such a rare treat. We returned to the hotel at eleven o'clock payed our 'little bill' and left Charlestown.

Having some purchases to make in Keith, we broke our journey there and went up town. We called on the Misses Maconachie, one of whom (Ann) has been lying for sometime in consumption. I was taken up stairs to see her, and judging from her appearance I do not think she will be long in this world.

We arrived at Hillfolds about four o'clock, Mr. Ross having come down to the station to meet us again. Mrs. and Miss McVicar, came over and took tea with us and after a pleasant chat for an hour or so we set out for home.

George Ross did not come home from Kirkton on Friday, and so his father was to drive us over and take him home with him. The evening was beautiful and we had a very pleasant drive.

On coming down the brae below Ardiecow, Katie gaze was fixed intently on what was to be her future home. Our eyes met and I easily read her thoughts. Miss Duncan had newly arrived with George Ross. She had seen us coming and had to run so as to get some cakes to break over the brides head. I was anxious to learn how things had been getting on in our absence. A cow that had been a cripple when we left, was not quite recovered, and everything else was just as it should be. And so our holiday was ended. I will not say our honey-moon. God grant that it may never end. From the bottom of my heart I can truly say that I never spent such a pleasant holiday all my life. We did not go to see anything grand, neither had we mingled with gay society but happy in the society of each other we had visited some of the quiet and beautiful spots of this fair earth;—we had looked with ravished eyes on pictures, fresh from the all creative hand of the Great Master Painter; and looking up from nature unto natures God, I truly believe that we had felt a happiness as near akin to that of Paradise as is possible on this sin stained earth.

8th

At last the clouds have dropped their precious treasure, and the parched earth has been refreshed with gentle showers. Hoeing turnips, cutting hay, and driving peats has been our weeks work. (It is work now and not pleasure of which I have to write. Is not our sweetest pleasure often found in doing our work). Half of the yellow turnips are hoed I believe.

They are all doing fine. I tried the reaper to the hay, but was not pleased with her work. Got Willie Duncan to help me for two days.

He came with me to the moss on Friday as we had the young horse. He was very quiet and I went with him in the afternoon myself.

Mrs. Seivwright left us on Wednesday night and Katie started housekeeping on her own account. She was twice over at Kirkton during the week. Her father was always asking if she had run awa', but she has always come back <u>as yet</u>.

15th

We have been hoeing for most part during the week. We have had occasional showers, and there is a marked improvement on everything. Our crop is to be fully an average one yet I think, and pasture has also been renewed with the moisture.

I went over with Aleck Duncan to Cornhill market on Thursday. There were few cattle and only middling sale. I have been busy taking off honey during the week. Have about fifty sections. Never saw them do so well in May and June. Got a swarm from each hive but one went to Cultain, and I sold one to James Gray.

22nd

No more cry for rain. Yesterday was a spate out and out.

We were to stay dinner at Kirkton after church but we were frightened to take out.

It has been warm however and turnips are doing excellent. Hay however is spoiling.

We only get the remainder of ours coled on Friday and we cut some of the seed on Saturday.

We were collecting earth for top dressing today and in the afternoon went up for two loads of lime.

We got an intimation of Ann Maconachie's death on Friday. She was to be buried on Saturday.

29th

We have had rather backward weather during the past week. Frost in the morning and then showers throughout the day. Late turnips, have now a little too much moisture, but early ones are doing well. Oats have lengthened out considerably and barley in early districts is beginning to mix. It has been bad hay weather however and the quality must now be inferior. Pasture is also getting scarcer and even where plenty it is now dry.

The United Banffshire Agricultural Association held their summer show at Cornhill on Tuesday last. Father went over and saw it. It had been a good show I believe, Mr. Beaton, Cullen House carrying most of the honours in the polled sections.

Father did not come home until Wednesday evening. Aunt of Finnygaud has been poorly and he went over to see her.

We had Miss Duncan and Aleck, Miss Smith from Aberdeen, and Miss McWillie to tea on Wednesday evening. The evening was lovely and we had a nice walk in the Greenhill plantation.

On Thursday afternoon we got in some of the hay in fair condition.

Friday was Peter Fair and it rained nearly all day. I got a drive over with Aleck Duncan. Fees were much about the same as last year. I engaged a bandster for £3.5.

Saturday was a great deal of rejoicing on the Fife estate, Lord Fife was that day married to Princess Louise, eldest daughter of the Prince of Wales.

We were all at church on Sunday. Katie and I stayed to dinner and tea at Kirkton. In the afternoon we went round the 'Kirkhill'—through the orchard,—down the burnside—and then took a look through the garden and had a feast of gooseberries.

This being the Deskford holiday Father set out in the morning for Aberdeen. He is to stay the most of the week I think. We led some more of the hay this afternoon again.

1889 August
5ᵗʰ

Leading hay, hoeing turnips, and driving peats has been our weeks work and a week of most excellent weather it has been. It has been mild and warm, and turnips have been growing splendid. We have the 'Den' all second hoed. I took off some more sections last week.

The bees did nothing all the month of July, but if the weather keeps favourable now I would expect a flow of honey, as the heather is in splendid bloom.

On Thursday evening I went down to Fordyce to pay an account to Mr. Brown. When I came home I found Aleck Duncan and Mr. Ross awaiting me. He had come over to try and buy the little mare, as one of his had died a few days before. I did not intend selling her until the foal was weaned, but when I considered that he was just in want of one, and when he was quite willing to keep the foal until the end of harvest, we soon made a bargain; £21 being the price.

We have had the young horse several times at the moss now, and he goes splendid. We have home eighteen loads but they are not so dry as they were.

We were expecting Father home on Saturday but he has not turned up yet.

We were both at church yesterday. Mr. Lamb's text was Galatians VI. 5. 'For everyone must bear his own burden.' There was two kinds of burden which he spoke of more particularly, the burden of business and the burden attending home duties. Our burdens he said were oftener looked upon as a doom than as a blessing but he was to try and show us that such ought not so to be. It was our burdens that made us strong. By manfully carrying them we were made better. Look at the successful business men, he said, and in nine cases out of ten they had in their early life had many difficulties to overcome and many burdens to bear. The man who was born with a silver spoon in his mouth; very rarely pushed himself much higher on the ladder of fame or success. What was true in regard to business was also true in regard to homelife.

12th

It was too wet for the hoe on Tuesday so we were turning the heap of lime and earth.

Father returned from Aberdeen on Monday night about twelve o'clock. He had come with a wrong train and had to wait two hours at Huntly. He also got a very wet night to come from the station, but except being a little tired next day he was none the worse of it.

On Thursday morning I rose at four o'clock and went to the moss. I then went over to Cornhill market. Sheep were selling well but cattle were stiff. The highest for beef might be 63/. Keepers were also cheaper than they have been for sometime. I paid Mr. Hutcheson for some corn manure we got from him, and bought a ram lamb. Katie and I went to Langlinburn after I came home. We were rather surprised to find Mr. Riddoch from India there. He had only arrived two days before. He had been very unwell and his Dr. had ordered him home for sometime. We commenced to thrash the hay on Friday but only got two loads done. It turned very gloomy and rainy looking in the afternoon so we just took it home and put it into coles.

We were to hoe on Saturday but it turned showery and they would not work. In the afternoon we went measuring all the fences, there being 4763 yards in all.

Uncle of Limestones and Jessie were over on Sunday afternoon. Their new house is finished now, but they are not into it yet.

On Friday we got word that Mrs. Ross, Hillfolds had got a son on Thursday morning. Elsie had been over seeing her and Mr. Ross came over with her on Sunday evening. Katie went back with him, and I will have to stop now and go and meet her with the cart.

19th

We have been driving peats for most part during the week, but they are not in good trim, as there has been a good deal of rain.

Tuesday was the Keith show. None of us went up to it, but I was hearing that it was a good bit back from former years.

On Thursday afternoon we went up to Backies and took tea with Miss McWillie. The evening was showery so we could not get to see the crops, but we inspected her cattle, and took a look at the garden. I was disappointed that her gooseberries were not ripe.

We were putting out topdressing on Friday forenoon. There was much rain on Friday night and a strong gale of wind, but since then we have had fine weather. Barley and oats are both changing colour fast, and at the coast side harvest is commenced.

26th

We have had two or three spates since I wrote last, which have done much damage to the crops.

Tuesday morning was dull but we started for the moss. Before we got there however it was raining heavy and it continued to do so the whole day.

I went over to the smiddy next forenoon with the reaper as she was needing some little repairs. As nothing was in very good season I went down in the afternoon to see the Cullen Flower Show and games. They were held this year in the grounds of Cullen House, the show being held in a marquee. The show was better than it has been for several years, but the prizes were mostly confined to a few. James Lorimer was the only competitor for honey. A large number of spectators were witnessing the games and they were all keenly contested, the dancing being specially good. The rain was on again before I got home and next morning the burns were bigger than I have seen them for several years. Crops are much laid and twisted and will not be good to take off the ground I fear.

On Thursday and Friday we were putting out topdressing. George Cowie and Annie were over on Friday. John Biddie took a very bad turn that day and next day he was worse and the Dr. at him. We heard today that he was a little better.

Father did not go to church on Sunday as it was wet. The attendance was very meagre but we got a very impressive sermon from Mr. Lamb.

1889 September
2nd

This Exhibition of the Deskford Horticultural Society has been the great event of the past week.

Wednesday morning was rather blowy, causing a good deal of anxiety to the owners of pot plants, and it was rather amusing to see these same personages carefully carrying their choice specimens, and all the while sheltering them with an umbrella. I had only five entries and I got four prizes. First and second for gooseberries, and the same for 1 lb sections. I had a wreath of white flowers but Miss Morrison, Clunehill, beat me. We went over to see the show about four o'clock, and went in past Kirkton for Elsie. The pot plants were a good bit back from former years, and also the cut flowers a little, but fruit and especially vegetables were excellent. There was also a good display of dairy produce and honey. James Lorimer and Miss H. J. Morrison were the medalists and Mrs Proctor got the brooch. Miss Duncan was also very successful with her exhibits, having eleven first prizes and several seconds and thirds.

We were thrashing and building the hay on Thursday and got a very good day.

I went to Portsoy on Friday for some coals, and in the afternoon we went to the moss.

On Saturday I went over to Kirkton for the gig and Katie and I set out for Ordiquhill. We first went to Hillfods where we found them all quite well. It is a very thriving baby and is named Alexander. After getting dinner we went out to see the crops. His barley is almost ripe and is a good crop. His lea is also good, but his yavels are only middling. His turnips are fair, and he has excellent pasture. We went over to Cairdswell about four o'clock. Annie had invited a few friends to meet us, and so after getting tea we went out to see Geordies cattle and crops. He is very bare of pasture, but he has good crops and good turnips.

We were at the moss today for four loads of peats but they are far from dry. Father and Katie were over at Blairock in the afternoon. A good few are commenced now to cut barley, but there is great complaints about it being bad to cut. Much of it is lying and the growth has come up through it. We are thinking of making a start about Thursday.

1889 September
9TH

Most excellent harvest weather. Bright sunshine and a breeze of wind. Every day a perceptible difference is visible on the crops.

We commenced on Thursday afternoon and we cut the barley on Friday and Saturday.

We were making roads today.

We got intimation on Saturday that James Cowie, Drakemires, was dead. He was to be buried today but Father did not go to the funeral.

It is rather against my inclination that I am writing tonight so I think I will lay past my pen and go to bed.

16th

Another week of fairly good weather, but rather quiet and warm. There are a great many stooks now in Deskford, in fact I believe Sunday had been stooky Sunday.

We did not push the cutting in the first of the week as we were easily cutting it as fast as it was ripe.

Tuesday morning was dewy and we were thatching the hay. We got a yokin at the lea in the afternoon.

On Wednesday morning I went to the moss for two loads of peats, and found them nice and dry. The boys were setting up the barley stooks. When I came home I was rather astonished when they told me that the bandster had run off. I was not much disappointed however as he was very useless. In the afternoon we got Lizzie Ritchie and took a yokin at the clean land.

Next day was Cornhill market so I went over and engaged another man. There were plenty of hands to be got. This is a mid aged man named Gray but he is to cut or build or anything I like. I have just engaged him by the day at 3/. There were but few cattle in the market, but a good many sheep and good sale for them too. The tailor bought three lambs and a ewe from me the night before but he did not get them all sold.

We cut until ten o'clock on Friday and it turned wet, and there was no more done that day. I was taking off the remainder of my sections, and found some well filled heather ones but not altogether sealed. A grocer in Edinburgh has offered me 9d for the clover sections, but I would be expecting something more for the heather ones.

Saturday was a splendid day, and I was at the scythe all day in the Den. We will not get the reaper into it at all this year, but it is a very good crop.

We were all at church on Sunday. It was a lovely day. Mr. Lamb gave us a very good sermon from the text, 'Ye are our epistle, written in our heart, known and read of all men,' II Cor. II. 3. Aleck Duncan and Elsie were up in the afternoon. Our new man came home this morning. We were cutting roads in the forenoon and in the afternoon we led part of the barley. It is bulking remarkably well.

23ʳᵈ

We have been broken at the harvest work a good deal during the past week, several days being rather showery. There has not been much leading done but except some patches about the hillside, the corn in our sight is all cut.

We cut the yavels beside the house on Tuesday also some in the Den, and also took up the remainder of the barley.

On Wednesday we finished the lea at the back of the byres, and went back again to the Den with the scythes but it turned wet at three o'clock.

Geordy Stephen came over on Tuesday afternoon to tell us that their little Jessie—(Jessie Wilson Stephen) had died that morning of hooping cough. The others had also been bad but were keeping better.

She was buried on Thursday in Deskford Churchyard. Father went over with Mr. Paterson, Netherblairock, and I went and met them at the Free Church. She was 2 years old past at June.

Friday morning was soft and we were putting out topdressing. We only got a few hours cutting. It turned very stormy before evening and during the night I heard some tremendous showers of hail. I was afraid the corn would be shaken but I could see very little next day.

As Saturday morning was still very wet looking I let the man away. We got a few hours in the afternoon.

Sunday afternoon turned hard and dry, with a sharp northerly wind. I was not at church as I was townkeeper and cook. It was over asking for Mrs McKay, but she is never improving any, and is always getting weaker.

We took clyack today, and got an afternoon's leading. The mason was putting up Mother's gravestone today. It is just an year past at Saturday since she died. Dear Mother may your memory be ever kept fresh in our hearts, so that our thoughts may be drawn heavenwards.

30ᵗʰ

Although we have not yet seen the month of October, we are already experiencing October weather.

Wednesday was exceedingly stormy, there being a strong northerly gale. We led the most of the day however from the lea.

Tuesday was soft. We made some stone foundations for the stacks, and set up the stooks. In the afternoon I went over to Cornhill Station with my honey. I had 51 lbs of section honey which I sent to Mr. Gilmour a grocer in Edinburgh, and 23 lbs of drained which went to Lizzie. We had a letter about ten days ago saying that she was very ill but we have had no word since.

Thursday morning the sun rose red and fiery but very soon went in behind the clouds again and by nine o'clock the rain was on and put a stop to the leading. We were cutting green thatch in the afternoon.

We had a splendid forenoon on Friday. We took up the potato oats from the Den, also the yavels beside the house, and commenced to the clean land. It turned showery about three o'clock and we had to unyoke. As we had not much more ready for leading I paid off my man.

Saturday was very stormy again, and we had some heavy showers in the afternoon.

Katie and I were both at church on Sunday. We had Mr. McDonald, Cullen preaching. He intimated that owing to Mr. Mackintosh having given notice that he wanted an assistant and successor, a meeting of the Presbytery of Fordyce would be held in Deskford Church on 10th October when the members and adherents were asked to attend.

I went down to Kirkton this morning for the horse rake and got a good forenoons yoking. The afternoon was showery and I was at the rapes.

1889 October
7TH

Very bad harvest weather. Much rain has fallen during the week, and work has made little progress. Crops that are still exposed must be some what damaged now I fear. We have about four stacks to gather in yet, but our neighbours, Ardiecow has not commenced the leading.

We were putting out topdressing on Tuesday.

Wednesday was a nice quiet day and we were thatching.

I was in the horse rake on Thursday forenoon, and in the afternoon we got in a stack off the yavels. It was not in very good order however. During the night there was a perfect down pour of rain and so there was no leading next day. We were making rapes in the forenoon and in the afternoon I went up to the Backies to order some oilcake.

Saturday was some what drier. I was in the horse rake while the others were driving the stooks out of the 'Den'.

Sunday was a beautiful day. We were all at church. Mr. Lamb preached to a large congregation from the text, 'Here we have no continuing city but we seek one to come.'

I was in the expectation of getting to the leading this morning, but at four o'clock I was awakened by the patter of rain, and during the forenoon we had another spate. I went down to Cullen in the afternoon to cash a cheque which I had received for honey—get a gun licence and some other errands.

14th

We finished the harvest work on Saturday having been five weeks two ½ days. The latter part of the harvest has been wet and unsettled, and some of the crop I fear has been taken to the stack yard in only middling condition. Thrashing machines will likely have a busy time for a few weeks and it will be a wonder if the rush of damp grain into the market do not take down prices. Oats at present are selling from 15/ to 16/6 and barley 22/6. We put kilns into all the stacks which we led this week. There are twenty in all and some of them are larger I think than we usually make them. I am expecting 17 qrs. barley and 90 qrs. of oats.

Thursday was Cornhill market I went over to try and buy a stirk and a calf, but got neither. There was a very keen demand for keepers and prices were high. Calves were selling from £5.10 to £7.10. We took in a stack when I came home, and the remainder on Friday.

Saturday was a great day of rejoicing at Banff. The Duke of Fife was that day to bring to Duff House his Royal Bride, and the citizens of the Royal Burgh were to make a grand effort to give them a warm and hearty reception.

One evening when Miss Duncan was up she was saying that Elsie and her were thinking of going in to see the rejoicing and as Katie had some messages she was also to go along. They went to Tochineal Station, Father put them down the road a bit. They got a beautiful day and enjoyed themselves fine.

Willie was over on Sunday and Father and him went to church. Mr. McVicar, Ordiquhill preached the church vacant and called a meeting of the congregation. They have a days leading at Cairdswell yet.

I was in the plough this forenoon and in the afternoon we cut the remainder of the tares.

21st

Those who have not got the crop all secured are having a weary time of it. There has been no leading all the week, and there has been a good rainfall, while there has been little or no drying. A good many stacks I fear are not in the best condition I was feeling a little heat in two of ours. There are no stooks in Deskford now except at Ardiecow and Greenhill, but in Bogmuchals scarcely any of them have it all secured.

I was in the plough on Tuesday, but the afternoon was wet. I am ploughing the piece on Ardiecow round about.

On Wednesday Josie and I were at Muttonbrae assisting at the steam mill. His corn was not in good condition.

Josie and Nellie were at Careston on Thursday and Friday.

On Friday afternoon I went over to Auchip and bought 10 old Cheviot ewes for 27/ the head. He is to keep them for three weeks yet. A fisherwoman from Portknockie came by a very sad and fatal accident that afternoon. She was attempting to cross a fence on the farm of Slackdale, and as is supposed she had placed her creel on one of the wires and had been going to take her rope over her head when the basket slipping from its precarious resting place she was instantaneously choked. Before the body was removed a policeman was sent for when she was afterwards taken to the farm of Slackdale.

When I came home Mr. Ross form Hillfolds was over with the foal. I know a good difference on it since I saw it last, and I think we are to have very little trouble with the weaning of it. As Katie and I were going over to Kirkton to tea Mr. Ross came along with us. The two new teachers—the Misses Watson were also there.

Saturday was a very wet day. I was cleaning harness the most of the day.

We had a minister from Aberdeen preaching on Sunday. He had a rather weak voice, but he gave us a very good plain sermon from the text. 'Blessed are the pure in heart for they shall see God.' 'The pure in heart were to see God' he said, 'not only in Heaven but also in a manner upon earth. Thy would see him in all his works around them, in the works of nature. Thy would hear his voice in the singing of the birds and in the sighing of the wind, and thy would see his smile in the sunshine.'

Father received a telegram today saying that Joan was dangerously ill with a sore throat and wanting him to come and see her. He is away over to Cairdswell, and is going in tomorrow morning.

28th

On Wednesday afternoon we received word that Joan died at six o'clock that morning.

Father and Annie both went in on Tuesday, but of course Annie had to return the same evening. She had a sore throat about the month of July, and it had never been altogether better. She was buried in Deskford Churchyard on Friday. The folks of Finnygaud and a few neighbours only were at the funeral. We went down and met it at Cullen station at 12 o'clock.

The weather has improved a little the last four days but the first of the week was very wet. A large portion of the crop is still in the fields in late districts and many stacks are said to be heating.

We took in part of one on Saturday which was pretty bad. It was lea corn too, and we thought there could be no mistake when we led it. The sap had not been out of the straw however. I have got the stubbles on Ardiecow all ploughed, and we are going to lift the potatoes tomorrow.

Father, Willie and I were at church on Sunday. Katie did not go further than Kirkton as her Aunt Mary and Mr. & Miss Dey from Botriphnie were down. I went down past and got dinner. When we came home Mrs. Riddoch and Miss McWillie were waiting us.

1889 November
7th

Thursday evening—I was at a meeting on Monday evening and another last night and so it did not get my Diary written. The meeting on Monday evening was to appoint a committee for the purpose of looking out a new minister. It was held in the church. Mr. McVicar moderator of the Kirk session presided, and there was a good attendance. A committee of 21 was appointed with Mr. Smith for Clerk, and Mr. Sim as Convener.

On Tuesday Katie and I went over to see the folks at Puttingbrae. The morning was very frosty. I saw ice on the water for the first time this year. We got a beautiful day however.

Yesterday Father and I were both at Mrs McKay's funeral. She died on Saturday evening. She has suffered long and painfully, it being about 8 months since she was first laid up. She was buried in Fordyce Churchyard.

I was at a Temperance lecture last night. Mr. Hall F.C. minister was the lecturer and he spoke very well.[6]

Last week we were lifting the potatoes on Tuesday and Wednesday. We had two women out of Berryhillock the first day and we lifted 9 loads. We had 16 loads altogether.

I got a drive up to Keith market on Friday with Miss McWillie. There was a very small cattle market as many were still working at the harvest. There were not many fat, but keepers were selling well. I bought a stirk for £11.12.6 and a calf for £6.10. They were both 10/ too dear I think. By the time I got home it was raining heavy, and it continued throughout the night, a perfect downpour, while the wind blew tremendous. In some places there was much thunder, and there has not been such a rainfall for some years.

We were at the drain on Saturday as the stubbles were too wet.

We were all at church on Sunday. It was the minister from Aberdeen we had preaching again, and he gave us a very good discourse on the brother of the Prodigal Son.

---

[6] F.C., Free Church.

11ᵗʰ

A week of most delightful weather for November. There has been more drying than there was all the month of October. I was ploughing down dung on Friday. It is a piece for potatoes which we have dunged. We were all at church on Sunday. Mr. Gibson, Portsoy, was to have preached, but he sent a Mr. Park from Aberdeen in his place. He is one of the candidates I believe and he has also been placed on the leet. There are over 70 candidates and they have selected six. These are Birnie, Gillespie, Philip, Park, Lamb and Black. Mr. Park who preached on Sunday is a tall dark man somewhere between thirty and forty I should say. He has a sharp clear voice and speaks very distinctly, but not a very pleasant voice to listen too. He gave us a good plain sermon from the text, 'We are do fade as a leaf.' Isaiah 64.6. The subject of man's mortality, is one which requires but little study to comment upon, for there is not another I believe upon which the Word of God touches so often. 'We all do fade as a leaf' he said was true not only as regards communities, but also as regards individuals. The leaves also do not all fall together. The frosts of Spring nips a few of the more tender. The storms of summer wrench a few more from their parent branches. In autumn the great majority fall, while winter sees the trees bare and leafless. 'We all do fade as a leaf' was also true as regards our religious feelings. How few he said, retained for any length of time, the warm feelings experienced at a communion service, and how short lived even was the sound of substance of a sermon.

18ᵗʰ

Never do I remember such a spell of fine weather in November. We had frost on Sunday only. The rest of the week was a fresh and mild as if it had been June. I have seen several bushes of whins in bloom, and I hear of strawberry blossom being seen in Banff; and ripe raspberries somewhere in England. It would be better however had we some more frost, for a longer continuance of fresh weather might make the turnips run to seed.

We commenced to store turnips today, and I am highly pleased with them. I never saw us have a better crop of yellows.

I was busy turning over the stubbles last week and they were in grand condition. I have finished all that is for clearing.

Wednesday was Hallow-Fair, and I never saw it such a fine day. There was a good deal of shifting, but little difference on the fees. I engaged a boy from Portsoy, George Priest, for £3.5.

On Saturday we were repairing some of the fences. We should have had them finished by this time, but I have never got the wire yet.

On Sunday we had Mr. Birnie assistant at Fochabers preaching. I never saw the church so well filled before. Mr. Birnie is quite a young man; with a nice, frank, open face. He choose for his text the first verse of the seventh chapter of St. Matthew, 'Judge not, that ye be not judged,' and I was highly pleased with his discourse. It was altogether a practical sermon. He has a soft, mellow voice, very pleasant to listen to and at the same time he speaks very plainly and distinctly. I cannot say that he in any way excels for fluency of speech, but his great attractiveness in my estimation is his decided earnestness. All he said seemed to come from the bottom of his heart.

1889 December
2nd

I have missed a week with my Diary writing having had other writing to do, and also being from home on several evenings. The week before last was excellent weather and we were busy storing turnips. Yellow ones. They are an excellent crop.

We pulled all day on Monday.

We had to go to the steam mill at Ardiecow on Tuesday. His corn was better kept than I expected and it weighed 43½ lbs.

On Wednesday we were driving our turnips up to the roadside. The sale at The Manse was that day. Mr. & Mrs. Ross came over in the forenoon, and George Cowie and a lot more Ordiquhill people were also over. They were all after the cows. Father went over, but I was anxious for the turnips gathered. There was a large turnout and everything sold well.

We were at the turnips on Thursday and Friday again when we managed to lift 58 loads.

We covered them on Saturday and in the afternoon I took a yokin at the yavels. I went up to the Backies that evening to pay for some oilcake.

We had Mr. Lamb preaching on Sunday but being the term time there was not a very large congregation. He had a splendid got up sermon however, but I must say that I do not like his manner. He makes such gestures and is so devoid of earnestness. I did not hear him in the evening as I went over to Limestones.

On Monday forenoon I went to Cornhill for some wire and in the afternoon we were thrashing and winnowing.

Sunday was very cold and Monday turned very stormy. The wind was north and there was driving hail showers.

Next morning the ground was white. I went over to the mill with two loads of corn. I was getting some of it hashed for the cattle. Five stots and three cows are getting some of it. For some hours in the evening it was snowing and drifting tremendous.

Next forenoon I went down to Fordyce for some paraffin, and in the afternoon I went over and paid the blacksmith and tailor.

On Thursday forenoon we were oiling the harness. I went over to Auchip in the afternoon and paid my ewes. I brought them home a week ago. I have them in the hill and giving them some turnips as I have not the other park ready yet. We were laying down some of the wire on Friday. It turned fresh that day a good deal of the snow went away.

Sunday was a wet day from noon to night. As the boy was away I did not get to church in the forenoon, and being wet Katie did not go either. Geordy Stephen was over and him and Father went. It was Mr. Philip from North Berwick who was preaching. He is quite a young man and is seemingly rather weak sighted as he wears glasses. He is a very earnest preacher however, and although he has not a very strong voice he speaks very slowly and deliberately. His text was the 10th verse of the XIX Chapter of St. Luke, 'The Son of Man came to seek and to save that which was lost.' He first spoke of the name which Christ took to himself. He then pointed out his suitableness for seeking and saving the lost, and showed how the good Shepherd went out to seek his lost sheep even before they thought of turning to him.

9th

Thrashing and driving away grain, has been our whole week's work, and the weather has been very favourable for the purpose.

On Tuesday we had Mr. Lamb and got our own thrashing done. I was extremely well pleased with the turn out of barley, but the oats scarcely came up to my expectations.

I was at Kirkton on Wednesday. The turn out of barley there was only middling but it was a very good sample.

Imlach was thrashing Sandy McKay and James Gray on Thursday, while Lamb was at Cultain. I had to hire a man so as to give them both a help.

On Friday we had down fourteen quarters of barley to Glenglassaugh. The first two loads weighed 55½ lbs but we put the rest through the fan and it stood 56. Altogether we sold 17 qrs. And there is 2½ qrs. small barley yet.[7]

We had 9 qrs. Oats to Portsoy on Saturday and it weighed 43 lbs. We had 16½ qrs. Out of the three stacks.

[7] p. bu., per bushel.

We were all at church on Sunday hearing Mr. Gillespie from Dundee. He is quite a young man and had a very good sermon but he speaks by far too fast, and his delivery is not in the least impressive. I rather fear he will not have many supporters.

We had a letter from Jessie last week, when she was telling us that Lizzie had been in Edinburgh in the Infirmary for some time and got an operation performed. She is keeping better now however and is home again. Jessie was also telling us that Willie Bidie, Jane and her had made up their minds to go to Australia in the spring. They will of course be home to see us before they go.

16th

We are always enjoying excellent winter weather. The first of the week was a little stormy and on Thursday we had a hard frost. Since then we have had fine fresh days.

We were at Portsoy on Tuesday again with corn, but it only weighed 42 lbs.

On Wednesday we commenced to pull the Swedes. They are the best crop that ever I saw us have.

Cornhill market was on Thursday, but I did not go over. Keepers are always selling well but fat is rather coming down from 60/ to 63/.

Friday was a very fine day, and we were pulling turnips all day.

We were driving them on Saturday, and we had Sandy Morrison covering them. We have over 50 loads of Swedes lifted.

We had Mr. Park from Aberdeen preaching on Sunday and there was a large turn out especially in the evening. We got two excellent sermons from him and every one seemed to be highly pleased. I liked him much better than when he was last.

I was ploughing yavels today.

23rd

Open winter weather still continues.

On Tuesday we had a tremendous gale of wind. About nine o'clock it lifted about the half of our straw 'Sow' and turned it over bodily. It did not blow much away but it gave us a good deal of work putting it on again. We had a herring net over it and plenty of rapes but we should have had chains or ropes.

It was pretty quiet on Wednesday morning, so we commenced to rebuild it, but we had not much done when the wind rose again and we had to let it alone.

I was ploughing stubbles on Thursday. In the afternoon I was at Tochineal for some oilcake. Katie was over that afternoon at Upper Blairock seeing Annie Smith's corpse. She died on Monday night.

Father and I were both at the funeral on Friday. The forenoon was quiet and we got the straw built.

We were gathering turnips on Saturday, which Mrs. Ogg pulled. Altogether we have now 144 loads stored.

Sunday was a very bad day. In the morning it was sleet which was falling and I thought we were in for a snowstorm, but it turned to rain and this has been a beautiful day again.

I commenced today to plough lea as the stubbles were too wet.

We had Mr. Black from Keith on Sunday but owing to the bad day there was a very thin attendance. I was alone in the forenoon, but Katie went with me at night. I rather fear that Mr. Black will not have many supporters. He gave us two very good sermons however but he is not at all a clear speaker. His texts were 'My Son go work today in my vineyard' and 'I have compassion on the multitude.'

30ᵗʰ

I was ploughing lea in the first of the week.

On Friday we were all pulling turnips in the parkie beside the wood. They are very good quality but there is not more than half the weight of a crop there was in the Den. We just put three rows together and covered them with the chilled plow.

On Saturday forenoon I was covering the tops in the Den. The chilled plow makes a good job of them.

We had Mr. Brown from Buckie preaching on Sunday. He gave us a fair sermon, but he has a miserable bad voice. He made a touching reference to the close of the year.

The year which has now so nearly run its course has on the whole been a fairly good one for the farmer. A commencement was made at sowing in the end of March but it was the middle of April before it was general. Altogether the seedtime was only middling and it turned worse at the close. The month of May however made ample amends for the backward April. I never remember such a warm genial month of May. Abundance of moisture and plenty of heat made vegetation spring rapidly and the braird was soon thickly covering the ground, while grass made such progress, that a large acreage intended for pasture had to be left for hay. The month of June was also warm but very dry. Consequently on light sandy soils the cereals, and more especially oats were burned up, while in many cases the seed of late sown turnips lay dormant in the soil for many weeks. Early turnips however came up remarkably well, and are in general a very heavy crop. Where there was deep soil, and in late districts the drought did not affect the crops, and the bulk was good. Owing to the drought in June, the hay crop was light, but there being more acres than ordinary there is lots of hay in the country. This may be learned from the fact that it has been selling from 5 to 6 the stone. Potatoes were in general a heavy crop and of excellent quality. July and August were both rather rainy months, causing much of the crops to be laid. Barley especially was terribly down and much second growth came up through it, making it very difficult to get off the ground. Harvest was commenced in the beginning of September and the first two weeks we had excellent weather. I have heard it said that the month of October never fails, but there is an exception to every rule. I never saw so little wind as there was in October this year. Never a great deal of rain but always showers and no drying. The harvest was consequently a most protracted one and much of the crop was secured in very bad condition.

Since harvest the weather has been remarkably fine. With the exception of three days in the end of November when we had a rather sharp snowstorm we have had no snow and but very little frost. Vegetation of all kind is springing. Grass is growing green, and the whins are in beautiful bloom.

All this is unseasonable however, and unhealthy too I believe. On the continent of Europe a fearful epidemic of influenza of thousands have been affected, in fact there are very few who have escaped it, and a good many deaths are reported. It is expected to break out in Great Britain in the month of January. All this it is said is an effect of the exceptionally mild weather.

Although crops of all kinds have in general been above the average in this locality, it cannot be said that the prices of all kinds of farm produce are satisfactory. Grain of every kind, is certainly fetching good prices, and since harvest it has always been rising.

At the present time good dry oats of the standard weight is selling at 17/ while barley 54 lbs per bushel is 25/. The weight is also most satisfactory our barley being 56 and some of the oats 43. A report of the same satisfactory nature cannot be given as to the price of beef however. The last Xmas market having been glutted, beef has never regained the same figure. In the middle of summer it perhaps, rose a few shillings, but since the month of September it has been coming down, down. The very choicest at the present time would not bring more than 60/.

Dull trade cannot be said to be the cause either. Workmen of all classes have been striking for higher wages, and their demands have in most cases been conceded. Consequently various articles have risen in value more especially all iron material. We must therefore look for a cause for cheap beef elsewhere, and it is to be found I think in the tremendous amount of imported meat. And not only has the dead meat import been very heavy, but a large number of lean cattle have also been brought into this country. Cattle food being abundant, the supply of home lean cattle was found inadequate to the demand. Large numbers were therefore imported, more especially from Canada. Many of these have now been fed off, and are being sent to the market. As a consequence of the scarcity of lean cattle the prices of such have ruled high, 70 to 75/ the cwt. I believe.

Speaking of our own crops more particularly I must say, that taking them altogether they have been the best I ever saw us have. There was perhaps fully as much straw last year, but then we have far more grain this year. Our crops of turnips are the heaviest I ever saw us grow, and we have about 180 loads stored. Having abundance of straw and turnips I bought some store cattle and although I do not except to make much off them, we will have an extra quantity of dung which we will expect to help future crops.

I also purchased ten breeding ewes in the end of the year, and they have been doing very well as yet, the fine open winter having been particularly favourable for them.

The year 1889 will always be a most memorable one to me, because on Friday the 28th of June occurred an event; which more than anything else I ever did all my life, will more closely affect my well-being and happiness.

After six months experience of married life, I must say that that I feel very thankful to Providence who led me to make such a happy choice.

May that Providence for the future guide and direct our every step in life, and trusting entirely to His Almighty care, we would look forward to the coming year with faith and hope, trusting, that not only for ourselves but for all our friends and relations it may prove both a happy and prosperous one.

A Journal of My Life and Everyday Doings

1890 January
6th

On the last night of the old year we had an invitation to tea at Mrs. Riddochs. Miss McWilllie and Mr. & Mrs. Duncan were the company. As there was to be a concert in the Schools we left a little before eight. The concert was in connection with the Temperance Society and the singers were all local. I cannot say it was of a very high class order but the charge was merely nominal, and Mr. Morrison F.C. gave us an excellent opening address. After wishing us all a very happy New Year, he pointed out to us two characteristics which would certainly help to make the coming year happier viz unselfishness, and self control.

We had Willie down from Keith on New Years day, and in the afternoon Aleck Duncan came up. We were out rabbit shooting but had bad luck.

I went up to Keith market on Friday getting a drive with Miss McWillie. It was far from being a large market, but calving cows and keepers were in keen demand, and fetched high prices. I saw several cows sold above £20. I bought a keeper and I also paid for him. £15 was the price, but I believe except beef rise that I will not make him worth more by the first of April. It will be a lesson for me to be more careful in future. I did not get him home either until today as he turned lame, and I had to leave him at Backies.

13th

The stot I bought at Keith market turned very bad during the week, in fact at one time I despaired of him getting better. I sent for the Cullen V.S. and his opinion was that he had got a touch of rheumatism in his legs, and his stomach disordered. He ordered his legs to be rubbed with sweet oil to keep in the heat, and he sent up powder for him. I knew a difference in two days, but his stomach is still weak.

The quey that has the sucking calf was also off his food the day he called. He prescribed a pound of common salt, dissolved in two bottle of water, and sent also some powders for her. She was chewing her cud next day.

On Tuesday evening we had Mr. & Mrs. Jenkins and Mr. & Mrs. Gray at tea.

Wednesday was the day for electing our minister and a beautiful day it was. The meeting was held in the church at twelve noon and 198 voters were present. Mr. McVicar moderator of the Kirk session presided, and explained the manner of voting. The church was divided into sections the names of the respective candidates being placed on boards at different parts of the church. The supporters of each then went to the parts assigned for them.

The candidates were all duly proposed and seconded except Mr. Gillespie, but Mr. Black had only one supporter and so his name was knocked down. Mr. Lamb was at the commencement at the top of the poll by a long majority he having 86 votes, Mr. Park 56, Mr Birnie 36 and Mr. Philip 17. Mr. Philip having the fewest votes was now knocked off and another vote showed Lamb 88, Birnie 50 and Park 58. Birnie having now the fewest votes his name was struck off, and a vote taken between the remaining two, when the whole of Birnie's supporters joined Park's thus giving him a majority of 20 over Lamb.

The Moderator then put the question, 'shall George Mathieson Park, Aberdeen be now elected minister of Deskford Yes! or No!.'

With the exception of about ten of Lamb's supporters, the whole of the congregation stood up to signify their assent. The Moderator then announced that Mr. Park had been duly elected minister and invited the congregation to come and sign the Call. A good many signed it before leaving the church but it is to lie for ten days with Mr. Smith.

Thursday was Cornhill market and Father went over. He only came home this afternoon, having been calling at Cairdswell and Finnygaud. Katie and I had an invitation to tea at Langlinburn on Thursday evening. We both had the cold, and she was otherwise unwell, but she thought she was able to go. Before we got home however, she was very bad and she has not been much up since. I fear it is the influenza which has been raging so badly elsewhere. The folks at Kirkton are also all laid up with it.

20th

Until Thursday the cold did not affect me so much, but that I managed to keep at the work but on that day I had to come home from the plough.

On Friday I went to Portsoy with a load of corn, and I have been much worse since. The symptoms are headache, feverishness, pains in the back and legs, and a severe cough. Katie has now nearly got over the cold, but she is far from right otherwise. We had the Dr. on Sunday, and he was also over at Kirkton. Jessie and Elsie are still rather bad. I see by the newspapers that it is spreading throughout all Scotland. The weather continues exceptionally mild.

27th

We have had three days of a snowstorm since I wrote last.

On Tuesday there was a bare frost, but on Wednesday morning it was snowing and it continued falling all the forenoon, there being about 4 inches.

Thursday was quiet and frosty.

Friday was milder and towards night a change appeared.

Early on Saturday morning the wind increased to a hurricane, and by day light the snow was all gone. Since the New Year we have had a gale every second day, but it was well it kept quiet when the snow was on the ground, for it was dry as powder.

On Wednesday and Thursday we had Davidson from Kirkton as I was never able to work. The boy and him were driving out dung.

I was about all right by Friday however. I was at the smiddy getting the young horse shod in the forenoon.

On Saturday I was at Tochineal for some oilcake.

Father was the only one at church on Sunday, as I was townkeeper and Katie was not able to go. She has been troubled with a sore side all the week.

I was ploughing lea today with the chilled plough as I had the other one over to the smiddy to be metalled.

I had a letter from Jessie last week. She has got word that her services will not be required after the 25th of March, and they are expecting to sail about the 25th of April. We also had a letter from Mary last week with a photo of them all.

1890 February
3rd

Excellent weather again. I was ploughing lea in the first of the week but went to the stubbles as it turned too dry.

On Saturday evening I set out for Cairdswell. It was a nice evening there being beautiful moonlight. The folks at Cairdswell were all well except the baby. Her face is always sadly broken out.

Sunday morning was frosty. After breakfast we went and had a look at the cattle. He has three young calves, and he has five cattle to sell yet.

About 12 o'clock Geordie went over with me to Finnygaud. Except Willie and Annie they were all at church.

There is never any difference on Mary. She does nothing now, and lies in bed for most part. I was disappointed when they told me that John had gone over to Deskford the night before. We had passed each other on the road I suppose. I met him as I was coming home. Their cattle are all in good condition, their year olds being particularly good.

The folks at Kirkton are now keeping better of the cold but Aleck is never able to work yet. Katie has been greatly troubled with a pain in her side all the week. The Dr. says it is the effects of the cough.

10th

Ploughing stubbles and casting drains has been my week's work. The stubbles are in excellent condition as the weather still continues dry. I also ploughed the haugh of clean land in the Den.

I had Sandy Morrison three days in he end of the week.

Willie came down on Saturday evening and Father him and I went to church on Sunday. It was a stranger who preached. He intimated that Mr. Wilson of the North Parish Church Aberdeen would preach next Sunday, and that Mr. Park would preach in the evening. Wednesday first has been fixed for the ordination, and there is to be a Soiree in the evening.

Last week some young ladies were collecting funds to purchase a pulpit robe with Bible and Psalm book for Mr. Park. They are to be presented to him on Wednesday evening I believe. They collected about £16.

17ᵗʰ

Except Sunday we have had another week of fine weather. A good deal of frost but nice quiet days. Everything as dry as mid summer. I have been ploughing stubbles when the plough would work and when frosty we were driving out dung. We have the court almost emptied.

Sunday however was a very bad day. It was snowing thick in the morning, and there fell about three inches. It turned to sleet however, and by evening it was rain, and this morning the snow was all away and I was at the plough.

The great event of the week has been the ordination of Mr. Park. The service was held on Wednesday at 12 noon.

Mr. Macdonald, Cullen, was the officiating clergyman. There is a rule I believe that the latest placed minister is always the one who officiates. He did exceedingly well I think. It was very impressive when the ministers all stood round Mr. Park, and placing their hands on his head as he knelt at the table, they prayed that the Holy Spirit might descend upon him in rich abundance.

Katie Cowie came over from Finnygaud the night before, and went with us to church. She then went up to Backies.

A Soiree was held in the evening when there was a crowded church. Mr. Macdonald, Cullen, Mr. McIntyre, Portknockie, Mr. Brown, Buckie, Mr McVicar, Ordiquhill, and Mr. McLean, Turniff, were the speakers. Mr. McVicar in name of the ladies of the congregation presented Mr. Park with a handsome Pulpit robe, Bible and Psalm book. Mr. Macdonald who up to this time was presiding now retired in favour of Mr. Park, who occupied the chair, the remainder of the evening. The speeches consisted chiefly of congratulations to Mr. Park and the congregation for the successful issue to which things had been brought finishing up with sundry advices, both to pastor and people. Mr. Reid of course had his choir and rendered several hymns during the evening, but I do not think they in anyway excelled themselves. I was very sorry that Katie was not able to attend either the forenoon service nor the soiree, the pain in her side having never quite left her. I am glad that it is now keeping better however.

On Sunday we had Mr. Wilson from Aberdeen preaching. He is an excellent preacher but not a very distinct speaker. He introduced Mr. Park to us, and spoke in the highest terms of his qualifications and abilities. His text was that from which Paul preached on Mars hill at Athens, 'Jesus and the resurrection.'

Mr. Park himself preached in the evening, and although the night was far from fine there was a good congregation. Phil. I. 21 was his text, 'For me to live is Christ' and he gave us a very impressive sermon.

24ᵗʰ

The good weather still continues, and I see by the newspapers that in some districts sowing has been commenced. They have peas, beans, and oats sown on Tochineal.

I have kept at the plough pretty steady during the week and I have turned over a good breadth. I finished the yavels at the back of the byres and other two days would plough all the clean land in the 'Den.' There has scarcely been any frost all the week.

We had a close mist today and very warm, more like the month of May than February. I saw rose bushes at Kirkton yesterday in leaf, and I was noticing our own gooseberries all budding. It is a wonder if they do not get a check yet. The influenza is always spreading I think. There is scarcely a house in Deskford escaped. In other districts it is also as bad. On some farms work was at a standstill owing to the horseman being all laid up. Schools in many places have also been closed, teachers and scholars being unable to attend. The death rate has been higher than for many years past.

Sunday was a beautiful day and we were all at church. There was a good congregation and Mr. Park preached from Romans XII. 1.

1890 March
3ʳᵈ

February has been an exceptionally fine month and still it has in some measure fulfilled the proverb of filling the dyke. There was no snow until the last two days but on Friday evening there was about three inches fell and also some blowing. It was all away on Sunday however. We have had several days of hard frost which will do much good, as the growth was getting too far ahead.

On Thursday Katie, Elsie and I went over to Hillfolds to see the folks there. The day was stormy, and it was very cold. They were to stay until Friday afternoon but it being a bad night they did not come until Saturday. Mr. Ross' cows are not in very good season this year some of them not being in calf. He bought a new one sometime ago for about £18. Calves are always very dear. He has four of his 'winterings' to sell yet but he has not been feeding much. I believe it will pay better this year to sell them as keepers. I have been giving ours 2½ lbs hashed corn and 1 lb oilcake but I am going to increase it a little now I think. The calves have scarcely been getting 1 lb of oilcake.

10ᵗʰ

The week has been stormy and on Friday we had a fall of snow, from 6 to 7 inches I believe. There was also a good deal of plowing between Saturday and Sunday. It has been fresh today however and much of the snow away. We were at Portsoy today with two loads of oats. We got 17/ for 41½ lbs but it is looking up. I was the only one at church on Sunday as it was a bad day. The church was very thin. Mr. Park preached from the first verse of the XXIII Psalm.

On Friday and Saturday filling the mill, thrashing and winnowing was the most of our work. During the past week I have been getting lots of price lists of seeds. I am not sure who I shall take the seeds from this year I have written for samples to Drummond Brothers, Edinburgh, to Bruce, Aberdeen, and Hutcheson's, Turriff.

17ᵗʰ

The snow got a quick dispatch in the first of last week. Since then we have had tremendous gales of wind, and everything was getting very dry. Had it continued a good many would have been sowing today I believe, but this morning the ground was white again, and snow falling fast. It turned to sleet and then to rain but it fell very heavy all the forenoon. We kept inside—working in the mill. In the afternoon I went to Craibstone for two loads of lime. I have driven 19 bolls to mix with earth to put on the grass.

Sunday was a beautiful dry and we were all at church. We got an excellent sermon from Mr. Park. His subject was the parable of the unjust steward, the words of his text being 'For the children of the world are in their generation wiser than the children of light.'

The yavels and clean land in the 'Den' are all ploughed now except the endrigs.

We had a letter from Jessie today saying that they would be home in the end of next week.

24ᵗʰ

The past week has not been a good one and I only got one yoking in the plough.

Wednesday and Thursday were both wet days. We were working in the mill and cleaning the harness.

On Friday we were fencing off a piece for hay. The social meeting of the Mutual Improvement Society was held that evening. Katie did not go but I went over and went up with Aleck. There was a full house, and after a sumptuous tea there was a short programme of readings and recitations finishing up with a dialogue in character. The school was then cleared and dancing engaged in. Mr. Park and Mr.

Morrison were both present and the former stayed for sometime and joined in the dance.

On Saturday morning the boy and I set out for Millagen for pailing posts. On arriving there however we were disappointed to find no one working at the Saw Mill, and no posts. A woman told us that the posts were at Grange Station and so we had there to go. They are 26/ a hundred this year. We found the folks of Cairdswell over when we came home.

Father was the only one at church on Sunday as the girl and the boy were both away.

We were repairing the road through the wood today and driving home turnips. I was also painting the stair and varnishing the front doors. We had the painter last week papering the lobby and staircase. I think we have made a good choice of paper.

1890 April
1ˢᵗ

We commenced sowing today and the land is in excellent condition. The past week has been dry and blowy. I ploughed the little parkie on Tuesday and Wednesday. It was firm but not too dry.

On Wednesday afternoon the steam mill came over the hill to us.

Thursday morning was nice and quiet and we were congratulating ourselves on getting such a nice day. About nine o'clock however the wind rose and it soon increased to such an extent that we had to stop. We got no more done that day, but on Friday we got everything finished up it being nice and quiet. The mill was also at Kirkton that day and I went over in the afternoon, but they had as many folk as could get wrought.

Father went over that afternoon to Cornhill Station and met Jessie and Jane and Willie Bidie came on Saturday.

I was ordering some corn and grass manure from Hutcheson, Turriff last week. I am going to give the barley some and the yavels. I am going to take the clover seeds from Drummond, Edinburgh this year.

7ᵗʰ

A week of fine weather in the first of April—I never saw—dry, fresh, and warm. Grass has made a good start and has a promising appearance. Everyone has been busy at the sowing during the week and the seed is being deposited in an excellent seed bed. I seldom or ever saw the lea harrow better.

We commenced sowing on Tuesday the 1ˢᵗ of April and on Wednesday we sowed the remainder of the lea.

On Saturday we sowed the ayvels at the back of the byres. The blacksmith has made a new brake-harrow for me and I am going to brake in the yavels and clean land with it. It is going to work very well I think and it will help to make a deeper mould.

Our visitors have been making calls nearly every afternoon all the week. They were at Cottartown and Kirkton on Wednesday at Swailend on Thursday and at Backies on Friday. On Sunday they were all at church with us.

Three of the ewes have dropped a lamb each. I do not think any of them would have lambed themselves as they are by strong lambs. I rise and look them in the middle of the night.

Tailor Reid, Berryhillock, died last week. Father was at the funeral on Thursday.

14th

The borrowing days have been rather long in coming this year, but they have far exceeded the proverbial number, and they have been very severe. In the first of the week we had strong gales of wind and excessively cold, while every morning the ground was white with snow. I saw ice on the watering trough on three mornings. I had a very disagreeable job sowing manure—one afternoon it being very blowy. I have given the yavels about 2 cwts. to the acre of millers xx corn manure. I am also going to give the barley some.

We sowed the yavels in the den on Wednesday and the clean land on Saturday.

On Tuesday Jane and Jessie left for Cairdswell. Willie and Father went over on Thursday. I was to go to the market with a fat cow but I sold her the day before so I kept at the harrows. Cattle of every kind are selling well just now. Beef is worth 63/ per cwt.

Father came home from Cairdswell on Saturday night and I went over on Sunday. We were all at church but it was a strange minister. Willie Bidie came to Muttonbrae with me in the evening.

28th

I have been very busy during the past two weeks. The weather has been all that could be desired for letting the work get on, indeed I do not think I ever remember a better seedtime. It has been cold and frosty however and as yet there has been very little growth. We would be glad now of a bite of grass for the sheep but we have abundance of turnips for the cattle. We have not got a large crop of lambs but they are good lambs. We lost one through carelessness, and there are two not lambed yet. I am not sure if they are in lamb yet. Only one has a pair so we have just the eight. They have been more trouble to keep in the park since they lambed, and we got over Jamie Stephen last week to notice them.

I sold a fat cow and two stots the week before last. I did not intend selling the stots yet as we have a lot of turnips, but I got a good offer and so I let them go. They were 12 cwts. and I got 65/. I am afraid that beef will come down for there are a great many cattle in the country and everyone is keeping up because they have plenty of keep.

1890 October
3rd

It is now nearly twelve years since I began to write down my weekly transactions, and only twice during all that time, as far as I can remember, did I allow a week to slip. Once for a few weeks during harvest; and again for three months after returning from a visit to Edinburgh. Here however is a bigger gap than any of these. More than five months have elapsed since I set pen to paper in my Diary. The most natural excuse that might be given for this negligence is of course 'I had na time,' but this is an excuse which I fear we make for too many neglected duties, and I am inclined to think that we might find time to do far more little odds and ends if were we only to husband it better. During the coming winter I am going to set myself certain tasks, and I shall try and give an account in my Diary of how I succeed. What tasks are to be, I have not yet fully determined.

Before commencing my regular writing I should like to give a sketch of the more interesting incidents, which have occurred during the summertime. Chief among these, has been the appearance amongst us of a little stranger. At nine o'clock on Monday morning the 2nd day of June I was presented with a nice baby boy.

The month of June is certainly a most eventful one in our family history. My grandfather and grandmother were married in June. Father was born in June, and married in June, and now another birth has to be chronicled in the merry month of June. At eleven o'clock on Sabbath night I went for Dr. Robb and he was very prompt in his attendance. I must also testify to his kindness and attentiveness during Katie's long and slow recovery. She was three weeks before she was able to get her bed made, and weary weeks they must have been to her. It was also other three weeks before she was anything like her former self, or able to attend to her ordinary duties. But although her recovery was slow, she never had any back turn, and very thankfull we felt to our Heavenly Father who had restored her to her wanted health and strength again.

We had old Mrs. Seivwright for a month after baby was born, and Elsie was also very attentive and staid with us for ten days or so. He was christened on the 31st of July, and we have named him Alec Duncan after his only uncle. May it be God's will to spare him to be a blessing to us, and may it ever be our great concern to teach him first the fear of The Lord which is the beginning of wisdom.

Our friends who were going to Australia left us in the end of April. They went back to Edinburgh for a few days to get their things in order, and on the 20th of April they set sail from London in the steam ship Orizaba, more than a thousand souls being on board. We heard from them twice during the voyage, and an excellent passage they got. Jane and William stood it out well, but Jessie I fear had not enjoyed the sail much. She was very sick at first, and she then took a cold and had to apply to the Doctor. However, they landed safely at Melbourne on the 4th of June, and after visiting Mary and Andrew at Stratford and staying a week or so with them, they returned to the capital, where they have taken a four roomed house with the intention of keeping lodgers. It being winter there, the dull time of the year, Willie did not get much work at first, but after a few weeks, he was pretty steadily employed, and his wages are ten shillings a day.

During the months of April and May we enjoyed excellent weather, and the seeds were got in, in good condition. The first half of the turnips land was also got well cleaned, but in the beginning of June we had a good deal of rain. We sowed some early yellows at Whitsunday which have done very well, but the rest of the land was all to make after that, and although we gave it an extra lot of work I was far from being satisfied with it. We sowed them on the 13th and 16th of June, and although they came well enough up to the hoe, I do not think they are to be a very heavy crop as the tops have kept too near the ground.

In the first of June, cereals were well advanced, and had the appearance of being an extraordinary crop. That month and the following one however were dull and cold, and the hopes of an early harvest were gone. Barley kept up its good appearance, and is in general an excellent crop, but oats after turnips fell away greatly. Still in the district there is in general an excellent crop. We are to have more bulk I think than ever I saw us have.

The wet weather in June and July was greatly against the drying of fuel, and it was the first of August before many peats were driven, and they were only in middling condition then. A few dry days allowed the hay to be harvested in very good condition, and we also had a fair crop.

We had two weeks of very fine weather in the first of August and barley was fast changing colour. On the 27th however we had a tremendous spate, the burns being bigger than I have seen them for several years. The Flower Show was held on the 28th of August, and an excellent turn out of everything. The day was also all that could be desired. We had two entries of honey and one of gooseberries and peas. First for honey super and third for clover sections, were all the prizes. It has been a very bad summer for the bees, I had no swarms and the poorest yield of honey since ever I commenced beekeeping. I have sold none yet, but I would expect the price to be rather better than for some years back.

We commenced the harvest on 12th September just a week later than last year. We had William Gray this year again by the day, and I engaged a woman for the harvest in Peter Fair. Harvest wages were up this year, women getting from £3 to £3.15 and bandsters from £4 to £5. We had excellent harvest weather for the first two weeks and we were busy at the cutting. Ardiecow sent down a lifter and bandster for two days, and we made good speed. We just had eight yokins of the reaper only the hallow in the den had all to be scythed.

We took clyack on the 24th and on the 10th October it was all in the cornyard. It is the largest cornyard ever I saw us have. There are 21 stacks but they are bigger than ordinary. I am expecting 18 qrs. barley and 100 qrs. oats. We were Ardiecow on the 16th October and gave them a days cutting with the reaper. We were also back yesterday the 15th and gave them a spell at the leading. His crop is not heavy.

On Tuesday we were at Limestones leading. They have a splendid crop and as the weather for the last few days has been remarkably fine it was in splendid condition.

21st

We had some extra fine days last week and some extra bad ones. Since Wednesday it has been cold and stormy, the wind in the north and a good deal of rain. There are no stooks in Deskford now however except on Ardiecow and he has more than the half to take in yet. We finished off on the 13th having been four weeks and three days, just one day later than last year. We got little done out of doors in the end of the week the weather being so boisterous.

I had some corn to the mill on Saturday for meal. It weighed 40½ lbs, but the miller was saying they had been getting as heavy as 45 lbs. I was very well pleased with the turn out of grain however.

Father was not been well for the last two days. He went to Cairdswell the last Cornhill market day and when he came home on Friday he felt very tired and he has never been right since. He sent for the Dr. on Friday last but he has been a little better the last two days again.

I was the only one at church on Sunday. The minister gave us a thanksgiving sermon so I expect there will be no thanksgiving day this year. He intimated that the sacrament would be dispensed on the first

Sabbath of Nov. and Mr. Birnie, Speymouth, is to preach on the fast day.

27th

There was only one good day all last week, and we were very fortunate in getting the good of it. I went over to Kirkton in the morning for the gig and Katie and I set out for Cairdswell. It was a splendid day and we got there about half past ten. Geordie was in the chilled plow and I went a few rounds with him before he unyoked. He has not a very big cornyard this year. Of course he will have more grain than us, but I scarcely think he has any more bulk of straw. He has his early potatoes lifted but a good many of them are diseased. He intended going over to Finnygaud in the afternoon but were too long in starting. We got home by seven o'clock.

The first of the week was warm and showery. On Tuesday and Wednesday we were pulling out topdressing lime and earth I commenced the plough that afternoon.

Seivwright was in the plough the most of Thursday, Friday and Saturday were stormy, showery days, but I scarcely expected to see so much snow as there was on Sunday morning. There was two inches at all event but in the upper end of the parish there was none.

I was the only one at church on Sunday. Mr. Park intimated that a thanksgiving day for the good harvest would be held on Wednesday week, when Mr. Kennedy minister of Birnie would preach.

It has been very stormy today with driving hail showers. I was down to Cullen in the forenoon to try and sell my honey. After a good deal of bargaining I gave it to James Grant for 9d for the best and 7d for the second quality. In the afternoon I went over to Auchip to try and buy some ewes, but he had none to sell but a few old ones.

1890 November
3rd

We were going to lift the potatoes today (and a very nice day we would have got) but there was a lot of rain between Saturday and Sunday and the land was too wet. We were casting a little bit drain in the Den and in the afternoon I went to Cullen for a 2 cwts. fencing wire. I have only got a few hours ploughing all the week.

I went to Cullen with my honey on Tuesday afternoon and brought home a load of tiles with me. On reading the newspaper that evening I saw that there were to be some Cheviot ewes for sale at the Keith Auction Mart on Wednesday.

I accordingly set out next morning and went over past Kirkton thinking to get the shalti but she was just going away to the smiddy to be shoed. Going past the Backies however I got Miss McWillie's pony and was in Keith by ten o'clock. There were about a hundred sheep and twenty cattle at the sale but trade was very dull. I bought 10 ewes for 24 shillings a head. It was gimmers that I should have liked but there is no getting them except you go to Aberdeen or Inverness.[8]

As Thursday was also the Fast Day in Keith Willie came down with me, he taking the pony while I drove the sheep. A good congregation turned out to hear Mr. Birnie on Thursday, but I do not think he has improved much since last year.

Mr. Park had no one assisting him on Sunday but he spoke very well himself. The morning was very rainy but it cleared up before church time.

10th

I have only got one days ploughing since I wrote last, it having been a very wet week. Of course there has been no potato lifting, and I don't know when there will. The earth is just as wet as it can be.

Wednesday was a thanksgiving day for the recent good harvest. We had Mr. Kennedy minister of Birnie preaching. He is quite a young man but a very good preacher. His text was Isaiah. It was a wet day however, and there was a very thin congregation.

Thursday was a cold blowy day. We were putting some extra wires on the fences for the sheep.

We were winnowing on Friday morning and cleaning harnesses the rest of the day. It was wet.

Saturday was a good day and I went to Portsoy with a load of corn. Katie went with me as she was going to buy some winter clothing. It was potato oats and it weighed 43 lbs. The price was 17/.

Saturday all night and Sunday all day it rained without ceasing.

Father was the only one at church as I was town keeper. Uncle George came up with him for church. He went up to the Backies the night before as Bidie is there just now. Father brought home word from the church that Mr. Proctor, Ardoch, died on Friday night. A shock of paralysis was the cause of death I believe and he was ill only a few hours. He was 78 years of age.

We were at the fences today again.

17th

We have been among the potatoes today and it has been a splendid day, but the land is still very wet. We had a good strength however and we lifted 10 loads. We had three hands from Ardiecow and a

---

[8] gimmers, young ewes.

woman hired from Milton. The champions are a very good crop and very few of them diseased. They are also splendid quality.

We were all at church on Sunday. It was frosty in the morning but it tunred cloudy and there were some showers in the afternoon.

Mr. Park intimated that he was going to open a Bible Class in the church at three o'clock.

Saturday was a fine day and I was ploughing.

Thursday was Cornhill market, but very few cattle went past this. I was to go with a calving quey but I sold her that morning to go to the Seafield Arms Hotel, Cullen. The price was £18 but I think she was well sold.

I was at Hallow Fair on Wednesday. Wages are much the same as at last term but I hear that a good many men are not engaged. Boys were in demand and getting good wages. I engaged Alex Findlay from Bauds of Cullen for £4.

24th

We had some very fine days last week. We were busy at the potatoes again on Tuesday but there had been a shower during the night and the land was very soft. The Magnum Bonums were scarcely so good a crop as the Champions and the 'Sandy McKay's' were badly diseased.

Wednesday was a splendid day and we got the land harrowed. I reckon there are about 18 loads.

We ploughed part of the land on Thursday. I was at a meeting that evening of the Committee of the Temperance Society. We are going to have a meeting in the month of January something the same as was last New Year.

On Friday evening Katie and I were over at Kirkton at tea. Old Kirkton is always in his ordinary health and going about.

We were at church on Sunday and got a very vigourous sermon from Mr. Park. He was advocating the cause of missions and at the close of the service he intimated that the elders were to call and get subscriptions from the schemes of the church.

1890 December
1st

Four days of very hard frost. Seldom indeed do we have it so severe, so early in the season. Being quiet however it was excellent weather for thrashing and we were fortunate in getting one of the fine days.

Lamb was at Careston on Tuesday and Wednesday. Imlach however was at Oathillock on the latter day and we had to go there, while I hired a woman to go to Careston.

We had Lamb on Thursday and a better day we could not have wished. We thrashed six and a half hours and I am expecting 40 qrs. of grain.

We had the barley down to Glenglassaugh on Saturday. There were 15 qrs. and it weighed 54 lbs except a few qrs. from the top of the stacks which was only 52. We are to let the oats stand for a week, as they are like to rise in price a little.

Imlach was thrashing at Kirkton on Friday, and it was also a good day. There was not an extra time out of barley and it only weighed a ½ lb more than ours.

Father and I were at church on Sunday. Mr. Park was from home and we had the old school master from Aberdeen again. The subject of his discourse was the unbelief of the inhabitants of Nazareth. 'Prejudice and envy were the two principal causes of this unbelief, and we might be apt to think', he said, 'that had we seen the many mighty works which Jesus did, and witnessed the extraordinary miracles which he performed we could not have done other than believe on his name.' Far more strange was it however, that so many were unbelieving in this nineteenth century, when the proofs of Christ's Messiahship were so many and so well established.

Today we were taking in straw and covering the potatoes.

8th

There has not been much frost during the past week but there has been a good deal of rain. We had a hired woman on Tuesday and were going to store turnips. The rain was on however before we had pulled an hour and it rained all day. We were dressing corn, and chopping firewood. Next morning I had the corn over to the mill, and in the afternoon I commenced to plough lea. It is very firm yet however for all the rain.

The steam mill was at Ardiecow on Thursday afternoon. His stacks were in good condition, and the grain of excellent quality. He weighed it up to 44 lbs but the natural weight was more. We had a few friends at tea that evening. Mr. & Mrs. Cowie, Inaltrie. James and David Smith, and Elsie, Alec and Miss Duncan.

We all started the pulling of the turnips on Saturday again, and it being a fine day we got on famous. It was swedes we were pulling but they are not nearly the crop they were last year, a good many of them having canker. The seed which I bought are better turnips, but that which came from Drummond has run to seed more than the others. We got 33 loads gathered and covered before it got dark.

Sunday was frosty. Father had a cold and did not go to church. Mrs. Stephen came over to see us, and Jane McCrae came up from church with us. Mr. Park gave us a very good sermon from the text,

'Be careful for nothing but in everything by prayer and supplication, with thanksgiving let your requests be made known unto God.' 'Be careful for nothing' he said did not mean that we were to take no care, but that we were not to be over anxious. We had a letter from Australia from Mary in the end of the week. Jessie was up staying with her again, but she has not been very strong since she went out. Mary is always highly pleased with everything.

15ᵗʰ

This forenoon I was ploughing lea but it was extremely hard, and I went to the stubbles in the afternoon.

Saturday and Sunday were very frosty. Katie was not at church yesterday as she has a bad cold. It commenced in her throat, but it is now into her head. I hope she may soon get over it.

We were pulling yellow turnips on Friday and we gathered them on Saturday but there was a little frost in them. We had 30 loads and we have 40 of swedes.

Father and I were both at Cornhill market on Thursday. There were not many fat cattle and they were a very dull sale 60/ being offered only for the very top. Keepers were brisker and more especially calves. I bought a yearling quey for £8. I think it was the cheapest beast I saw in the market. We took over some potatoes and meal with us for Lizzie and Maggie, and Father had up the cart to Cairdswell. After I came home I went up to Backies to pay some oilcake and order some more. Miss McWillie is not feeding so high this winter as formerly and she has not so many of them either. It will not pay now to buy cattle to feed, the beef is so cheap.

22ⁿᵈ

The Almanac says this is the shortest day, but we had plenty darker days than this has been. We have had a week of dryer weather I believe than has been for two months. Except a slight shower of snow there has been no rainfall. On Tuesday we were pulling swedes all day and except a few drills we have them all lifted now.

We gathered them on Wednesday afternoon, 29 loads.

There was a sharp frost on Thursday and we commenced to drive out dung. We are driving the rank into a 'middin' and putting the short on to the stubbles to plough down.

We were at it again on Friday.

On Saturday we went to Portsoy with 9 qrs. of potato oats. The roads were nice and dry with the frost. The corn weighed 43½ lbs, and the price was 17/3.

Willie Cowie, Finnygaud, came over to see us on Sunday. I was making ready to go to church when he came, but did not go then, as he was not inclined.

We were at the dung today again as the frost is still keeping a hold. Turnips that are not lifted will be damaged I fear, there being nothing to protect them.

We have got a pony since I wrote last. A subscription was lately made to get a new pony for the postman and Alec Duncan and A. Morrison, Berryhillock, went to Keith market and bought me one. The post only had it a few days however when it turned dead lame, and so another had to be bought and so this is the first one. They asked if I would keep it for a week or so to see if it would get sound. It is not lame in the least now, and although it is old it is a grand eater. I am going to try it in the plough whenever it comes fresh. If it works I believe I might do worse than buy it. As the mare is in foal we would be better of it in the spring.

29th

Driving out dung and taking in straw and turnips has been our week's work. We put all the dung out on Friday. It has always been frosty but never very severe and there has been no more snow.

We heard today that Mr. McCombie, Leitchestown, had taken paralytic shock when over at Inaltrie and was not able to be taken home. This is the third attack he has had.

It has been my custom at the close of the year to take a look back over the year that is past and give a short sketch of the different seasons.

Taking it all together the winter of 89 and 90 was an exceptionally mild one. Indeed, it was thought to be too mild, and would have been more healthy had there been more frost and snow. An epidemic of influenza prevailed over nearly the whole globe and the death rate was exceptionally high, and even yet you will hear of the death of those who never fully recovered from its effects.

January and February were both very open months and work was well advanced. A few patches in early districts were sown in the end of the latter month.

We had a rather sharp snowstorm in March but it was not of long continuance. Sowing in general begun in the first of April, and I seldom remember a finer month. The seed was all deposited in an excellent seed bed.

May was also a good month for clearing the land and sowing turnips. An unusual sight in the month of May was the tremendous quantities of turnips everywhere to been seen. In fact there were hundred of loads never eaten.

June and July were both wet months and late turnips were sown in bad condition while crops of every kind made but little progress. Hay was a fair crop, although deficient in clover, and was harvested in good condition. It was a bad season for peats however, and although the most of them was got home they were far from dry.

August and September were better months with more sunshine, which greatly helped the ripening of the crops. In this district the cereal crops were far above an average. Barley was the best on clean land, but it has scarcely thrashed in proportion to its bulk, and the weight of the grain has scarcely come up to expectations 54 and 55 lbs being the usual sum. Oats on the other hand are thrashing and weighing remarkably well. We have had 6½ qrs. on the acre of potato oats and some of it weighed 43½ lbs.

The harvest was a long and protracted one. In late districts stooks were seen standing in the month of November. That month and the preceding one were both exceedingly wet, and ploughing has been proceeding but slowly, in fact I never saw so many stubbles to plough at the New Year. Turnips in general are only a fair crop. There is a good deal of finger and toe, and many of the early sown ones have rotted. A good few of the swedes have also run to seed. Before harvest it was thought potatoes were going to be a complete failure, as the early ones were nearly all diseased. When lifting time came however it was found that the late varieties were comparatively free from disease, and they were also a good crop. They are selling at 1/6 a bushel, I believe. Barley is much about the same price as last year viz. 25/ but it is rather looking down. Oats are cheaper than at this date last year. The best variety of common oats bringing only 15/6. The greatest cause of complaint among farmers however, is the price of beef. 60/ being the top price for top quality. Keepers are a good deal more for their weight that that however and more especially calves and year olds.[9] Calving cows have also been selling very high.

A Journal of My Life and Everyday Doings

1891 January
12th

After nearly four weeks of frost a soft, fresh, westerly wind is again blowing. It has been very seasonable weather for holding Christmas and the New Year, but farmers have been chafing a little at being kept so long from the plough.

---

[9] keepers, animals, in this case calves, kept for fattening.

On New Years day Geordie Cowie and Annie and little George came over to see us. Everything was very quiet in Deskford there being no shooting match this year. A week past at Sunday we had a fall of three inches of snow, and since then the frost has been very severe.

On Monday I went over to Finnygaud, it being Auld Yule. As the roads were still slippery I went to the smiddy and got the shalt sharpened before I started. There was quite a family gathering at Finnygaud, twenty sitting down to dinner. They have two young calves already, and they have some good two year olds feeding, but think three year olds are all away.

We went to Portsoy with two loads of corn on Wednesday. The price is up 6d the quarter. It was potato oats and weighed 43½ lbs and we got 17/9.

Thursday was Cornhill market. I went over with a two year old stot intending to buy a younger one, but I bought him home unsold. Fat was a very stiff sale. Keepers were not so dear as formerly, but year olds were exceptionally dear.

We went back to Portsoy again on Friday. As we had 10½ qrs. we got a cart from Sandy McKay and took the shalt. The roads were very slippery and we had to be very careful, but no accident befell us.

On Saturday I went over to see the folks at Hillfolds. The bairns had all been bad with the hooping cough but are now keeping better. Mr. Ross bought a calving quey in the market, and he has two young calves already. He has sold two fat cattle, and he is feeding two farrow cows. His year olds are far better than last year. That evening it turned fresh, during the night a strong breeze of wind got up and next morning the snow was all away.

I was ploughing stubbles today but they were rather soft.

Last Wednesday evening there was a meeting to the members of The Temperance Society. Part of the evenings programme was a debate, 'Is a Teetotal Farmer justified in selling his barley to a Distiller?' Mr. & Mrs Gordon supported the affirmative while I had the negative.[10] There was a very keen debate good many of the members taking part, while Mr. Morrison, the Chairman summed up in a very able manner. Those present declined to vote however.

19th

We have got a whole week at the plough and every one has kept busy. In the first of the week I was ploughing down dung, but in the end of the week I was at the lea. Father was driving home some turnips with the shalt.

---

[10] Printed in Appendix 2.

I did not go to church yesterday as a cow was like to calve. She dropped a fine black cow calf in the afternoon. We are going to put it to suck along with the quey's calf. She calved a week ago. I am going to commence and give the cattle some potatoes now I think as I am afraid the turnips will run short. I am giving the feeders 2½ lbs of bruised oats and 1 lb of oilcake while the calves are getting 1 lb oilcake.

26th

We have had a week of frost again and there has been no ploughing. The roads have been almost impossible with ice. We were putting in a few yards of a drain in the stubbles.

On Friday evening there was a concert in the Schools in connection with the Temperance Society. It was a fine evening and there was a good attendance. It was all local performers. Mr. Reid had a choir who rendered several choruses in good style. Miss Duncan sang Bonnie Prince Charlie. Miss Morrison gave Rothesay Bay. Miss Milne, The Blue Bells of Scotland. Miss Hay, Twas drink that killed my Darling and Miss H. J. Morrison, I'm glad my heart's my ain. There were also several readings and recitations. I gave the 'Seven Ages of Women' as a recitation.

There is word of Mr. Park having a Soiree in the end of February. I was up one evening seeing Ardiecow's Canadians. He has not got them very fat yet, but he is thinking of selling them as his turnips are going done. Their average girth is fully 6ft 4 and I valued them at £16.15 the head. He got them in the month of August and they cost him £12.

1891 February
2nd

Fine fresh weather. We have got a whole week at the plough. If the old saying about Candlesmas be correct we have more than the half of the winter to go yet for it has been both fair and clear. I have been ploughing at the stubbles for clearing and have got them finished now. The lea is the stiffest to plough I ever tried.

Katie and I were up at the Backies on Wednesday afternoon. Miss McWillie is not feeding so many cattle this winter, but she has a few of them in prime condition. I am increasing the corn and cake for ours now. They are getting 3¼ lbs oats and 1¼ cake and they are also getting about 5 lbs potatoes each. Beef is always a very stiff sale. It must be prime quality before you get £3. The potatoes have got up terribly in price during the past week or so £5 and even £6 being offered for the ton. This has been caused by Government buying up a large quantity of Champions to go to Ireland for seed. As soon as they have supplied prices will doubtless come down again.

9th

Although the weather has been fresh I have not ploughed much during the week. We were at the steam mill at James Gray's on Wednesday afternoon at Cultain on Thursday and at Careston on Friday. Cultain's barley was in very bad condition. Careston thrashed a stack of barley and 4 stacks of tares. The tares were well kept and fine and fresh.

I was ploughing yavels on Saturday and today. They are in grand conditon. We were all at church on Sunday. Mr. Park gave us a sermon from the text, 'Train up a child in the way he should go and when he is old he will not depart from it.'

16th

We had showers of snow and a little frost in the middle of the week, but the last three days have been remarkably fresh and warm. Turnip tops are commencing to grow, and Father says the berry bushes are all budding. He has been pruning at them for some days.

I have been ploughing yavels all the week and finished them on Saturday.

Wednesday forenoon was wet. We winnowed up 8 qrs. corn and as it cleared up at twelve o'clock I had it to Portsoy in the afternoon and got 17/3 for 43½ lbs. Father got James Gray's spring cart, and went over to Cairdswell that afternoon.

I went over to Cornhill market on Thursday and bought a calving quey—a black poll for £17. She is scarcely two years old and her time was up yesterday. Katie and I were at a grand party that evening at Limestones. It was the 'fire kindling' and a proper one it was. There were over twenty guests, and after tea we had some music and songs. Mary has got a splendid new piano just now, and we also had two fiddlers. The tables having been cleared away dancing was commenced, and we all kept hearty until past twelve o'clock. Supper was then laid and a grand supper it was too. There was a round of beef and a roast turkey, two cold fowls and a roast duck. Then there was plum pudding, apple pie, prunes and macaroni, pears and jellies. We left between 2 and 3 o'clock but the others were started the dancing again.

I was town keeper on Sunday but I went over to the Free Church with Alec Duncan in the evening. It was a Schoolmaster from Buckie who was preaching, but there was not a large congregation.

I commenced to plough clean land today.

23rd

A week of finer weather no one could have wished. There has been no rain, and everything is getting extremely dry. Sometimes a little frost in the mornings and then bright sunshine all day. I have been ploughing clean land all the week, and it is in splendid condition. I have it all ploughed I will get in the meantime as we are going to put in a few drains below the house.

I sold two cattle to Ardiecow on Tuesday. I fear we are to be rather short of turnips, and as he offered a good price I thought I might do worse than let them go. One of them was 6 ft in girth, the other an inch more, and the price was £38. I believe a butcher would not have given me more than £30. 56/ and 57/ a cwt is all they are giving just now.

Alec Duncan was up on Friday evening and I bought the shalt from him for £6.15.

We were all at church on Sunday. Mr. Park intimated that a congregational Soiree would be held in the church on Wednesday evening.

1891 March
2nd

The above mentioned Soiree was held on the evening named. A most beautiful evening it was—bright moonlight, mild and quiet. There was consequently a very large turn out, over four hundred it was reckoned. Tea having been served by a large band of stewards and stewardesses, Mr. Park made a few introductory remarks, and altogether I was very well pleased with his conduct in the Chair. The first speaker was Mr. Lumsden the new minister of Grange. He is quite a young man and is a fluent speaker. As he is to be married this week he made the excuse that he had not had time to get up a lengthy speech. He believed greatly he said in Social meetings, but would prefer them in the form of a conversazione! Mr. McDonald, Cullen, was the next speaker and he gave us a rather lengthy address. To begin with, he had a message to deliver from Mr. Mackintosh he said. Having been in Aberdeen lately and speaking to Mr. Mackintosh about coming to the Deskford Soiree, he was told to remember him to all his friends there, and to say that although now removed from our midst his heart was still in the old place. Mr. McDonald then went on to speak of the necessity for both pastor and people making all due preparation for attending the services of the sanctuary. That the minister should have a well prepared sermon was not enough, the people also should prayerfully prepare themselves for hearing the word. The newly placed minister of The Ord—Mr. Aitken came next. He seems to be a very earnest man, but no great speaker. The next item on the programme Mr. Park said was Mr. McIntyre, Portknockie, but this worthy bachelor objected altogether being called an item. Mr. McIntyre spoke a good deal in a humorous strain, but having a very weak voice he could not be heard far from the pulpit, and toward the end of his discourse they turned exceedingly noisy. The folks could not expect great speeches he said, as the tickets were far too cheap. They ought to have been a shilling instead of sixpence and then there might have been something over, which would have helped to paint the church, which was greatly in need of renovating he said. He was greatly against drinking and smoking but believed in a cup of good tea. Mr. Reid of course had his choir in full strength and between each of the speeches gave some beautiful hymns.

The weather still continues dry and work of every kind is now well advanced. Careston and Nether Blairock have been sowing tares and in several places a good breadth of oats has been put in. We have been draining nearly all the week and they have been nice and dry. I have the clean land ploughed close to the turnips. I have still three or four days ploughing of lea, but unless it come rain I fear it will be too hard to plough.

9th

A change of weather fairly—severe frost and intense cold. The whole week has been stormy with strong gales of wind. We were driving stuff off the road several yokins. We are making up a hollow with it at the end of the clean land.

Friday was Keith market. Father went up with Alec Duncan. It was a very stiff market, fat cattle being almost unsaleable, 56/ is the highest they are giving just now.

On Saturday we had a coating of snow. I went over to see the folks at Cairdswell in the afternoon. Anna is far from well yet.

I was the only one at church on Sunday as the servant was away and Father had sore eye. I went down this forenoon to see Mr. Michie about some brushwood, I also spoke to Mr. Smith about a porch for the kitchen door. He is to call in by some day and see it. The V.S. came up in the afternoon to see a stot that is not well. His stomach seems out of order he says. He ordered nearly a bottle of linseed oil and he is to send up some powders. He is an agent for insuring horses. I insured the in-foal mare for a twelve month and her foal for a month for the sum of £25. The premium is to be £2.5. I have the sheep on the Hill just now as they got a pluck of heather. They are getting a large barrowful of cut turnips, but I was obliged to put them to the Den tonight for shelter.

16th

March weather fairly. A good deal of snow has fallen and we have had severe frost. The sun however melts a good deal of the snow in the afternoons and yesterday and today being a little soft some black patches are beginning to appear again.

I went to Portsoy on Tuesday with a load of corn. The price is now 16/ for common corn and it weighed 43½ lbs. There was a cow calving when I came home at 2 o'clock, but she did not calve until half past six and the calf was dead. As she did not <u>clean</u> I went down for the V.S. on Thursday morning and he took the clean from her and sent up some powders. She is now keeping better. We bought another calf for £3.17.6 and put it and the queys on to suck. The bought calf has turned stiff in the legs however, and I went down to the farrier today again and got some ammonia liniment to rub into its joints as they are swollen. We are going to take it away from the cow, and I bought another today from Jeffrey Sinclair for the same money.

I was at a meeting on Thursday of the Temperance Society. It was proposed to make the business meeting in May a social meeting and instead of having tea I was on for having something in the form of supper. The proposal however was not very warmly received a great many difficulties appearing in the way but the ladies were to be consulted.

On Friday and Saturday I was driving sand for James Gray's new house from Little Cultain.

23ʳᵈ

The weather has improved a little but it is still stormy. I have been ploughing the remainder of the lea. George Cowie and Annie were over on Friday. Annie went across to Swailand to see Mrs Reid who has been laid up for some time with a sore leg.

On Saturday I went over to Kirkton for the gig and Katie and I went in to Portsoy. I went past Redhythe to buy some seed corn. I also spoke for 5 qrs. for Miss McWillie. Mr. Wighton grows nothing but sandy oats, so we should get it clean.

30ᵗʰ

I was ploughing clean land in the first of the week, and the land was fine and dry. Had it continued sowing would soon have been commenced but the weather turned very stormy in the end of the week again.

Thursday and Friday morning's it was snowing and blowing excessively. There was a Social meeting in the Schools on Friday evening in connection with the Horticultural Society. There was a crowded house. After tea Mr. Michie gave an address on Botany, with which I was greatly pleased. Some Cullen ladies and gentlemen also gave solos, readings and recitations. A two hours dance finished off.

I went down to Glassaugh Station on Saturday morning for some manure from Kynoch, 10½ cwts corn manure and 4½ potato manure. I am also taking a ton of XX from Hutcheson, and I have ordered the seeds from him. I also went into Banff on Saturday and ordered a metal roller, and an American pump, and three metal troughs for Kirkton. Our old pump is completely done.

1891 April
28ᵗʰ

Being so busy getting in the seed, the ewes lambing and the many other items which call for attention at this season. I have got no time for writing all the month of April. Had it not been that I am sitting watching the mare, as she is likely to foal tonight, I might not have been writing yet. She is just a week past her time today, and I have been beside her the last two nights. There has been wax at her teats since Sunday, and this evening the milk was running out. We have had an exceptionally good seedtime, and the cereals are all in now in this district. There has scarcely been a shower all the month of April but it has been terribly cold. There has scarcely been any growth yet, and turnips in many cases are done.

I was up at Backies on Thursday last, and saw several of them with the cattle out grazing. We have more than two weeks turnips yet, but we will sorely need them all as the sheep are getting a few, there being no grass yet. Eleven of the ewes are lambed, and there is just one pair. I am doubtful if two of them are in lamb. They are all good lambs, and I am giving the ewes about 4 lbs oilcake and 4 lbs corn.

We were greatly surprised and shocked on Saturday morning (the 25ᵗʰ) when a boy came up and told us that Old Kirkton had been got dead in bed. He has been ailing for the last five weeks and not taking much food. The Dr. was seeing him several times but he was never confined to his bed. He was out as usual on Friday and went to bed about nine o'clock. Alec (who sleeps in a bedroom close beside him) heard him making some movement on the night. He asked what time it was and on Alec looking he found it a quarter past three. About half an hour afterwards he asked again how he felt himself and he answered 'fine'. On Alec rising at five o'clock he thought he was sleeping and went out softly so as not to disturb him, but the poor old man was past all disturbance for his spirit had quietly flown away. When Elsie came but a short time afterwards she was terribly shocked to find him dead.

The last time I saw him was on Thursday, which was the fast day. I knew a great difference on him. He was very restless, but he was quite resigned and it was very touching to hear him speak with so much thankfulness of the long life, which he had enjoyed; and how free from sickness it had been. He was quite prepared to go now he said, whenever it should be God's will to take him. He was eighty past at

October and it was truly wonderful for a man of so great an age, never scarcely to have been a whole day in bed.

The funeral was on Wednesday and it was very largely attended. He was buried in the churchyard of Botriphnie beside his wife Margaret Shearer who died 23rd October 1857.

1891 November
2nd

Once more the long days of summer have come and gone, the busy days of harvest are past, and the short dull days of winter are upon us. During the busy season I could not find any time for writing, but now when the evenings are lengthing out I shall once more put pen to paper, and strive to jot down some few items, which may be interesting to look over in after years.

The summer of 1891 will be a long remembered one, but indeed it scarcely deserves the name of summer.

April and May were good months for putting in the seed but very cold and no growth.

On Sunday the 24th of May there was a good fall of snow, and several degrees of frost and braird and grass looked miserable for sometime afterwards. The month of June was remarkably dry but still cold, and pasture was in most cases very bare. A good deal of what was intended for hay having to be eaten. We had abundance and I bought other three stirks, but I fear when selling time comes there will not be a large margin of profit. In the end of June some rain fell and the weather turning warmer we had two weeks of excellent growth. From showers however it turned to daily rains, and from daily rains to spates, and the month of July and August was nothing but rain. June having been dry of course hay was a very poor crop, and it is selling as high as 10d the stone. We had just three loads off 1½ acres.

Corn and barley were fully an average crop, but terribly laid with the rains. In some cases there was a good deal of second growth among barley, and the quantity and quality are both inferior. I have scarcely heard of any coming up to the standard weight. Oats are always the most profitable crop in a wet summer. There may not be an extra turnout of grain but I think it will be a very good sample and of fair weight. The price of both oats and barely are advancing, the former being quoted from 20/ to 22/ and the latter from 27/ to 30/. The cause of this advance in price is partly the limited quality in this country, but principally the great deficiency of the crop in Russia. Except wheat, the exportation of all other kinds of grain has been prohibited. In some parts of The Czar's dominions there is said to be terrible famine; so great that the people are dying for hunger.

Our potatoes were a good crop but a good many of them diseased. In general however, there is a great deficiency and already they are selling at 3/ a bushel.

The greatest loss to the farmer however is the failure of the turnip crop. I many cases they are a complete failure, while the best of them are not much more than half a crop. We have more than 2 acres not worth pulling. We drive the cattle on to them and eat up what is. As a consequence the price of feeding stuffs is rising, linseed cake having advanced £1 per ton since the month of August. I got a cask of feeding treacle about that time and have been cutting straw and mixing it. The cattle are very fond of it, and the cask is nearly done.

The summer being so wet, no peats were got home. The week before we commenced the harvest however was dry, and we went up and took out what was dry and set up the others, and when harvest was finished we also took them home in excellent condition.

I never drove peats in October before, and many are driving still. A better harvest we could not have got. We were just three weeks from the time we commenced until it was all in the cornyard. There were some tremendous gales of wind however, and some corn was shaken.

On the evening of the 14th October we had a perfect hurricane of wind and rain, and much damage was done. About the middle of October we had a week of showery weather, but since then it has been delightful. Calm and dry, sometimes a little frost in the mornings, but bright sunshine throughout the day. I have just seen ice once this season on 29th October.

Cattle are still being kept out of doors. When it was seen that the turnip crop was to be a failure the price of store cattle came down more than £1 a head but beef is selling fairly well. At the present time you might realise from 63/ to 65/ per cwt. Store sheep are a very stiff sale.

I sold four ram lambs in July for 23/ thinking it a very small price. I have all the others still on hand, and will have difficulty to get rid of them I fear. I have been giving them corn and oilcake for a month past or so.

In the month of June our worthy pastor Mr. Park was married to a Miss Ruth, daughter of a salesman in Aberdeen. A sister was staying with them at the Manse and one day in the end of July the minister and her went to see the grounds of Cullen House, Mrs Park staying at home with a headache. When they returned Mrs Park could not be found, and although they searched all night no trace of her could be found. The fact of her being missing however was kept close except to a few, and next morning the minister went in to Aberdeen with an early train, thinking she had doubtless returned to her fathers, but No! They had heard no word of her. On returning to Cullen however, the news was brought to him that some fishermen had found her body at the foot of the rocks between Cullen and Portknockie. Mr. Park was almost beside himself with grief and it was three or four weeks before he could occupy his own pulpit again. Many were the surmises as to what could have been the cause, but nothing was known for certain. One thing however seems to give little cause for doubt her death was not the effects of an accident. Oh! how sad and how very sad! My heart bled for the poor man. The minister of one of the most desirable parishes in the north of Scotland. A stipend above the average of country ministers, a beautiful home, and a young and attractive wife, all these seemingly left nothing to make his cup of happiness full, and yet how soon was it dashed from his lips. How strange are God's dealings with man! And yet we know that 'all things work together for good to them that love God' May not this sad trial be a blessing in disguise, may it not be that 'tribulation which worketh patience.'

In the month of July James Stirling and James and Minnie Carmichael were North for their holidays and two weeks ago Lizzie and John Carmichael paid us a short visit. Lizzie's baby is a nice thriving boy, and she is looking remarkably well herself.

9th

We had the steam mill on Saturday afternoon, and it was nice and quiet. We thrashed in the close this year, and out the chaff into a shed to use with treacle. The grain did not turn out very well however and I fear the barley will be light. I was at Careston today. His barley is a good weight, some of it being 56 lbs.

I was at Keith market on Friday with Alec Duncan. It was very stiff market for all kinds of stock. Calving cows are generally selling well at this season, but they are a very low price in the meantime. A great many are being bought from the south, and the scarcity of keep is doubtless the cause. We have one for sell, and Alec Duncan bought a stot and quey from me on Friday for £23.

16th

I went to Portsoy on Tuesday last with two loads of corn, and brought home coals etc. The corn weighed 43 lbs and I got 23/6. Corn and barley are rising in price almost everyday. I would get 25/ for that same corn now. I am rather afraid however that the prices will not be long maintained. 54 lbs barley is giving 30/.

Wednesday was Hallow Fair. It was a very bad day. Wind and rain the whole day. I see by the papers that a great deal of damage has been done especially to shipping. It was not a large market but fees were a little up. I would have kept the boy we have, but he was asking too much wages. I engaged a boy, George Gray, for £6.10. Mr. & Mrs Ross, Hillfolds, came over in the morning, and he came down to the market, but we were home again by twelve o'clock.

Next day was Cornhill market. I had over a calving quey and 16 sheep. I had plenty of merchants but the prices were very small. Mr. Ross bought the quey for £14 and I sold 7 lambs and two ewes.

On Friday afternoon I went down to Glenglassaugh Distillery with a sample of the barely. The manager advised me to go into Portsoy as he thought I would get more for it there than he was giving. I sold it to Mr. Ewing for 27/ and weigh it up to 52 lbs.

I got railway bags and had it down to Glassaugh Station today. There was 17 qrs. but there is about 4 or 5 qrs. small barley.

23rd

There was ice on the watering trough for the first time, this morning. There has been frost more or less every morning during the past week, but it was always showery through the day, and on some days we had a good deal of rain. The frost today however has kept a hold, and tonight it is very keen. Some have commenced to plough lea. I still have about an acre of stubbles yet. We have been putting out the dung to plough down.

I went up to Craibston on Thursday evening to pay my lime. I was to go to Langlinburn to ask for Old Mr. McWillie but I met Elsie Duncan, who told me that he died that afternoon at two o'clock. He had taken a very bad turn on Monday morning, and never rallied again. He was 82 years of age, and I was at his funeral today. He was buried in Deskford Churchyard.

30th

The last day of November, and still the weather continues remarkably good. We have had a pretty hard frost on some days, and on Friday the roads were awfully slippery, there having been a shower of sleet the previous evening. We were driving out our dung last week, and we cleaned out the court. We put 20 loads of the rank into a dung pit and the rest on to the face to plough down.[11] We put 30 loads on to an acre for turnips, and 24 loads for potatoes.

On Friday afternoon I went down to Cullen. I was putting some money into the Bank, and I also put £2.5 into the savings bank in Duncan's came, being small sums which he had received. I was ordering some new harness from the saddler two collars and two

---

[11] rank, uncomposted dung.

bridles. The collars are to be 16/ each and the bridles 14/. I also bought a lantern and leggings.

I was in the plough today. Another yokin will finish the stubbles for turnips.

1891 December
7th

Fresh breezy days. The wind was on some days almost a gale, but there has been no snow and except today no frost. Everything is remarkably dry.

I finished the stubble on Tuesday and on Wednesday I tried the lea. I have seen it far firmer when I commenced.

I was ploughing down dung for potatoes on Thursday and on Friday and Saturday we were storing turnips. They are just about half a crop. We gathered 14 loads on Saturday afternoon. I would like to lift all the swedes and also some yellow ones, as the rabbits are chipping them.

The new woman and boy came home on Monday night. They are both going to do very well I think.

I was the only one at church on Sunday. Mr. Thomson, Skeith, was proclaimed. His intended was a teacher at Cullen for sometime— Robina Mary Gillie.

George Stephen was over yesterday. Kate and the baby are both keeping strong. It is about two months old now and is named William.

18th

I did not get written in the first of the week as another Kate and another baby were needing some attention. At five o'clock on Tuesday afternoon the 15th inst, a little baby girl appeared in our midst. I went into Portsoy on Monday for Mrs Seivwright, and we had Mrs Murray, Berryhillock, over as Mrs Gray is laid up with influenza. Katie is, as yet, making a very good recovery, and it is a nice strong baby, (so the wives say).

I went over to Cornhill market and sold the white quey for £12.2.6. It was a very small market and a dull sale for all classes of stock. I went up past Hillfolds with Mr. Ross and then went up to the Barry to see a foal of Mr. Taylor's. I offered him £12 but he was needing £14 so we did not make a bargain. I got a letter from him yesterday however saying I would get it at my offer so I went over for it today.

We had a good fall of snow on Tuesday evening but it turned to rain and most of it melts. The ground was white before however and it is not much broken yet. Yesterday was very frosty, but it has been soft today.

21ˢᵗ

Saturday and yesterday were two excellent days and the snow has been all blown away. I went to the mill and smiddy on Saturday morning and in the afternoon I went to the plough. There was an entertainment in the Schools on Friday evening in support of the funds of the Library. I did not go over but it had been a success I believe, there being a crowded house. It finished off with a dance. Mr. Smith was chairman.

Father and I were at church on Sunday. I saw Mr. Thomson and his newly wedded wife.

As we heard that Robert Gray was leaving his croft at Hoggie I went down to the Factor's Office today to see about it for George Stephen. There is 8½ acres and the rent at present is £9 but as the houses are to pay for, the rent is to be raised to £10 but I think it would be cheap yet. There are a great many after it however. Katie is always mending, but has not been up yet. This baby is very quiet.

28ᵗʰ

There has been no ploughing during the week, but still it has been very reasonable weather, and far from severe. It has been frosty every day, but generally quiet, and sometimes a good deal of sunshine. The steam mill was at Oathillock on Tuesday and at Knowes on Wednesday and both days were good for thrashing. None of them had a large outcome of barley however. I sent the boy over to Limestones on Thursday to assist them with the steam mill.

Friday was Christmas Day. Mr. & Mrs. Ross came over from Hillfolds to see us. They went down to Kirkton in the afternoon and I went to Tochineal Station for some linseed cake and cotton cake.

Saturday was a little soft and we took in some turnips.

Father and I were at church on Sunday. The minister gave us a very impressive sermon as to the close of the year, and when referring to the losses and sorrows which many had sustained during the past year he was greatly affected, remembering no doubt how his own cup of joy had been so suddenly dashed to the ground.

Today we were taking in straw, thrashing and winnowing.

A Journal of My Life and Everyday Doings

1892 January
22ⁿᵈ

What with nursing and other little odd and ends I have got no time to write any since the New Year. It has been very stormy weather since then, often high winds and we have also had a considerable fall of snow. At one time we had eight or nine inches, and there was also considerable drifting, roads, railways being partly blocked. The frost on some days was very severe. As we had some turnips stored we were at no inconvenience, but they could not have been in good condition putting them in the field. Beside providing food for the cattle we have done little else at farm work all the month.

We commenced to drive out dung today. Two weeks ago I went over to Buckie and bought some wood, and since then I have been making bar frame hives. I have got two finished. I have made them for open sided hanging frames as I thinking of buying an extractor and working for drained honey. I was taking a look into my hives one day and I find that some of them are in a very weak condition. I will need to give them some food directly.

I sold two fat stots last week to Mr. May for 63/ the cwt. He offered me £31.10 but I was wanting to see them weighed. They were just 10cwts 12lbs and the price came to £31.16.8. I think the day is not far distant when we will sell all our cattle by weight, and I decidedly think it ought to be so. I am beginning to fear that the turnips will go done before the month of May. The cows are getting about half the usual quantity twice a day. They get treacle and chaff at night and at nine o'clock 2½ lbs mixed oats and barley and 1½ lb cotton cake. The calves get chaff and treacle in the morning, a few turnips at dinnertime and 1½ lbs oilcake at nine o'clock beside all the barely straw they can eat with treacle upon it. I bought home the third cake last week.

26th

I was at Banff yesterday hearing the trial of George Smith, Limestones, on a charge of perjury. The beginning of the case was on this wise. About harvest time Mr. Garden, Begburn, says he sold George a foal. George denies he ever bought the foal. Mr. Garden then takes it to Cornhill and stables it, and summoned George Wilson to a small debt court. George went to court but said his name was not George Wilson but George Alexander Smith and produced his birth certificate. The Sheriff put him into the witness box and asked him if he ever went under the name of George Wilson or did business on his own account under that name. To this George answered 'no'. A short time after he was apprehended and lodged in gaol on a charge of perjury. He was liberated on bail of £20. The court room was crowded, and a great many witness were examined. Although there is no doubt but he had often gone under the name of George Wilson and signed himself as such, the Sheriff said that denying this did not imply perjury. Mr. Watt an eminent lawyer from Edinburgh defended George, and the jury after a short absence delivered an unanimous verdict of not guilty.

APPENDIX 1
A SELECTION OF POEMS BY JAMES WILSON

Spring

Some praise the beauty of the flowers, as beneath a Summer Sun, —
They scatter fragrance all around, in the merry month of June.
Some love the Autumn of the year, when ripe fruit the earth doth crown
And the green leaves change their lively shade, to red and russet brown.

Cold surly winter others say, is the best of all the year,
For then comes merry Xmas round, with joy and right good cheer.
And they love to see the ice-bound stream, and the snow-flakes as they go
To wrap up Old Mother Earth in her spread of white and fleecy snow.

But of all the seasons of the year, I love sweet Spring the dearest.
For then the fields are fresh and green, and all Nature looks her fairest.
How pleasant it is on a fresh Spring morn, to hearken the wee birds sing,
As each tiny minstrel adding its note, makes wood and valley ring.

But spring is the time for busy work, and no idlers there should be,
For the soil must be ploughed and harrowed and sowed,
if a full crop we must see,
How I love to see on an April morn, all the white sacks dotting the field,
With the sower sowing the seed as in faith, he expects it a crop to yield.

Our Youth is the Spring-time of our lives, and we all our seeds do sow,
Be they good or bad they shall all take root, and in after-years shall grow.
And as if in Spring we mispend our time, and sow not the proper seeds
In harvest the fields will no ripe fruit show, but a mess of noxious weeds.

Even so in our Youth, if we do not our words and actions guard,
Our after-life will no pleasure yield, but sorrow be all our reward.
But Oh! may it always be our Aim, As the years of youth fly past,
To sow in our hearts no seed but the good and true for truth shall last.
So that when the harvest of life shall come, and our seed to fruition has grown
The tares may be easily rooted up, if no tares have at all been sown.

November

The trees have doffed their summer dresses,
The flower stems hang their dripping tresses,
All Flora's children hide their faces,—November.

At early dawn dull silence reigns
No more are heard the blackbird's strains,
The thrush his joyous note restrains,—November.

A doon by dark green planten's gate,
No amorous cushal woos his mate,
But sits in sullen, silent state,—November.

Of all the joyous choir of spring,
No member now attempts to sing,
Sma' cheer evok robin's twitterings bring,—November.

The miry beasts come frae the plow,
The sun,—lang set ayont the knowe,
The stirkies stan' at gate an' lowe,—November.

But cheer ye up my cantie lass,
Dark days o' winter soon will pass,
On croquet green, ye'll gar him face, Surrender.

A Wish

Oh! may we strive, each day we live,
For higher, better, thoughts to gain;
With all our might to keep the right
And all that's ill and wrong disdain.

May onward, upward, be our course,
And higher may our aim still rise
May we aye keep the goal in sight
And strive to win the immortal prize.

Shadows

Tis the quiet hush of an autumn eve,
And love's spring is in our hearts.
And the fair light gleams in thy soft brown eyes,
As above a meteor stars.
The noiseless feet of the moons white rays!
Trip soft through the silvery air,
Brown leaves lie low on the shaded path,
And two shadows are walking there.

Two shadows—come nearer my loved one, list,
Must I say it once again,
That the moon may change and the stars grow dim
Yet my love for thee ne'er wane?
The crisp brown leaves bear witness now,
As their ruddy embers shine
Two shadows flit o'er their gentle sleep-
The shadows are mine and thine.

Oh, doubting heart if hope was there
Thou'd'st chide when thy spirit grieves,
And in secret thought to the future haste
When all doubts have shed their leaves,
I see it now—'tis a narrow path
Where but two may have a share.
There are lights above, there are leaves below,
And two shadows are walking there.

Two shadows—ah! yes life indeed, is sweet
If we strive but to make it so;
In blossom those flowers are dearest far
That tears may have helped to grow,
To lighten that path in the future years
Love's stronger prayers combine,
Two shadows are there though we seen them not-
The shadows are mine and thine.

Life Aims

I live for those who love me,
For those who know me true,
For the Heaven that shines above me,
And waits my spirit too.
For the cause that lacks assistance
For the wrongs that need resistance
For the future in the distance
And the good that I can do.

The Water Mill

Oh! listen to the water mill, though all the live-long day
How the clinking of the weary wheel, wears hour by hour away
How languidly the autumn wind, doth stir the withered leaves
As on the field the reaper sings, while binding up his sheaves
A solemn proverb strikes my ear, with meaning deep and vast
The mill will never grind again with water that is past

Soft summer winds revive no more, leaves strewn on earth and main
And the reaper never more will reap, the yellow garnered grain;
And the rippling stream flows ever on, as tranquil deep and still
But never glideth back again to the clinking water mill
This solemn proverb speaks to all with meaning deep and vast
The mill will never grind again with water that is past

Oh take the lesson to thyself dear loving heart and true
For golden years are fleeting past, and youth is fleeting too
Oh learn to make the most of life, nor lose one happy day
For life will ne'er return sweet joys, neglected, thrown away
Oh take the lesson to thyself, do take and clasp it fast
The mill will never grind again with water that is past

Work while yet the sun doth shine thou man of strength I will
For never doth the streamlet glide, all useless by the mill.
Wait not until tomorrow's sun beams brightly on thy way
For all that thou can'st call thine own lies in the phrase 'today'
Posessions, power, and blooming health, must all be lost at last
The mill will never grind again with water that is past.

Oh! the wasted hours of life that swiftly flitted by
Oh! good we might have done, all gone without a sigh
Some that we might once have saved by a simple kindly word
Thoughts conscious but in e're repressed perishing unpenned unheard
Oh! take the lesson to thy self do take and hold it fast
The mill will never grind again with water that is past.

Oh! love thy God and fellow man, thy self consider last,
For come it will when thou must scan dark errors of the past
And when this fight of life is past, and earth recedes from view
And Heaven in all its glory shines, where all is bright and true
Then will you see more clearly still this proverb deep and vast
The mill will never grind again with water that is past.

Charity

Meek and lowly, pure and holy.
Chief among the blessed three;
Turning sadness into gladness
Heaven born art thou charity.

Piety dwelleth in thy bosom,
Kindness reigneth o'er thy heart;
Gentle thoughts alone can sway thee
Judgement hath in thee no part.

Hoping ever, failing never
Though deceived believing still
Long abiding—all confiding
To thy Heavenly Fathers will.

Never weary of well doing
Never fearful of the end
Claiming all mankind as brothers
Thou dost all alike defend.

Meek and lowly, pure and holy,
Chief among the blessed three;
Turning sadness into gladness
Heaven born art thou charity.

Memories

Around the memories of youth,
A halo clings;
We heard it almost in our hearts
Like sacred things.

The faces of the friends we loved
In years gone by;
Are dearer now; their memory
Will never die.

Dear are the memories of home,
The first we knew;
And dear the memory of that time
When hearts were true.

In these short happy childish days,
Our hearts were light
And free as air; to us the earth
Was fair and bright.

And full of sunniest loveliness,
To our gay eyes.
What thought had we of sorrow then
Of tears or sighs.

Ah! Well for us we did not know,
That earthly life
Brings tears, and care, and weary toil,
And bitter strife.

That comes with years we learn too soon,
The sad, sad truth;
Ah! Then we hoard the memory,
Of our lost youth.

But there is left for us to taste, a deeper joy
Ours may be still a happiness, without alloy
Our Fathers hand still guides our way, and he knows best
To weary toil-worn heart-sick souls, He can give rest.

The Hay Fields

The sun had risen, the air was sweet,
And brightly shone the dew,
And cheerful sounds and busy feet
Pass'd the lone meadows through;
And waving like a flowery sea
Of gay and spriry bloom
The hay fields rippled merrily
In beauty and perfume.

I saw the early mowers pass
Along that pleasant dell,
And rank on rank the shining grass
Around them quickly fell;
I looked and far and wide at noon
The fallen flowers were spread
And all, as rose the evening moon
Beneath the scythe were dead.

'All flesh is grass', The Scriptures say,
And so we truly find;
Cut down as in a summer's day,
Are all of human kind;
Some, while the morning still is fair,
Taken in earliest prime,
Some mid-days heat and burden bear
But all, laid low in time.

A fable full of truth to me,
Is this the mower's tale;
I soon a broken stem shall be
Like hay that strews the vale;
At early dawn, on closing light,
The scythe of death may fall;
Then let one learn the lesson right,
So full of truth to all.

The Rose

The rose the sweetly blooming rose,
Eve from the tree tis torn;
Is like the charms which beauty shows,
In life's exulting morn.

But oh! How soon its sweets are gone,
How soon it withering lies;
So when the eve of life draws on,
Sweet beauty fades and dies.

Then since the faintest form that's made,
Soon withering we shall find;
Let us possess what now shall fade,
The beauties of the mind.

The Year Just Gone

Hark! How the solemn midnight bell,
From yonder turret lone,
Proclaims with loud and startling knell,
Another year is gone!
And shall we drain the wassail-cup,
Or raise the song of glee,
As swiftly surely winding up
Our thread of life we see?

No! if in youth's unthinking day,
Ere care had marked the brow,
We trifled months and years away
Let us be wiser now;
And conscious of the mighty debt
We to our Maker owe,
No longer struggle to forget
We reap that which we sow.

No! let us seek, with holy dread
Through his exalted Son,
A pardon for the year that's fled
And grace for that begun,
Grace to improve the little hour
For peace and safety given;
Grace to resist temptation's power
And tread the path of heaven.

Time

Oh! Never chide the wings of time,
Or say tis tardy in its flight!
You'll find the days speed quick enough,
If you but husband them aright.

Thy span of life is waning fast;
Beware, unthinking youth, beware;
Thy souls eternity depends
Upon the record moments bear!

Time is indeed a precious boon,
But with the boon a task is given;
The heart must learn its duty well,
To man on earth, and God in heaven.

Take heed, then; play not with thine hours,
Beware unthinking youth beware!
The one who sets the part he ought,
Will have but little time spare.

All Work Is Holy

Work while life is given
Faint not although tis hard,
Work is the will of heaven,
And peace is the reward
All work is holy.

What though thy lot be hidden,
And proud ones pass thee by?
Feel duty as God-bidden,
Act as beneath his eye!
For work is holy.

Cleave to thy humble place
Ennoble it with zeal
Work with a manful grace
Make fruitless cumberers feel
That work is holy.

Scorn nought as plain or mean;
All with thy worth impress?
That all where those hast been
May day by day confess
That work is holy.

Work while life is given,
Nor shrink though hardships scars;
True suffering fits for heaven,
There Sin alone debars!
For work is holy.

Angels' ears now listen
Thy earth-spurred plaintive tale;
Angels' eyes shall glisten
While they thy scars unveil!
For work is holy

They'll know these are the proof
That thou hast striven well;
Nor idly stood aloof,
While other brave ones fell,
For work is holy.

Work while life is given;
Pine not although tis hard,
Work is the will of heaven,
And peace is the reward
All work is holy.

Forgiveness

The fairest action in our human life
Is scorning to revenge an injury,
For who forgives without a further strife
His adversary's heart to him doth tie,
And tis a firmer conquest truly said,
I win the heart, than overthrow the head.

If we a worthy enemy do find,
To yield to worth it must be nobly done;
But if of baser metal be his mind,
In base revenge there is no honour won.
Who would a worthy Courage overthrow,
And who would wrestle with a worthless foe?

We say our hearts are great and cannot yield;
Because they cannot yield it proves them poor.
Great hearts are tasked beyond their power, but seld
The weakest lion will the loudest roar,
Truth's school for certain doth this same allow,
High-heartedness doth sometimes teach to bow.

A noble heart doth teach a virtuous scorn
To scorn to owe a duty over long.
To scorn to be for benefits forborne,
To scorn to lie, to scorn to do a wrong;
To scorn to bear an injury in mind,
To scorn a free-born heart slave-like to bind.

But if for wrongs we needs revenge must have
Then be our vengeance of the noblest kind
Do we his body from our fury save,
And let our hate prevail against our mind
What can 'gainst him a greater vengeance be
Than make his foe more worthy far than he?

My Wish
Written in Miss Georgina Grant's Autograph Book, Brodiesord, May 1914.
The above lady was confined to bed for 16 years with rheumatism in her arms
and legs. She is deceased now.

Goodness and mercy all your life
Each day I hope may tend you;
Oh! That our Heavenly Father's hand,
Richly his gifts may send you.
Grace, mercy, peace, love, hope and joy,
In fullest measure be your lot;
No cross, no care, but with strength to bear
All these I wish, —and forget me not.

Lines written on the fly leaf of 'The Lame Dog's Diary'
presented to the above lady, 30th August 1916

The Lame Dog's ploy, may you enjoy,
As bees rejoice 'mang clover,
Your winning smile, be deepened while
These pages you turn over.

Lines written on fly leaf of 'Laddie'
given to my daughter on her birthday, 15 December 1916

Many happy returns of this day be yours,
And tho dark be the clouds of December;
May sunshine as June, effulgent as noon,
Flood your heart with a peace true and tender.

Lines given to my Daughter, along with a small present,
on her 21st birthday

Oh! Peggy, Oh! Peggy, you're nae mair a lassie
But noo a woman full grown;
Birthdays twenty one, have flown past wi' a run,
And Dovie's got wings of her own.

But tho the wings you have got, I hope you may not
Leave the old nest for many a day;
For hangin's too good, for the rascal who would
Steal my one bonnie wee lamb away.

So on the your Birthday, I hope and I pray
Best blessins upon you may fa';
Sae lively and cheery, tho never sae weary,
Cheers the hert o' your ain Daddy's Da.

The Sweetest Time of All
Written in reply to some verses received from my sister Annie (Mrs Cowie)
entitled 'The Hardest Time of All', December 1886

There are days of sweetest gladness
In the course of every life;
There are seasons when all sadness
Seems quite banished from the strife;
There are times of strong emotion
When the tears of joy do fall,
But the waiting time, my sister
Is the sweetest time of all.

Love and youth may be impatient, but impatience is no crime
For if properly divided, it oft leads to heights sublime;
For the greatest zest of pleasure, in anticipation found,
In pursuit more pleasure is, than in possession safe and sound;
Altho 'fore the fruit be gathered, we must see the blossom fall.
Sure the waiting time my sister, is the sweetest time of all.

Love and youth they are twin sisters,
And their pleasures none may name,
'Tween the gloaming and the mirk
When the kye come lowin' hame;
Or when at the trystin' tree
The shades o' evenin' sweetly fa'
Oh! The waiting time my sister,
Is the sweetest time o' a'.

An acrostic Christmas wish sent to my grand-niece Miss Bessie Bell, Vancouver B.C.
1916

Bessie Bell, Grand-Niece to thee
Each day my thoughts are roving
Such happy thoughts across the sea,
So pleasant and so loving.
I send you Christmas greeting true
Each year as it comes round,
Bright be your prospects as the blue
E're clouds in sky are found.
Leal Friends, contentment, peace and joy in twins,
Lo this is sent to you with love from Burns.

Verses recited at the Silver Wedding of Mr. and Mrs. Findlater, Brodiesord Farm, 18th
July 1916

It's five an' twenty years I'm taul, since 'Brodie' took the wife
An' gin the twa can be believed, they ne'er hid lect a strife.

Be that's it may, we'll no gainsy, nor split hairs wi' a knife,
But it's plain they baith been thrivin', and specially the Gude wife.

An' gin they ever come tae grips, an' hae a stan up fecht,
She nae doot wid the advantage hae, wi' her fourteen stane doon wecht.

But noo my friens, I'm sure ye'll jine wi' me wi' richt gude-will
In houpin that the couthy pair, o' joy may hae their fill.

Wi' bumper craps o' corn an' neeps, the haddin aye weel stockit,
An' aye the tether thirvin' colt, preparin' tae be yokit.

O' warl's gear may they ne'er wint, nor yet ae ither thing,
An' may the gear that disna roost, be heapin up the bing.

Their gowden wadin' may they see, conteenin' hale and herty
An' may their bairns be, nae ane or two, but thirty.

Lines sent to my Niece Alice Ross, on hearing that she along with other two ladies, had
been seen out walking with two gentlemen named Peter and John

Three ladies fair, in dresses rare, with Peter and (James) and John,
Went out for a walk, and a sweet little walk, but one was a chaperon.

But 'James' sure he, must a wee bean be, and yet far from the nubile state,
But Alice dear, never shed a tear, he'll grow if you only wait.

Given as a Recitation at Brodiesord Farm 27 July 1916

In an upper room so coz, where or when I'll not disclose
A meeting once was held, with one in bed,
It was named 'The Georgie Club', and we all denounced the Pub,
And upheld some other social joys instead.

On that eventful night, hearts full of joy so light,
The worthy Mr. F. did there preside.
And supporting him erect, with her face in smiles bedecked,
Was his bonnie, blooming, buxom, silver bride.

There were ladies young and fair, sporting side-sheds in their hair,
Their blouses latest modes from Lobban Crichton.
Other ladies too beside, some from Glasgow on the Clyde,
And tho single, sure their age it was uncertain.

One lady tho not old, silver threads amongst the gold,
Devoutly worships at Fair Flora's beauteous shrine,
And last tho far from least, comes the Princess of the feast,
Who plays at 'Polyanna' all the time.

Mr G, from fair Edna, with his charming little Rena,
And a rovin' shymin' rascal they ca' Burns;
The nickname Willie loon, mair than nits are in his croon
Ane an' a' took up the cudgels in their turns.

The programme it began, every maiden, every man,
Without the slightest hitch or hesitation,
Did produce some dainty bit, some of wisdom some of wit,
For the peerless, Princess, private delictation.

Come all ye maids and swains, who sport about in trains,
On bikes and motor cars so fast and furious;
Come join 'The Georgie Club', the go-by give the pub,
You'll find those fancied joys are wholly spurious.

Here you'll find some other thing, treasure fit for prince or king,
A pleasure that is pure, without a flaw.
But in case that you are weary of my ditty, dull and dreary,
I shall say gude nicht an' joy be wi'you a'.

An Acrostic Christmas Wish Sent to Miss Julian Stewart, Banchory House, Banchory
Devinick, Xmas 1916

Christmas Greetings warm and true,
High o'er the hills I waft to you.
Right hearty are the season's greetings
I send in memory of our meetings.
Sincere I wish that peace and joy
To you be given, without alloy,
May all that's good, and pure and true
Attend your life right through and through;
Such is the wish I send to you.

Christmas Greeting
Sent to my Niece Minnie Carmichael, Xmas 1916

May Christmas Day be fair and bright
Into your life, come naught but light,
Naught that would cause a sigh or tear,
No vain regrets to close the year.
Into your life come pure and true,
Each longing wish desired by you.

Not Christmas toys, but Christmas joys
Not merriment, but sweet content,
This gladsome time I send to you
On this blest morn, when Christ was born
May wars all cease, may His own be peace,
And all that's good attend to you.

Sent to two Old Friends
Xmas 1917

A New Year's wish I send you,
May all that's good attend you,
May the even-tide of life, bring only peace,
May the old year with its care,
Be laid aside like broken ware,
May the coming year in happiness increase.

June
<u>The</u> *Month of all the Year*

Oh! June, Oh! June, you are in tune
Your breath so sweet does fan my cheek;
And I too am in tune.

The clover fields, a fragrance yields,
Delightful beyond measure;
The honey-bee from flowery lea
Wings homeward with its treasure. Oh! June.

The tasselled larch, and silvery birch
Have donned their summer dresses;
The woods and glades, in varied shades
Display their wondrous tresses. Oh! June.

The broom and whin, by loch and linn,
Present their gold to view;
The hyacinth bells to lover tells
The story ever new. Oh! June

The morning mist, the vale has kissed,
Soon, soon the sun is shining;
His genial say, the live-long day
Keeps sorry hearts from pining. Oh! June.

When fields are dry, and farmers cry
'Oh! for a shower of rain';
A cloud appears, down drop the tears
Refreshed is earth again. Oh! June.

As 'Robbie' sings, 'all nature sings
Her joy-bells', come along
With heart and voice let us rejoice
And join the gladsome throng. Oh! June, Oh! June.

The Flowers of Spring

The flowers of June are rich and rare,
July brings a wealth of roses;
In August plots are seldom bare
Of gems from Nature's posies.

The Summer flowers do well deserve
The meed of praise I bring;
But the warmest tribute I deserve
For those that come in Spring.

The snow-drops first kind Nature sends
Beside the snow-wreathe peeping;
The harbinger of other friends,
That still are soundly sleeping.

In yellow, blue, and purest white,
The crocus comes in order;
The pollen-laden bees invite
To view the gay decked border

The 'dancing daffodils' come next,
In all their golden glory;
Their bounteous blooms with green leaves mixed,
Proclaim the Easter story.

In rich variety of shades
The auricula delights me;
The first of Spring's florescent maids,
Whose perfume sweet excites me.

To one and all a meed of praise
My rhyming ranter renders,
Yet still there's one to whom my muse
Her warmest tribute renders.

The lily fair in purest white,
Beloved alove all other;
My heart has captivated quite
In memory of Mother.[1]

If those fair flowers, from earth's plain bowers,
So charming are to view;
What rare delight must be the sight
Where flowers are ever new.

[1] The lily was his Mother's favourite flower.

APPENDIX 2
LECTURES AND ESSAYS GIVEN TO THE DESKFORD AND BALLINDALLOCH MUTUAL IMPROVEMENT ASSOCIATIONS

An Essay on Love
Read at a Meeting of Deskford Mutual Improvement Society, November 1883

Of all the passions that reign in the heart of man, love is the most productive of good. Writers of all ages have touched on this subject, and still it seems to be a subject unexhausted. It is the poet's theme, and the artist's study, and dry indeed would that volume be, in which the love of some object, secular or sacred, was not portrayed.

Many and varied are the definitions of love. You have all heard the well known rhyme, 'Oh love, love, love, love is a dizziness, it winna lat a body be, tae gang aboot their busieness'. This I think is a very erroneous description of love. Instead of being a hinderance, love should be a very great help, in any ones business.

You have also no doubt heard the old song, which says of love, 'It's just as if you tumbled into honey or some-one died and left you all their money, it's so peculiar and funny, Oh! So funny when you feel that way'. As the song speaks of tumbling, I suspect it refers to that catastrophie known by the phrase, 'falling in love'.

I have already made the assertion that love is productive of good, and I would further say that love is productive of good only. Some may deny this and state that the love of certain things is the source of much evil, the love of gambling, or the love of strong drink, for instance, but such is not love in the true meaning of the word. Love is that secret hidden power, which touching a chord in man's inmost heart, makes it vibrate and resound with joy and gladness in sweetest harmony.

A sermon has generally a text, an introduction and so many heads, and I see no reason why an essay should not have the same. I have given my text, and made some remarks by way of introduction. I would now say a few words first on the love of home and country, second on the love of music and nature, and third on the love of woman.

I have placed the love of home first, because it has been to all of us, our first love. The love of home is implanted in the breast of every true man and woman born. Home is said to be one of the three most beautiful words in the English language, viz. Home, Heaven and Happiness. Home is a word most dear to all of us, and there are many reasons that it should be so. The poet says, 'Mid pleasures and palaces though we may roam; be it ever so humble, there's no place like home'. 'Tis there that the love and sympathy extended to us, can be depended on as being real and genuine. 'Tis there that we appear in our true colours, without the mask of concealment which the world enforces us to wear in self defence. 'Tis there that all that is lovely should have its centre.

The love of country is akin to that of home, and yet it is widely different. Every true Scotchman loves his country and many are the songs which he sings in its praise. 'It's a bonnie wee lan', oor ain wee lan', as a' the warl maun say. Its hills and dells, its moors and fells, an' torrents white in spray. Its lochs an' linns, its broom an' whins, gae match them whaur ye may. Oh it's a bonny wee lan' oor ain wee lan', as a' the warl maun say'.

The love of country has in many instances been the means of inciting great men to great actions–to noble deeds of daring. It was the love of country that burned in the breast of Nelson, when at the battle of Trafalgar, from the deck of his good ship Victory he made his last signal, a signal which will be remembered as long as the English language exists: 'England expects every man to do his duty'. It was the love of country that prompted Wellington to meet the veteran Bonaparte on the field of Waterloo, and shall we forget The Bruce and The Wallace, Scotland's greatest patriots, who fought, and who bled on so many a battle field, and all for the love they bore their fatherland.

To those of us who live in days of peace, and to those who know not what it is to leave their native land, the deep-rooted love of country may never have been truly felt, but still I am sure that it burns in every breast, and should fate so will that any of us should cross the sea, and roam in foreign lands, when all is left behind that is near and dear to us, the place of our birth, the scenes of our boyhood, the burn, the bogs and the braes, the woods and the hills where we used to ramble. When we think of all these as we stand a stranger in a strange country, then will the lines of Montgomery come home to us in all their truth and beauty:

> There is a land of every land the pride,
> Beloved by heaven o'er all the world beside.
> There is a spot on earth supremely blest,
> A dearer, sweeter spot than all the rest.
> Where shall that land, that spot on earth be found,
> Art thou a man, a patriot, look around;
> And thou shalt find, how e're thy footsteps roam,

That land thy country, and that spot thy home.

Or again, should a foreign foe but dare to set his foot on Scottish soil, with the intent of wrenching from us by force, our freedom and our faith, then shall we feel as did our forefathers of yore our blood boil in our veins, then shall we know how Sir Walter Scott felt, when he penned the often quoted lines, 'Land of brown heath and shaggy wood, land of the mountain and the flood, land of my sires what mortal hand, can e'er untie the filial bond that knits me to thy rugged strand'.

The love of music is a most enobling love, and exercises a great power over the mind of man.

Under the hands of a skilful player, music can be made the means of elevating our thoughts, of raising us above the petty cares that trouble and annoy our every-day life. It can soothe us when we are weary; it can lull us to sleep when we need 'Nature's sweet restorer'; but it can also rouse us to action, and fire our dormant energies, as when the drum and pibroch are played to march our soldiers to battle array.

Scotland is said to be, not a very musical country. Why this should be, I know not. I am sure it would amply repay any time or trouble bestowed on it.

The musician may not be a naturalist, but the naturalist ever is a lover of music, for nature is full of music. The singing of the birds, the murmuring of the brook, the sighing of the wind, and the moaning of the ever restless sea, are to him but so many notes in the great organ of nature, all joining in happy chorus, in unison, and in harmony.

Who has not looked and listened with rapture and delight, to the sky lark, springing from the dewy grass, mounting up into the azure sky, and all the time pouring forth its morning song of praise?

How pleasant it is in the fresh spring morn
To hearken the wee birds sing;
As each tiny minstrel adding its note
Makes wood and valley ring.

If the music of nature be a source of pleasure to the lover of nature; how much more are the many and varied scenes that daily meet his eye. The rare and delicate plants of the hot-house, are beautiful to look upon, the sweetly blooming rose, the scented lily, and the lovely violet of the garden are well worth cultivation; but above all others in my estimation, are the flowers that bloom by the way-side. Needing no culture, nursed by the winds, and watered by the dew of heaven they are free to all, 'A' body's garden, A'body's flowers'.

The more closely you inspect the workmanship of man, let it be the highest achievements of Art or Science, the more defects you will find in it, while in the works of nature, though it be the humblest flower that blooms, the longer you look, the greater beauty you will behold.

The revolving seasons, and the ever changing aspect of nature, have been most wisely ordered. A perpetual Spring or a never ending summer, would soon lose for us their charms. But when the storms of winter have scattered the withered leaves, and the biting frost has nipped the tender grass, how beautiful to us seem the buds upon the tree, and the return of verdure to the fields, with what delight do we hail the snow-drop as it peeps forth beside the snow-wreath, or the primrose starting from its mossy bank.

I now come to the third Head of my Essay viz. The Love of Woman.

On the love of Home and Country, and on the love of Music and Nature, I have partly spoken from experience. What I have now to say, is from study and observation only.

George MacDonald the celebrated novelist speaks thus of the love of woman, 'Whatever it is that keeps the finer faculties of the mind awake, wonder alive, and the interest above mere eating and drinking, money making and money saving, whatever it be that gives gladness or sorrow or hope, this, be it violin, pencil, pen or highest of all the love of woman, is simply a Divine gift of holy influence for the salvation of that being to whom it comes, for the lifting of him out of the mire, up on the rock'.

To reduce this to plain language, does it not imply, that to take a wife would make you nobler, and a better man?

The love of woman has been a failing of the Lords of Creation ever since Adam took the hand of Eve and led her through the Garden of Eden. How many of their sons and daughters have acted Romeo and Juliet since then, it would be hard to say; but after the lapse of nearly 6000 years, it still seems to be, the old, old story, that is ever new.

The love of woman is not only the privilege but the duty of man. Woman was made for an helpmate to man, therefore that man who thinks he can live without her help, who stifles that finer feeling, and constitutes himself a bachelor, not only breaks one of the great laws of Nature, but he also does monstrous injustice to Society, he compels some delicate frame to bear the burden of life unaided, he suffers her to pine in loneliness and neglect, without that love and sympathy which are his to bestow, and which are so much justly her due.

Love is said to be blind, but I do not credit it. The poet says, 'Tis not the lily brow I prize, nor rosy cheeks, nor sunny eyes; Enough of lilies and of roses, a thousand fold more deal to me, the look that love alone discloses, the look that love alone can see'. Now if love can see that which nothing else can, how can it be termed blind?

Cupid the god of love is represented as having a bow, with quiver full of arrows, which he shoots with unerring aim at the hearts of his worshippers. The poet La Teste speaking of his spouse says, 'I thocht ye was an angel Jean, when first we cam together; till twa three rompin bairnies Jean, played bump aboot their mither'. After the latter episode I would infer that in the poet's estimation, her angelic form had taken wings and flown away. You will be saying perhaps that his love had been blind, but not so. He had only drunk too deeply of the potent draught, or allowed Cupid to pierce his heart too sharply with his arrows, and so had abused love.

Love has a language entirely its own, a look, the warm pressure of the hand may speak volumes, but it often needs no language. Between two hearts knit by the ties of love, there is as it were an electric wire, so that the thoughts of the one, can be known and read by the other. A homely incident that lately came to my notice, may illustrate this a little.

Two rustic cronies were having a talk about their love affairs. In the course of their confab one says to the other, 'Man Geordie foo div ye get Kirsty tae come oot t' speak t' ye, fan ye gang t' see her'. 'Weel, weel Tam ye are a green ane. I jist gie the pump hannel a dirl, an' syne a hoast, an' she's oot in a jiffy'.

From an electric wire, to the dirl o' a pump handle may be looked upon as a descent from the sublime to the ridiculous, and yet a similar effect may be produced by both.

These few remarks on love, and its several objects will do all they were ever intended to do, should they help us however feebly, to cherish more sacredly in our hearts, the love of the good, the beautiful and the true.

Whether Are The First Or The Last Six Months of the
Year The More Pleasant?
A Paper read at a Social Meeting in Connection with Deskford Mutual
Improvement Association supporting The First Half of the Year, March 1884

Ladies and Gentlemen,
As it has fallen on me to support the claims of the first half of the year, I shall strive to do so to the best of my ability. I have been greatly aided in my task, not only in the belief that the majority of you will support me, but also by the consciousness that I have the right end of the string.
January is the first month of the year, and it is a winter month. Still it is more pleasant in general than either November or December. When at School we were taught, 'January brings the snow, makes our feet and fingers glow', while December was said to bring sleet. Now I am sure you will all agree with me in saying that snow is far more pleasant than sleet. But suppose that we had snow during both these months, still I

hold that January is the more pleasant of the two, for by the end of that month we can perceive that the sun has once more commenced to climb towards the zenith, and although we may have some dark days, still we will occasionally have some bright ones, the sun will at times look out from behind the clouds to cheer us with his pleasant beams, and remind us of the coming Spring.

Of all the seasons of the year, Springtime is without doubt the most calculated to inspire us with pleasant thoughts and feelings. Writers of all ages, poets of the highest order, and all true lovers of nature, agree in praising the beauties and pleasantness of Spring.

From the writings of King Solomon, the wisest of men, we can infer that he was an ardent lover of Spring. In reference to the same he says, 'For lo! The winter is past, the rain is over and gone: the flowers appear on the earth, the time of the singing of the birds is come and the voice of the turtle is heard in our land'. One of the pleasures of Spring, he says, is the appearing of the flowers on the earth. Now why are the flowers of Spring the means of producing so much pleasure? They have little or none of the sweet odour which the flowers of summer possess, they are not arrayed in gorgeous colours, like those of July or August, and yet I maintain that a snow-drop in February gives far more true pleasure than a rose in July. The price of an article is not always in accordance with its real value, but it is often governed by its supply. So it is with the flowers of Spring. They are few and we cherish them accordingly. But there is another reason. During the long hard months of winter, there has been nothing to cheer the eye, nothing but withered leaves and broken stems, with what delight then do we hail the snow-drop peeping forth beside the snow wreathe, and the primrose starting from its mossy bank. Tennyson, the sweet singer, says, 'in the Spring a young man's fancy lightly turns to thoughts of love'. If such be the case, and I see no reason why that pleasant season should not produce the same feeling in the gentle sex, surely we have a very strong argument in favour of Spring.

I have already referred to the pleasure derived from the flowers of Spring, but who can describe the enjoyment from listening to the singing of the birds, and this is a pleasure which the first six months of the year almost entirely claims. Not only do we listen with greater pleasure to the feathered minstrels in Spring from the fact that they have been so long silent, but their songs are at that season far sweeter than at any other time during the whole year.

Allow me to try and picture to you a Spring morning, we shall say in the month of April, such as I have often seen and admired, and such as you will all very soon have an opportunity of beholding. The sun has just dispelled the thin white mist that was hovering in the hollows, the air is calm and still, a sweet odour arises from the newly awakened earth. From each tiny blade of grass glistens a drop of pearly dew, while the bright morning sun is shedding a ray of glory over all the landscape. As we stand and admire the pleasing scene, from the dewy grass beside us upstarts the sky-lark. Shaking the dew-drops from its wing, it mounts up into the azure sky, while from its little throat there issues such a flow of music as fills you with admiration and delight, and which the pen of man has never yet found to adequately describe.

From the branches of the larch tree, already hanging forth its tassels of delicate green, the blackbird and the mavis seem to vie with each other which will produce the sweetest song, while all the other members of the sylvan choir, each in its own peculiar key, yet all blending together in sweetest harmony, are pouring forth in joyful strains their morning lay.

Where in all the other seasons of the year, can you produce a scene so pleasing alike to the eye and ear, as this one I have feebly tried to portray?

That the other seasons have pleasures I must readily allow. It is pleasant indeed in the Autumn of the year to behold the ripe fruits of the earth which Nature hangs forth in tempting clusters before our eyes and it is more pleasant still to partake of them: but is it not the pleasure chiefly of satisfying our appetites, a pleasure which lasts only for the time being, and not to be compared to the rapturous enjoyment derived from listening to the sky-lark's song? Here we have a pleasure of a higher order, a pleasure that stirs us to the very depths of our beings, a pleasure that elevates our thoughts that raises us above the petty cares that trouble and annoy our everyday life, and tends to make us better, nobler holier beings.

I have already stated that poets of all ages have been loud in their praises of that season when as Burns so finely puts it, 'Now in her green mantle blythe Nature arrays, and listens the lambkins that bleat o'er the braes'.

No doubt we have also many poetical effusions in praise of Autumn, but is there not always a sadness in the lines, is there not always a melancholy blended with the sweetness? And so it ever must be, for however beautiful is the variegated colour of the leaves as they change from red to russet brown, we cannot forget that it is the forerunner of coming winter, it speaks but too plainly of death and decay, and such to our natures are ever saddening.

Youth and Spring are often compared to each other, and the comparison is a most suitable one. Now I am sure no one will attempt to deny that youth is the most pleasant period of all our life-time. It is in youth that hope, that well-spring of all our sweetest joys, that bright star which beacons us onward over the rocky road of life, I say that it is in youth that hope burns must brightly in all our breasts. Have we not all our day-dreams? Do not we all build our castles in the air, and do we not derive much pleasure from this exercise? Are not the same feelings produced by the return of Spring? Is not Spring the season of hope, the time of looking forward, and it is a fact well known and often proved that, pleasure derives its greatest zest from anticipation?

Farmers are proverbially a race of grumblers, and of course one outstanding subject of discontent, a subject on whose head epithets, many and varied are heaped from day to day, is the weather. Now of all the seasons of the year when the weather is the least liable to be attacked is the Spring, and the reason is not far to seek. If we have a spell of dry weather, everyone is delighted for dry weather is pleasant, and it is also most suitable for getting in the seeds, but should a week of wet weather prevail, still there are no crops to spoil, and although it may protract the seed time a little still the hope that the latest sown may prove the best crop restrains any very pointed remarks.

But should a few weeks, or even a shorter period of drought occur in July or August, and behold an outcry most loud and lamentable is the consequence, 'There's sure to be a short crop! The neeps are a fa'in ower wi' canker!' And such like. Of course the clouds in due time make their appearance, and drop their treasure on the thirsty ground, but still contentment does not follow. Another race of grumblers springs up like mushrooms. The blessing which the moisture has bestowed is all too soon forgotten, while any little inconvenience it may have produced is magnified most enormously, 'I never saw weather like this a' my life! Is'n the mess in an awfu' splash? There'll be nae mair peats this year. The hay'll be a' rotten, or it be gotten aff o' the grun! etc., etc.'

So much for Spring, but before concluding I must say a few words on Summer, the earlier part of which belongs to the first six months of the year.

With what pleasure do we witness the tender bud bursting into leaf under the gentle influence of the Summer sun? What more beautiful than the hawthorn when covered with its load of snow-white blossoms, and shedding far and near its perfume so rich and rare? Who has not felt themselves lightened of a load of care after witnessing on a sweet May morning, the gambols of a score of young lambs. Types of all that is pure and innocent. So full of life, of love and liberty. Jumping, frisking, racing and chasing, scampering hither and thither yet ever and anon returning to the side of their fleecy dams.

I shall now as the lawyers say, sum up the evidence. That portion of winter that falls to the first six months of the year is the more pleasant part, because the day is not so short and dreary, because we see more of the sun, and everyone knows that light is a pleasant thing to the eyes.

That Spring is more pleasant than Autumn, I think nobody will deny. Surely it is more pleasant to look on the opening bud, than to see the falling leaf. The beginning of Summer has also many advantages over the end of it. In early Summer everything is so fresh and fair, so full of life and hope, that we also who are much influenced by our surroundings are also inspired with new hope and new strength. Have we not all felt our steps lighter, aye and our hearts lighter too, when all Nature is reviving and springing into life and beauty.

Such are a few, but only a few of the many pleasures we enjoy during the earlier half of the year. That it is the more pleasant half, there can be no doubt. That the gentleman who opposes me will have arguments many and strong in support of the latter half, I am also certain, yet after hearing all he has got to bring forward in support of his cause, I still hope that with me you will say, 'Of all the seasons of the year, I love sweet Spring the dearest'.

Reply to Mr. McWillie's Paper In Favour of the Last Six Months of the Year Being The More Pleasant, 1884

Mr. Chairman Ladies and Gentlemen,
I am sure we have all listened with very great pleasure indeed to Mr. McWillie's excellent paper on the pleasantness of the latter half of the year, but there are few assertions in the same, that I can scarcely allow to pass unchallenged.

He commences with a review of the first six months, and he would fain try to make us believe that there are no pleasures whatever during that period. Not one redeeming feature does he find from beginning to end of it. Extreme cold, frost and snow; cold high winds, dull monotony; hard disagreeable work and scanty fare. 'These', he says, 'are the real characteristics of the period extending from January to June. Now all this sounds very fine but the excellent weather we have been enjoying for some time past is far from corresponding with Mr. McWillie's picture.

First of all he says, 'It is only in January that that we experience extreme cold'. A little before this he told us that our climate was a temperate climate. I fail to see how these two statements can be reconciled.

Then he tells us, that frost and snow are great hinderances to the farmer, but anyone with even a very limited knowledge of agriculture could tell him, that they are quite the opposite. The action of the frost upon the soil is so necessary and so beneficial, that no amount of labour can produce the same results. Cold high winds are another source of unpleasantness to Mr. McWillie, during the first half of the year, but I would remind him that cold high winds prevail at other seasons, as we have often experienced to our cost, and when they visit us in Autumn or the end of Summer, they are far more unpleasant, because more destructive.

Again he says that monotony and hard disagreeable work, are characteristics of the Spring months, but I think if our heart is in our work, we will find it neither monotonous nor disagreeable. On the contrary the consciousness of having performed our duties, that we have finished our work to the best of our ability, is ever a source of true and lasting pleasure.

All the farmer's work (with the exception of harvest), he would fain have us believe, is performed during the first half of the year, and the other half he says is thus left wholly for enjoyment.

Let us glance for a little at the source from which he derives his pleasures, in his estimation so great and so manifold. The sum and substance of all his enjoyment seems to be, to have nothing to do but eat and drink, and attend pic-nics, games. shows etc. etc. From the time, he says that we get new potatoes and fresh herrings in July, until the roast goose and plum pudding of Xmas, scarcely a week passes but some new dainty can be added to the table. That new potatoes and fresh herring, are quite good in their season, I will not deny, but that they are a source of such unbounded pleasure, such exquisite delight, such unspeakable joy, as they seem to possess for Mr. McWillie, we will scarcely admit. That our Annual Pic-nic is a most enjoyable meeting, most of us here present can testify, but is it a source of wholly unmixed pleasure? Is there not usually a something that mars our enjoyment? Does not the following morning generally disclose some keen regrets? So it ever must be with all such pleasures. What is it that makes the Pic-nic, or any other holiday, a source of pleasure at all? Is it not the hard disagreeable work, that my good friend complains about? Take away the work and give us Pic-nics for all, and I rather fear they would very soon become both disagreeable and monotonous. The greatest, the truest and the purest pleasure, is that of looking forward to the holidays, when busily engaged at our work in the Spring. The only source of enjoyment in which I agree with Mr. McWillie is that derived from the flowers. The pleasure obtained from flowers is ever true and ever pure, but those of Spring and early Summer, have for me a charm, which the gaudy colours and gorgeous display of July and August can never possess. By that time the eye has grown accustomed to bright colours, that they cease to impart to us the keen pleasure of admiring those that first appear on the earth.

Mr. Cruickshank brings forward the argument of the pleasure obtained from feasting on the honey which the bee supplies us with. I am sure you will agree with me however, when I say, that the study of the bee's habits, and the watching it in early Summer as it flits from flower to flower in its unwearied search for pollen, is a pleasure of a far higher order than either robbing it of its treasure, or feasting on its hard earned stores.

Not even the tempting honey, and not even the delicious odour of the new potatoes, and the fresh herrings will tempt me to forgo the rapturous pleasure of a sweet May morning, that season when trees do bud and flowers do bloom.

Should The Church of Scotland Be Disestablished?
A Paper Read at a Meeting of Deskford Mutual Improvement Association Supporting the Negative Side, 17th November 1885

Mr. Chairman and Gentlemen,
The subject which we have chosen for discussion this evening viz. Disestablishment, is a subject which most intimately concerns us all. It is in my opinion one of the most important questions that has been raised, at least in our day. It behoves us therefore to give it that consideration which it merits.

As an aid to the better discussion of the subject I have resolved to treat it under four different heads viz. 'What is Disestablishment?' 'Who wants Disestablishment?' 'What arguments can be brought forward in support of it?' and, 'What objections do we have against it?'

First then what is Disestablishment?

The Established Church of Scotland is the Church of the majority of the people. It is the National Church, and as such it remains as a witness in the land of the national recognition of religion-as a witness of the great truth, that Christ is King and Head of nations, as well as of individuals. This is a truth which all sections of Presbyterians, however separated now, were once united in asserting, and none more so than the Fathers of the United Presbyterian and Free Churches.

Disestablishment therefore means the abolition of this sacred institution, but it also goes much further than this. For many generations the people of Scotland have enjoyed the advantages of a free Christian ministry. Many hundred years ago, certain portions of land were set aside for the benefit of the Church, exclusively for religious purposes. The patrimony derived from these lands has been

handed down to us by our forefathers. The funds of the Church
therefore are clearly national property, and if all the people of Scotland
do not take advantage of this property, it is entirely their own fault, for
it is free to all.

It is intended by Disestablishment to deprive the people of this
their lawful property, to take from them these funds so long devoted to
the maintenance of religious ordinances, and to apply them to other
purposes.

This brings us to consider the next point, 'Who wants
Disestablishment?' There are two parties in this country, and two
parties only: from whom such a proposal might come with any show
of reason. The Episcopalians or the Roman Catholics. Any of these
bodies might with some show of reason say, 'it is not fair that the
Presbyterian Church of Scotland should enjoy endowments which
once were ours. But gentlemen they don't say so, and they don't say it
for a very good reason, they know there is no possibility of having any
Established Church in this country other than the Presbyterian Church
of Scotland.

But it is the Free Church, or rather a section of the Free Church,
and the United Presbyterians, who are pressing this question forward.
Before proceeding further therefore, let us look for a little at the
position of these bodies.

They came out from the Established Church no doubt for high and
conscientious motives which I think in the opinion of most men,
rebound highly to their credit. Every one certainly admires the sacrifices
they have made since they did come out, for men will make great
sacrifices for objects which are dear to their hearts, but why should they
complain of the inequality which they themselves have created.

They were perfectly free to remain. They chose to go out, because
they preferred to be free. They have the utmost toleration, the utmost
freedom to prosecute their worship as they please. Their courts are
supreme, and are not interfered with by law in any one way, and the
only thing they don't possess are the endowments which they
deliberately rejected. Is there any shadow of a reason here, why those
who are content with the National Church, and who wish the
endowments to remain as they are, should have their Church pulled
down about their heads?

These then are the parties who want Disestablishment. They are
not atheists, they are not Episcopalians neither are they Roman
Catholics, but they are a sect of Presbyterians, whose creed is the same,
and whose form of worship is the same as those they wish to injure.

We will now look for a little at the arguments brought forward by
these parties in support of their contention.

In a recent manifesto issued by the Committee on Church and State of The Free Church, on Disestablishment, we find that the main argument set forth in support of the same is religious equality. Now religious equality is a very fine sounding phrase, and unthinking persons are apt to be carried away with it but let us look at in the face for a little, and see what it really means. Religious equality of course means this- that it is not fair that one community should enjoy State endowments because other unions don't. Now gentlemen, I think I have shown you plainly enough already, that if there be any inequality, it has certainly been created by those parties who complain.

But although religious equality seems to be a very fine principle, I think we do sometimes get an inkling of what is really meant by those who are so highly applauding it. At a meeting at Keith the other week, a Reverend gentleman in the course of his speech, made an illustration in connection with the Church question. 'How', said he, 'would any of the merchants in Keith be pleased, if the Government were to open a shop next door to them, and sell all their goods for nothing? Would it not be likely that the customers would all leave the other merchants and flock to the government store?' This shows us all too plainly, that it is not the interests of religion that are really aimed at, but that the question is solely one of trade jealousy.

Another argument set forth in the manifesto before mentioned, is that Disestablishment could greatly help towards the union of the different Presbyterian Churches. Now gentlemen, the disunion of the Presbyterian Churches of Scotland is a standing disgrace to the history of Scotland. It is a disgrace towards which the enemies of Protestantism are continually pointing the finger of scorn, and I am sure there is not one here present this evening, who would not rejoice to see that union accomplished. But can any of you honestly and conscientiously think that Disestablishment would in any degree help toward the furtherance of that end? Is it anything like reasonable to suppose that the adherents of The National Church would be in anywise ready to forgive, far less to unite with the party who had been the means of depriving them of these funds, which for so many generations had been devoted to the supplying of religious ordinances in every parish in Scotland.

No gentlemen, far from helping towards the union of the churches, Disestablishment, even the mentioning of Disestablishment, is completely tending towards the other extreme.

Another proof of the fallacy of the assertion that the removing of the funds would help to join the churches, is found in the fact that although no such barrier exists between the U.P. and The Free Church, still they cannot be got to unite.

We have now considered what Disestablishment means, who wants
it and what arguments are being brought forward in favour of it. We
now come to the fourth point, viz 'What objections have we against
it?'

The Disestablishing of the Church of Scotland is clearly a question
for the people of Scotland to decide. If the majority of the people were
in favour of it, or if it could be proved that the Church of Scotland
was failing properly to supply religious instruction to the people, then I
would say, and say decidedly; let that Church be Disestablished. But
the majority of the people are not in favour of Disestablishment, and
instead of failing in usefulness, there is ample testimony to prove that
the Church of Scotland is year by year increasing in efficiency, in the
number of churches she is endowing, in the number of her
communicants, in the number of Sabbath School scholars, and in the
number of Young Men's Guilds and Christian Associations. In short,
The Church of Scotland was never so thoroughly in earnest in
fulfilling her duty to the people, was never more efficient in the means
she is employing for promoting Christian work and Christian activity
than she is at the present day.

This is an assertion which none of her adversaries have ever
attempted to gainsay, but it is also an assertion that beyond doubt can
be clearly proved.

As to the number of her communicants, according to a
Parliamentary Return, the number in connection with The Church of
Scotland was given as 464,000 in 1874, while this number is now
increased to 555,622.

Compare this with the strength of The Free Church which can
only muster 254,000 while the U.P. has 174,000. Altogether 428,000,
or more than 100,000 less than The Established Church.

Another proof of the truth of the assertion that the majority of the
people of Scotland are in favour of The Church of Scotland might be
found in the 600,000 signatures attached to the petition got up against
Mr. Dick Peddie's Bill.

It is not her own adherents only who are in favour of the
continued connection between Church and State. It is not many days
ago since a memorial signed by over 200 of the leading elders of The
Free Church was sent up to Mr. Gladstone, praying him to have
nothing to do with the disestablishing of The Church of Scotland.

Apart from this altogether however, is certain that many difficulties
would be felt in maintaining a purely voluntary ministry. This is often
gainsaid, but look at the facts in connection with The Free Church.
Out of 1081 churches, 722 are not self supporting. When such is the
case with The Free Church, whose supporters are voluntary, what

might be expected if after depriving the people of Scotland of their lawful patrimony you compel them to support a Christian ministry?

Many objections are often made to The Church of Scotland as it is at present. What these objections are, or on what grounds they are made, I will not at present enter into, but be they what they may, surely they form but a very sober plea for the entire dissolution of that sacred institution.

I will close with an extract from a pamphlet issued by a Committee of The General Assembly of The Church of Scotland. 'The power in Church and State alike now belongs to the people, and it remains with them to mould both according to their highest sense of justice and well being. Make of your Church then, all you would wish it to be. Reform and improve it. Remove any barrier that may still prevent other Presbyterians from uniting with us on the widest possible basis. Reorganise it but do not overturn it. It will be a dark day for Scotland, and the old religion of Scotland, if you yield to the clamours of English secularism and sectarian rivalry'.

We see from this the weakness of the argument of those who would completely disannul the Church because it may not be altogether perfect, as existing at present.

Here are The Heads of the Church willing that the Church should be reformed and reorganised to meet the views of the people, and reformed also in such a manner as to allow other Presbyterians to unite with it.

Since the union of the Churches is the one great end which is aimed at, and since I am totally opposed to Disestablishment as in any way tending towards that end, it may be asked, what would I propose as a help towards the accomplishment of that object?

Well gentlemen, this is perhaps a rather difficult question to answer, but one thing seems to be very clear in my mind viz. that the funds of the Church are not the chief cause of division, for The Free Church at least is as ready to accept of the national funds as any party. I rather think that some of those abstract principles which the Duke of Argyle says are so hard to define; but which from the mind of the Scottish people are yet so hard to dispel, have more to do with the disunion than may be supposed. Anything therefore that would help to set aside these principles, or that would in any degree help to lessen their influence; anything that would bring more prominently into view what ought to be the one great end and aim of all Christians, whether collectively or individually viz. the furtherance of the interests of true religion. Let this once become the aim of all men, let this be the one grand ideal towards which all their efforts will be directed, and soon all this sectarian rivalry and petty jealousies will cease to exist, and the union of the Churches be an easy achievement.

An Essay on Time
Read at a Meeting of Deskford Mutual Improvement Association, 1886

Time is one of these things which cannot be defined. It is only by referring to those periods into which time has been divided, that we can speak with any degree of intelligence concerning the same. The space of time occupied by a year, a month, or a day, is easily comprehended by everyone. From history we hear pretty clearly what has been going on upon the surface of the earth for the last 4000 years, and the conception of this is quite within the range of an average intelligence. Geologists however inform us, from the examination of the crust of the earth, that our planet has been in existence for a prodigiously longer space of time than that, a period computed by hundreds and thousands of years, but yet even of this vast space of time we might conceive some faint idea. So entirely dependent however is our ideas of time upon measurement, or so purely rather may it be said to consist of measurement, that a beginning or an end of time, is to our senses altogether inconceivable. To illustrate this I shall relate an anecdote I remember being told when at School. 'A German peasant boy had become famous for the wise and ready answers which he gave to all questions. The Emperor had even come to hear of him, and sent a message that he should present himself at the palace. Says the Emperor to the boy, 'if you answer rightly the three questions which I shall put to you, I shall regard you as my own son, and you shall dwell with me in my royal palace'. One of the questions was, 'how many seconds are there in eternity?' The boy without the least hesitation answered, 'In East Pomerania there is a diamond mountain, a league in height, a league in length and a league in breadth. Once every hundred years there comes a little bird and rubs its bill on that mountain, and when it is all rubbed away one second of eternity will be gone'. At first sight the seeming impossibility of a bird ever rubbing away a diamond mountain, might lead us to suppose that the boy had answered rightly. But had the bird actually rubbed away a portion however small, and had it been possible for it to continue doing so, it would in time have reduced the whole. Still even this inconceivable length of time would bear a smaller proportion to eternity than a second does to time. We thus see how dependent on measurement our ideas of time are.

The natural division of time into days, months and years must have been apparent to mankind at a fairly early period. We may very naturally suppose that the first human ideas regarding time would be the day.

The rotation of the earth on its own axis; bringing a succession of light and darkness, a waking and a sleeping time, a time to work and a time to rest, must have impressed the simple fathers of the race, as soon as reflection dawned in their minds.

The time taken by the earth to rotate on its own axis is strictly speaking the length of a day. This has been ascertained to be 23 hours, 56 minutes, 4 seconds. The earth however, has an additional motion in its orbit round the sun, and it therefore takes other 3 minutes, 56 seconds before the sun appears in the same place, and the length of the day is therefore 24 hours. While the day absolute is thus seen to be measured by a single revolution of the earth, the day practical is a very different affair for places having different meridians have each a practical day of their own. On going westward we gain time, going eastward we lose it. If two people therefore were to start to circumnavigate the globe, the one going west, and the other going east, it is certain that when they met their nominal day would not agree. It would be say Tuesday with the one, and Wednesday with the other. When the Sabbath was first instituted in the Garden of Eden, it only occupied 24 hours, but since Christians are now to be found in every quarter of the globe, it takes 48 hours from its commencement to its final close. It is curious to remark that in the extreme west of North America, while one race of people are calling the day Saturday, another at no great distance are observing the Sabbath, this being occasioned by the people who first colonised the places coming from different directions.

The week is deemed by some to be a natural division of time, being determined by the observation of the principal phases of the moon. Chambers in his Book of Days does not agree with this because, he says, the week does not consist of the same number of days in all countries. The week, says he, with its terminal day among the Jews, and its initial day among Christians observed as a day of rest and devotion, is to be regarded in the main as a religious institution.

Considering however that the days have only various names in the range of one week, and that by this period many of the ordinary operations of life are determined and arranged, the week must always be reckoned a time division of the highest order.

The natural division of time determined by the revolution of the moon, has doubtless been the origin of the year being divided into twelve months. The month of nature, or the time taken by the moon to revolve round the earth is 29 days, 12 hours, 44 minutes, 3 seconds, and there are of course twelve such periods each year, and about eleven days over. From a very early period there were efforts amongst most civilised nations to arrange the year into parts accordant with the revolutions of the moon, but they were all of a rather irregular character, until Julius Caesar reformed the calendar by deeming that there should be 365 days in each year, and an extra day every fourth year. The number of days assigned to each month by Julius Caesar was 30 and 31 alternately with a day less in February when it was not a leap year. His successor, Caesar Augustus, altered this order however. It was he who gave names to all the months, naming the 7th one after himself, and these names, and the numbers of days which he assigned to each, are now used in all Christian countries except Holland.

The length of a year is strictly expressed by the space of time required by the Earth to revolve round the Sun, viz. 365 days, 5 hours, 48 minutes, 49 seconds and 7/10th of a second, for to such a nicety has it been ascertained. For convenience in reckoning however, it has been found necessary to end the year with a day, and then add the fractional parts together and form another day.

About 45 years before Christ, Julius Caesar saw the necessity of having an extra day every fourth year for the purpose of using these odd minutes. For several hundred years this system was followed, but as an extra day every fourth year is in reality too much by 11 minutes 10 seconds it came to be seen that the natural time was falling behind the reckoning.

In 1582, the reckoning being 10 days wrong, Pope Gregory decreed that the 5th of August should be reckoned the 15th, and to keep the year right in the future, the over plus being 18 hours, 37 minutes in a century, he ordered that every centurial year that could not be divided by 4 should not be a leap year, as it otherwise would be.

The Gregorian style soon obtained sway in all Catholic countries, but it was not till 1752 that it was adopted in this country. By that time there were 11 days between the Julian and Gregorian style of reckoning, and 1800 not being reckoned a leap year there are now 12 days between the styles.

Of all the Christian countries Russia is the only one now in which the old style is still retained.

The division of the day into hours, minutes etc was an arrangement that could only be adopted after means had been invented of mechanically measuring time. We accordingly find no allusion to hours in Scripture history until we come to the Book of Daniel who lived 552 years before Christ.

Both the Jews and Romans divided the day into 24 hours, but they assigned an equal number to the day and to the night. The hours with them therefore were a varying quantity of time according to the seasons and the latitude. Before the hour division was adopted, men could only speak of the different parts of the day by such vague terms as morning, evening, forenoon or afternoon, or by alluding to their meal times. This custom has still some hold upon us, partly because they are so natural and obvious, and partly I expect from tradition.

We also have some terms of rather an original and practical nature for certain portions of the day viz. the gloamin', the dawn and the skreigh o' day, meaning the cry of the coming day.

So much for the division of time, and the causes which have led to its being so divided.

Let us now look at it in another aspect. To illustrate its fleeting nature time is often represented as having wings. 'Time flies' is an oft used expression.

The poet says, 'Oh never chide the wings of time, nor say they're tardy in their flight, you'll find the days speed quick enough, if you but husband them aright'.

Although time strictly speaking cannot be defined, yet it is often compared to a variety of things, and more especially to those things which illustrate its transient nature. Time's a hand-breadth, 'Tis a tale, 'Tis a vessel under sail, 'Tis a short lived fading flower, 'Tis a rainbow on a shower, 'Tis a torrent's rapid stream, 'Tis a shadow, 'Tis a dream.

Time also is not only fleeting, but it often flies past unperceived. Joanna Bailllie says of time, 'Still on it creeps, each little moment at another's heels, till hours, days, years and ages are made up of such small parts as these'.

When engaged in tasks that are uncongenial to our tastes, when on beds of sickness, or when held in suspense as to the ultimate result of any project closely connected with our welfare, time may sometimes seem to lag, and we may mark its progress with anxious careworn faces. But when in health, and performing with a will those duties in which our heart is centred, when eager in the pursuit of some object that is dear to us, or when in the company of these we respect, esteem and love, time generally, as Burns puts it, 'flies past wi' tent less heed'. It is said of Jacob, that the seven years which he served for Rachel seemed to him but a few days.

'Time is money' is a maxim often quoted by men of business, but surely time has a greater value than can ever be counted in coin. The proper improvement of it is self culture, self improvement and growth of character. An hour wasted daily on trifles or in idleness, would at then end of a few years, if devoted to self improvement greatly add to our knowledge.

The following advice is said to have been given by Lord Chatham to his son. 'I would inscribe on the curtains of your bed and on the walls of your chamber. If you do not rise early, you can make progress in nothing. If you do not set apart your hours of reading, if you suffer yourself or anyone else to break in upon them, your days will slip through your hands unprofitable and frivolous'.

An economical use of time is the only sure mode of securing leisure. We should have a time for everything, and everything should be done at its time. If our work be thoughtfully planned, and our time properly apportioned, be our business what it may, we will be enabled to accomplish it, and carry it forward.

On the other hand a miscalculation of time involves us in perpetual hurry, confusion and difficulties. Lord Nelson once said, 'I owe all my success in life to having always been a quarter of an hour before my time'.

Take care of the pennies and the pounds will take care of themselves, is advice we often hear given to youthful spendthrifts. As truly might it be said, with reference to time, 'take care of the minutes and the days will take care of themselves'. Smiles says, 'lost wealth may be replaced by industry, lost knowledge by study, lost health by temperance or medicine, but lost time is gone forever'.

When we soberly consider the great value of time, given unto us as a talent to improve, when we think also of its fleeting nature, so that as we speak, like the electric current it flies past and is gone forever, how ought we to bestir ourselves, to make the best possible use of it?

It is a saying of Fullers, 'He lives long who lives best, and time misspent is not lived but lost'.

I will conclude by quoting the lines of a Deeside poet.

> Work while yet the sun doth shine, thou man of strength and will
> For never doth the streamlet glide, all useless by the mill;
> Wait not until tomorrow's sun, beams brightly on thy way,
> For all that thou canst call thine own, lies in the phrase today.
> This solemn proverb speaks to all, with meaning deep and vast,
> The mill will never grind again, with water that is past.

Whether is Nature Or Art The More Beautiful To The Eye
A Paper Supporting Nature Read at a Meeting of Deskford Mutual
Improvement Association, February 1887

Mr. Chairman and Gentlemen,
I do not think the subject we have chosen for discussion this evening (is) a very suitable one, my reason for saying so being, that it is too one-sided.

Before entering upon the discussion of the relative claims which Nature and Art put forth as regards beauty, let us consider for a little what these two really mean. Our dictionaries tell us that Art means skill or cunning. In connection with our debate therefore Art means whatever the skill or cunning of man has produced.

Nature on the other hand is what man's Creator has made. Taking it for granted that this is the true meaning of the respective terms, is it needful think you to go any further? Can any stronger argument than this be brought forward to prove that beyond comparison Nature has the stronger claim to beauty, nay does it not almost seem irreverent to compare them at all.

For the sake of the debate however, let us take a few specimens of Art and Nature, and placing them side-by-side, look at them clearly and calmly without prejudice and without partiality.

That the Art of man has produced works of wondrous beauty will never be denied. Painting in these latter days attained to such proficiency, the outline of the object can be drawn so naturally, and with such exactness as to shape and symmetry, and the blending of the colours can be performed so delicately, that in certain cases it almost appears like inspiration. Who does not admire the works of the great Master Painters, many of whom have given the work and the study of a lifetime to be able to produce on canvas a scene of rarest beauty, deepest pathos, and life-like loveliness?

Let us suppose that the picture before us is that of a storm at sea. A gallant ship riding at anchor, and the billows breaking in a line of foam along a rocky coast. Or it may be a peaceful rural scene. The summer sun has newly set, and a glow of glory is lighting up the western sky. A cosy farm steading stands in the foreground, the farmer wearied with the labours of the day is sitting in the summer seat of his garden, enjoying his evening pipe. The lowing kine are being driven home from the grassy lea, while the milk maid stands awaiting them her milking cog under her arm. Or perhaps the painter may present to us a view of some of our famous highland scenery. A beautiful loch studded with islets, trees over-hanging the water, and mirrored in its glassy surface, the surrounding hills covered with the purple heather, a wild mountain stream tumbling over its rocky bed, and to make the scene complete, an eagle soaring in the azure sky above.

Pictures such as these we have all seen, and greatly admired, and all honour to the artists who can produce them. Let us confer on them that eulogium they so rightly deserve. Let us compare their works of beauty with other works of Art, but here we must halt, for after all what are these fine pictures whose praises we have been sounding so highly? Only imitations are they not and rather poor imitations the best of them are of those real wonderful pictures hung up above, below and around us in the great Art Gallery of Nature.

What a poor substitute for the reality is the picture of a storm at sea. The mighty thundering of the billows is not at all to be heard. That rolling, seething, never-tiring motion of the ever-restless sea can never be transferred to canvas. The costliest, the most beautiful, and the truest picture of the mighty ocean, that was ever produced, can never impress us with a sense of our own littleness, nor fill us with such vast ideas of the Eternal and the Sublime, as crowd into, and fill our souls as we walk by the sea-shore, reminding us so forcibly of our own weakness, and of His greatness who holdeth the sea in the hollow of His hand.

There is a beauty in the sea as it sparkles beneath the summer sun, which no artist ever yet portrayed, and there is a grandeur in the storm-tossed billows of the mighty deep, which the most consummate skill and the greatest Art of man has totally failed to produce.

It may be argued however, that the sea is a very different subject for the painter to study, and that the other pictures we have alluded to might compare far more favourably with nature. This may to a certain extent be true. The rural scene, which I have feebly attempted to depict to you, and the picture of the highland loch with its surrounding hills, may indeed be rare and beautiful works of Art, and may convey to us a very true idea of what they are meant to portray, but will anyone dare to assert, that the most life-like picture of rural peacefulness, can in any way compare with the simple beauty of the reality? Can the most striking reproduction of peace and plenty in any degree produce in us that calm contentment which we feel on a balmy summer's evening 'tween the gloamin' an' the mirk when the kye come hame'.

Or again, never can a picture of the hills and glens of Scotland convey to us a true idea of their sublime beauty and majestic grandeur. They must be seen before their beauty can be truly realised. We must stand in person beside the highland loch, we must see its tinywavelets rippling on its pebbly shore, we must follow the lordly eagle soaring far above us, as he seeks his eyrie on some rocky cliff, we must gaze upwards to the lofty summit of the everlasting hills, we must mark their rugged outline and their bold and striking features. Then shall we realise the true beauty of Nature, then shall we feel our hearts rising upwards from Nature unto Nature's God, and then shall we be constrained to confess how feeble is the Art of man when compared with the perfection of Nature.

Let us now look on painting in another light, and compare the beauty of man's Art in that respect with the beauty of Nature.

The wild Indian paints his skin, tattoos his body with figures of animals, trees etc. and is thereby distinguished from members of other tribes. In our own country however, with its boasted civilisation, and its refined culture, the painting of certain parts of the body is not altogether unknown. There are those in all ranks of society, but more especially ladies connected with the stage, who are often suspected of being quite lavish in the use of rouge. Painting of this nature, this tinting of nature's roses as we might term it, may pass muster beneath the moon's pale beams, or even in the brighter glare of these artificial lights which man has invented, but let not the sun arise upon it, or like the morning cloud and the early dew, its beauty will soon vanish away.

Nature's painting on the other hand will bear a closer inspection. Indeed like everything else in Nature the more closely we inspect it, the more beauty do we behold.

What has been said in reference to the painter holds equally true in regard to the sculptor. His ingenious brain may design, and his skilful hands may execute a work of passing beauty. The symmetry of mould, the grace of limb, and the lineaments of the human face, may all be produced with a striking resemblance, but at least it is only life-like. The rosy hue of health, the glowing cheek and the sparkling eye, are Nature's beauties, and altogether beyond the reach of the sculptor's chisel.

Music is another of the fine arts, but then we also have music in Nature. The ingenuity of man has produced a variety of musical instruments many of which under the hands of a skilful player can certainly discourse sweet music. With all his vaunted skill however, he has never yet invented an instrument that can equal the human voice.

Singing however may be claimed as an Art, but even allowing that it is so, how hoarse and croaking, how tame and flat, how lacking in sweetness and melody is even the sweetest human voice when compared with songs of the feathered minstrels, Nature's accompaniment to the Spring mornings, the music of the grove, the Cantata of the Sylvan Choir.

In the Industrial Arts we also find, that the beauty of the workmanship executed by Nature's artisans (if we may call them so) far excells that which man's greatest skill produces. The bird is an excellent architect, the beaver a most skilful bridge maker, the silk worm the most beautiful of weavers, and the spider the best of net-makers.

All these execute their work in a manner which the art of man can neither rival nor excel.

We might continue without limit to present to you examples of Art and Nature, but the comparison of their respective claims to beauty, would invariably be the same. It stands to reason that Art must always be second to Nature, for Art is limited, while Nature is unlimited, Art is defective, Nature is perfect. Art is the work of man, Nature is the handiwork of man's Creator.

A Paper Read at a Temperance Meeting in Deskford School, February 1889

Mr. Chairman Ladies and Gentlemen,

When I was asked sometime ago to make a few remarks at this meeting, it was with some reluctance, and after a good deal of consideration that I consented to do so.

Not for lack of interest in the Temperance Cause by any means, but simply because I was doubtful if I would be able to say anything that would interest or edify you.

There are few if any present who will deny that drunkenness is not only a vice, but that it leads to other vices, to crime, misery and degradation. There are few also who do not allow that some remedy should be tried to suppress this evil.

What then is to be the remedy? What means are we to employ? What cure can we prescribe? It is here that the divergence of opinion exists. Some hold forth moderation, others advocate Total Abstinence.

It is in this light therefore, I think that Total Abstinence and moderation should be viewed. Which of them is most calculated to suppress, what on all hands is allowed to be a great and terrible evil? Of course my convictions are very strongly in favour of Total Abstinence, but I am inclined to think that sometimes we are inclined to be a little hard on those who differ from us, forgetting perhaps that their convictions may be as dear to them, as ours are to us.

I shall therefore try and refrain tonight from being too severe on the moderate drinkers, for although Total Abstinence is, and ought to be the guiding principle of the Temperance Movement, still in my opinion, moderation ought always to characterise the language we employ in advocating the cause.

Before discussing the relative claims of these two remedies (so called) for the abuse of intoxicating drink, it might not be uninteresting to say a few words as to the origin of the Temperance Movement also the meaning of the words Teetotalism and Good-Templarism, and how and when they came to be used.

Like many other new inventions, the Temperance Movement was first promoted by our cousins across the water, the Americans. About the beginning of last century it appears that the vice of drunkenness had reached an alarming height in the United States. In the year 1808 a Society was formed at Saratoga in the State of New York, consisting of 43 members. 'No member shall drink rum, gin, whisky, wine or any distilled spirits or compositions of the same, except by the advice of a physician or in the case of actual disease (also except at Public Dinners) under the penalty of 25 cents, provided that this article shall not infringe on any religious rite'.

This Society continued to exist for 14 years, but whether from the laxity of its rules, or from some other cause, it does not seem to have done much good. Gradually however, the clergy began to take an interest in the subject, and after a series of sermons had been preached and publicised against this degrading and ever increasing vice, another Society was formed in 1829 called the New York State Temperance Society. This movement seems to have been attended with a marked degree of success for before the close of the year, 1000 local Societies, with 100,000 members were in existence, and a periodical entitled, 'The Journal of Humanity', was established to promote the cause.

Rumours of the progress of this movement soon reached the Old World, and in August 1829, a Society was formed at New Ross in the county of Wexford, Ireland, the members of which pledged themselves to abstain from the use of distilled spirits, except as a medicine in the case of bodily ailment, and further neither to allow the use of them in their families, nor provide them for the entertainment of friends.

Most brilliant success seems to have attended this movement in Ireland. In 1838, the Rev. Theobald Matthew, commonly known as Father Matthew, commenced his extraordinary career, and in less than two years 1,800,000 men and women were enrolled in Ireland's Great National Total Abstinence Society.

This Father Matthew had truly been a most extraordinary man, and the reformation which he effected in the habits of his fellow countrymen was really marvellous. His zeal and enthusiasm in behalf of the Temperance Cause won for him the title of 'The Apostle of Temperance'. In Chambers' Encyclopaedia (to which I am indebted for several of these items) we read, 'he died in 1856 but the fruits of his labour are still visible. The general tone of the public mind in Ireland as regards the use of intoxicating drink may be truly said to have undergone a complete revolution, which continues to the present day'.

Meantime Scotland has not been uninfluenced. As early as October 1829 Mr John Dunlop of Greenock, a Justice of the Peace in Renfrewshire, after lecturing on Temperance in Glasgow, and surrounding district, succeeded in forming a Society in Greenock, the first in Scotland, and the precursor of the Glasgow and West of Scotland Temperance Society. Mr Dunlop may thus be called The Father of Temperance Societies in Great Britain.

The zeal and activity of this Society was remarkable. During the first year of its existence it circulated no fewer than 425,000 tracts and 20,000 pamphlets, while its adherents in Glasgow alone numbered over 5000.

The notable word Teetotal is said to have been first used in September 1833. Up to that time Total Abstinence was not the recognised principle of Temperance Societies, ardent spirits only being prohibited. It being seen however, that porter and ale were also the cause of intoxication this new and more stringent application of the principles began to be advocated. Many of the old members, who were now called 'moderates', objected to this. Large meetings followed where lively and animated discussions were held as to the merits of the two principles.

In the County of Lancashire, a certain Dicky Turner was a very warm supporter of Total Abstinence, but Dicky had a stutter in his speech. They have a very peculiar dialect in Lancashire, and one evening when Dicky was making a thundering speech against the 'moderates' he happened to say in the course of his harangue, 'I'll have nowt to do with this moderation, botheration pledge. I'll be reet down tee-tee-total for ever and ever', and so Dicky's supporters came to be called Teetotalers.

This origin of the word however has been disputed, and it is affirmed that the term is simply a Lancashire phrase for final, thorough or complete.

The most recent development of the Temperance Movement is that known as Good Templarism. It originated in New York about the year 1851 and rapidly spread through the United States. In 1868, the Order established itself in England, and the following year found its way to Scotland. Its progress has been singularly rapid. Some years ago it was estimated that in England alone its membership exceeded 200,000. These figures of course do not represent absolutely new adherents to the Temperance Cause. In many cases they were members drawn from the older Temperance Societies, but it is an undoubted fact that The Order has been very successful in making fresh converts to the cause of Total Abstinence.

The name is derived from the famous Knights Templars, a religious and military order founded at Jerusalem in the beginning of the Twelfth century, for the purpose of protecting the Holy Sepulchre, and pilgrims resorting thither. The title of Good Templars originated therefore in a fanciful analogy between the functions of this order of military monks, and the modern disciples of Temperance. As the former were enrolled to defend the Holy Sepulchre and the interests of religion, so the latter are branded together to protect Christianity against the drinking institutions of the land.

It owes its great popularity to certain peculiarities in its constitution, to its picturesque or showy ceremonial, and its aim to combine social and festive amusements with missionary zeal.

Such then was the origin of the Temperance Movement and such the manner in which the terms Teetotaller and Good Templar came to be applied to its supporters.

At the commencement I said that I should try and refrain from being too severe on the moderate drinkers, as I have already trespassed quite long enough I fear on your time and patience, I think that I had better keep strictly to my resolve, by saying no more in the meantime. Perhaps by the time I have another opportunity of saying a few words at a public meeting, there may be no moderates, nor yet immoderate drinkers in Deskford.

When the time comes that such a happy state of matters shall exist, a state of matters which would certainly greatly help to make Deskford truly entitled to be called a Model Parish, I shall then feel quite at liberty in denouncing the practice in the severest of terms.

We shall at least strive to live in the hope so well expressed in the lines of the poet, a little parody of which may suit our case in the meantime:

There's a good time coming friends, a good time coming,
The folks shall join the Temperance cause,
And they shall love to keep its laws,
They will not use, what's so abused
But strive to make virtue stronger,
The reformation has begun, just wait a little longer.
There's a good time coming friends, a good time coming,
Then let us aid it all we can
Every woman, every man,
Smallest aids if rightly given
Will make the case aye stronger
It will be strong in Deskford one day, wait a little longer.

Is a Teetotal Farmer Justified in Selling Barley to a Distiller?
A Paper Supporting the Negative Side Read at a Meeting of the Vale of Deskford Temperance Society, January 1891

Mr. Chairman Ladies and Gentlemen,
The subject which we have chosen for discussion this evening is one upon which all Total Abstainers should have a very decided opinion, and more especially those Total Abstainers who are in any way connected with agriculture.

We have listened with pleasure I am sure to the very able paper delivered to us by my friend and opponent Mr Gordon, and after hearing the arguments so many and strong, which he has brought forward in support of his cause, I fear your opinions will be so decided, that it will be needless of me to try and alter them.

I would try to remind you however, that there are two ways of looking at things, that there are two sides to every question.

The subject for our consideration tonight is, 'is a teetotal farmer justified in selling his barley to a distiller'? Mr Gordon says he is, while I say he is not.

To begin with then, who is a teetotal farmer and what are the principles which he upholds in regard to the use of intoxicating drink, and the drink traffic?

A teetotal farmer is one who has pledged himself to abstain from all intoxicating liquor as beverages, to do all in his power to suppress the drink traffic, and to discountenance all the causes and practices of intemperance.

We find then that a teetotal pledge affects in the first place his own personal conduct, but in the second place it affects his conduct towards his neighbour, and all with whom he comes into conduct for he promises to do all in his power to remove the causes, and to discountenance the practices of intemperance.

If a teetotaller's pledge affected himself only, there might be some reason in saying that he was justified in selling his barley to a distiller, for as long as he continues a total abstainer, it matters little to him how much drink is made or sold. But when we consider that his promise goes much further than this seeing that he has pledged himself to do all in his power to remove the causes of intemperance, on what grounds can his conduct in this transaction be justified? Is not drink the cause of drunkenness and is not a farmer when he supplies the material for making the drink, promoting instead of suppressing the cause of intemperance?

It may be said however, that the simple fact of a farmer supplying a distiller with barley does not in any way implicate him as a partner in the making of the drink. I do not think it will require any round about logic however to clearly prove the contrary. You will all doubtless remember the School book story of an Uncle who invited his nephew to dinner on Xmas day, and promising to give him a pudding which had taken a thousand men to make it. The desert consisted of a plain plum pudding. The Uncle in enumerating the different persons who had helped to make the pudding, included the farmer who grew the wheat from which the flour was made. Far more closely connected with the making of the drink, than any of those who were with the pudding, is the farmer who directly supplies the material for the making of whisky.

Having thus proved that a farmer who sells barley to a distiller is one of the principle agents in the making of intoxicating drink, let us now try to show how unjustifiable is the conduct of a teetotal farmer who engages in such transactions.

To bring the matter more clearly and forcibly home to you, let us consider a case for a different although somewhat parallel nature.

A judge in a court of justice is supposed to do all in his power to uphold the law of his country. In fact he has sworn and pledged himself to do so. His principles are, you must obey the laws of your country, or suffer the penalty due for the transgression of the same. As St. Paul puts it, 'he is a terror to evil doers, and praise to those who do well'. Suppose now that this judge was in the habit of attending, and taking an active part in Socialistic or Bolshevik meetings, setting forth as his decided opinion that society as presently organised was not on a proper footing, upholding the theory of a new distribution of means of property, and thus inviting those who before were law loving, and law abiding subjects, to discontent, perhaps to riot of rebellion. Must you not allow that his conduct in thus acting was the opposite of being consistent with his professed principles?

Or take another example. A young man in the prime of life offers himself to go to India as a missionary. Having been solemnly ordained as a preacher of the Gospel, he sets sail full of zeal and enthusiasm for the great and noble work to which he has dedicated himself. The conversion of the heathen to Christianity, their improvement, mentally, morally and physically, the preaching of the glorious Gospel of Our Lord and Saviour, and the setting forth of his belief in the one true and the living God all receive his earnest and undivided attention.

His sacred duties are all performed conscientiously, fearlessly and faithfully. Suppose now that this young man should begin to contribute a series of papers to some monthly periodical supporting the belief in Deism or Atheism. Or suppose that he should write, print and circulate a number of leaflets having for their title Protestantism versus Romanism, denouncing therein in no measured terms the religion of his forefathers, and the form of worship he so zealously professed to support, and for which he had striven so hard to get converts, while at the same time he upheld with equal fervour the tenets of the Church of Rome.

What would our opinion of such a man be? Would he be justified think you in so acting? Would we not be unanimous in condemning his conduct?

He would certainly in my opinion be guilty of the gross inconsistency of striving to build up with one hand a noble structure, while with the other he was actively engaged in pulling it down.

In what respect does the conduct of our teetotal farmer when he sells his barley to a distiller, differ from those characters we have feebly tried to portray? His conduct is as inconsistent as theirs, his action in so doing as unjustifiable.

As a Total Abstainer we must give him credit for supporting a noble cause, for lending a helping hand to push forward that movement, which ultimately aims at the suppression of crime, the raising of the degraded, the relief of the poor and the indigent and the making of the home happy, while on the other hand by selling his barley to a distiller he is (whether intentionally or not) undermining all these beneficial results. In supplying the material for making intoxicating drink, even although we make the allowance that he is 'as the man who slew and did not know it', still we cannot get rid of the fact in some measure he is responsible for the slaying of thousands, that indirectly he helps to fill our prisons and lunatic asylums, to raise our poor rates, and to greatly increase the misery, the slavery, the ignorance and ungodliness, that still exist in this enlightened nineteenth century, in this highly favoured land of boasted liberty and Christianity.

An Essay on Courage, undated

Courage is a trait of character, of which few are altogether lacking, and yet which few at all times possess. Most persons however, have a desire to be considered courageous, for true courage is everywhere honoured and respected, while cowardice on the other hand is universally despised.

In the lowest grades of society, even amongst those who make thieving a profession, courage is considered a virtue, while cowardice is a crime.

It is not courage of this nature however, of which I intend at this time to treat. I will rather in the first place strive to say a few words on those callings of which courage is generally supposed to be a necessary attendant.

I will then try to enumerate a few actions, in the performance of which true courage is always displayed, and which, although seldom awarded public applause, still in the highest sense merit our warmest commendation.

Foremost among those whose actions generally are considered courageous is the soldier.

In times of peace the soldier's courage may be put to no severer test than that of any common citizen. The craven hearted and the coward may then pass muster for brave men. But when war, that fearful calamity overtakes a country, when our soldiers are called forth for service in the field, called it may be to a foreign country, where the heat of a tropical sun makes action nearly impossible, and life almost a burden, when the line of battle is drawn, and the foe stands facing him in stern array, when the cannon belch forth their thunders, and a line of muskets are levelled at his breast, when he feels that except a comrade's body shields him, death must certainly be his doom, then is the soldier's courage tried, then it is seen who are the weak and wavering, and who have the hearts of steel.

The British soldier has always been specially noted for his courage and bravery. Many a hard battle has he fought, and many a victory has he won.

Napoleon Bonaparte fancied he could conquer Europe, but the Scots Greys at Waterloo forced him to change his opinion. The Emperor's exclamation at that famous battle, 'How terribly those Greys charge', is a lasting tribute to the courage of our gallant soldier lads. The Charge of the Light Brigade at Balaclava, when a handful of men made an attack upon an army in position, will also always remain a red lettered page in the record of British daring. The battles of the Nile and Trafalgar, where the greatest naval hero the world has ever seen so gallantly fought and fell, the battles of Corunna, Sebastapol, and Tel-El-Kebir all tell the same tale, all testify to the truth of the lines, 'Hearts of oak are our ships, hearts of oak are our men'.

And shall we forget the courage displayed by the Bruce and the Wallace, Scotland's greater patriots who fought and who bled on so many a battlefield, and all for the love they bore their fatherland.

Looking then to the victories of the past, and to the laurels which are yet being won by Britain's loyal sons, are we not justified in our enthusiasm when we say:

Rule Britannia, rule the waves
Britons never shall be slaves.

Next to the soldier the sailor claims our attention in reference to the courage necessary in the pursuit of his calling. Those who have never gone on a sea voyage, and whose only experience off terra firma may have been a sail on a summer day down the Clyde, through the Kyles o' Bute and Rothesay Bay may have fancied that the duties of a sailor were but a pleasant pastime. Let them but for once however, experience the stern realities of a storm at sea, when the waves lashed into fury by the angry elements, are rolling mountains high, and threatening every instant to engulf them, when the cordage creaks and strains, and the bare masts bend before the blast, making the strongest ship appear such a puny thing, as it is tossed to and fro at the mercy of the wind and waves. Then will they feel as they never felt before, how much courage is required by those who encounter the perils of the deep, by 'those who go down to the sea in ships, and who trade in the great waters'.

Let us also follow for a little the fearless Greenland whaler, as year by year he steers his trusty bark towards the regions of snow and ice. What a brave heart must he possess, as he glides out and in among the mighty icebergs, which towering above him like crystal mountains, may at any moment draw together and imprison him, or worse fate, crush his frail bark like a nut shell.

But what need is there to go so far from home to find examples of courage and bravery. Are not the fishermen of the Banffshire Coast noted for their hardihood and daring? The coast is rocky, the storms that visit us are wild and frequent, the harbours in many instances are insufficient, and yet our hardy fishermen are ever the foremost in the prosecution of their dangerous calling.

Before enumerating more instances however, let us look a little deeper into the subject and see if we have not been attributing a greater amount of courage to the soldier and the sailor, the fisherman and the whaler than what really belongs to them. The performance of one action does not necessarily require the same amount of courage from different persons. What may be of extreme difficulty to one, may be the performance of daily duties to another. A good deal depends on the training received, and also on the circumstances in which we are placed. The severe training received by the soldier, and the strict discipline which he undergoes, must therefore detract somewhat from his supposed courage, and would not the daily duties of the sailor, the constant battling with the wind and waves, have a hardening influence on his nature, so that the duties which so sorely tried the courage of the cabin boy, on his first voyage, would soon come to be looked upon as trivial tasks.

From what has been said it might be supposed that I meant to infer that courage was a qualification of The Lord's Creation only. Far be it from me ever to insinuate such a thing. Has not the courage and hardihood displayed by Grace Darling, rendered her name a household word, and doubtless there are many such whose deeds are as worthy to be remembered, although they have not been kept in record?

Rev. E.P. Roe in his novel, 'Opening a Chestnut Burr' remarks (and I agree with him entirely) 'In the sudden and awful emergencies of life, woman's fortitude is often superior to man's'.[1]

---

[1] Edward Payson Roe was the most popular American novelist in the mid-nineteenth century with his books outselling even those of Mark Twain. His other novels included *Barrier's Burned Away* and *A Day of Fate*.

APPENDIX 2: LECTURES AND ESSAYS

This brings us to consider the second part of our subject viz. those actions in the performance of which true courage is always displayed, and which although seldom awarded public applause, still in the highest sense merits our warmest commendation. Circumstances for the display of such courage, is ever occurring in the daily lives of all.

They are often circumstances too which try our courage far more severely, morally if not physically than even being placed in positions of danger. How many a soldier is there whose bravery would sustain him in marching up to the cannon's mouth, and who would yet allow the sneers of his companions to dissuade him from reading the Bible, and many a soldier's courage would completely fail him, even after he had taken the pledge, if his prodigal comrades were to taunt him that he could not take a glass of grog, who would fearlessly mount to the giddy top-mast on a stormy night at sea.

Let us bring the subject a little nearer to home however. How many opportunities for the exercise of our courage in the matter of self-denial, occur in our everyday life?

Selfishness is one of the deceiving of the many evil tendencies to which we are heir. It tempts us to gratify our desires, at the expense of others, holding forth as the result a happiness which never comes. If we could only call our courage to our aid, and by practicing self denial, strive to make others happy, how much more real happiness we would ourselves possess.

Another instance in which courage is often sadly lacking is that of standing up alone for a good cause. How often do we find ourselves asking the question, 'what will the world say, or what will the world think?' And thus we allow our conduct to be governed almost wholly by public opinion.

Among the many examples of courage of this description which we have in sacred history, that of Daniel the Prophet is the most striking. The courage of Daniel has indeed become proverbial. Against kings and princes he was not afraid to stand up alone for the truth, and he dared to do the right independent of the frown or the favour of man.

From whence did Daniel's courage spring, and how may we attain a like strength of character? These are questions worthy of our earnest consideration. Dr. MacIntosh in the course of his New Year's Sermon made the remark, 'a guilty conscience makes cowards of us all'

It requires but little reasoning to show from this where lies the source of all true and lasting courage.

Of how much service is good courage also to the man of business. In these depressed times, when the prospect is far from tempting, will it be the despondent and the doubting, or those full of courage and hopefulness who will succeed? Would it not speak well for our courage, were on all occasions to take as our motto, 'Hope for the best, be prepared for the worst, and be content with whatever comes'.

Whether are Large or Small Farms the most beneficial to the Community
A paper supporting the Large Farms read at a Meeting of Ballindalloch Mutual Improvement Association, 5th January 1888

Mr. Chairman and Gentlemen,
Whether are large or small farms the most beneficial to the Community, is a question about which (at first sight) there might appear to be some doubt. A little consideration will however, suffice to show to any unprejudiced mind, that by far the greatest amount of benefit is derived from having a goodly number of large holdings.

It having fallen to my lot to support the large farms in this Debate, I shall strive to lay before you as clearly and concisely as possible a few arguments in support of the same.

In doing so however I would not have you suppose that I would advocate the doing away with all the small farms in the country, for I do not at all believe in that practice which certain landlords have, in dismantling small farms, in order to form large holdings.

Let us look at the county however, divided as it is into large and small farms alternately, and I maintain that the large farmers have done far more for the advancement of agriculture, and therefore for the good of the Community, than the small farmer.

You must all admit that during recent years, there has been in this part of the county, and indeed all over Scotland a very marked improvement in the breed of cattle. Instead of the thin scraggy animals that might have been seen pasturing in the fields some forty or fifty years ago, an entirely new and improved breed has been substituted,- a breed whether it be the Shorthorn or the Aberdeen Angus, that will produce a half more beef in the same time; and beef also of better quality. It is entirely to the large farmers that we are indebted for this important improvement. Whether it be our soil or our climate, but Scotland has certainly come to be looked upon, as the breeding ground, par excellence, of these two valuable breeds of cattle, and although a large percentage of the plums are being sent abroad to improve the native herds across the seas, still our own home cattle are steadily being improved through the same agency.

It was the large farmers also, who first saw the necessity of and the advantage to be derived from an Agricultural Society and who by joining together and forming the same, have done so much for the advancement of agriculture.

For the improvement of the breed of horses no less than the breed of cattle, we are indebted to the large farmer. By introducing pure-bred stallions of good stock, and sending them through the country the small farmers have got the advantage of them, and a better class of horses is the result.

During the past twenty years a marked improvement has also been made on the implements used on the farm. It is the large farmers we have to thank for introducing these new and labour-saving implements. When any new tool or implement is brought to the market, there is always some risk in purchasing at first, because it may not be suitable for the purpose for which it was intended. The small farmer is therefore afraid to venture, and he must needs leave it to his richer neighbour to make the first investment. In doing so we must admit that the large farmer does by far the most good to the community.

It is not only the want of means however that handicaps the small farmer, but also lack of sufficient horse power. You are all aware that certain soils can be rendered far more productive by being sub-soiled. The small farmer with his pair of horses, is unable to do so, and must be content with simply ploughing. The large farmer with more strength at his command, can put the sub-soil plough to follow the ordinary one, the result being a large increase in the yield of grain, roots and grass, and surely he who makes 'two blades of grass to grow where only one grew before', not only benefits himself, but also benefits the Community.

Another reason why large farms are the most beneficial to the Community is because they are in general cheaper rented. So many people have the mistaken idea that a small farm would be a desirable and profitable investment that in general they are rack rented. Their possessors therefore have to toil and moil from dawn to dark in order to make a bare subsistence, while their hard won earnings but too often go to maintain the landlord in luxury.

The large farmer on the other hand, being cheaper rented, has more money to lay out on improvements. He employs more work people. He gives more work to local tradesmen, and instead of giving his money to the proprietor to spend abroad, he diffuses it amongst the people at home.

It is therefore clearly to be seen, that the large farms are the most beneficial to the Community.

APPENDIX 3
A SHORT STORY BY JAMES WILSON

Rustic Courtship or Farm Life in Banffshire:
A Story in Two Chapters

Chapter 1

It was half past eight o'clock one Saturday night, and Mysie Brown, the servant lass at Brackenknowes, had just finished milking her cows. She had 'syed' her milk, carefully washed her milking cog, put everything into its accustomed place, and had now seated herself at the cosy kitchen fire to have an hour at her stockin'.

A sonsie, weel-faured lass was Mysie, with dark curly hair, red rosy cheeks, and a merry twinkle in her eye. She had been cook or kitchen lass at Brackenknowes for more than five years, and being an honest active servant, always considering the interests of her Master and Mistress, her wages had been steadily advancing and being thrifty, and of a saving disposition far above the average of her class, she had the reputation of having 'a gye triffle laid by'.

It being Saturday night the farm lads were all away, excepting Willie Andrew, the foreman, who being 'toon keeper', was seated in his usual corner, beneath the lamp, eagerly perusing The People's Journal.

'Od Willie fat are ye sae earnest at, cudna ye read something till's' says Mysie. Willie laid down his paper, drew his chair a little nearer to the kitchen maid, and looking earnestly into her face said, 'div ye ken lassie fat I'm thinkin' aboot'. 'No ye gomeril fat wye cud I dae that'. 'Weel I'm gaun awa tae Canada at the turn'. The bloom suddenly left Mysie's face, but keeping her eyes steadily fixed on her knitting, she rather dryly remarked, 'Oh ye are'.

'I wis jist readin' here', continued Willie, 'aboot a plooman that gaed oot tae Manitoba aboot sax year syne wi' only £10 in his pouch, an' no he's laird o' 160 acres, an last year he thrashed mair than a thoosan' bushels o' wheat. Noo fan cud we ever dee onything like that in this quintry'.

The click, click of Mysie's wires, and the tick tock of the little alarum clock on the kitchen mantle piece was the only sound that broke the silence for the next few minutes. At length Mysie, rather faintly remarked, 'An' wid ye gang awa an' leave me Willie'. 'Oh I've a' that planned' says the foreman, 'I wid jist gang oot mysel' for an year or twa, an' syne fan I'd gotten a bit lan', an' a hoose biggit, ye'd come oot till's, an' we'd get marriet'. 'But fat aboot my mither', says Mysie, 'Oh Willie I cud never gang sae far awa an' leave my mither'. 'But cudna yer mither come oot wi' ye, I wid like awfu' weel tae hae yer mither wi's. She'd look aifter the poultry, an', an', an' the young fouk maybe', and Willie gave Mysie's ear a gentle squeeze with the hand that was resting on the back of her chair. Mysie's roses were in full bloom now, but giving no direct reply to his last remark, she dropped her knitting into her lap, and facing round to her companion said in a firm and decided tone of voice, 'Na, na Willie, we wid never get my mither tae cross the sea, an' I'll never gang sae far awa an' leave her, so if ye'r gaun to Canada I doot ye'll hae tae gang yersel'.[1]

To let you understand Mysie's mother was a widow. Her husband had been a tenant of a 20 acre croft on a rather bare hillside, but being an intelligent, hard-working, God-fearing man, he had done his best to make ends meet, and to bring up decently a family of four sons, and a daughter. Dying however when they were all young, his widow had most reluctantly to give up the little homestead, and remove to a 'tane' house in the village of Fordyke. By retailing some groceries to her neighbours, by boarding one of the female teachers in her room end, and by dint of the strictest economy, she had managed to bring up her family in a most respectable manner, making it a strong point, that every one of them should go regularly to Church and Sunday School.

Often would she remark to her boys on a Saturday night when hearing them their catechism, 'Yer father widnae bide frae the kirk in rain or snow, an' I wid jist like you tae be as gude men as he wis'. And truly it was a pleasant sight to see on a Sabbath morning, Widow Brown with her four sturdy boys in front of her, and with little Mysie in her hand, marching to the village Church as regularly as the parson himself! By the time our story opens however, they had all grown up, and been at service for several years. The second son was married, but the others as yet were single, although the gossips alleged that Mysie was not likely to continue so for long.

To return to our narrative however. Willie's plans having been thus rudely knocked on the head, the pair sat in silence for some time. At length Mysie remarked, 'Od Willie, I wis hearin that Robbie Stewart wis likely to get a big fairm awa doon the Turra wye. If that be true, fat

<hr />

[1] This story on courtship may have been influenced by Wilson's own experiences in courting Katherine Duncan. The Journal also contains many references to the advantages of emigrating.

wid ye think o' tryin' Robbie's placie. I'm sure the maister wid pit in a guide wird for you w'i the Factor. There's a richt nice dwallin hoose on Burnfit wi' bow windows in't, an Robbie got a new hen-house biggit last year, an' dod widna the aul' hen-house mak' a richt place for a breedin' soo. We wid keep a breedin' soo widdna we Willie? I cud manage the piggin brawlies; ye see the mistress aye taks me wi'er fin the soo's piggin'. 'Stop! Stop! Mysie, od sakes yer jist rinnin on like a hoose on fire'. At the same time it could be plainly seen that the picture which Mysie had drawn, had considerable attraction for Willie.

'Do ye raily think that the maister wid pit in a gude wird for me, I wis to try't 'oman'. 'Think it, man I'm sure o't. The mistress wis jist telling me yestreen that Brackens hid been sayin', he niver hid a mair carefu' foreman, nor a better plooer'. 'Did she tho!' says Willie, aye weel pleased like, 'He's nae an ill breet Brackens, but gosh lassie here ist aifter nine o'clock, the mistress will be ben on's I'm thinkin'. 'Oh! I'm nae ony feart', says Mysie, 'she's tell't me ower an' ower again, that if lads and lasses wid only be open an' stracht-oot-the-gate wi' their coortin, she wid never fin faut wi' them. But od here she is noo I'm thinkin', she'll be comin ben tae min' me to pit the ream pig to the fire, for Monday's aye churnin' day ye ken'.

They are now standing at the outer kitchen door, and Willie putting his arm round the buxom lass says, 'Weel! Weel! Mysie come awa wi' that kiss than, an' I'll nae hinner ye'. 'A kiss', says she, 'I'll rather gie ye a clap on the lug ye big sumph' and freeing herself from his embrace she roughly pushed him out, shut the door and turned the key. Standing thus with a happy smile on her face, she can hear Willie saying, as he makes his way towards the stable, 'Daiget bit ye'r an' awfu thrawn craitur Mysie'.

Chapter 2

It was Saturday night once more, and it was also the night of the Martinmas term. Altho' wages were slightly down, Widow Brown's sons were all staying on in their places.

There is a custom prevalent among farm servants that when a master speaks of reducing their wages they will on no account be persuaded to stay. The Browns being sensible lads however, did not conform to this custom. They knew that if they left their present places, they would most likely have to accept less wages than that offered by their present employer, and they also knew that when times changed for the better, their masters would readily give them a rise.

There was always a little extra stir in the village on Saturday night, but this being the term night as well things were more than usually lively.

On his way home, and coming past the corner where the village inn was situated, Geordie Brown was accosted by an old acquaintance. This young man was in a rather elevated condition, and seemingly had being paying Sunday visits to the bar. 'Come awa in Geordie man, an' lats hae a nippy, jist for aul' lang syne, an' fat are ye aye deein man? Ye hinna gotten a wife yet hiv ye?' 'Na, na Sandy, I've aye stucken tae my aul mither'. 'Weel, weel, come awa in an' we'll jist hae a bit taste'. 'No Sandy', says Geordie firmly, 'I'm nae gaun in wi' ye, ye've hid over mony tastes the day already an' I think ye should gang awa hame noo'. 'Hame Geordie, man hame wis never like this, I'm, I'm jist awfu happy. As Robbie Burns says I'm just glorious ower a' the ills o' life victorious, man Geordie ye see I'm a poet'. 'Come awa doon an my mither will mak a cup o tae tills Sandy, I think that'll dee ye mair gude'. 'Teuch man gae wa hame tae yer aul' mither yersel'. Man I widna be tied to my mither's apron strings like you', and with this parting salute, he swaggered away in to the inn once more, while Geordie made his way down the street very thankful that his mother had instilled into him the principle of total abstinence and musing over the manifest evils that drink leads to.

Besides his brothers, Geordie on reaching home found his sister Mysie and Willie Andrew.

After long consideration, and many calculations in conjunction with Mysie, Willie had at last resolved to face the Factor, and put in an offer for the small farm of Burnfoot. His task however had been made comparatively easy, for Brackens had readily consented to accompany him, and by giving him a good recommendation as a first class servant and also a steady well doing man, and likely to make an improving tenant, Willie had been fortunate in securing a lease of the tidy little farm.

Now that a suitable home had been secured, Willie and Mysie had mutually agreed that the marriage should take place the week after the Whitsunday term, that is if Mysie's mother was willing to entrust her into Willie's care and keeping, and it was just to ask Mrs. Brown's consent, that Willie had come down this evening.

Before Geordie arrived, Willie and the Widow had the matter through hand, and everything had seemingly been arranged in a most satisfactory manner to all concerned, for it certainly was a very happy company that sat down that evening at Widow Brown's board there to partake of that good woman's hospitality.

After tea the women folk retired to the room end to inspect the contents of a parcel of drapery goods that Mysie had that afternoon being purchasing at Mr. Dunns in the neighbouring town, while the brothers and Willie interchanged ideas about the work of the farm, the changes among farm servants, and other kindred topics of interest. Geordie related to them his interview with Sandy Willox, and took occasion to ask Willie Andrew if he was a total abstainer. 'Weel no', says Willie, 'I can tak a dram or wint it, but I'm fairly doon on them that's aye tippling, or them that makes a beast o' themsels'. 'Surely! Surely!' says Geordie', but seein' that a healthy man his nae need for't, an' considerin' that we never ken foo far we may be led awa if aince we begin, divna ye think it wisest jist to lat it aleen a'the-gither'. 'Oh! but I would never mak a beast o'myself I fairly ken fan to stop', says Willie confidently. 'Weel lats look at it fae anither pint than Willie. Supposing your moral courage is strong enuch to keep you in moderation, we hiv proof positive that a' body hisna that strength. Noo gin ye tak a wike brither into the inn an' gie him a dram, micht'nt jist be like gein him a push over a precipice'. 'Dod I never lookit on't in that licht, Geordie, but maybe ye'r richt man'. 'There's nae may-be aboot it', says Geordie firmly. 'Does'na' St Paul say, 'If meat make my brother to offend I will eat no flesh while the world standeth'. Noo in oor day there's nae mony offences throu' eatin butcher meat, but it canna be denied there's hunners an thoosans o' offences throu drink so if we're to tak St Paul as an example in self-denial and Christian Charity, I think oor duty's as clear as day licht'. [2]

At his juncture Mysie and her mother appeared from the other end, the former remarking that she would need her time now to be at Brackenknowes by eight o'clock which was milking time. This trail of punctuality was one on which Mysie rather prided herself and truly she had some reason for doing so, for during all the years she had been at service, she had never yet been five minutes behind her time.

As they were preparing to leave Geordie remarked, 'wis ye in at Portsoy the day Willie'. 'I wis that man I hid tae gang to the bank, an I was in by seein' the Dr.' 'Are ye no weel Willie', asked all the company at once. 'Oh fairly, fairly, ye micht ken that by the supper I took, but I'm thinkin' o' insurin' my life so the Dr. hid to examin' me'. 'Od I think naething o' that insurin', says Geordie. 'Supposin' noo that ye live to be four score, an' Mysie here, an' your family are a' awa afore ye, faur's ye'r profit, ye'r maybe jist layin by siller for them that disna care tippence for ye'. 'Oh! but its Endowment Insurance that I'm gaun in for', says Willie, 'an' I'm to get my siller fin I reach 55'. 'I think it wid be as weel in the Bank', says Geordie. 'Weel I dinnae', says Willie, 'if ye insure in a gweed office, ye'll get far better interest

---

[2] Wilson expanded on the theme of Temperance in a paper delivered to the Deskford Mutual Improvement Association, 1889, printed in Appendix 2.

than ony Bank, an' then it's a gran' provision for them that's ahin' ye, if ye'r taen awa yersel'.[3]

'There was little wird o' insurin' in my young days', says the Widow. 'Oh mither it wad made a gud difference tae ye tho', gin father hid haen his life insured', says Geordie. 'Weel, weel, maybe it wid laddie, but we've aye been providit for, and sae will we yet, but Willie man I aye think the mair o' you fin ye'r sae anxious to provide for my lassie, in case o' onything happenin' tae yersel'. My best blessins on ye baith, but gang awa Mysie, gang awa an' dinna be ahin ye'r kye'.

Bidding each other a hearty good-night, Mysie and her intended took their way up the hill. They had not gone far, when a lady and gentleman met them on cycles. After they had passed, Willie says, 'I'm near sure yons your Minister an's wife they've been awa' upthrou veesitin'. 'Oh I widnae winner, they gang a lot amon' their fook. The Minister mair noo aince his come hine to Brackenknowes to see me'. 'I think the Ministers sud a' tak mair interest in the fairm servants, and veesit them aftener than they dee', says Willie. 'I've been nine year a servant in this pairish, an' fourer year a member o' the au'l kirk, an' I've never seen the Minister yet cep' in the poopit, or fin I meet him on the road. Of course we should aye gang tae the kirk, fither the Minister comes tae seeos or no, but I ken lots o' young chaps that wid be awfu' easy advised, if the Minister wid only come an' hae a frienly crack wi' them'. 'Od Mysie speaking aboot kirks an' ministers fatna kirk are we tae gang till aifter we're mairiet? Ye've aye been a Free Kirker ye ken, but sidan the wife gang wi' the man aifter they're spliced'? Mysie took some time to consider before she answered. 'I believe ye're richt Willie, but Burnfit's an awfu' lang road fae the pairish kirk, an' of course we canna afoord a shultie an a machine yet, michen we jist gang ower tae The Free Church at Cornhillock'.

'Weel that wid be fine an' near han' in a coorse day ony wye', says Willie, 'an weel-a-wite I care-na muckle faur we gang, as lang's he's a gude Minister. Mr. McDougal's a fine hammel kin o' a chiel, jist a gude bit o the fairmer in him. Od Mysie I think we'll jist say that's settled'.

The approaching marriage of our homely pair, and their venture in taking this small farm, being of such vast importance in their eyes, their conversation for the rest of the way, naturally turned a good deal on these topics. Who should they invite to the marriage? Where should it be held? What furniture would they require? Would Willie need a loon to assist him with the work? How many cows should they keep? All these questions, in their several pros and cons were discussed at

---

[3] In April 1887 Wilson insured his own life, see p. 208 above.

length, Mysie being always firm in her determination that they should keep a breedin' soo.

By this time they had now reached their destination, and taking shelter for a few minutes at the neep shed door, Mysie asked her young man to 'crack a spunk an' see fat time it wis'! 'Jist five meenits tae aucht lassie, gosh yer jist in the nick o' time'. 'Oh! I'll need my meenits', says Mysie, 'afore I get my claes changed'. 'Weel, weel, gies that kiss then, an' we'll be lattin ye gang', says Willie.

The night being dark it would be difficult to describe with accuracy the proceedings of our worthy couple during the next few minutes, but from sundry sounds and shufflings, we can form some conjectures.

Willie at all events seemed to be in the very best of humour, for as the pair turned the corner we can hear him saying, 'Gosh! Ye'r nae an ill crater yet Mysie'.

INDEX